WHO KILLED HUNTER S. THOMPSON?

Hunter Stockton Thompson, age 9

Sebastian released Miss Frost from his arms. Your gray sweater and their shape in there. And your hips have a nice swell. Want to press a warm nose in your white cool ear. And smelling this new bread. Get the juices well around the teeth. I think, Jesus, we're just two little bread breakers. I want a big loaf. Big enough to get inside. Safety. Miss Frost, take my clothes off and put me in with a big loaf of bread. A touch of gold on the crust. Float my ears and eyes. Do that, put me in there and save me. Little naked body, shriveled with fright of the world and cock by which I'll poke my way to poverty and my tiny buttressed buttocks, fold me all up like those noiseless nomads and put me in the bread. Don't burn my balls, just brown and cozy, fat with fine crust. And take me out in the morning baked to a fine turn and put it on the table. And I'll be there inside. My little self with my lovely strange eyes looking better than ever. Then, Miss Frost. Eat me.

-- from "The Ginger Man" by J. P. Donleavy, Hunter's favorite book

WHO KILLED HUNTER S. THOMPSON?

The Picaresque Story Of The Birth Of Gonzo. Illustrated.

Edited, with an Introductory Essay by Warren Hinckle

Contributors

Roger Black, Susie Bright, Phil Bronstein, Jerry Brown, Bill Cardoso, John G. Clancy, R. L. Crabb, Robert Crumb, Johnny Depp, Emory Douglas, Dennis P. Eichhorn, Wayne Ewing, Christopher Felver, Timothy Ferris, Ben Fong-Torres, Deborah Fuller, Jeff Goodby, William R. Hearst III, William Kennedy, Paul Krassner, John R. MacArthur, Terry McDonell, Matthew Naythons, Martin F. Nolan, Dan O'Neill, Stephen R. Proctor, Jonah Raskin, 'Dr. Hip' Schoenfeld, Jonathan Shaw, Winston Smith, Barbara S. Solomon, Ralph Steadman, Michael Stepanian, Dugald Stermer, Jack Thibeau, Juan Thompson, Garry Trudeau, John Walsh, Wavy Gravy, S. Clay Wilson, Barbara Wohl, Tom Wolfe

Cover Design by Roger Black
Cover Illustration by Ralph Steadman

PUBLISHED BY LAST GASP OF SAN FRANCISCO

ISBN 978-0-86719-855-3
Book Design by Warren Hinckle
Consulting Editor, Pia Hinckle
Copy Editors, Layla C. Lyne-Winkler & Leslie Kaye
Index Editor, Leslie Kaye
Typesetting and Production, Layla C. Lyne-Winkler & Kim Tavaglione
Pre-Press, H&H Imaging, San Francisco
Printed in China by Prolong Press Ltd

First Edition, August 2017

Published by Last Gasp of San Francisco
Ron Turner, Proprietor
777 Florida Street
San Francisco, CA 94110
www.lastgasp.com

From The Publisher:
Gentle Readers, please note: Great effort has been taken to allow your curious minds access to the unfettered and raw writings of these contributors so that you may hear their voices and see their 'Hunter' in their unedited words and styles.

TO HUNTER, WHOSE DEATH MADE THIS BOOK HAPPEN, AND TO HIS GOOD FRIENDS JOHN CLANCY AND BILL CARDOSO, WHO WROTE THEIR FINE PIECES FOR THIS VOLUME, AND THEN DIED, TOO

&

TO SANDY AND DEBORAH ... WHO HAD, IN ONE WEIRD WAY OR THE OTHER, TO PUT UP WITH MOST OF US

&

TO HUNTER'S FRIEND JIM MITCHELL, WHO JUMP-STARTED THIS PROJECT

&

TO RALPH STEADMAN, WHO HAS INHERITED, FOR GOOD AND EVIL, THE UNSTEADY TORCH OF GONZO

&

TO LINDA CORSO, WHO PUT UP WITH THE UNNATURALLY LONG GESTATION AND BIRTHING OF THIS PROJECT

Ralph Steadman's drawing for the VHS box cover of "The Crazy Never Die"-the movie about Hunter Thompson made by the Mitchell Brothers, but never released.

TABLE OF CONTENTS

BOOK ONE

"The Crazy Never Die"

WARREN HINCKLE

INCLUDING *The Night Manager*

Begin in the middle of things. Hunter Thompson walked into my office on North Beach's topless strip and tossed his knapsack on the couch by way of introduction. I poured whiskey while Hunter engaged the office monkey in one-sided conversation. We went up Broadway to have dinner at Vanessi's and the monkey got out of his cage and into Hunter's knapsack and opened many bottles of pills and gobbled the contents. When we returned a few drinks later the poor thing had gone bananas and was running at ferocious speed along the railing atop the office cubicles with his leash clanging dementedly against the frosted glass. Lovable Henry had turned into Cujo. No one could pacify him. It took a day and a half for him to slow down. "Goddam monkey stole my pills," Hunter said.

I had named the monkey Henry Luce to hopefully piss off the eponymous founder of *TIME* and *Life* magazines. Luce once asked a *TIME* reporter if I really kept a monkey in my office that was really named after him, and such are life's little triumphs. The office where Hunter fed Henry Luce was in the corner of a squat-ugly two-story building on the exit to a freeway ramp, which had previously housed a government agency researching poisonous substances. It overlooked a freeway exit pouring cars packed with topless-bound rubes onto Broadway; two doors up a girl scant of costume was gyrating to an inner music in a glass cage high above street level, a live advertisement who got a piss break every hour and free white powders to tune her engine. The building was the tatterdemalion headquarters of *Ramparts* magazine, which began life as a right-leaning Catholic literary quarterly and which I had misdirected, critics said, into a New Left slick that cut a deal with the mob to get on the newsstands

nationally and was the upfront journalistic shit disturber of the generally shit-disturbing sixties. This was in 1967 and *Ramparts* was where the action was, and where the action was, was Hunter.

Hunter was then, justly, famous for his fine book on the Hells Angels with whom he had ridden to get the story and was beaten in gratitude to within an inch of his existence by some bad Angels. I was known as an editor-pirate because I wore an eye patch (I lost an eye in a childhood automobile accident) and ring-mastered the unruly school of left wing researchers, genuine eccentrics, and retired national security whistle blowers who stocked the *Ramparts* trout pond. It was somewhere written in the star-crossed stars that Hunter and I would become friends: We were two journo-lefties who both liked the unlikeable Ayn Rand, were both immodest in our pursuits and had no respect for authority in its many guises. We both had no sense of time and were habitually late. It is a wonder we ever met at all.

Fast forward nearly 40 years later: He wanted his ashes shot out of a cannon. A great funeral was what he wanted, he had told his son. Then he sat in his command-post kitchen in Woody Creek and shot himself dead in the head.

That was the end of my old friend, Hunter S. Thompson. But the end is only the beginning of the story.

His last writing was a sports column, for ESPN's *Page 2*. His editor was John Walsh, a mutual friend who Hunter met in San Francisco when Walsh was enduring a Foreign Legion stint at *Rolling Stone*. Walsh is an enterprising editor, a cheery albino who looks like Santa Claus, and a part-time prankster whose credits included the stewardship of the A to Z Bar Tour, in which a merry group bussed it to 26 Frisco bars, arranged alphabetically, all in one day of unclocked hours of beer bottles and stained glasses emptied of traveling cocktails, and vials of amyl nitrate lifted from gay bars on the route clashing and clattering in the bus aisle like shipwreck detritus after a storm; Walsh, who was addicted to schedule, tooted a serious whistle to blow tardy drinkers back into the bus for the uphill haul to the next stop.

Hunter had begun his professional career as a sports writer for his Air Force newspaper, and he came full circle to end it that way--his off-base ESPN sports columns were politically prophetic and ice-cold righteous. In the first years of the new century, while the paycheck press was resting with its beak tucked in its armpit,

Hunter S. Thompson wrote the most prescient criticism to surface in the mainstream media of the Bush *fils* Administration. He called George W. Bush the "boy president," which was the kindest thing he had to say about the truffle pig. It is curious to the point of cliché that the herd of professional critics who bared their chest hairs to make the plaint that Hunter was on a downward slope as a writer in his last years conveniently take no notice of the fact that Hunter S. Thompson was virtually alone among the boys-on-the-bus political commentators in sounding the battle shofar against Shrub's follies --and in high-style brilliantly vituperative prose. Someday someone will write a "Why England Slept" book about the big snooze of the Eastern Establishment press corps/liberal media intelligencia during the formative years of Bush's criminality--but Hunter S. Thompson was not sleeping.

Hunter considered it quintessentially American that he was able to toss off his political blue meanies on a major sports network. He usually viewed corporate journalism through the same prism of suspicion he observed professional politicians. We shared a mutual affection for the bromide that the sports page box scores were the only part of a newspaper you could trust because there were too many witnesses for anyone to lie--although Hunter, quite typically, was not ready to give even the box scores a free pass.

Thompson's demise at age 67 on February 20, 2005 at his "fortified" redoubt, Owl Farm, in Woody Creek, Colorado shook his San Francisco friends and admirers with the rigors of a psychic earthquake. His unexpected death registered way up on the upper Richter scale in the hang-loose, cynical city where life and death are usually taken casually, and one can find a ready taker for a bar bet over whether it was Kool-Aid or Flavor Aid (don't get suckered, it was the latter) that the Rev. Jim Jones of Frisco's People's Temple served for a mass suicide cocktail to his transplanted faithful in a Guyana rain forest. Hunter's favorite San Francisco hangouts were decked in gloom. On the night of his death, on a slow rainy Sunday in North Beach, in the back room of the old Tosca, an operatic bar that was to the art and movie-making crowd in San Francisco what Elaine's was to the glitterati in New York, Hunter's friends were sitting shiva. Tim Ferris, the author and black hole expert, was in the back room with Tosca owner Jeannette Etheredge; Jonathan Moscone, the son of assassinated San Francisco Mayor George Moscone, was there,

as was the city's mayor, Gavin Newsom, listening to Hunter's BFFs swapping stories. Recalled fondly was the night of Hunter stacking every brandy snifter not immediately in use in an increasingly unstable pyramid on two cocktail tables he had pulled hastily together to support the pile. The glasses were undulating in the manner of a giraffe's neck. Hunter stayed focused on the task at hand. "I've got to get this sucker up there," he said of the last glass. Thompson, when the occasion seized him, could get pissed off real fast and he took sudden ire at a helmet-haired lad he had in tow whom he had introduced as "a cousin of the Kennedys who needs to have his tooth pulled." Thompson brought pliers with him to do the job. "You touch that table and you'll eat every glass that breaks, you shit-eared hyena," he told the fat-lipped Kennedy. The Kennedy kid touched the table to steady it and the glasses went down with all the clatter of a drunk climbing the Macy's Christmas tree. "Swine!" Hunter yelled at the hapless Kennedy.

Ferris would often sojourn to Woody Creek, to greet the dawn outdoors with Hunter, gaming the mysteries of the stars. He placed a $100 bill on the Tosca back room pool table as a coaster for a glass of Chivas Regal on the rocks, poured for Hunter. Chivas was a popular detergent Hunter washed his teeth with many of his mornings, which were most people's afternoons. The next day at the O'Farrell Street Theatre, Hunter's other Frisco home away from home, the flags above the marquee--"Live Girls! Bambi the Barbie Queen! Open at Noon!"--were lowered to half-staff. Hunter had bonded with the brother-owners, Jim and Artie Mitchell, and enjoyed many full moons as the designated Night Manager, on assignment, he said, from *Playboy* to write an article about the sex industry. Hunter became a permanent O'Farrell fixture, roosting on his high director's chair up in the wings from where the spotlights played down on the strippers on the stage below. He said he might have a novel in mind. I asked him the name; "Polo Is My Life," he said.

A word about Hunter's friends. Tim Ferris has said that if you wanted to know who Hunter S. Thompson was you should check out his friends--as the plaque in St. Paul's Cathedral to the great London architect Christopher Wren states, "Reader, if you seek his monument, look around you." Hunter, his good friend Ferris said, modestly, had great taste in friends. Hunter picked his friends, and they were few, but it was never the other way around. Hunter had the not-so-eccentric attitude that anyone who *wanted* to be his friend

must be some sort of bottom-feeding weirdo. Friendships to him just happened, like the collision of atoms, the felt recognition of mutual madness certified by actions signaling same. His old friend and lawyer John Clancy first said, "We may be lunatics, but we are pros." One of Hunter's signature lines, "We are, after all, professionals," was a hallowed motto in which we all took refuge, sometimes chanting it in chorus after a night, or nights, of writing madness and acrobatic editing acts of Making It Work--deadline-defying professional bravado that the straight publishing types who had the keys to the asylum of journalism held, as a matter of faith, that the inmates could not perform.

San Francisco and Northern California were a seminal part of Hunter's life, from his first escapades in Big Sur to the early 60s when he lived in San Francisco writing his Hells Angels book, to *Ramparts* and then *Scanlan's*, to life as the Night Manager of the Mitchell Brothers O'Farrell Theatre, which only in Frisco could become a hallowed if harassed civic institution. In this book, journalism professor Jonah Raskin, in an appreciation of Thompson from the left, notes that Hunter possessed a keen moral compass--and he was never off course. Hunter always always knew what side he was on, and it was, invariably, the (lower case) right side. Hunter built his nest in Woody Creek in the shadow of the Rockies, but further west San Francisco was his second home, where he was continually drawn to, at the end of the continent, where the wild things were, towards The Edge ... that place to which Hunter always was heading and of which he wrote: "The only people who really know where it is are the ones who have gone over."

This book is also about the journalism and politics and art of the 60s and 70s in two magazines, *Ramparts* and *Scanlan's Monthly*, and how Hunter was attracted to them for the ruffian, ball-busting ways they changed the game plan of journalism in America, and how the government went after them both and tried to put them out of business (with *Scanlan's* it succeeded, rather dramatically.) Hunter was forever warning me about the perils my shit-disturbing publications were inviting and in typically impious fashion took a perverse delight in seeing his worst fears come true.

Hunter quite enjoyed tilting at windmills with Irish guys. He once wrote his old friend, the great novelist William Kennedy, that he wondered "why my life was so bound up in the failed dreams of crazy Irishmen (Clancy, Hinckle, you ...)" But Hunter was a man on his own

mission; Ahab had his Whale, and Hunter had The System which he pursued with a Pauline zeal. He took his allies wherever he could find them and he found in these two cutting edge magazines--journalistic comets that would inevitably flame out but what a pretty sight they made--a port in the storms, so many of them self-created, that raged around him. Hunter appreciated that *Ramparts* and *Scanlan's* were not run by the men of the probity and property and caution of the establishment publications he dueled with throughout his long professional life, but by familial lunatics--who for a glorious, frenzied time possessed a real freedom of the press which comes so rarely in America.

He said he was drawn to *Ramparts* for its rather brazen use of commercial art and graphics to package its anti-establishment message. This was unheard of for a left publication and became cheekily known as Radical Slick. The art of *Ramparts* and *Scanlan's* that is extensively reproduced here was for its time revolutionary, and a seriously attractive nuisance to Hunter, who always pictured himself an art director. (In 1993 when I resuscitated the august 19th century San Francisco publication, the *Argonaut*, Hunter immediately announced that he would be the *Argonaut* art director--he wrote me that he saw this was a first step toward his goal of "becoming head of the art department at Stanford.")

Discussions about fucked-type faces and fuck-nosed art directors and the otherwise appropriate use of graphics filled our phone conversations with expletives for decades. That Hunter was himself a conceptual artist there is no doubt--his Shotgun Art is reproduced in this book, and another Exhibit A is Hunter's Midnight Faxes (in Book Five) where he designed nut-case stationery from the droppings of political campaigns and his own made-up letterheads and sausage-factory-floor graphics and turned them into wacky communicative art through his adornments, always drawn with heavy black felt-tip pen. If one of Hunter's communiqués ever cluttered out of your fax machine at dawn, you knew you were getting something... different.

This book has been many years in the gestation and now double its original size, as rekindled memories and lost art kept popping up like wretched children, and through the indulgence of its publisher, Ron Turner, of the venerable house of Last Gasp. Many of Hunter's friends have written original essays for this volume--the aforementioned John Walsh of ESPN; John Clancy, one of Hunter's oldest

buds and co-conspirators; gonzo linguist and meticulous writer Bill Cardoso; editor and sexologist Susie Bright; publisher and advanced mathematics brain Will Hearst; the Pulitzer Prize novelist Kennedy, who first met Hunter when Kennedy was editing the *San Juan Star* and Hunter was looking for work; Deborah Fuller, who for more than two decades had the unenviable task of maintaining order in Hunter's life, generously plucked some plums from her personal photo album of life at Owl Farm; Gene "Dr. Hip" Schoenfeld, M.D., Hunter's sometimes attending; attorney Mike Stepanian, one of Hunter's band-of-brothers friends; and many others who have dipped into their memoirs-in-progress for this book. The one compatriot of Hunter's from his San Francisco years who did not contribute to this volume was Jann Wenner, who started the *Rolling Stone* while working as a copy boy for *Ramparts*. After sufficient consideration, Wenner, the brat, said that he had to save his Hunter material for "his" book, which turned out to be a transcription of "interviews" which came out a few years ago and sunk, if you will excuse the cliché, like a stone into the remainder ponds.

"Gonzo" appeared in the vernacular, and then quickly in the dictionaries of usage as adjective, noun, and then verb. Once, when Hunter was on Night Manager duty at the O'Farrell, he took off his glasses, professor-like, and said that looking back--a direction infrequently on his compass--what had attracted him about *Ramparts*--and led to our hooking up for both good and evil--was that *Ramparts* was "the first gonzo publication." He meant it. "You beat up the government viciously and shoved it in the face of the rest of the press, you kept doing the unexpected and behaved outrageously--it was gonzo, goddammit." *Scanlan's* was the devil's womb which gave breach birth to the gonzo genre and inflicted on Hunter, like the blind bats of the Nile, the wilderbeast, artist Ralph Steadman, a monster of purpose beyond Dickens' most colorful nightmares. Hunter had never met Steadman until I teamed them up for the Kentucky Derby piece in *Scanlan's*. He said I would be held accountable for all this in Hell, if there was one.

Ramparts and then *Scanlan's* changed the landscape of opinion journalism in the last half century. There were, literally, no magazines like these freakoids--for even a taste you had to go back to the 20s and 30s of *The Masses*, which had art and verve but no mass circulation. These bastard 60s magazines which Thompson admired reached further back for precedents, to the late 19th and early 20th

century popular muckrakers, and further back still to the foul-mouthed partisan enjoyable looniness of the journalism of the screed that nurtured the weaning years of a new and then hardly United States.

The 60s black lotus explosion of left mass journalism, howsoever brief, unmoored the psychic chains confining American journalism and forced truly dissenting ideas into mainstream media, effectively digging the media out of the living grave where it had been buried by smothering consumerism and political centrism, and prompted a return to when American journalism was as iconoclastic, novelistic, imaginative, profane and shocking as the Bible at its best.

There is now a small library of books and articles on how the 60s forever changed American culture and politics. Despite this overkill, surprisingly little attention has been paid to the fact that the 60s also changed American journalism. The story of *Ramparts* and *Scanlan's*, the originators of radical slick and gonzo publishing, is a story heretofore largely untold. It is both a snapshot in time and a graphic documentation of journalistic change in frenzied motion.

There have been many previous volumes about Hunter S. Thompson, floating icebergs in the Sargasso Sea of books, and doubtless there will be more to come. But in the growing library of Thompsonalia this large book for the first time places Hunter and gonzo on the broad canvas of the art and artists and cheery wackos and culture vulture-hero pornographers of the dare-to-do city where he was so at home.

Maria Kahn, Thompson's dauntless and invaluable editorial assistant, recalls Hunter always saying that the essence of gonzo was putting the writer in the middle of the action, and making the thrust of the story about himself. "Some things should be subject to ambiguity," she said about fact-checking Hunter's titles. Thus the title of this book is very much a title Hunter would have used if he had written about his own demise. "Why?" As Hunter would say when explaining the inexplicable, "It was the Right Thing to do."

[MEET STEADMAN]

Steadman was waiting for me in Cookie Picetti's Blue Star Buffet. The artist's hands were in angelic repose around a glass of Scotch. The rest of him was a rattled venetian blind, vest hung open over a blue dress shirt that had escaped the Laundromat, eyes wet firecrackers

looking for a way out of his head. The sight of me brought back memories, horrible memories; "Teddible, teddible," he said in Brit-speak.

This was on a hung over morning early in the 80s. I had not seen Steadman for maybe ten years. In the intervening decade since I had introduced him to Thompson he had become, for all practical purposes, the man's caboose, and time had not treated him well, or perhaps Hunter had not. For looking the worse for wear he had come to the right place. Cookie's was a magnificently inelegant San Francisco cop bar. The clientele included generous helpings of defense attorneys, judges, mailmen, police inspectors, bail bondsmen, private dicks, highway patrolmen, poultry salesman, and the drinking press. Cookie's was where Jake Never-Plead-Guilty Ehrlich always stood drinks for the jury after he inevitably humiliated the prosecutors next door in the old Hall of Justice where they shot "The Streets of San Francisco." The buffet was simplicity itself: if you wanted a burger you banged on the wall to get the attention of the cook in the Chinese restaurant on the other side. You entered the premises through a stained wooden door framed by once-lovely blue tile with a crack as wide as an earthquake fault and soiled for eternity with the grim patina of diesel bus exhaust from Kearney Street. The air inside was permanent nicotine yellow.

Cookie's was a narrow dim room, like a railroad car in a tunnel with the lights off. The weathered wooden bar was marked like smallpox scars from the sweating of a million cocktails. Above the bar was a hand-crafted sign noticing those among the regulars who had borrowed money from the Bank of Picetti, "Youse Wanna $ee Me?" The wall opposite was lined with petite black formica cocktail tables at which uniformed employees of the Special Delivery Unit of the United States Postal Service were daily engaged in ritual games of dominos; their motor scooters were parked in the bus stop outside, forcing the Muni buses to let passengers off in the street to dodge the oncoming traffic--the bittersweet joke among Cookie's regulars was never send anything special delivery, regular mail is faster. A framed page of dialogue from a "Dragnet" script posted a note of levity unusual in that sturdy police procedural which had dominated the gray age of television--Ben Alexander, Jack Webb's sidekick, asks where they should go for a drink in Frisco and Webb says, "Cookie's. Where else does anyone go?"

In this living wreckage of old-town San Francisco, uncertain of foot, at the bar stood Ralph Steadman, arguably England's greatest living artist. "Is this place on the San Andreas fault?" he asked. Sitting on a stool next to him was a mannequin of Sigmund Freud, naked from the waist down, with whom he had been sleeping. The artist made his hands into a claw cradling his giant head like a condor egg. He shivered at the very mention of the name of Hunter S. Thompson. Steadman said I had destroyed his life, damned him to everlasting perdition by pairing him up with The Beast, Thompson, and sending the two of them off to cover the Kentucky Derby in 1970, beginning the artist's psychedelic Sancho Panza-like adventures with Thompson which, he insisted, had driven him into years of therapy and his unhealthy relationship with Freud. Steadman was driven by the furies to draw a book on Freud, and *Penthouse* was promoting an excerpt by sending him on an American tour with the proviso that he sleep with a life-sized dummy of Freud for the publicity; bloody humiliating. Steadman had dragged Freud from his room at a Fisherman's Wharf motel to Cookie's after a long and sleepless night. The artist blew his nose in a bar rag. "You got a big honker," Cookie said.

Cookie had a spot-eye for the proboscis. Steadman has a nose like a burglar's jimmy, prominent in a face resembling battered type, a face cheerily animated in a lock-down gaze of perpetually amused astonishment. Never one to forget a perceived wrong, Steadman sat at the bar muttering about it being all my fault: how he lost his shoes after I sent him, following the Derby, to the America's Cup races in Newport, R.I. there to rejoin Thompson and do the nasty to Rhode Island High Society. Hunter fed Steadman psychedelic substances in fishcakes and sent him underwater with a can of spray paint clenched in his teeth, on an aggressive mission to draw "FUCK THE POPE" in red on the lead yacht, the *Intrepid*. There were screams and sirens and the local constabulary was closing in as they escaped into the night. Both assignments were for *Scanlan's Monthly*, the successor magazine to *Ramparts*, a provocateuring publication very much unloved by the Watergate White House. Steadman reminded me that the Kentucky Derby assignment was a personal disaster, he lost his tools and had to draw in borrowed lipstick and eyebrow pencil and then Thompson had maced him at the end of the article just for the fun of it. Thus began the form of journalism now in the dictionaries as gonzo.

The artist had escaped Newport without his shoes and fled the country, saying that any money he got from *Scanlan's* would be "danger money" and vowing never to return to the States. Yet he did return, to fitfully collaborate with Thompson on continuing Fear and Loathing articles and books on Vegas, Hawaii, and other altered states, most of them published in *Rolling Stone* after the astonishingly short-lived *Scanlan's* imploded when the Canadian Royal Mounties, on the urging of the Nixon administration, arrested an entire edition's press run, which had been printed in Canada, while it was in trucks headed for the border carrying an incinerating issue titled "Guerrilla Warfare in the USA."

The scribbler deserves soothing ink here because his psychic wounds are real, although when he says repeatedly that "Hunter ruined my life" there is the scent of bullshit on his lips. As a result of all this he said he had, go figure, become addicted to Freud's fart jokes. When I sent him to the Derby with Hunter I only knew of Steadman from his early days at *Private Eye*, vilifying the mighty of England high and low. He soldiered on, becoming unhinged in the way a great artist should be. He illustrated the works of Lewis Carroll--"Alice In Wonderland" and "Through The Looking Glass"--in a death-head's style that gave Tenniel and Rackham a run for the money; Steadman's Cheshire cat wears what can fairly be described as an existentialist Werner Herzog smile. Steadman did many editorial drawings for *Scanlan's*, including several of the dreaded Nixon who was a paint card in the pantheon of Ralph's favorite candidates for caricature. (One of Steadman's ruder takes was Nixon leaning long-nosed over the lectern at the microphones with his ass morphed into another face, eyes, nose, and mouth vilely coughing, or, if you will, farting.)

Steadman has the devil's very appreciation for the queer detail. I stumbled into him at the bar in the Jerome Hotel in Aspen during the wake for Hunter the month after he died. He stared at my feet, which were dutifully in mountain-man shoes as snow was still on the ground. I have been long addicted, for reasons best left unexplored, to wearing black Brooks Brothers patent leather dancing pumps with little goose grain bows. Steadman gave me the artist's evil eye. "Where are your fairy shoes?" he demanded.

That morning back at Cookie's, Steadman was suffering a hangover out of Baudelaire. He complained that his mind had been forever twisted by "sour mescaline a dwarf sold me in Canada." His hair

was in disarray, like an Ann Miller wig run amuck. He was stressed from being subjected to that peculiarly American form of tortures, the book promotion tour. Freud was out in a rental car in a suitcase when Steadman walked in and asked Cookie, "I say, do you mind if I bring a friend in for a drink?" Cookie looked at the Englishman through dark eyes under black eyebrows thick as garbage bags. He was chomping on an ever-present unlit cigar in his mouth.

"I ain't cashing no checks for nobody I don't know," Cookie said.

A woman walked into the bar. She carried the missing parts of Freud and put him together under Cookie's watchful eye. It was hard to tell the difference between the dummy and a lot of Cookie's regulars, Steadman said. She was introduced as an English sculptress who had made his faux Freud, for *Penthouse*. She was dressed for duty in an artisan's smock with her breasts bobbing like Halloween apples. She assembled Freud at the bar while Steadman went on muttering about Freud as if Freud wasn't sitting next to him. "Freud's middle name is Schlomo. That's not very well known," he said with the satisfaction of the scholar. Steadman traveled to Vienna to the Freud Museum and lay down on the wet spot where Freud's consulting couch had been and immersed himself in all the fun parts about Freud--the cocaine and the train phobia and the stuff about seeing his mother naked twice, and how Freud discovered the testes of an eel and so on. Steadman became addicted to Freudian fart jokes and therapeutically produced a coffee table book that was an illustrated and annotated riff on Freud's 1905 barnburner, "Jokes and Their Relation to the Unconscious." Hunter made light of the book as "Ralph's gibberish about Freud's gibberish." Steadman said, defensively, "There's some good farting jokes in there."

Steadman asked Cookie for another Scotch. He was still shaking from a month on a Hollywood lot with Hunter and Bill Murray, who played Hunter in the first Hunter flick, "Where the Buffalo Roam." The movie under-exceeded expectations but has become a cult classic--the scene of Bill Murray-as-Hunter pretending to be a *Washington Post* reporter shaving in the john when Nixon comes in to take a piss is worth anybody's money. Hunter had been in a foul mood in Hell-Ay during the shoot because he felt ripped off by the producers--Hunter had ferocious fights with anyone who dared to try to make a movie about him. The "Buffalo" producers paid Thompson $100,000, a nice round sum, to film his life. Steadman said Hunter spent it "in a mean and joyless frenzy." He bought a speedboat and under the influences

Self-portrait by Ralph Steadman from the Argonaut, reprinted from "The Grapes of Ralph." (Houghton Mifflin Harcout)

of evil substances fell against the throttle and the thing took off like a scalded cat and cut another boat in half. The way Hunter viewed the world, the producers should pay the damages and buy him a new boat.

Steadman and Thompson had previously worked on a movie of their own, an ill-fated BBC documentary in which Hunter--an incurable hypochondriac who always believed that death was imminent--discussed his burial plans with thoroughly freaked out morticians. Hunter wanted a skywriter to put a "Re-Elect Nixon" smoke signal in the sky over Watts, and then have a 150-foot red fist shoot off a mortar shell every half hour from a hill near his house in Woody Creek--eerily presaging his actual memorial send-off decades later. The BBC film was largely takes of cars burning in the desert with Hunter asking a West Hollywood funeral director, "Do you handle this type of memorial?" It didn't play too well on the BBC and the only station in the U.S. that showed it was an educational TV station in North Carolina. Steadman wasn't depressed about the failed film venture: "Freud said, 'Life's a new hat,' " he said.

Steadman drew a sketch of Cookie on a cocktail napkin and gave it to him. Cookie looked at it suspiciously. "You gave *me* a big honker," he said. In fairness, Cookie did have a big honker. Steadman

some years later took an unnatural interest in the wine business and began promoting a London wine seller called Oddbins. He drew wild mail order catalogues urging connoisseurs to buy the better brands. The artist visited the great wine growing regions of the earth to steel himself in the vinous arts. He produced a hilariously illustrated book, "The Grapes of Ralph," which can be found on most upscale remainder tables. He sent me a copy and I shamelessly hustled the book and his penetrating depiction of "The Great American Wine Slob" in the *Argonaut*. Among Steadman's sketches of the Napa Valley wine kingdom in the *Argonaut* was a hideous self-portrait of himself in dread of the horrid phylloxera bug, which I presumed was a metaphor for Thompson.

["A PERFECT SOUTHERN GENTLEMAN"]

"Hunter knew where every ice machine was at every motel in San Francisco." Jeannette Etheredge, the former proprietor of the landmark Tosca Cafe and one of Hunter's closest Frisco confidantes, was talking. Hunter was not much into sleep at the routine times and often after a night when the Tosca had to shutter at the puritanical San Francisco hour of 2am and the night's receipts had been tagged and bagged, he would take Jeannette out for what he called a "ride" in a top-down rented convertible, or at times a jeep. Wild, daring, conversation-strewn, wind-blown rides with the stars looking down in the pre-dawn hours when the cable cars were still in the barn snoozing for the night and there was none of that Tony Bennett sentimental Frisco ooze about little cable cars climbing halfway to the stars. Hunter's choice of transport was always well-stocked with provisions for a roader--a bottle of Wild Turkey, two six packs of Heinekens in an ice bucket, and drugs in an enclosed inhaler lest the wind get in the way. He once took Jeannette in a jeep down the Pacific Coast Highway south of San Francisco, hard past the Zoo, and drove down a rough road to a beach below Pacifica where he did doughnuts in the wet sand with the jeep in the dark before dawn intruded. He sometimes ran out of ice. One night out by the Cliff House he abruptly braked the car outside the Seal Rock Inn and climbed out of the driver's seat without benefit of opening the door. He had to enter quietly because he had been banned from the Inn for repetitive destruction of the premises. "When he came back, he had a new bucket of ice," Jeannette said. While having lunch with

Jeannette and the Mitchell Brothers at the original Original Joe's, a journo, sports-buff Old Boy hangout in the Tenderloin, my daughter Pia noticed that Hunter had a watch on each wrist. She asked him why he wore two watches. "Time is very important," Hunter said.

Tosca regular Sean Penn called Jeannette "the mayor of the San Francisco night," and Tosca became Hunter Thompson's adopted bar, which he worked in as a combination rec room and office-waiting area, the way he utilized the Woody Creek Tavern in his hometown. He once brought a Mitchell Brothers' dancer dressed in a

Photo: Deborah Fuller

Jeannette Etheredge and Juan Thompson, Hunter's son, at Spec's 12 Adler Place Saloon in 2007 at the wake for Hunter's friend Bill Cardoso, who invented the word "gonzo."

gorilla costume with notably no clothing underneath into the bar for a drink and the movie gang didn't even notice. When he broke his ankle performing a ballet misstep on the top of the bar Thompson didn't want to go to the hospital, concerned that it might affect the bar's insurance rates. He insisted on taping the ankle himself with black electrical tape fetched from the nearby Chinatown Walgreen's. Jeannette doesn't drink at all--she didn't stop, she just never started--but she accompanied Hunter on some of his epic San Francisco foraging expeditions.

"He was always a perfect Southern gentleman," she said.

[HOTEL ROOMS AS CANNON FODDER]

Hunter's favorite spot to stay in San Francisco was the Seal Rock Inn at Land's End. He trashed the place so often--there was once, regrettably, something about a fire--that management barred him for eternity; they would rather have had Osama bin Laden as a guest than Hunter S. Thompson. When I was an editor at the Hearst *San Francisco Examiner* in the mid-80s, I talked to publisher Will Hearst (who had hired me away from the larger morning *Chronicle* to raise hell at his afternoon broadsheet), about bringing Thompson aboard as the columnist from hell. It took no persuading, as Will was a big fan of Hunter's but there was a bean counter issue--it was not so much Hunter's salary as the amount the paper would have to set aside for accrued damages, given Hunter's penchant for using hotel rooms as cannon fodder--from vague memory a Hilaire Belloc jingle springs to mind: *Like many of the upper classes/He loved the sound of smashing glasses.* Hunter's weekly *Examiner* column--contrary to expectations he met every deadline--increased both the frequency and velocity of his visits to San Francisco. It also seriously diminished the city's rental supply of IBM Selectrics, always Hunter's writing weapon of choice. Some of them ended up on the composing room floor, the composing being Hunter's and the floor his hotel room. Come with me now, for a moment in the present tense, back to a halcyon San Francisco night:

We are at the Hyatt Regency, a compost heap of modern design by the Embarcadero. The hour is just before dawn. The hotel is one of those upside-down-cake designs with the lobby open to the skies, interior balconies looking out into the emptiness and elevators going up and down in see-through glass tubes. It has been, what we call in Frisco, a long night: Earlier there was a bit of a dust-up in the publisher's office at the *Examiner*. Will had invited some staffers to meet Hunter for drinks but Hunter has locked himself in the publisher's private bathroom. Suddenly the toilet door bursts open and Hunter cannonballs out in a total summersault and lands upright holding an unspilled glass of Chivas Regal, grinning in his sheepish, disarming way. There is a commotion in the street outside the publisher's window. Below printers are staging a wildcat strike over a perceived sin of management. Hunter looks out the window, mutters goddamnit and disappears back into the bathroom. He emerges with a large pot of hot water and opens the window and dumps the water in the direction of the impromptu pickets below. They look up.

Boiling water! From the publisher's office! Medieval! "We must flee," Hunter says, something he has said to me on more than one occasion. The office is promptly vacated and we reposition at the M&M, the newspaper bar down the street. Thence to Tommy's, a Mexican eatery on Geary Boulevard, Thompson's favorite restaurant, for a serious sampling of obscure tequilas with Julio Bermejo whose family owns the place. Thence to Gino & Carlo, a North Beach anchor bar pioneered by garbage men (there is no Gino and no Carlo but never mind); then to visit Ward Dunham, the night bartender at Enrico's on Broadway who is 6-foot-6 and as big as a house in Texas but one of the finest calligraphers in the country; then to the Tosca and its next door neighbor, Spec's 12 Adler Place, where longshoremen are playing chess; then to an after-hours crap game in the Tenderloin hosted by Jimmy the Glove, a beloved City Cab driver who used to be a baseball pitcher, Jimmy is in a tux and people are playing who have names Damon Runyon would die for--Monty the Duck and Hydro Willy the Cucumber and Cactus Jack; then for a drink at the law offices of Michael Stepanian, Esquire, a rugby-playing, deep sea-fishing, African safari-hunting dope lawyer and Thompson running buddy. Stepanian accompanies Hunter back to his room in the Hyatt Regency so Hunter can retrieve his knapsack of black beauties.

Thompson is muttering, "people may be following us." The hotel room is a campground scene in Hades. There are half-eaten club sandwiches, burned out Sterno cans, crumpled linen napkins, a face-down tape deck murmuring Jimi Hendrix sweet nothings into the carpet, several crashed IBM Selectrics, sofa cushions tossed about like clothes at an orgy, spilled Heineken bottles everywhere like dead soldiers. Wilted cantaloupes. There is a feeling that *maneuvers* have occurred here.

Hunter is wearing gear for battle journalism--white duck shorts and oversized basketball sneakers. Ibsen said that a man should put on his best suit when he goes out to fight for freedom and truth. Hunter's oval head is large like Humpty Dumpty, his forehead high and bald; his eyes appear to be almost in the middle of his head, like eggs on a plate; beneath the yellow-orange lenses of his gold-rimmed aviator glasses, the eyes have a jalapeño pepper shine. Thompson opens beers. He continues to mutter. The night sun is setting, the bastard of the day must be dealt with, and nothing can help us now, not even the black beauties. In the vampire light of dawn Thompson morphs into his alter ego, Raoul Duke, Famous Weapons Consultant,

a Hunter nom-de plume. Out of his knapsack comes something that looks like a miniature MX missile launcher. "Air pistol," Hunter says by way of explanation. "Stand back! This is an evil bugger! It shoots weird darts. It's the most advanced state of the science. It electrocutes people. Watch."

Stepanian protests. "Don't shoot that thing in here!" Thompson points the gun at the wall. There is an ear-engulfing roar. It is like shooting off a .45 in a vacuum-sealed can. The framed pastoral print on the hotel room wall turns into breadcrumbs. The space where it was is full of little darts with tiny nylon threads dangling down like sperms in a sex-ed video. There is smoke in the room, then the stillness of a casket. Gas curls out of the small cannon in Hunter's hands. He reloads and fires again as the lawyer yells, "No! No Mas!" There is more smoke, and the sound of plaster decomposing and tinkling like cheap chimes, the sound of something broken. There is frantic pounding on the wall from the room next door. "We must flee!" Hunter says for the second time that night.

["THIS GUY IS BEYOND ROUST"]

Michael Stepanian is a believer in the immortal advice George M. Cohan, the father of American musical comedy, gave to Spencer Tracy, "Whatever you do, kid, always serve it up with a little dressing." He is an admirer of Thompson's style: "It's like this guy Thompson is beyond roust! It's another dimension entirely. We're walking through the airport. He's like got knives and long chains and heavy metal-looking things and he's carrying a bottle of booze and two grapefruits. Hey, everything I know about the laws of search and seizure says this is probable cause for a roust. He walks right through the cops. It's so outrageous, they like just don't want to deal with it. He gives this insane look out of the corner of his eye, a left punch from under the glasses, and the cops just take a pass. It's fabulous. I've been with a lot of crazy people, but I've never seen anything like this. Beyond roust. He-a-vy."

Stepanian is one of three lawyers who contribute to the character of Dr. Gonzo, the lawyer in Thompson's phantasmagoric, dope-drenched escapades in the Hunter movies "Where The Buffalo Roam" and "Fear and Loathing in Las Vegas." The first is Oscar Acosta, a Samoan; the second is John Clancy, Irish; Stepanian is Armenian. In

the "Buffalo" movie he is played by Peter Boyle; in "Fear and Loathing" he is played by Benicio Del Toro.

The mouthpiece doesn't just speak, he marches verbally; he paces as he talks, he gestures, he jumps up and down, he's a mariachi band. Stepanian is a big, burly rugby player with flashing eyes and curly hair like a bunch of black soap bubbles and a Frito-Bandito mustache. He's a crusading, successful defense attorney who is always busting the prosecution's balls. His law office is out of a San Francisco wet dream, a Victorian on Eddy Street with a garden in the back that is both run down and well maintained at the same time in the special way old houses in Frisco can be. The office is a shrine to San Francisco left wing history, although the gunkies and zits have now been mostly cleansed from the face of the Old Town by the dermatology of political correctness. His office mate was the great mouthpiece himself, Vincent Hallinan, a lion in court, a lion in winter who once ran for Vice President of The United States on the Socialist Party ticket while he was doing time in a federal pen for putative tax evasion. The combative Hallinan not infrequently went to court with a gun in his pocket to protect his clients from the Law, and at age 88 he beat the shit out of a mugger who made the mistake of presuming him weak prey. Vince Hallinan was, put simply, probably the best, most ballsy trial lawyer in the world--he once sued the Catholic Church in a wills case demanding that it prove the existence of Hell.

Stepanian as a youth worked as a bouncer for Art D'Lugoff at the Village Gate in Greenwich Village. His job was telling crazed hoodlumnized maniac dopesters to act cool. "One thing about me, I'm never afraid to go up to a heavy guy and say what does this heaviness mean. Because I'm heavy, too ... I can be as totally crazed as the next maniac and they get the idea." The lawyer broke into life in Frisco as a bartender at the hungry i; he learned a lot of his courtroom stand-up shtick at the hungry i watching Lenny Bruce and the early Woody Allen and the early Barbra Streisand putting a little dressing on what they were serving up for the customers. What he learned about style he says made him understand the philosophical underpinnings of gonzo.

Stepanian speaking: "Madness is no good without style. Like Hunter and his room service bit. Fine tuning. He hits the hotel and he's in the room and on the phone to room service ... two cases of Heinekens, a tub of ice, a bottle of Chivas, a bottle of Absolut, a

bottle of Wild Turkey ... and two IBM Selectric typewriters and eight grapefruits and be quick about it! Bam! The phone's down. Action!"

Stepanian had a bit part in "Where the Buffalo Roam," playing a creepy lawyer who gets trashed by the Acosta-Clancy-Stepanian lawyer played by Peter Boyle. The trashing scene was shot in Jerry's, a Third Street bar where *Rolling Stone* staffers used to go to drink their Boone's Farm before the rock culture tabloid took its 70s bad-skin journalism to the Big Apple. Stepanian loved going to see the movie and watching part of himself trashing himself on the big screen. The "money-grubbing, scumbag goniff lawyer" he played in the movie was taken from Stepanian's real-life courtroom experiences. "You can't imagine how many of these total assholes there are who hang around the courts... they were forever siding up to me back when I was representing a lot of hippies, doing millions of cases for two hundred bucks, and they say, 'Mike, how much are you getting? These kids got parents you know ... we can work it out, fix it up so you can really charge them ... Mike, you got to learn how to play ball.' "

Stepanian was Hunter's wingman on many road trips and a frequent tripper to Owl Farm. He stayed with Thompson at the Universal guesthouse in the Hollywood Hills during the shooting of the "Buffalo" flick. Thompson and Bill Murray were having a good old time. The caretaker was crying to Stepanian to please get these maniacs out of there. Thirty years of seeing movie people screw-off and he'd never seen anything like this! The place was wrecked. It looked like an overused public toilet on the moon. When Stepanian arrived, there were stereos tossed up in the trees, all the chairs in the house were at the bottom of the swimming pool and Thompson and Murray were arguing over who gets to be Richard Widmark. Stepanian said if they shot that instead of the movie, it would have been a great movie.

The gonzo lawyer speaks about Thompson with the vehemence of an Old Testament prophet--the Prince of Gonzo's creative craziness and the heart-felt paranoia in the 70s and 80s were harbingers of the bad things that were to come. The drug lawyer said we are moving closer and closer to an informer society and that Thompson's moral paranoia was a way of sniffing out the finks. Thompson saw politics as a gaggle of rip-off artists screwing each other and the country while trying to control shrinking power bases which atrophy as people get turned off from politics as usual.

"Hunter was into the anarchy vibe. That's the weather forecast and he was the weather vane, pointing the way the wind was blowing." Stepanian loved and understood Hunter so much that for decades Thompson had an American Express card in Stepanian's name. Until he died, Hunter never stiffed him.

[RADICAL SLICK]

Ramparts entered the great hall of journalism through the backdoor of Catholicism, a world of whiskey priests and segregated communion rails and New York's Cardinal Francis Spellman, the Vicar of the United States military and the chief ecclesiastical sponsor of the Vietnam War, and a pervert. U.S. Protestants' taxpayer monies were funneled to Vietnam through the Catholic Relief Agency primarily to the minority Catholic population of Vietnam with bumpkins for the Buddhist majority, who lived in squalor. It however didn't take long for us to realize that for all the Church of Rome's faults everything wasn't the Church's fault, it was all part of a system that was... really fucked-up. *Ramparts* became famous as a "New Left" mag, but the reason it was called New Left was that the etymologists of media didn't know what to call it--it was clearly not Old Left but it was definitely Left. (In full-brat mode I once sued George Wallace, the racialist governor of Alabama, for libel for saying that *Ramparts* was "Communist." I found that defamatory because Communists were so yesterday and much, much too conservative.) *Ramparts* was enigmatic politically. It was not about ideology but about moral outrage--the war and torture and racism and other injustices were simply wrong per se and to be opposed, without the usual leftist bother of trying to invent a new system of government, or the usual liberal fussing with fixing the existing broken one. *Ramparts* exposed the sins of the CIA and FBI that other left publications had prayed over--the left press of the time had a lecturing tone and a butcher paper look and its readership was of the choir. *Ramparts* became the first mass circulation Left magazine in U.S. history. It was a slick with high-tone graphics and New Journalism-type writing. American mainstream journalism in the 60s was a journalism of sheep, and *Ramparts* broke from the herd with its sensationalistic "Front Page" foot-stomping, hard-drinking Old School journalistic approach to high-minded matters formerly in the exclusive domain of the keepers of the Left's tabernacle. It made being out of the mainstream somehow mainstream. *Folio: The*

Magazine for Magazine Management wrote in a 2004 look-back: "It was slick, printed on heavy, shiny stock with classy graphics that looked good on a Danish Modern coffee table. *Ramparts* was the only New Left magazine that could penetrate middle-class households." I used all the methods available to the Other Side, and in the doing offended both old and new Left cultural sensibilities. I had no docility about utilizing sex to sell copies although the New Left part of *Ramparts* thought I was culturally incorrect: I shrugged--people don't visit the newsstand to buy a sermon.

The story of Donald Duncan is the quintessential *Ramparts* story. Duncan was a hero Green Beret Master Sergeant who made his medals in Vietnam and came away from the experience thinking the whole thing sucked. The handsome Duncan was resplendent on the cover of *Ramparts* in February of 1966 in his bottle-green uniform with his Green Beret beanie and chest full of medals, saying in display Times Roman type, "I Quit. The Whole Thing Was a Lie." Duncan's story helped significantly alter the public perception of the Vietnam War--he had a bird's-eye view of American forces routinely torturing and killing Vietnamese civilians, white GIs openly racist to black GIs, military brass wildly inflating "kill" figures to make it appear we were winning when we were in fact losing. Duncan's story became a big story in the *New York Times* after the hero bemedaled soldier first spoke out in *Ramparts*--except that he didn't first speak out in *Ramparts*. Duncan first spoke out at a mammoth Berkeley teach-in with 70,000 attending and the national and local press covering it--but not a reporter, or an editor, heard what he said; deaf editorial ears. I took his story and, in the term of art, re-packaged it and sold it to the rest of the media that had ignored it until it was served up to them on coated paper.

The ex-soldier remained possessed of the military mindset. When I put Duncan on the *Ramparts* staff--as, what else, Military Editor--I had to restrain him from saluting when he came to work. He was still a soldier, now at war against the war, soldiering on to do his duty as he saw fit. The Green Beret was a very decent man. We often had drinks together as he continued to shake off the madness of Vietnam. *Ramparts* was a career change enabler that pulled up the welcome wagon for a magnificent succession of decampers from American institutions who followed Duncan into the magazine. Out of the Cold War shadows of academia came university professors such as Stanley Scheinbaum of Michigan State University who

Ramparts *staff writer William Turner, a former FBI agent, told all about being "a burglar, wiretapper and spy for the FBI" in the magazine.*

fessed up to his school taking CIA money to do the government's dirty work in building a dictatorship in Vietnam. Scheinbaum joined the *Ramparts* board of directors and married Betty Warner and went on to become a prominent civil libertarian and civic leader in Los Angeles.

Ramparts had more than its share of CIA tattletales, many of whom were bound tight as Chinese feet by secrecy oaths punishable by jail time, and many of them thus must remain unheralded. But into the disinfecting sunlight direct from the FBI came William W. Turner, a ten-year veteran of the Bureau, a nice Catholic boy from Buffalo and a former semipro hockey player who made perfect soup meat for the FBI pot; Turner was a "sound man," which is FBI-speak for a wiretapper. He also carried a black bag and did domestic break-ins to plant electronic bugs. Turner had a promising future in the Bureau but had a fatal streak of independence--he inquired into why FBI field offices spent so much time dummying up stolen car statistics to log as solving crimes "across state lines" and so little time going after organized crime. Turner requested through official channels to discuss this heresy with J. Edgar Hoover himself, who was on record as denying the Mafia existed. Such questions were not considered to be in the "best interests" of the Bureau.

Turner soon found himself in Hoover's cross-hairs. He was fired for conduct unbecoming a eunuch, hired Beltway powerhouse attorney Edward Bennett Williams to sue the FBI, and wrote his confessional ("I was a burglar, wiretapper, bugger, and spy for the FBI") for *Ramparts*. He became an editor, in the magazine's grand tradition of professional flip-flops from right to left.

As *Ramparts* investigative fullback, Turner was in charge of overseeing our deconstruction of the Warren Commission's Katzenjammer Kids-style investigation of the Kennedy assassination. In the process he became involved in one of the more bizarre entanglements of *Ramparts* history of strange bedfellows--the Minutemen volunteered to help *Ramparts* find out who really killed JFK. Turner was secretly approached by the Minutemen after he wrote a *Ramparts* piece about the menace of the armed paramilitary right in which Turner once again took issue with his former boss J. Edgar Hoover, who had pooh-poohed the militant anti-communist Minuteman as a "paper organization" that was no threat. Turner wrote to the contrary that the Minutemen were dangerous, well-armed, well-financed, well-disciplined vicious right-wing paramilitaries with the trustworthiness of electric eels. By writing that, Turner had a friend for life in the Minutemen, who loved being feared. None other than the Moses of the Minutemen, Robert DePugh, a Missouri biochemist in his day job who posted stanzas of the Hail Mary on the old Burma-Shave signs along the state highways, asked *Ramparts* to take a meeting. DePugh was worried about Minutemen sprawl--he said he had 8,000 trustworthy, dues paying regulars but there were some 80,000 wannabe Minutemen bursting out of their britches all over the country. DePugh told Turner there was no way Oswald had acted alone and Kennedy was slain in a classic guerrilla crossfire involving many gunmen. He was concerned that some self-proclaimed Minuteman, nutcase John Birch Society sharpshooters, might have been involved in the nastiness at Dealey Plaza and he wanted to clear the good name of the real Minutemen. Welcome to the world of *Ramparts*.

The Minuteman probe didn't pan out, but DePugh stayed in contact; he sent Turner a postcard from jail, proud that the Minutemen softball team had beat the John Birch softball team, 1-0, on the diamond at the federal pen in Atlanta.

Ramparts' arguably biggest hit on the Muckraker's Top Ten was the CIA's manipulation and secret funding of American institutions—a direct violation of the 1947 National Security Act creating the CIA, which specifically prohibited it from doing what *Ramparts* caught it doing. *Newsweek* labeled the story the CIA's "most damaging scandal since the Bay of Pigs" and reported that to CIA officials "almost as galling as the story was the vehicle of its disclosure—*Ramparts*." Hunter Thompson was more succinct: "You swine, you have royally fucked our government," he told me.

This began with me treating Michael Wood, a former employee of the National Student Association, an organization consisting of all the college student body presidents in America, to bourbon and grapefruits and many helpings of chocolate cake in the dining room of the Algonquin Hotel in New York City. Wood was as jumpy as an owl in a popcorn machine. He had a tale to tell out of *Astounding Stories*. He had brought a plastic bag full of copies of the NSA's financial records that showed the CIA had been clandestinely financing the student leaders and telling them what to do for almost two decades. This was difficult to believe. It was accepted wisdom that the FBI spied in the U.S. and the CIA spied abroad, and never the twain could meet; it was so written in the stone of the national security apparatus. The records Wood offered me showed only that the organization received its funding from many distinguished foundations, but Wood said these foundations were secret "conduits" for CIA money. He was nervous as hell and fearful he might go to jail for what he was telling me and fessed up that he had recently suffered some sort of nervous breakdown and was not, on balance, your average trustworthy source. If true, which it turned out to be, such a revelation would shake the CIA to its foundations, which it did, but at that moment the story was as shaky as his trembling hands. I assigned our New Left researchers to dig into the foundations. Nothing suspicious was found until we came across a brief and long-buried *New York Times* story from a decade before in which Texas Congressman Wright

Patman had in open hearings in the House of Representatives named eight philanthropic foundations as undercover "financial conduits" for the CIA. The *New York Times* printed the story in a two-paragraph shirt tail and did not follow up. Congress did not investigate. It was as the cynical Italians say *insabbiata*, buried in the sand.

To my amazement, among the foundations identified by Patman were the very foundations funding the NSA. The CIA was so stinking lazy it hadn't bothered to change its fronts. I was astounded--anyone who has read a John le Carré spy novel knows you have to change your fronts. Thus armed with a one-paragraph I.D. we interviewed former student leaders who filled in the blanks and discovered that some of these foundations existed only in mahogany drawers in Brahmin law firms. We had the story ready to go to press when two things happened: 1) I found out that the CIA had infiltrated the *Ramparts* staff and knew every word we were writing about them and 2) a double agent told me that the CIA had corralled the current student leaders and intimidated them into calling a press conference to denounce the CIA for 'attempting' to manipulate them, thus obscuring and blunting the *Ramparts* story which would not hit the newsstands for two weeks and would by then be old news. Angus Mackenzie of the Center for Investigative Reporting, in "Secrets: the CIA's War at Home," his fine book of the CIA's illegal activities in the United States, recounted what happened next:

> However, Hinckle discovered the plan before the press conference could be held. "I was damned if I was going to let the CIA scoop me," recalled Hinckle. "I bought full-page advertisements in the *New York Times* and *Washington Post* to scoop myself, which seemed the preferable alternative."
>
> Hinckle's ad read: "In its March issue, *Ramparts* magazine will document how the CIA has infiltrated and subverted the world of American student leaders over the past fifteen years." On February 13, 1967, the day before Hinckle's advertisements appeared, the news that they were forthcoming panicked the CIA, the State Department, and the White House. The acting secretary of state drafted a secret memorandum for President Johnson suggesting a Plan B for handling this fiasco. The State Department, making a

"bare bones" admission, would claim that the student operation was "tapering off" and would soon come to a complete halt.

Even as the fallback plan was being developed, a new surprise was in the works. Although CIA officers had already told the students not to talk, one of the student leaders confirmed to reporters the accuracy of the *Ramparts* allegations. Hinckle was astounded yet again:

"It is a rare thing in this business when you say bang and somebody says I'm dead."

On the next day the informational dam broke. February 20, 1967, the *New York Times* ran two front page stories about *Ramparts* --"CIA WILL NOT PROSECUTE STUDENTS OVER DISCLOSURES" and "RAMPARTS: GADLFY TO THE ESTABLISHMENT" and we 26-year-oldish editors got our picture on the front page. Beltway reporters lined up sixteen deep outside the IRS building in Washington to get their copies of the conduit foundations' records. Soon the major papers in the country were doing their own "The CIA illegally funded (fill in the blank)" story, black-eying institutions from the AFL-CIO to *Encounter* magazine to the Boy Scouts. The most counter-intuitive revelation was the extent to which the CIA had used liberal and leftwing groups to further its Cold War purposes. Allen Ginsberg caught spot-on the outrageousness and the absurdity of it all in a letter to then CIA director Richard Helms:

"I am the treasurer of a tax-exempt nonprofit corporation, properly registered and approved by the government. Our national and international activities, tho small, are extremely useful in the artistic world: we supply cash and comfort to artists and poets harried by society, police, themselves, and the universe. Monies I receive from poetry readings are made over to the Committee on Poetry (COP, the short) Inc., and given to poets far less fortunate than others. I notice that the CIA in the past has been giving money to groups rather arbitrarily chosen. I am therefore asking for a proper redress of that secret balance, by means of a large grant from the CIA thru its fronts,

Wirephoto of The New York Times

PLANNING THE NEXT EXPOSE: In San Francisco office of Ramparts magazine are, from left, Warren Hinckle 3d, editor; Sol Stern, assistant managing editor and author of the article on C.I.A. links with student group, and Robert Scheer, the managing editor.

Ramparts: Gadfly to the Establishment

Special to The New York Times

SAN FRANCISCO, Feb. 19 —Resplendent in a pink shirt, red suspenders and a deep blue and maroon striped necktie, Warren Hinckle 3d paced between the rolltop desks.

He lifted the telephone off its stand, a black-painted keg with gold-painted hoops falling in rings on the floor. He talked to his pet monkey, Henry Luce by name, caged in the next room.

He talked, too, about his magazine. "Next month we have Stokely Carmichael on the origins of the Black Power movement," he said. "Then we're going to go out after the world of the foundations, following up what we found out about the C.I.A. Just decided that today. Got to do it."

Mr. Hinckle, a pudgy six-footer with a flowing Edwardian mane of hair, is 28 years old and the editor of Ramparts, the splashy magazine that won front-page newspaper notice last week when it scooped itself.

It bought advertisements, which soon became news, to tell what its March issue would say about the Central Intelligence Agency's undercover relationship with the National Student Association.

This was the latest in a series of publicity coups for Ramparts, which was founded in 1962 as a five-times-a-year journal aimed at liberal Catholic intellectuals.

The magazine's conversion into a busy gadfly on the liberal-to-left side of politics began two years ago. Two business consultants (who have since become stockholders) recommended a change in direction. And Mr. Hinckle, whose first connection with Ramparts was as a public relations man, was named editor.

The consultants, Howard Gossage and Dr. Gerald M. Feigen, have a company here

Continued on Page 18, Column 5

"CREATING A MONSTER:" Ramparts *had so many scoops reported in the* New York Times *that the* Times *sent a reporter, Marty Arnold, to San Francisco to find out how these darn kids did it.*

> or preferably, directly. I don't see why, in the balance of things, COP--President Peter Orlovsky, Vice President Ed Sanders of *Fuck You: A Magazine of the Arts* and the Fugs--doesn't deserve equally to receive government stipends as did more conservative socially minded organizations. Investment in some hip community is only fair. The sum of $10,000,000 would be useful in the next few years."

The Ivy League mugwumps running the Central Intelligence Agency were not pleased. Mackenzie reported that the CIA set up a supersecret task force of twelve black-ops types to go after *Ramparts* "on a high priority basis"--the CIA had the IRS vacuum our tax returns, and CIA agents "identified and investigated 127 writers and researchers, as well as nearly 200 other civilians with some link to the magazine." He reported that the agency also asked the FBI to scrape up derogatory information on *Ramparts* to use in a disinformation campaign against the magazine and plotted to scare off the few brand-name advertisers it had--Eagle shirts, Paul Mason Wines--a tactic that proved succesful.

Ramparts was broke and $1 million in debt when I took command of the unseaworthy vessel in 1964. The quarterly had just gone monthly, at my urging, and imagine my surprise when the publisher, Ed Keating, over cocktails in the Algonquin lobby in New York, with a tear running down his nose, sobbed that he was broke, busted, had spent all his wife's money, and in the asset department was down to one, heavily mortgaged, shopping center. I recall, as if it were yesterday as the memorists say, reaching in my pocket to make sure I had my return-trip ticket to San Francisco.

Circulation thereafter grew so fast that half of my time was spent in New York in a desperate, constant fundraising quest to feed the growing beast. The *Ramparts* bunkhouse in New York was the Algonquin Hotel on 44th Street, home to the ghosts of the Dorothy Parker-Robert Benchley bitchy literary Round Table salon of the 30s and 40s. I often met Hunter for drinks in the Algonquin lobby, crowded with cocktail tables and overstuffed chairs, and introduced him to old leftists like Carl Marzani, who stared at Hunter as if there was a snake growing out of his ear, and new leftists like Phil Ochs and, Bernadine Dohrn, before she went underground. Meanwhile, in

San Francisco, *Ramparts* became part of the city's High Society Left. There were editorial board meetings at Howard Gossage's converted Firehouse-office and on chic industrial designer Walter Landor's converted ferry-boat office, and soirées at Jessica Mitford's house in Oakland, which was a 24-hour Old Left salon and debating society. One night at the Mitford house Bill Turner was chatting with Decca's husband Bob Treuhaft, a gentleman of the Old Left, and Turner said, "I'm sure I know you, where did we meet before?" But Treuhaft said nowhere, you worked for the FBI for God's sake, so how could I have known you? Then it came to Turner--"It's your voice that's so familiar," he said. "I used to wiretap you!" Decca thought this just screamingly hilarious. Decca also just happened to have an island for sale. It was called Inch Kenneth, a barren scrub off the west coast of Scotland in the Inner Hebrides, where Dr. Johnson once squatted. We tried to sell it through full color back cover ads in *Ramparts*. We had a few nibbles, but never closed the deal.

Decca Mitford was a most delightful and witty woman. She became a great friend who always annoyingly addressed me as "Hink III" since the magazine masthead listed me as "Editor In Chief, Warren Hinckle III" because we naively thought it would help in fundraising. The *Ramparts* gang would often have drinks with her and her best bud Sonia Orwell, the widow of George. Orwell was a hero to Hunter and me, in particular for "Down and Out in Paris and London" which Hunter and I had both youthfully committed to memory. Hunter was jealous when he heard that I was having drinks with the Orwell widow and demanded to get in on the action. The next time I hooked up with Sonia Orwell was in London but I forgot to tell Hunter in advance and waited until we were on a second martini to call Hunter and ask, "Where are you? Sonja is dying to meet you." He said I was a fucking swine and pledged to cut the balls off my office monkey. For a guy who kept a lot of nasty peacocks at his house in Woody Creek, Hunter hated my monkey who he insisted should be arrested on general principles of cleanliness.

Text continues on page 48

"The whole thing was a lie!" *by a Special Forces Hero*

Ramparts

February 1966 Seventy-five Cents

"I quit!"

DUNCAN

"I QUIT! THE WHOLE THING WAS A LIE!" Hero Green Beret Master Sgt. Donald Duncan quit on the cover of Ramparts*. His story helped change the American public's view of the Vietnam war. He went to work for the magazine as "military editor."*

Understanding Marshall McLuhan / Felix Greene at f5.6

April 1966 **Ramparts** Seventy-five Cents

The university on the make

[*or* how MSU helped arm Madame Nhu]

MICHIGAN STATE

MSU

Paul Davis

A UNIVERSITY ON THE MAKE: Ramparts' *cover depicting Vietnam's Madame Nhu as a buxom cheerleader, for a story exposing Michigan State University's complicity in setting up a dictatorship in Vietnam.*

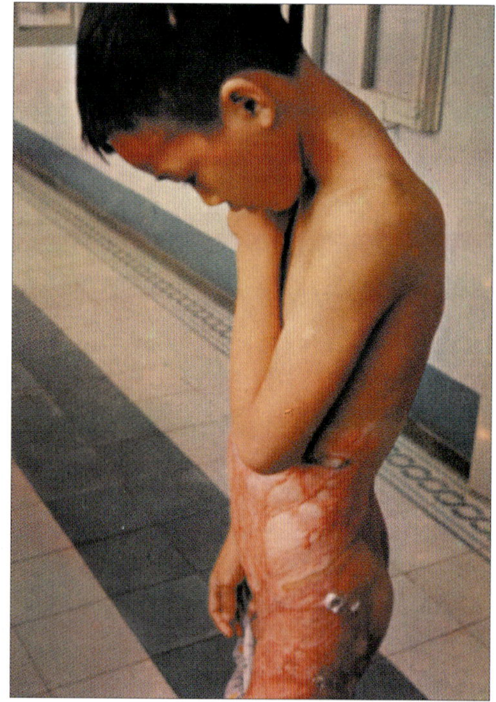

(Top) Hinckle's much-anthologized essay critiquing the hippie/consumer culture attacked Bill Graham and caused a counter culture storm. (Below) (L) "The Children of Vietnam" cover. Dr. Spock says, "a million children have been killed or wounded or burned ..." (R) Ramparts *printed color photographs of napalmed Vietnamese children that shocked the nation. Martin Luther King, Jr. said on seeing the* Ramparts *issue that he decided to publicly oppose the Vietnam War.*

Art by Robert Grossman

THE 60s IN PASSING: Ramparts *portrayed LBJ as crapping bombs on Vietnam; accused the CIA of executing Che Guevara; and celebrated Bob Dylan.*

Art by Gene Holtan

September 7, 1968: A Ramparts Exclusive: Sirhan Sirhan's Family Reveals His Motives; Chicago's Power Brokers; Biafra—The Politics of Starvation; Bugging Cops; What Makes Al Lowenstein Run; The HHH/Shriver Axis, by Jack Newfield; An Anti-Pope? 75¢

Ramparts

(A recently declassified CIA portable tape recorder, weighing 11 ounces: it bugs both in mono and stereo. See page 39)

SEX AND THE NEW LEFT: Ramparts' *occasional use of sex on covers infuriated some among the New Left seraphim. This cover illustrated a story about new government bugging techniques. The cover model was San Francisco's famed 60s topless star, Carol Doda.*

Jean-Paul Sartre on Genocide

Ramparts

February 1968 Seventy-five Cents

Women Power

JEANNETTE RANKIN For President

"WOMEN POWER:" *A controversial cover. Hinckle said the woman's head was cut off to obviously satirize the commercial use of sex in U.S. magazines; Feminist critics said it was selling cleavage more than making a cultural point. (Jeannette Rankin (pin) was the first woman elected to the United States Congress, where she voted against entering World War I.)*

October 1965 **Ramparts** Seventy-Five Cents

Art by Barnaby Conrad, Sr.

CATHOLIC EXPOSÉ: *When cover artist Barnaby Conrad, Sr. asked Hinckle if he could have the original art back after the cover of Pope John XXIII, crying over his trashed reforms, had been printed, Hinckle asked why. The artist said he could paint out the tear and sell it again.*

A Profile in Courage: J. William Fulbright

Ramparts

June 1966

Seventy-five Cents

Ben Shahn

Art by Ben Shahn

HERO WORSHIP: Artist Ben Shahn did this cover of one of Ramparts' *heroes, Arkansas Senator William Fulbright, for coming out against the Vietnam War.*

AMERICAN IMPERIALSIM: Ramparts *carried out Twain's design idea for the American flag and printed it as a four-page fold-out cover.*

l: The White Olympics; LBJ & the Racketeers

c

n & Other Enduring Characteristics of The Republic." (*Pg.64*)

December 1967 Ramparts Seventy-five Cents

The Ramparts *editors were summoned before a federal Grand Jury after they burned their draft cards on the cover.*

FOLDOUT: Ramparts *classic eight-page gatefold cover, "The Aviary," portrayed the Vietnam War's instigators and supporters. (Art by Edward Sorel.)*

to purchase an island?"

NOVEMBER 67 · 40. Woche · Zinstage 277-83

S		5	12	19	26
M		6	13	20	27
D		7	14	21	28
M	1	8	15	22	29
D	2	9	16	23	30
F	3	10	17	24	
S	4	11	18	25	

Sonnabend

7

OKTOBER

Se cumplieron los 11 meses de nuestra inauguración guerrillera sin complicaciones, bucólicamente hasta las 12.30 hora en que una vieja, pastoreando sus chivas entró en el cañón en que habíamos acampado y hubo que apresarla. La mujer no ha dado ninguna noticia fidedigna sobre los soldados, contestando a todo que no sabe, que hace tiempo que no va por allí. Sólo dió información sobre los caminos; de resultados del informe de la vieja se desprende que estamos aproximadamente a una legua de Higueras y otra de Jagüey y unas 2 de Pucará. A las 17.30, Inti, Aniceto y Pablito fueron a casa de la vieja que tiene una hija postrada y una enana; se le dieron 50 pesos con el encargo de que no hablara ni una palabra, pero con pocas esperanzas de que cumpla a pesar de sus promesas. Salimos los 17 con una luna muy pequeña y la marcha fue muy fatigosa y dejando mucho rastro por el cañón donde estábamos, que no tiene casas cerca, pero sí sembradíos de papa regados por acequias del mismo arroyo. A las 2 paramos a descansar, pues ya era inútil seguir avanzando. El Chino se convierte en una verdadera carga cuando hay que caminar de noche.
El Ejército dió una rara información sobre la presencia de 250 hombres en Serrano para impedir el paso de los cercados en número de 37, dando la zona de nuestro refugio entre el río Acero y el Oro. La noticia parece diversionista.
h = 2000 m.

DEZEMBER NOVEMBER OKTOBER

REVOLUTIONARY PENMANSHIP: A page from Ramparts' *edition of Che's Diary—in Che's own handwriting. The CIA raced* Ramparts *to get out its own version.*

January 1968 **Ramparts** Seventy-five Cents

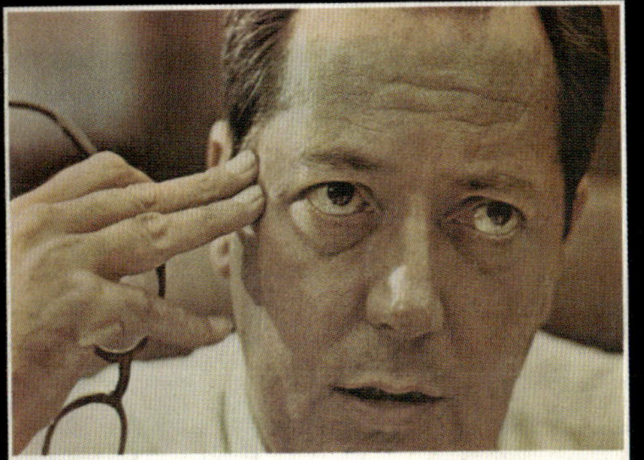

"Who appointed Ramsey Clark, who has done his best to torpedo the investigation of the case? Who controls the CIA? Who controls the FBI? Who controls the Archives where this evidence is locked up for so long that it is unlikely that there is anybody in this room who will be alive when it is released? This is really your property and the property of the people of this country. Who has the arrogance and the brass to prevent the people from seeing that evidence? Who indeed?

"The one man who has profited most from the assassination—your friendly President, Lyndon Johnson!" — *Jim Garrison*

U.S. Plane Shot Down by China

WASHINGTON

CHINA SHOT down an American Navy plane on Tuesday -- China time -- but in contrast to the recent case of the USS Peublo, the Pentagon this time admitted that the plane was where it wasn't supposed to be.

Specifically, the plane was one of two A-1 Skyraiders which, the

—Continued on Page 3

HERB CAEN

Pocketful of Notes

MY NEW HERO is Lew Alcindor, the sensational UCLA basketball star. Asked by a New York newsman where he'd like to play as a professional, he said "Well, I wouldn't mind playing in San Francisco—that's a *CITY*. But Los Angeles—you know—it's just out there." How come I haven't read that in an L.A. paper? . . . All kinds of mumbo-jumbo is being used these days to figure how long the S.F. newspaper strike will last—black magic, Ouija boards, tea leaves and so on—but the theory I like least has it that the Ford Foundation really KNOWS. The Foundation has given $50,000 to KQED to finance the nightly brightly "Newspaper of the Air," which costs $5000 a week. Ergo, goes the dejected reasoning, the Foundation's mighty computers decided at the very beginning that the strike would last ten weeks. You go argue with computers. They're winning the war in Vietnam, aren't they? Actually, according to the computers, we won it two years ago . . . While marching in the picket line at Fifth and Mission Tues., Congr. Phil Burton was asked if he agreed it's "inconceivable" that we would use nuclear weapons in Vietnam. "Everything about this war his been so inconceivable," he sighed, that even THAT is conceivable." Burton, by the way, is still ashamed that he voted for the Tonkin Bay resolution. That happened, he reveals, because he promised Pat Brown he would go along with Administration policy for one year—in return for Brown's support in his race for Congress. Like most deals, a bad one.

• • •

HERBERT the Furrier supplies the solution to the mystery: Thomas Nelson Truax is really Teddy Nelson grown up! Truax is the feller you've been reading about who made off with $510,000 from the Assoc. of Bay Area Governments—while Teddy is the young man who worked as a messenger for an Oakland bank several years ago: he delivered his final message by walking out of the bank with over $190,000 in cash in a paper shopping bag. The tipoff is that both Thomas Nelson and Teddy Nelson are described as "clean-cut." Moral: hire hippies. They don't care all that much about money, especially yours.

• • •

JOE ALIOTO is aging fast in the Mayor's chair: he was 51 when elected and now all of a sudden he's 52. Happy birthday, caro Giuseppe!

—Continued on Page 7

ThursDay
San Francisco's Only Daily Newspaper
PAY NO MORE 15c
San Francisco February 15, 1968 Vol. 2, No. 36

100-Year War In Vietnam--CIA

WASHINGTON

THE HEAD of the Central Intelligence Agency has privately warned a Congressional committee that at the present rate, the Vietnam war could last another 100 years.

The profoundly gloomy assessment by CIA Director Richard Helms was leaked to newsmen by a Republican

—Continued on Page 3

China Won't Let Us Enjoy Our Little War, Gavin Says

THE UNITED STATES is moving steadily up the escalator in Vietnam toward a war with Red China, Lieutenant General James M. Gavin warned yesterday.

And he predicted the Red Chinese will resume the Korean War when then sense the U.S. is hopelessly mired down in Vietnam.

—Continued on Page 3

Abortion Doctors Found Guilty; Verdicts Are Protested

TWO DISTINGUISHED San Francisco physicians were punished by the State Board of Medical Examiners yesterday for violating California's abortion laws.

Dr. J. Paul Shively, chief of obstetrics at St. Luke's Hospital, was found guilty of performing illegal abortions and given a 90-day suspension of

—Continued on Page 3

Bringing It All Back Home

By Maitland Zane
1st of a series

CONFLICT - of - interest scandals have been sprouting like noxious toadstools all over Ronald Reagan's front

—Continued on Page 5

The Sunday Ramparts

Signed Opinion by: Robert Scheer, Paul Jacobs, Stokely Carmichael, Howard Gossage, Jessica Mitford, Ralph J. Gleason, Etc.

SAIGON CABLE: 'DEMOCRATIC ELECTIONS' WERE A FARCE

THE CREATION OF RONALD REAGAN

Brown aides help right-winger, then Birch-bait him to get liberal votes

A new McCarthyism?

Sexual Freedom League rumors

MRS. JOHNSON'S VISIT

Nurses at USF feel Viet pinch

Faggot Ball to be casual dress

A night at Port Chicago

On Other Pages

JULY 27, 1968: EXCLUSIVE U.S. EDITION OF CHE'S DIARIES. SPECIAL PRICE, 75¢

Ramparts

THE DIARY OF CHE GUEVARA
INTRODUCTORY ESSAY BY FIDEL CASTRO

NEWSPAPERS AND MORE: Ramparts *put out a daily newspaper during the 1968 San Francisco newspaper strike ... and published a Sunday newspaper ... and won the race to be the first to print Che Guevara's diary in book form--an international publishing scoop.*

[HUNTER'S R.I.P. FOR RAMPARTS]

My candle burns at both ends;
It will not last the night;
But ah, my foes, and oh, my friends-
It gives a lovely light!

Hunter sent me this dogeral when *Ramparts* went under in 1969. A lot of people on the left still cherish the idea that *Ramparts* went crash because I bought people drinks.

A very rough rule of thumb of what it costs to launch a successful national magazine: It took in 1960's terms approximately $1 million to get each 100,000 of circulation, and around 400,000 stable circulation is desirable if the magazine is going to have a reasonable chance of attracting enough advertising to allow it to make money. Those figures were operative only if you didn't make any mistakes. In the five years I ran *Ramparts*, in addition to Keating's two million--which didn't exactly count, since he spent most of that when the paper was a 2,000-print quarterly--we raised another two million, give or take some.

The highest circulation *Ramparts* reached was some 450,000; so I suppose the paper was potentially somewhere in the ballpark of making it, although we did make a lot of mistakes along the way. In 1967, for instance, one critical editorial on Israel cost the paper $1 million from a stockholder--if you like that sort of example. It's the old story of the monkey pissing into the cash register--it all runs into money. In this case, a lot of money.

I figured that as long as I had to go to the bother of raising loot, I might as well try to raise enough to make the paper over into something more than the Catholic penny dreadful that it had been. Joe Ippolito, *Ramparts* accountant, found a book about publishing in a used bookstore and that was the extent of our technical knowledge, although I did become rather artful about putting togther P+L spreadsheet projections to show prospective investors. Ippolito was my companion on frequent fundraising forays. When we struck paydirt, he would invariably tell my then wife, Denise, "put meat in the spaghetti sauce." Hunter and his wife Sandy and their infant son Juan would often come over for taco dinners at my house, a haunted

STUFF OF LEGEND: The hippie-dropout-LSD-Tim Leary-"Lucy in the Sky With Diamonds" ethic, which was a nuisance to Ramparts' *political-first priorities and was pilloried by Hinckle in his "Social History of the Hippies" cover story in* Ramparts, *became so pervasive in the late 60s that it subverted even square syndicated comic strips like Rex Morgan, M.D. (above)*

Victorian on a hill overlooking the Castro, a neighborhood then on the hinge of transforming from bi to uni-sexual.

There was certainly no great call for another liberal magazine with Catholic flavoring, or, God forbid, yet another plain vanilla leftist sheet. *Ramparts* was different because I added a healthy dash of muckraking. The left-wing press, such as it was in the United States, had been the product of shadow circulation caves and butcher paper ghettos--magazines and newspapers of the committed, by the committed, and for the committed. The intramural left press posed no threat to the prevailing wisdom reflected in the so-called "middle of the road" commercial media with all its stuffy egocentric nationalism. That point is, I daresay, not especially arguable--one has only to recall the sad story of the *Nation's* printing the story of the Bay of Pigs preparations--five months before the invasion--and being almost totally ignored in its pitiable attempts to alert the rest of the American press to the story.

The experiment I tried with *Ramparts* was to attempt to break out of the circulation boundaries and audience of fellow basket-weavers of the traditional liberal-left press. The goal was to escalate dissent from the soapboxes to the newsstands of America. That the gamble succeeded, to the limited but still surprising extent that it did, is comment enough on the Big Sleep of American journalism through

Photos: Wayne Ewing

ZAPPED: Hunter put down the bouquet of flowers in his hand and zapped Jann Wenner in his office with a fire extinguisher blast. Filmmaker Wayne Ewing got the zap on camera but Wenner threatened to sue if the frames of him being hit in the face with the hideous foam were released for publication. Thus the reader here sees only Hunter taking aim at his then boss but is denied the indecent pleasure of seeing Wenner get it smack in the puss. (From "Breakfast with Hunter.")

most of the 60s. If the rest of the press had been halfway on the ball, there would have been no way for a cocky kid like *Ramparts* to muscle onto the block.

An even more radical change than process color was the paper's approach to the truth, which, on the left, had been virtually synonymous with the correct line. I barred such theoretical essays from *Ramparts*, and substituted old-fashioned muckraking journalism with its bias on the left but reported facts--or, to give my critics their day in court, purported facts--which made the political points stick. There is nothing ideological about the facts, I would say to many a young leftist as I blue-penciled his theorems. Along with this hard-nosed approach to digging up dirt, *Ramparts* developed a branch of new journalism that interpolated social and political criticism with trendy you-were-there stylisms. And believing that the truth has to be marketed just like everything else in America, I promoted the blazes out of our stories so that the larger media, should it be inclined to ignore our screeds, ála the example of the *Nation*, would find it difficult to do so. This Kamikaze approach to journalism became known as "radical slick.' It was on these terms of taking liberal-left journalism for a ride uptown that *Ramparts* went for broke.

Hunter thought *Rolling Stone* should never have left San Francisco for New York, one of his many battles with Wenner, including a hilarious beef when Hunter accused the publisher of canceling his life insurance after *Rolling Stone* sent Thompson to Vietnam. Wenner mostly denied this.

Wenner, to indulge in understatement, frequently had staff problems, which he would usually resolve by firing. Talent such as Jon Carroll and Greil Marcus were fired (Marcus was canned for writing a record review trashing Bob Dylan's "Self-Portrait" album; the review never ran) and editors often quit on their "little Hitler." A former editor, John Lombardi, wrote thus of Hunter's relationship with Jann: "He asked to have his name taken off the masthead, and Wenner fought it for as long as he could, finally settling for 'Raoul Duke,' Hunter's pseudonym, as 'sports editor.' They quarreled about content and style, with Hunter saying privately that "Jann has reduced the *Rolling Stone* to a Gap catalogue." Much of this conflict was Hunter's unwillingness to put up with the Love Generation as a substitute for politics. Ralph Gleason actually believed that Bob Dylan and the Beatles *et al* had started something that was "beyond politics" which would end up "changing the heads of the world."

Witness Gleason on the future of political action:

"Out of it (the music) will come the programs. Out of it will come the plans. When the time is right."

The time was right at Altamont, where the Hells Angels cracked the heads of the flower children, speaking brutal truth to the power of the Love Generation.

When *Scanlan's* was busted in Canada, Hunter tried to save it by writing Wenner and one of his financial backers to see if the *Rolling Stone* and *Scanlan's* could be published in an umbrella operation ..."it strikes me as a fetching sort of idea. What comes to mind, right off, is some kind of 1970s version of a *Time/Life* empire; two entirely different publications locked in the same nexus ... real freak power ..." But Wenner would have none of that. There was tainted blood. Wenner got his start working for the *Sunday Ramparts*, a newspaper offshoot of *Ramparts* that art director Dugald Stermer and I created out of overset one afternoon when we were sitting around Enrico's bored with nothing to do after finishing an issue of the monthly magazine. We figured why not put the rejects into a newspaper?

I let Wenner use the *Ramparts* art department to produce the first issue of the *Rolling Stone*. I had no interest in producing a music magazine and Wenner little interest in a political magazine, which was evident when the *RS* led the parade to put the revolution in stores. Wenner's partner in the *Stone* was Ralph Gleason, a venerable music writer for the *San Francisco Chronicle* who moonlighted as a *Ramparts* editor. I liked Ralph who helped enormously in developing *Ramparts*'

cultural coverage, which was far mellower than its hard-ass New Left staff. Ralph was a middle-aged nice guy who took to wearing beads and thought the Summer of Love ethic would change America. We differed over the efficacy of flower power and when I wrote a controversial *Ramparts* cover story dumping on the hippie phenomenon, a furious Gleason resigned and helped Wenner start the *Rolling Stone*. (Arnie Passman, the historian of disk jockeys, who wrote for *Ramparts* and *Scanlan's* penned a letter to the editor about Gleason's resignation, asking if "Gleason was three 18-year-olds or four 16-year-olds?") The controversial *Ramparts* hippie article said the naïve purveyors of free love and free music and flower power over politics were being ripped off by consumer capitalists and the exploiters of star power like rock-promoter Bill Graham.

Where do dead magazines go? I suppose there is a place, as in a conversation in a bar where one person imagines his life re-lived and the other person says, "I used to subscribe to *Ramparts*, too," but the speaker doesn't really hear him because his thoughts are of himself and times back then. Wherever that place is, if it is it, is not a place of quiet; there are emanations--novelist Gertrude Atherton once explained the craziness of San Francisco as emanations from the old gold mines nearby--memories as stimulants. *Scanlan's* is tangled in the memory of Hunter S. Thompson and gonzo and Nixon killing *Scanlan's*, but *Ramparts* stands singular like that fleeting glory that once was known as Camelot--it was around so briefly and did so much to bring back muckraking and put a smiling face on it, that it is well positioned in the deep springs of memory of the century.

What made me start thinking about all this was a telephone call one day from Kathleen Cleaver, widow of Eldridge Cleaver, the Socrates of the Black Panther Party, the rapist-essayist who *Ramparts* sprang from prison and into print in the 60s. She had lost my telephone number and tracked me down through the Tosca's communications network, and called my number in New York with an urgent request for something she needed from *Ramparts* and, as she explained, in desperately seeking *Ramparts* she found there was nothing left of *Ramparts* but me. She was teaching at Yale and I told her to come into the city and meet me for a drink at the Players, the venerable old actors' hideaway in an elegant Stanford White brownstone on Gramercy Park. The years had treated her well and she made nothing short of a terrific entrance where the boys at the downstairs bar greeted her as a rad Michele Obama.

One day I took Eldridge Cleaver to Cookie's for a drink. He noticed that he was in a cop bar (an easy guess with signs like "Thank God for the Tac Squad" plastering the walls). Cleaver wanted to know why I had brought him to a right-wing bar. I asked him if he knew of a decent left-wing bar. He surrendered the discussion, and bought a drink for all the cops in the joint.

[WHO KILLED JOHN F. KENNEDY?]

The New York investigative journalist Peter Maas was a friend of Bobby Kennedy and invited me at the Senator's behest to dinner at the Oak Room in the Plaza Hotel. This was about three months before Bobby ate that indigestible bullet in L.A. Maas said Kennedy wanted to make nice and share some information about Vietnam with the editor of *Ramparts*. It went without saying that the predicate of the meeting was that Bobby believed the leading magazine against the war was all wet. Assured that Kennedy would pick up the check, I went.

Bobby was as humorless as a priest's jock strap and only wanted to talk about the Ho Chi Minh Trail, which, he maintained religiously, was a heavy military supply line for weapons of Red Chinese or Russian origin to be lugged from North to South Vietnam. *Ramparts* had reported the Trail was about as real as the yellow brick road of Oz and that many of the weapons used against our soldiers were stolen or captured by the indigenous Viet Cong. It was Mao's old tale of the guerrilla as a fish in the sea v. Cold War theology; cunning natives v. foreign power invaders. I impiously changed the subject by asking who Bobby thought had really killed his brother. He stared at me fish-mouthed when I asked if he believed the sitting president, Lyndon Johnson, for whom Bobby famously had no love lost, could have been involved.

Bobby recited the catechism of the Warren Commission--Oswald was the lone assassin and so on--and I knew he was lying like a rug. It wasn't until years after his own death by an assassin's gun (or guns) that it became known that he had been tormented by the worry that his brother could have been the victim of blowback from the Kennedy brothers' own murderous plots against Fidel Castro. Bobby as much believed in the Oswald story as I did in the tooth fairy. "That went well," Maas said afterwards.

When I recounted that unpleasant dinner conversation to Hunter, the Southern Gentleman in him came out. He said I shouldn't have badgered Bobby about such a grievous family matter.

Hunter loved a good conspiracy theory. I had many a late night phone conversation with Hunter about the JFK assassination and the latest version of who done what. *Ramparts* had championed the theories of eccentric New Orleans district attorney Jim Garrison--that CIA anti-Castro Cubans and the mob were prime among the unindicted co-conspirators. Hunter wasn't so sure about Garrison but he was certain that someone other than Oswald or the butler had done it. He loved the stories I told him about the Warren Commission-busting small town Texas editor Penn Jones, Jr. whom I was then promoting for national hero status.

Hunter's fascination with JFK conspiracy theories weighed heavy on my mind when conspiracy theories flooded the internet about *his* death. This harkened back to the glorious days of yesteryear when the cottage conspiracy industry about Who Killed John F. Kennedy? blossomed like a Luther Burbank hybrid in the sun of governmental screw-up and cover-up.

I share here some of the *Ramparts* JFK stories that so intrigued Hunter because I believe they played at least a subliminal role in forging the wild speculation about Hunter's death. I know--as the tooth knows where the cavity is--that this stuff was deep in his head and I can't help but wonder if Hunter, the evil bastard, didn't plant the seed of speculation--Who Killed Hunter S. Thompson?--about his own demise in the 9/11 conspiracy conversations and interviews he gave before his death on February 20, 2005 in Woody Creek.

Musing over the theories about Hunter's demise, I went back in time, a not-so-distant-time in real time, to Midlothian, Texas in 1966, sitting in a rocking chair on a ranch house porch drinking branch water and bourbon with Penn Jones, Jr., the editor of the *Midlothian Mirror*--"the only paper that gives a shit about Midlothian." Penn's ranch boasted the only working water wheel (you had to run up the hill and give it a good whump to get the wheel going) in Ellis County, a formerly prosperous cotton county some 30 miles out of Dallas. Penn was that rarest of late-20th century breeds, the populist, fighting country editor--the marquee American editorial position that was once occupied by William Allen White in Kansas and is now well filled by the estimable Bruce Anderson, who terrorizes the Mendocino coast of California with his *Anderson Valley Advertiser*.

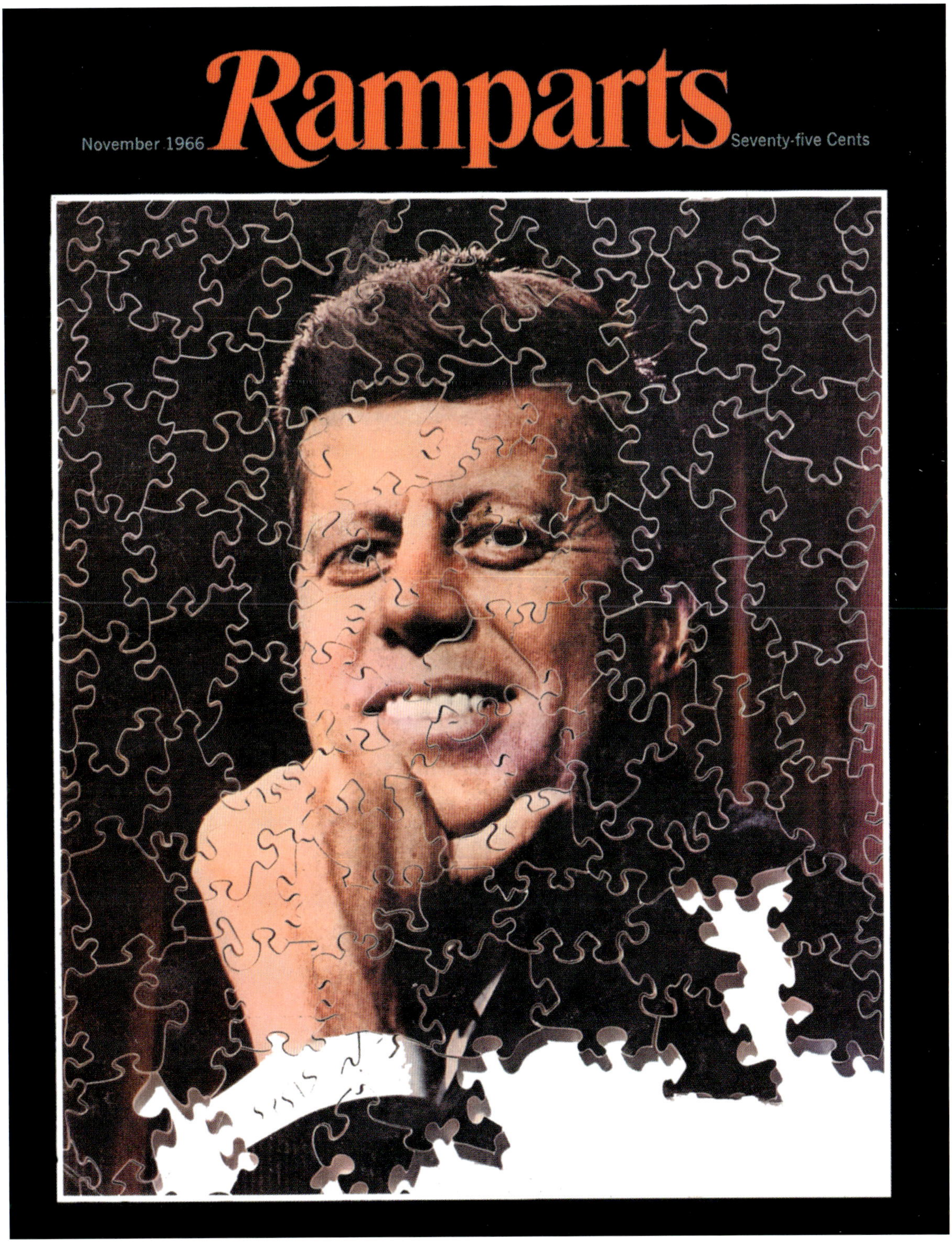

November 1966 **Ramparts** Seventy-five Cents

Ramparts *Kennedy Assasination cover by Dugald Stermer.*

Penn's weathery face sagged like a broken windmill. His eyes were bright as he boasted of his collection of antique barbed wire that he knew was the largest in the U.S. And he *knew* who shot Kennedy, or, at least, who didn't. Penn would talk for hours in his dusty Texas drawl about his investigation of the Warren Report and why it was a spit bucket of lies, not worth the paper it was printed on.

I was in Texas to see the country editor because he had himself one hell of a story, maybe the story of the century. Penn had published a gotcha' series of "investigative editorials" in the *Midlothian Mirror* detailing an astounding series of deaths of potentially key witnesses to the Kennedy Assassination. Not a one had testified before the Warren Commission--because they had all died, mysteriously, before they could testify. There were thirteen mysterious deaths when I first talked to Penn, and this number was to thereafter expand exponentially. An army of *Ramparts*' amateur sleuths began to dig into the parts the Warren Commission left out about the president's murder. (If you are inclined to give the Warren Commission the benefit of the doubt, please welcome Arlen Specter, the party-switching Pennsylvania senator who was a stalwart defender of the Warren Commission and enthusiastic promoter of the ridiculous magic bullet thesis.)

"How mysterious were these mysterious deaths?" Hunter demanded of me when I first told him about our hero, the amazing Penn Jones. One for-instance: a meeting in Jack Ruby's Dallas apartment was convened by Ruby's sometimes roommate, George Senator, after Ruby shot Lee Harvey Oswald, the president's putative assassin. Senator gave his occupation to the Warren Commission as that of a "beggar" but told a remarkably incurious Commission that he was darned if he could remember anything about the meeting he had called. Three of the five people present that night in Ruby's apartment died, mysteriously if you want, or freakishly by any standard, shortly after that fateful, for them, meeting. Two were newsmen. Jim Koethe worked for the *Dallas Times Herald*. He was killed by a karate chop to the neck when he stepped out of his shower, and the notebooks on his Kennedy assassination investigation disappeared. Bill Hunter worked for the *Long Beach Press Telegram*. He investigative-reported from Texas about the assassination, and on his return to California was shot dead in the Long Beach press room--two cops explained that they had been horsing around when a gun went off, killing the reporter. That type of thing doesn't happen every day. The third

death was that of attorney Tom Howard, a Dallas ambulance-chaser who spent the two days and two nights interviewing Jack Ruby after he shot Lee Harvey Oswald. Howard was almost immediately thereafter found dead, at 48, of a "heart attack," although no autopsy was performed. There was also no autopsy for Oswald's landlady, Earlene Roberts. Also found dead of a "heart attack," she had enticing information about a Dallas Police car pulling up in front of her rooming house and giving a toot-toot horn salute for Howard a few minutes before Oswald left, in a hurry, on Assassination Day. These were some, among many others, of the key players with intimate knowledge of the Dallas assassination, who shared the common denominator that they were all, as a matter of absolute fact, dead.

This was a genre story right out of the Curse of King Tut's tomb: *death shall come on swift wings to him who touches the tomb of the pharaoh.*

When I got back from Texas I asked *Ramparts*-man Bill Turner, ex-of the FBI, to make damn sure all of these thirteen witnesses were really, really dead. They were. So I shit-canned a lengthy, studiously detailed analysis of the Warren Commission's many sins of omission and commission that *Ramparts*' New Left sleuths had been slaving over for more than a year, infuriating them one and all, to put the Kennedy/King Tut curse on the cover with a commanding illustration of JFK's pretty face cut up as an incomplete jigsaw puzzle. The daily papers had relegated the many critiques of the Warren Commission back with the truss ads, but when *Ramparts* ran Penn Jones' modern King Tut curse story, *caramba*! Kennedy-assassination mania swept over the national press. A crew from Huntley-Brinkley hung out for two days at *Ramparts*' North Beach offices. Before he went on the air with the story, Walter Cronkite Himself, went to Texas to tell America that all these potential witnesses were, oddly, actually dead.

The resulting tumult gave *Ramparts* its own ink blot on the map of publishing. Hunter suggested that *Ramparts* send him to Idaho to explore his theory that somewhere in the rugged Idaho terrain NASA had faked the moon landing against a computerized backdrop of space.

[WALLPOSTERS, CHICAGO AND ASPEN]

The pilot speaking: "Well folks I am afraid we will have to hold over Dodge City for about 35 minutes because of a sudden influx of military aircraft into Chicago to protect the Democrats."

"...Folks, I am normally kind of a law-abiding guy, but this is something else today. I am advised by Air Traffic Control that 45 military troop transports have been unexpectedly brought into the Chicago area. We had no previous knowledge of such military flights. Air Traffic Control tells us they knew nothing about it. You folks fly your planes and buy your tickets and don't know anything about this. I think this is worth a note to your Congressman."

This was on a plane from San Francisco to Chicago, to the 1968 Democratic Convention & Riot. The pilot was pissed off. I was sure he was a registered Republican who had had it with all this disruption of his air space so the corrupt Democratic Party bosses could hold a closed-door convention in the face of party rank and file protests that burgeoned into the mother of all street demonstrations. Liberal delegates expected the cops to be reasonable. But the iron heel of the state came down in Chicago as it had so many times before in the 60s at pressure points of protest from the Oakland Army Depot to Selma.

There was this awful smell in the lobby of the monolithic Conrad Hilton Hotel, the official Democratic headquarters. The residue of a stink bomb set off by an enterprising demonstrator in the hotel's air conditioning system had not been eradicated and the eating and sleeping quarters of the party in power smelled like a lion's asshole. Some delegates pretended not to notice and went on with party hack business as usual, amid the usual pretensions of representative democracy. It was like pretending that you had not stepped in dog shit.

Even the proscription of the Third Amendment to the Constitution against the quartering of troops in peacetime--which Mencken noted in the *Roaring 20s* was the only part of the Bill of Rights that had not been taken from us--was violated in Chicago. Even the city's elder statesman of high culture, Hugh Hefner, was not inviolate--Hef was clubbed in the ass while checking out the yippies being gassed by the cops.

Hunter had trouble getting this issue of his Wallposter printed.

Chicago was the end of the line for the vestiges of 60s good liberal beliefs in orderly change through The System. The lesson of Chicago was that disorder comes out of the failure of the orderly process. The democratic system had corroded arteries and channels of dissent and the gears of democratic decision-making were frozen. The Constitution's promise of the redress of grievances was kaput; few in power were hearing the thunder from the streets, or if they heard, they didn't listen. Dissent took over Main Street, disrupting commerce, which at the end of the day was why the war in Vietnam had to be ended--the rioting in the streets was interfering with the business of America, which, as Calvin Coolidge so cooly observed, was business. But LBJ outfoxed the theoreticians of the New Left. When he removed himself by saying that he would not run for re-election, he removed the symbol of protest that held together the disparate branches which made up the tree of the New Left--which never had a coherent philosophy. Without LBJ to kick around, the DNA of the New Left broke down like atoms into its parts--gay rights, women's rights, green rights and so on--that had made it whole in opposition to the war. There was no more LBJ and, after a time, there was no more New Left.

Hunter had been roughed up pretty bad in front of the Hilton Hotel by the cops. He and Pete Hamill had signed on with the disparate *Ramparts* task force covering the convention. Hunter was a frequent drop-in at the *Ramparts*' city room, a suite in the Ambassador East Hotel, where he replenished himself and found skullduggery afoot. Sydney Schanberg, the *New York Times*-man and later Pulitzer Prize correspondent in Cambodia, was also moonlighting for *Ramparts* in Chicago and noticed suspicious characters entering and leaving the room next door. Schanberg organized a scouting posse, followed one lug into the room next door and found it crowded with recording devices and overweight men in golf caps and polyester pants. Hunter figured it for some sort of Chicago police or state law enforcement eavesdropping operation because he said the equipment seemed too outdated and clumsy for a CIA or FBI op. The buggers were scattered the righteous way Jesus chased the moneychangers from the temple.

Hunter had a deep moralistic faith in the American dream, and he left Chicago horrified that it had been violated. For Hunter, Chicago was a fantastic watershed in American politics and in his own head; as his friend and biographer Douglas Brinkley has observed, the

shock of Chicago propelled him into electoral politics and his 1970 campaign for sheriff in Colorado.

Hunter needed a horse to ride in his charge into politics, and in Chicago I provided him with an unlikely mount. The New Left seraphim had asked *Ramparts* to publish a daily newspaper for the convention. I warily agreed. I didn't think a conventional paper would make sense since the streets were in such chaos; I couldn't see anyone having the time or the convenience of sitting still long enough to digest a daily left analytical tabloid. The thought then hit me like a thunderclap from the Witch of Endor--a Wallposter! After all, that was what Mao had done to communicate with the masses during the Revolution--put up wallposters! "Two pages," I explained, "Front and back. A Wallposter! Immediacy!"

The first issue of *Ramparts*' Chicago Wallposter was produced by Fred Gardner and a staff of volunteers and academics who shocked me silly by putting words of left political analysis, in small print, on the front. I was flummoxed. Any dummy should know that the front of a wallposter is supposed to be the poster part. The paper had been produced at great expense at a left-leaning Chicago printing plant that had no qualms about charging me capitalist prices. By the time they got the thing off the presses, the next morning's paper, full of yesterday's analysis, came out in the afternoon when nobody could read it because most everyone was otherwise occupied being beat up by Mayor Richard Daley's goons. I stripped that crew of their epaulets and summarily brought in a crew of newspaper pros--including Schanberg and my old friend Sidney Zion, also then at the *Times*--(Zion later became my partner in *Scanlan's*.) The next morning's edition of the Wallposter came out on time and looked like a poster--but unfortunately created a cultural collision with the New Left. I was hosting a nightly table in the fabled Pump Room in the Ambassador East Hotel where Hunter would drop by to schmooze with the gaggle of political insiders and establishment reporters drinking *Ramparts*' booze. The night before there had been a police riot outside and tear gas came through the Pump Room doors and windows. The wealthy customers, among whom we were drinking, began gagging and puking. I was elated--Class Warfare at last! It reminded me of a G.K. Chesterton line, something about the upper classes and the sound of smashing glasses. The AWOL *Times* men went to work on the lead story and the next morning's Wallposter announced class warfare under the huge headline TEAR GAS IN THE PUMP ROOM! The story

was set in wire service capitals in typewriter type with an AP-style lede datelined THE PUMP ROOM.

In that issue the High Left analysis was printed on the back, where the paste went to glue it to the wall. Our incensed New Left distributors gave the issue sewer service.

That ersatz product of the Chicago madness created a little known chapter, well, perhaps, a footnote, in the strange story of 20th Century agitprop journalism--the short-lived Wallposter phenomenon. At that time Thompson and I both thought Wallposters were the bee's knees. Hunter fell in love with my Chicago Wallposter and decided this was the perfect medium to connect with the common folk during his campaign for sheriff in Pitkin County. Hunter thought this big news and excitedly wrote Herb Caen at the *San Francisco Chronicle* with these suggestions for items in Caen's locally famous three-dot column: "Wallposters were a 'totally new form of journalism' ... Caen should recognize 'Hinckle as the father of the Modern Wallposter'... Thompson would soon begin printing an Aspen Wallposter to be published by 'the judgment proof Meat Possum Press'... "

I had promised Hunter I would run a subscription ad for his Wallposter in *Scanlan's*; all he had to do was send in the copy. As hard luck would have it, the issue his Wallposter ad ran in was the Guerrilla Warfare issue that was seized by the Mounties in Canada.

Hunter put on his copywriter's beanie and wrote his ad copy, a detailed exposition of his fiendish plans for Colorado once he was elected sheriff. I published Hunter's ad, fabulously illustrated with the rejected cover for an Aspen Wallposter (a doctored version of an old *Time* cover, giving Nixon zombie eyes, blood dripping from his mouth.) Hunter couldn't get that cover printed in Colorado and the heretofore unpublished Nixon cover of the Aspen Wallposter found unsafe harbor in *Scanlan's*.

Hunter's instructions for the placement of his advertisement are of interest to students of the man because it is so typical of the jeweler's eye for detail he had as he focused on his first love, which was print publications.

Dear Warren...

Here's the Wallposter ad, along with a few space problems that I've hopefully solved, to wit:

1) Drop the subscription box and run my copy in that space. Given the vicious subscription prices, I think we'll be better off soliciting $2 sample shots... and that way we'll also have room to run the copy, which says a lot more than the box.

2) The other alternative is to do whatever you want with the fucker. Rearrange the whole goddamn ad, for all I care. And by the way of explanation, this "Agnew Sucks Fireplugs" thing was the cover we had planned for WP #3--but the local printer refused to print it.

All this clearly proves to me is that I'm not worth a shit as an ad-writer--and particularly not as an ad-writer cum politician cum publisher. So I leave the bugger to your hands, for good or ill. Since my last dreary letter, our finances have taken a fast turn for the better. We are not only in the black, somehow--that kind of fatness embarrasses me--WP #5 is in the works & this one will fuck us all. I have made a list of all our enemies--and many of our friends--involved in the local land-rape enterprises, and we intend to savage them all... and along with this list of greedheads & their transgressions, we will publish a score-board--showing that we have whipped, terrified & destroyed all those we have attacked. --Hunter

[BY DR. HUNTER S. THOMPSON,
ADVERTISING COPYWRITER:]

Are you ready to drop out? Flee the city? Screw off to the Rockies and seize a ripe chunk of the Good Life?

If so, first do yourself a favor--read the Aspen Wallposter and be the first on your block to have your illusions come home in a tube.

The Rape of Aspen is a mushrooming horror story, designed by experts to drive even the most zealous freak/liberal/would-be agrarian escapist straight to his knees. What began in the 1950s as a chic seduction by ski-mongers and jet setters soon became a frenzied gang-rape of the whole valley.

Aspen has been skillfully merchandised from coast to coast as a weird little ski-commune & culture-spa, full of happy refugees from the Nazi/plastic nightmare of Urban America. And a lot of people came here, believing that treacherous swill --most of it written by hired geeks in the pay of such monsters as Boise Cascade, American Cement, First National

City Bank of New York, Texas International Petroleum, Minnie Pearl Chicken, Head Ski and Holiday Inn. The hype was compounded by greedheads like John Wayne, Leon Uris and Robert McNamara, who lent the dubious prestige of their names to some of the ugliest "development" schemes since the Florida real estate boom of the 1920s.

Meanwhile, all political power was centered in a Nazi-oriented cartel of local businessmen who instructed the cops to do whatever was "necessary" to protect the town's image--and their own foul investments--from desecration by freaks, hippies, dope-suckers & other strange weeds that were threatening, by the end of the 60s, to take permanent root in the merchants' profit-garden.

Then, with no warning--in the fall of '69--Aspen's long-smoldering Underground suddenly flexed its political muscle and came within six (6) votes of electing a twenty-nine year-old head, lawyer & bikeracer as mayor. Joe Edwards lost by a hair--but the establishment lost three of its crucial City Council seats, and the mayor's tie-breaking vote is now all that keeps the greedheads in control of Aspen.

The Wallposter was created in the wake of that campaign, to maintain the energy & keep the swine off balance--a full-size poster, on heavy paper, with the Brute/Color graphics of Rev. Thomas Benton on one side, and the savage screeds of the Rev, Hunter S, Thompson on the other.

After only four issues the Wallposter has grown from an esoteric local handbill to a nationally distributed monster that drives the local cops and greedheads completely crazy each time it appears. The first issue blew the county attorney out of office; #2 introduced Jimson Weed & the sexual aspects of Sumo wrestling to local newsstands; #3 caused banks in New York & Boston to pull out of a huge land-rape project, which soon collapsed; #4 destroyed the sheriff.

Issue #5 will very likely destroy the Wallposter, the Meat Possum Press and all those associated with it. But we are now whipping it together, for good or ill, and if our infrastructure survives this next one, #6 will carry

UP AGAINST THE WALL

The Ramparts Wall Poster

COMPLETE CONVENTION COVERAGE

8:00 AM CITY EDITION — Wednesday, August 28, 1968 — TEN CENTS

(CHICAGO BEGINS TO FALL APART)

TEAR GAS IN THE PUMP ROOM!

(BOMBED)

BY JAKE MCCARTHY

© 1968 The Daily Wallposter

THE PUMP ROOM — BRUTAL POLICE SUPPRESSION OF DISSENT IN CHICAGO WAS AN IMAGINARY WORLD OF NEWSPAPER HEADLINES AND TELEVISION FILM FOR DELEGATES AND VISITORS UNTIL THE WORST HAPPENED TUESDAY NIGHT AS THE TOWN BEGAN TO FALL APART.

TEAR GAS SEEPED INTO THE FAMED PUMP ROOM THROUGH TWO SMASHED WINDOWS AS CANISTERS BLASTED OFF EIGHT BLOCKS FROM LINCOLN PARK IN THE BIGGEST POLICE FORAY OF THE WEEK.

PLUMED BLACK BUS BOYS (DRESSED ACCORDING TO THE COAT OF ARMS OF PRINCE FREDERICK) WEPT ALONGSIDE DOWAGERS AND FIXERS WHO COULDN'T GET PASSES TO THE CONVENTION FLOOR, OR DECIDED TO DANCE INSTEAD.

"CHRIST, SOMETHING MUST REALLY BE HAPPENING OUT THERE," SOMEBODY GASPED AT THE BAR.

THE BUSTED WINDOWS IN THE PUMP ROOM--AND THE DRIFTING TEAR GAS— SHOCKED THE CELEBRATORS AS MUCH AS THE SIGHT OF DOZENS OF HIPPIES TAKING REFUGE IN THE LOBBY OF THE AMBASSADOR EAST.

THE FURIOUS NEW ASSAULT BY CHICAGO POLICE WAS PART OF A SCENE OF DEEPENED INTENSITY IN THE CONFRONTATION BETWEEN COPS AND YOUNG WHITES IN MAYOR DALEY'S "SHOOT TO KILL" TOWN.

A HALF-DOZEN POLICE CARS WERE SMASHED, FOUR BUSES WERE HIT BY BRICKS AND DOZENS OF PEOPLE WERE HURT AND HUNDREDS ARRESTED TUESDAY NIGHT AS THE BATTLE BETWEEN POLICE AND PEOPLE IN CHICAGO WENT INTO ITS THIRD NIGHT.

(MORE DETAILS)

© 1968, Ramparts Magazine, Inc.

SEWER SERVICE: Ramparts *daily Wallposter at the riotous Chicago Democratic Convention got sewer service from its New Left distributors over this headline.*

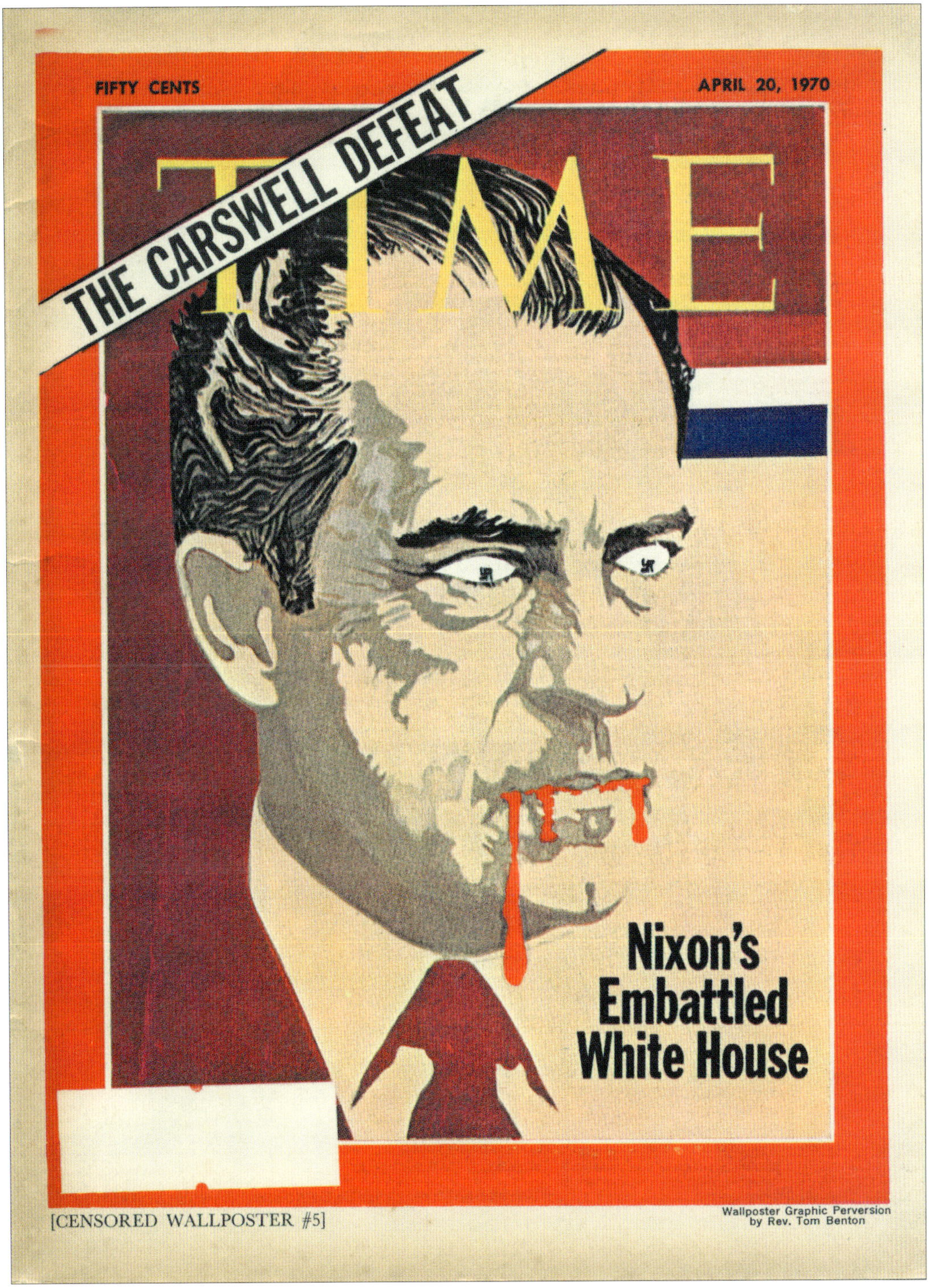

FIFTY CENTS

APRIL 20, 1970

THE CARSWELL DEFEAT

TIME

Nixon's Embattled White House

[CENSORED WALLPOSTER #5]

Wallposter Graphic Perversion by Rev. Tom Benton

Art by Tom Benton

TIMID PRINTERS: Hunter had trouble getting Colorado printers to print his Wallposter. Covers making nasty with Spiro Agnew and Richard Nixon were unprintable in the state. This (unprintable) Wallposter cover was finally printed in a promotional ad for Hunter's Wallposter in what turned out to be the last issue of Scanlan's.

the Reverend Thompson's declaration of candidacy for the office of county sheriff--along with his platform, now being hashed together with the help of Sgt. Sunshine & Wes Pomeroy, the main cop at Woodstock.

Further issues will detail the Rout of the Greedheads & the collapse of the local money/politics establishment... and the implications of this battle plan extend far beyond Aspen. The question here is not How to Work Within the System, or How to Destroy It--but rather How to Seize It, how to drive the pig off the ship without sinking the ship itself & putting us all in life rafts. It is the simple assumption that political power in this country is stagnant & static, until the people learn how to use it.

Maybe not--but on the basis of last Fall's experiment, we're ready for another run at the bastards, and this time we plan to win. The Wallposter will be the main voice of this effort. It was conceived more as a political tool than either a newspaper or a poster but it has evolved, very quickly, into a combination of all three. And on this basis we intend to run the bugger full bore for as long as there's room to run.

During his campaign for sheriff Hunter developed a grand plan for what he called "ecology-type law enforcement." He was going to stop the Rape of Aspen by developers and chalet-builders-from-Gstaad by turning the blue line green. He wrote me describing his vision for a Green Iron Fist:

> "I'd enforce laws with the same lunatic zeal which the incumbent sheriff once brought to bear on the drug laws. Drive the fuckers crazy, keep them in a state of fear and loathing--midnight raids to search for sewer violations, attaching their cranes & cats with writs of seizure, have them constantly in court & defending themselves on strange charges."

The election was in November of 1970, and Hunter damn near won.

Scanlan's Monthly was named after a much-disliked Irish pig farmer, John Scanlan. My friend Sidney Zion, then the legal correspondent for the *New York Times*, and I were vacationing with our

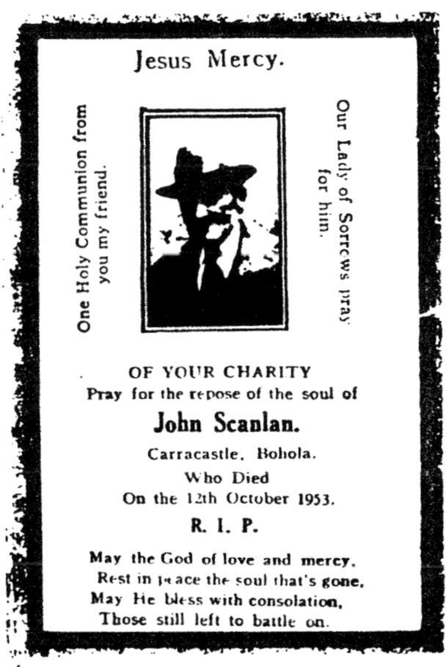

Jesus Mercy.

One Holy Communion from you my friend.

Our Lady of Sorrows pray for him.

OF YOUR CHARITY
Pray for the repose of the soul of

John Scanlan.

Carracastle, Bohola.
Who Died
On the 12th October 1953.

R. I. P.

May the God of love and mercy,
Rest in peace the soul that's gone,
May He bless with consolation,
Those still left to battle on.

The mass card of Scanlan's *anti-hero and namesake.*

wives in Ireland in 1968 and we met up with Paul O'Dwyer, the great Irish defender of American civil rights. O'Dwyer took Zion and I to an annual banquet in a suburban Dublin hotel. The diners were toasting the long-ago demise of this fellow John Scanlan. No offense to any living relatives, but John Scanlan was the most disliked man in his village, a charming cad who neglected his bar bills, failed to support his many illegitimate children, let his crops lie fallow while he sat in the pub and generally was a black mark on the civic community. The locals gathered annually to drink to his death. At the time Zion and I joked that John Scanlan would make a great name for a magazine.

We forgot about that until *Ramparts* folded and we found money in the stock market for a new muckraking magazine. I had a crazy idea to more or less continue *Ramparts* with a new corporation, free of its years of accumulated debt. However the New Left majority on the staff felt that would be somehow immoral. (Only David Horowitz, who had been Bertrand Russell's private secretary and was the fartherest to the ideological left of the *Ramparts* crew, understood the

capitalistic brilliance of such a solution. "Corporations have no soul," he told his fellow lefties, "They aren't people. There's nothing wrong with killing the corporation." But the consensus among the beaten and beleaguered *Ramparts* stalwarts was that we should never have tried to be so big in the first place. Horowitz later had a Light That Failed moment and went over to the conspiratorial right. I always felt sorry for David. He traversed from the far left to the far right without getting as much as a blow job from Ayn Rand.)

I had a name for the new magazine--*Barricades*! But Howard Gossage besieged me not to call the new mag anything like *Ramparts* but something entirely different. "Don't remind the readers of *Ramparts*. They'll be pissed-off at you," he said in his signature stutter. What to call it? Zion and I came to the same, obvious conclusion: name it after the hated pig farmer. Call it *Scanlan's*.

The magazine was financed by an over-the-counter stock issue scared up by Zion and myself in that smoke-filled temple of free-wheeling capitalism, the Sardi's second floor bar. We cornered Bob Arum, the fight promoter, at the time a partner in Louis Nizer's law firm representing the IPO genius Charlie Plohn. Zion convinced him that "Hinckle could work that old *Ramparts* magic" with a new magazine unencumbered by *Ramparts* debt. The red herring for the stock sale was unusual for its bluntness, warning investors that there was hardly any chance in Hell that *Scanlan's* would ever make money. The cover of the first issue struck a gonzo blow by printing on the cover the check from the underwriter Plohn & Co. for $675,000 (which was a helluva lot of money in 1970.) The bold-face

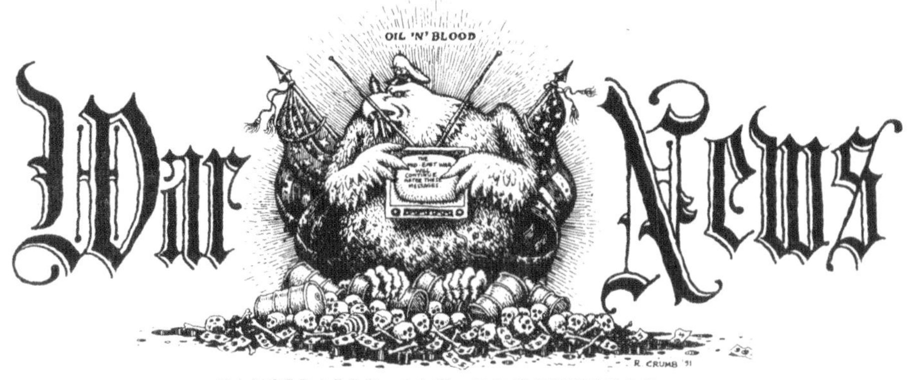

The irrepressible Hinckle kept starting up publications. (Above:) Robert Crumb's nameplate for War News, *an occasional 200,000 run newspaper in 1991.*

editorial beneath the check bragged that *Scanlan's Monthly* was funded by selling stock to the gullible, greedy public, and that there were not among the many small investors who peed into the *Scanlan's* pot enough souls who could get together to agree on anything, so *Scanlan's* could do what it damn well editorially pleased. We pledged, in fierce red type, to be "fiercely independent."

Hunter had been curious about the rumored new magazine. Turning down a writing assignment from the ongoing, deflated and more predictably and boringly-left *Ramparts*, which continued to publish after Elvis left the building, he wrote Peter Collier, Horowitz's better angel and a surviving *Ramparts* editor, about his "abiding curiosity as to Warren Hinckle's action these days." Hunter wrote he missed the old, exuberant *Ramparts*--"the simple fact of Hinckle sitting there in his office full of bad debts and strange animals lent a sense of possibility to the task of confronting my mail, some slim and wild chance that the fiendish daily stack might yield up something with a terrible zang and rattle to it."

He asked Collier: "Is Warren serious about putting out a new magazine? If I had a lot of money I'd be tempted to give him some, if only to watch it burn and hear the screams of the afflicted."

Scanlan's, the magazine, was a throwback to the phantasmagoric 19th century western journalism of the days of the code duello. *Ramparts* was conflicted over whether it was the *Front Page* or the *The Masses* and that kinetic energy worked. *Scanlan's* was conflicted with a cultural tug of war between its offices in San Francisco and New York, Hunter S. Thompson v. Ben Hecht, and the resulting magazine, typos and all, burst out of the gate an exuberant and wild beast of print. I was concerned about what John Scanlan's new monthly should look like. It couldn't look like *Ramparts*--art director Dugland Stermer's Times-Roman powerhouse design, and the *Ramparts* "look" had spread like the flu through the precious world of opinion publishing and by the end of the 60s almost every publication--*Harper's Monthly*, the *Atlantic*, the aging *Evergreen Review*--had redesigned or otherwise suffered a typographical hysterectomy so that they all resembled *Ramparts*; no greater compliment than imitation.

Text continues on page 80.

Scanlan's

Volume One Number One March 1970 Price: $1.00

CHARLES PLOHN & CO. 44 BEAVER STREET NEW YORK, N. Y. 34894
MEMBERS
NEW YORK STOCK EXCHANGE
AMERICAN STOCK EXCHANGE

11/25/69 19 1-30/210

PAY TO THE ORDER OF Scanlan's Literary House Inc. $675,000.00

DOLLARS

MANUFACTURERS HANOVER TRUST COMPANY
40 WALL STREET, NEW YORK, N. Y.

We must be fiercely candid about who owns and controls this new magazine.

Over 700 people in these United States bought stock in a public issue floated by our underwriter.

Frankly, we don't even know the names of our stockholders.

Moreover, we don't care.

Our deal with the underwriter was that the editors have absolute and dictatorial control of the magazine.

Such virgin promises of editorial freedom are usually a joke. There are few investors or owners who can conquer the very human temptation to influence editorial policy, and we know of no editors with sufficient nerve or desire to fight such pressure.

So before the public put up its money, at $3 a share, the two editors bought enough stock at a nickel to give them control of the magazine. We had to borrow from relatives to do this because, even at a nickel, effective control of a publicly owned publishing company takes cash.

All this was fully disclosed to the public before they bought in.

We would be dishonest if we didn't allow our surprise at getting this sort of dough with no strings attached.

This was a wingdinger of a stock issue to come through the great Bear Market of 1969, especially considering the well-known economic sand traps that magazines have become. Then there was the implicit promise by the editors of Scanlan's Monthly to carry out an unreasonable editorial policy which would vilify the institutions so dear to the hearts of most investors.

But we are not ones to look a gift magazine in the mouth. Then again, we think we pulled off quite a caper in this otherwise co-opted world of publishing.

Since the halcyon days of the great muckraking journals of half a century

[Continued on Back Cover]

Australia .90 cents Brazil 5000 cruzeiro England 8s 6d France 5.55 F Germany 3.63 DM India 7.5 rupees Ireland 8s 5d Israel 3.5 Pounds Italy 620 L Japan Yen 360 Mexico 12½ pesos Sweden 5.1 Krs

FULL DISCLOSURE: The new magazine's inaugural issue reproduced its stock market funding check from the underwriter on its cover and promised to villify everyone who invested.

Scanlan's

Volume One Number Six August 1970 Price: $1.00

THIS DIRTY MAGAZINE IS ONLY ABOUT POT AND DOPE SMUGGLING AND POON-TANG MOVIES AND LEFTWING INDIANS AND PENTAGON FRAUDS AND CHARLIE MANSON!! SO DON'T HAND ME ANY OF THAT CRAP ABOUT WINNIE THE POOH (P. 28)

R. CRUMB

Australia .90 cents Brazil 5000 cruzeiro England 8s 6d France 5.55 F Germany 7.00 DM India 7.5 rupees Ireland 8s 5d Israel 3.5 Pounds Italy 900 L Japan Yen 550 Mexico 12½ pesos Sweden 5.1 Krs

'KEEP ON TRUCKIN': *Artist R. Crumb of Zap Comix fame, was a favorite* Scanlan's *illustrator.*

Scanlan's

Volume One Number Three

May 1970 Price: $1.00

Russia's Underground Political Pornography

Exclusive:
NEW HOT WATER FOR TEDDY KENNEDY

The New York Times & The Supreme Court

Graham Greene on Graham Greene

Hemingway's Cub Reporting

Jean Lacouture on Nkrumah

J. Edgar Hoover's First Woman

Australia .90 cents
Brazil 5000 cruzeiro
England 8s 6d

France 5.55 F
Germany 3.63 DM
India 7.5 rupees

Ireland 8s 5d
Israel 3.5 Pounds
Italy 620 L

Japan Yen 360
Mexico 12 ½ pesos
Sweden 5.1 Krs

PROTEST ART: Scanlan's Art Director, Barbara Stauffacher Solomon, jazzed up Russian underground mimeographed "samizdat" protest literature mocking the new Soviet State to produce this striking newsstand cover.

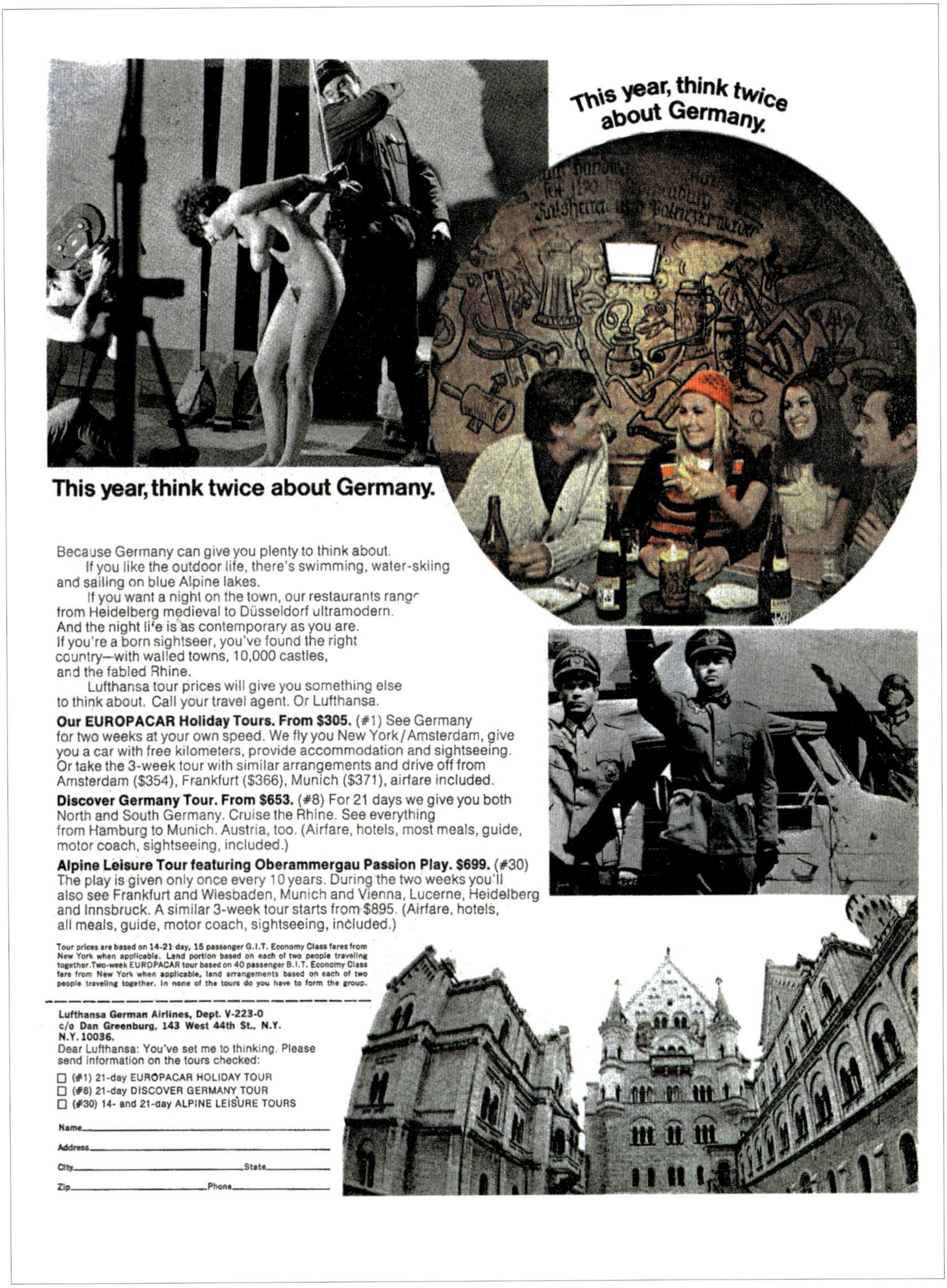

This year, think twice about Germany.

This year, think twice about Germany.

Because Germany can give you plenty to think about.

If you like the outdoor life, there's swimming, water-skiing and sailing on blue Alpine lakes.

If you want a night on the town, our restaurants range from Heidelberg medieval to Düsseldorf ultramodern. And the night life is as contemporary as you are. If you're a born sightseer, you've found the right country—with walled towns, 10,000 castles, and the fabled Rhine.

Lufthansa tour prices will give you something else to think about. Call your travel agent. Or Lufthansa.

Our EUROPACAR Holiday Tours. From $305. (#1) See Germany for two weeks at your own speed. We fly you New York / Amsterdam, give you a car with free kilometers, provide accommodation and sightseeing. Or take the 3-week tour with similar arrangements and drive off from Amsterdam ($354), Frankfurt ($366), Munich ($371), airfare included.

Discover Germany Tour. From $653. (#8) For 21 days we give you both North and South Germany. Cruise the Rhine. See everything from Hamburg to Munich. Austria, too. (Airfare, hotels, most meals, guide, motor coach, sightseeing, included.)

Alpine Leisure Tour featuring Oberammergau Passion Play. $699. (#30) The play is given only once every 10 years. During the two weeks you'll also see Frankfurt and Wiesbaden, Munich and Vienna, Lucerne, Heidelberg and Innsbruck. A similar 3-week tour starts from $895. (Airfare, hotels, all meals, guide, motor coach, sightseeing, included.)

Tour prices are based on 14-21 day, 15 passenger G.I.T. Economy Class fares from New York when applicable. Land portion based on each of two people travelling together. Two-week EUROPACAR tour based on 40 passenger B.I.T. Economy Class fare from New York when applicable, land arrangements based on each of two people traveling together. In none of the tours do you have to form the group.

Lufthansa German Airlines, Dept. V-223-0
c/o Dan Greenburg, 143 West 44th St., N.Y.
N.Y. 10036.

Dear Lufthansa: You've set me to thinking. Please send information on the tours checked:

- ☐ (#1) 21-day EUROPACAR HOLIDAY TOUR
- ☐ (#8) 21-day DISCOVER GERMANY TOUR
- ☐ (#30) 14- and 21-day ALPINE LEISURE TOURS

Name____________________

Address____________________

City____________ State________

Zip____________ Phone________

THINK TWICE ABOUT GERMANY? Scanlan's *created quite a dust up on Madison Avenue when it doctored a Lufthansa magazine ad promoting tourism to Germany with Nazi horror pictures and ran it without permission as its back cover ad.*

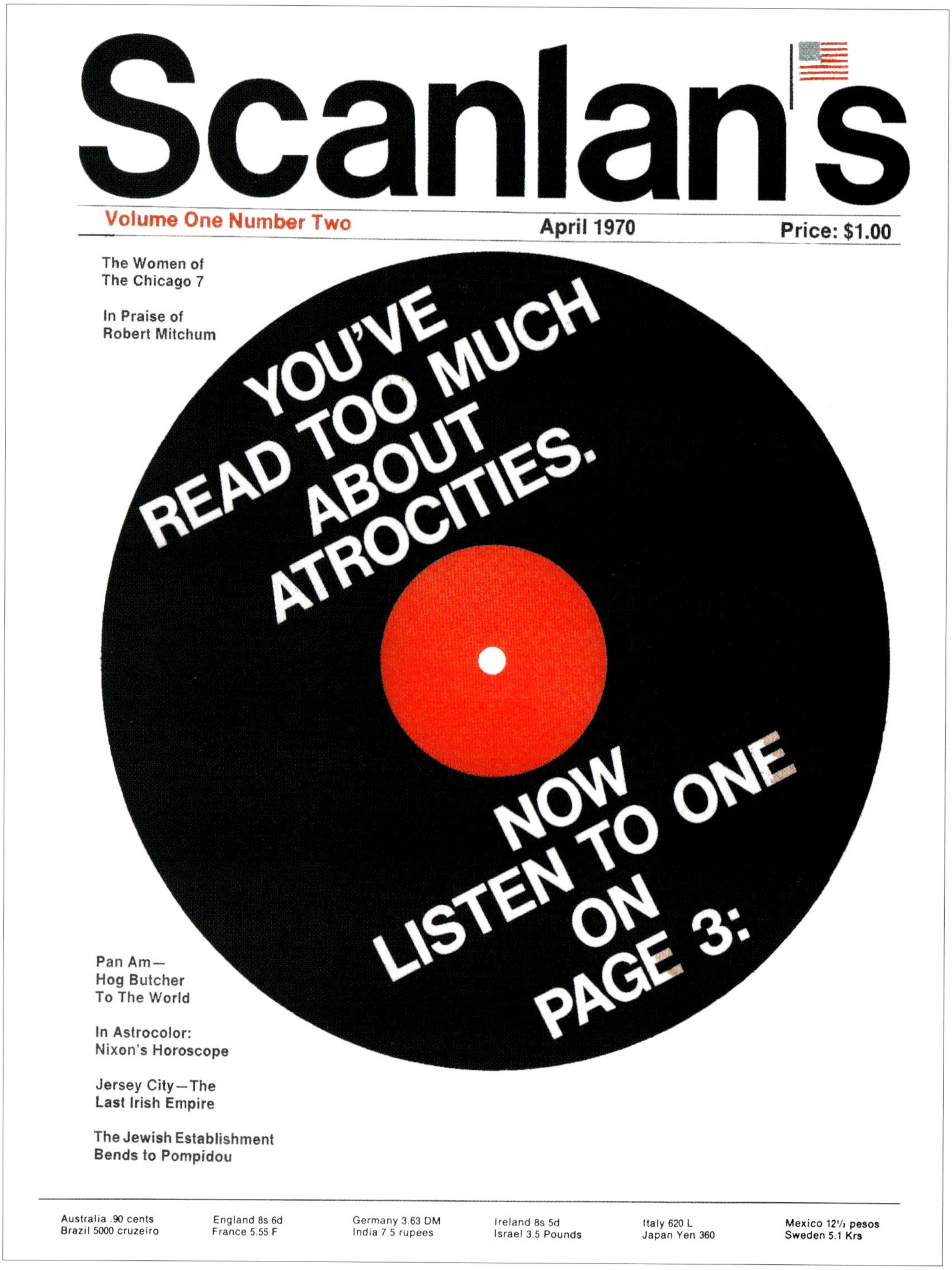

Scanlan's

Volume One Number Two — April 1970 — Price: $1.00

The Women of The Chicago 7

In Praise of Robert Mitchum

YOU'VE READ TOO MUCH ABOUT ATROCITIES.

NOW LISTEN TO ONE ON PAGE 3:

Pan Am— Hog Butcher To The World

In Astrocolor: Nixon's Horoscope

Jersey City—The Last Irish Empire

The Jewish Establishment Bends to Pompidou

Australia .90 cents · Brazil 5000 cruzeiro · England 8s 6d · France 5.55 F · Germany 3.63 DM · India 7.5 rupees · Ireland 8s 5d · Israel 3.5 Pounds · Italy 620 L · Japan Yen 360 · Mexico 12½ pesos · Sweden 5.1 Krs

NOW HEAR THIS: Green Beret war hero Donald Duncan, who went anti-war in Ramparts, *continued to write about Vietnam war atrocities in Scanlan's. He secured a frightening tape recording of an Army interrogation of one soldier's heinous acts that Hinckle had made into a record and bound into the magazine.*

NIXON AND THE BUMS.

AN EDITORIAL

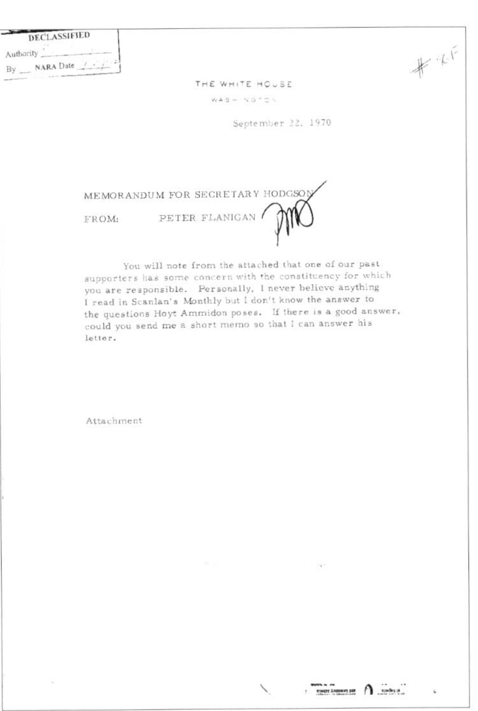

DECLASSIFIED
Authority
By NARA Date

THE WHITE HOUSE

WASHINGTON

September 22, 1970

MEMORANDUM FOR SECRETARY HODGSON

FROM: PETER FLANIGAN

You will note from the attached that one of our past supporters has some concern with the constituency for which you are responsible. Personally, I never believe anything I read in Scanlan's Monthly but I don't know the answer to the questions Hoyt Ammidon poses. If there is a good answer, could you send me a short memo so that I can answer his letter.

Attachment

THE GREAT WHITE HOUSE TEA PARTY: The Nixon White House decided that Scanlan's *had to go after it published an account of the president meeting with New York hard hat labor leaders and detailed suspected criminal connections.*

How Ralph Steadman saw Nixon's meeting with New York union leaders.

Scanlan's

Volume One Number Five July 1970 Price: $1.00

San Francisco's
Film Bastards
Cookbook Frauds
The CIA's Cancer Cure
Maoists in Limerick
&
Revolutionary
Latin American Poetry

Australia .90 cents
Brazil 5000 cruzeiro
England 8s 8d
France 5.55 F
Germany 3.63 DM
India 7.5 rupees
Ireland 8s 5d
Israel 3.5 Pounds
Italy 620 L
Japan Yen 360
Mexico 12½ pesos
Sweden 5.1 Krs

CURTAINS, LAST EDITION: The cover of Scanlan's *last regular issue.*

To: Hinckle

GONZO NATION

WARREN

I SHALL SURFACE WHEN THE ROCK IS ROLLED AWAY. YOU CAN HELP. I WANT TO BE APPOINTED IMMEDIATELY AS HEAD OF THE ART DEPARTMENT AT STANFORD. MY FRIEND BILL WALSH HAS RECOMMENDED ME VERY STRONGLY, BUT HE SAYS I NEED SUPPORT FROM THE INTELLECTUAL COMMUNITY IN SF, ALONG WITH A TORRENT OF AFFIRMATION BY LOCAL ARTISTS.

I KNOW YOU CAN DO THIS, WARREN -- AND, ONCE IT"S DONE, BILL HAS AGREED TO SIGN ON AS SPORTS EDITOR OF THE ARGONAUT. INDEED, HE LOOKS FORWARD TO IT WITH GREAT EAGER-NESS & POLITICAL ZEAL, AS DO I. SO LET US PROCEED.

AS FOR ART -- WELL, SHUCKS. WHY NOT? I WOULD BE HONORED TO HAVE MY ART ON THE COVER OF YR. MAGAZINE, WHICH IS LOOKING VERY SHREWD, CRUEL & ELEGANT A/O VOL. 2. I HAVE, AS YOU KNOW, ALWAYS MAINTAINED THAT YOU ARE THE FINEST EDITOR OF YR. GENERATION & PERHAPS THE MOST GENEROUS WITH ARTISTS.

IN CLOSING, LET ME SUAVELY REMIND YOU OF THAT $10,000 YOU OWE ME FOR THE WORKS (OF MINE) THAT YOU PUBLISHED IN VOL. 1 -- AND BE ASSURED THAT I DO UNDERSTAND THAT THE RICH PAY LATE & THE DOOMED PAY FOREVER. SELAH.

SO , WHO DO YOU WANT SHOT? ALL I NEED IS A FINELY-MOUNTED HUMAN PORTRAIT, CORPORATE LOGO OR EXPENSIVE ANIMAL IMAGE. YOU SEND IT, I"LL SHOOT IT. NO QUESTIONS ASKED. I AM, AFTER ALL, A PROFESSIONAL. OKAY

HUNTER

HST

In 1993, Hinckle brought back to life the Argonaut*—a venerable San Francisco magazine first published in 1867, with the late Ambrose Bierce as a founding editor. Hunter demanded to be the* Argonaut*'s art director and enlisted the now re-born magazine's aid in his efforts to become head of the art department at Stanford, where Hunter's old friend Bill Walsh, the legendary coach of the San Francisco 49ers, was then coaching. Hunter, in full bribe mode, said that Walsh had agreed to "sign on as sports editor" of the* Argonaut.

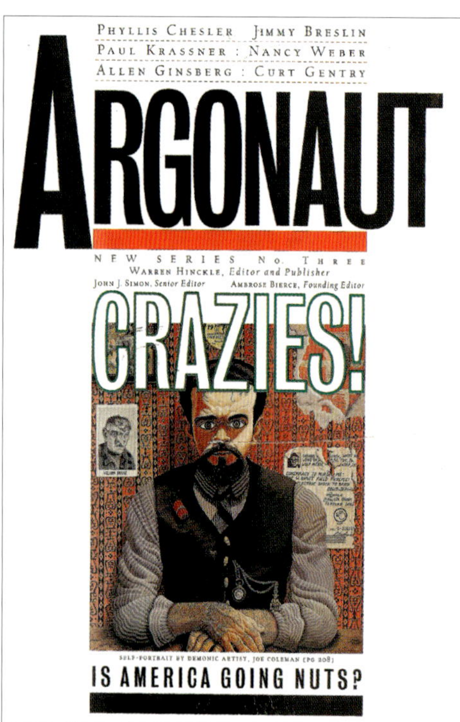

Cover Art by Joe Coleman

Cover Design & Typography by Roger Black

Cover Art by Spain Rodriguez

ARGONAUT

The Whole Family Is Crazy!

The Dysfunctional Crumbs:
Robert's Troubles with Women
Maxon's Brooding Aestheticism
Charles' Suicide Syndrome

Art Scandals!

The deYoung Museum's Giant Sucking Sound

The CIA's Mutant Fly — New Fiction by Richard Miller

YEAH, LOCK US ALL UP!

NO, NO, NO on Prop. 226—The Far Right's Assault on California

Cover Art by Robert Crumb

A TRADITION CONTINUED: The Argonaut *was printed in quality paperback book format and distributed nationally in bookstores. Its covers in the first decade of the new century continued the tradition of* Ramparts *and* Scanlan's *covers in midcentury. The* Argonaut *has featured Ralph Steadman, many Scanlan's artists and new artists including S. Clay Wilson and Spain Rodriguez. It moved to the web in 2007 (www.argonaut360.com) and continues to publish occasional print editions in San Francisco.*

MONDO WORLD [Confidential]
P.O. Box 420178
San Francisco, CA. 94142

"LIVIN' LARGE"
with J. EDGAR HOOVER & DA VERY SECRET SECRET SERVICE [CIRCA 1950]
Before Victoria's Secret there was J. Edgar's.
A strollin' diorama

See the 12 ft. J. Edgar Hoover with his coterie of hand picked Very Secret Secret Service Agents out for a stroll down Market Street as part of San Francisco's annual Lesbian/Gay Freedom Day Parade.

JUNE 27, 1993 11 AM

ALLEN GINSBERG
℅ ARGONAUT
2250 GEARY BLVD
SAN FRANCISCO, CA
94115

"LIVIN' LARGE" created and produced for Mondo World [Confidential] by-
Mondo Jud Hart & Stan Huncilman 415- 647- 9504 510-849-2470

Proudly sponsored by Westec Roofing

After he published a poem in the Argonaut, *Allen Ginsberg was delighted to receive an invitation care of the magazine to a gay parade featuring J. Edgar Hoover in drag. (Below Right)*

S. Clay Wilson (Below Left) continued drawing his wildly distinctive illustrations for the Argonaut.

Art by S. Clay Wilson

Art by J. Edgar Fag

I remembered my old friend the San Francisco fine arts printer Lawton Kennedy telling me that what he wanted most was to design the label for a can of peas--his would use a medieval woodcut drawing of a pea and the word PEAS in simple Caslon capitals and it would be printed in stark black and white. He said that amid the four-color clutter on the supermarket shelves this would be the only can of peas that would stand out. So I asked a San Francisco friend, Barbara Stauffacher Solomon, a landscape architect and graphic designer who was known as the Queen of Helvetica for her lectures about the use of the sans serif font as simplicity itself, to take a whirl at designing a magazine. The result was the anti-design, postmodern look of the newborn *Scanlan's*, which was about as different physically from *Ramparts* as an eagle from a turtle. Hunter said he had a hard time finding the page numbers.

BETWEEN MAGAZINES: After Scanlan's *was rudely arrested by the Mounties, Hinckle edited the San Francisco weekly,* City of San Francisco, *for Francis Ford Coppola. The first issue sold out.*

Paid circulation grew within months well past our original goal of a 100,000-copy first-year circulation due to very funny full-page advertisements we placed in the *New York Times* headlined "YOU TRUST YOUR MOTHER BUT YOU CUT THE CARDS." (Zion's favorite phrase). The *Times* ads promoted *Scanlan's* counter-culture Consumer Guide "How-To" articles such as "How To Smuggle Dope from Mexico," and an illustrated twelve-easy-steps piece on "How To Counterfeit Credit Cards And Get Away With It"--alongside the story of how the Chicago cops assassinated Black Panthers, written by John Kifner of the *Times*, a story the *Times* didn't see fit to print.

The *Scanlan's* ad was an irreverent exception to your usual buy-me pitch. It bragged on the magazine's corny but hilarious journalistic pranks, such as reprinting the official newsletter of the Republic of South Africa's Mission to the United Nations, pirated with its official

logo on the top but with the text changed to articles about keeping those darkies in their places and praising the Republic's Nazi heritage. Our quite official-looking bogus newsletter was printed as a four-page insert in *Scanlan's*. We didn't stop there and ran off copies sufficient to fulfill the Mission's mailing list (which we had, er, stolen) and mailed the phony to its regular recipients, in the process violating several Post Office regulations punishable by felonies. As the TV infomercials say, Wait! There's more. *Scanlan's* printed in the same issue a doctored back cover ad for Lufthansa airlines. The glossy ad was running in the major national slicks promoting the German tourist industry with the theme "*Next Time Think Twice About Germany*" and presented lovely photographs of German castles and river valleys and buxom Bavarian ladies-of-song in costume. The ad included a coupon to be mailed to the actual German Tourist Board.

True to *Scanlan's* promise to pay for advertising it liked, we paid the brilliant copywriter-funnyman Dan Greenburg $500 for his version of the Lufthansa ad printed in *Scanlan's*. (Greenburg also wrote the popular *Scanlan's* subscription ads in the *New York Times*.) Dan changed only two of the original advertisement's illustrations--adding a *Sieg Heil* salute picture in place of a Bavarian castle and a photograph of a Nazi storm trooper whipping a naked woman. *Advertising Age* reported that Topic A on Madison Avenue was the "complete consternation at Lufthansa" over what to do about the brazen appropriation and mutilation of its copyrighted ad. Lufthansa of course threatened to sue. Zion, a former assistant United States Attorney in Jersey, said be our guest--we'd love to get a Nazi airline in front of a jury of New York Jews. Thinking twice, the airline cancelled its ad campaign for "Think Twice About Germany."

There had been little of this type of outlandish merriment and cheerful fraud in New York journalism since the lunar man-bat stories in the *New York Sun* in the 19th century. *Scanlan's* was far to the left of mainstream journalism with essays by leftist intellectuals Jean Lacouture and K.S. Karol. It also published Auberon Waugh on the West's atrocity-making in Biafra; and articles promoting Third World independence from the U.S. (Congolese freedom fighter Patrice Lumumba was a *Scanlan's* hero); Latin American revolutionary poetry; an account of the CIA messing with third world writer Frantz Fanon; and exposés of Washington's corporate welfare for the Bank of America, Pan Am and Lockheed. Alongside Hunter's gonzo screeds, you could read Graham Greene (yes, that Graham Greene)

examining his pinko conscience. *Scanlan's* cultural critiques slammed High Left snots for dumping on American Indian politics as single-issued and "nationalistic" (translation: what's wrong with just demanding give us back our land, white man?), and gave my dear old friend, the literary critic Maxwell Geismar, open season on the suspect Mark Twain scholars that ignored Twain's radicalism and scathing anti-imperialism and tried to whitewash the man as a non-political humorist. *Scanlan's* was also, impishly, ahead of its time with Robert Crumb's artwork, debuted Tintin comics to America, and bound a 33-rpm record into the magazine of a recording of Special Forces soldiers torturing a suspected Viet Cong agent so readers could hear for themselves the U.S. use of torture. (The recording, and the article, came by way of Donald Duncan who kept soldiering on against the war from *Ramparts* into *Scanlan's*.)

Hunter debuted in *Scanlan's* Vol. 1 No. 1 with a piece that had been kicked out of bed by *Playboy*. The pink had assigned him to profile Olympic-icon skier Jean-Claude Killy. This was a money assignment for Hunter, who always needed money. His copy nonetheless trashed the crude mercantilism of the celebrity-endorsement sport world of the star he had been assigned to profile--endorsements for the products on which *Playboy* relied financially for advertising. Hunter made Killy look like something between a pimp and a dork, "the world's richest ski bum." *Playboy* rejected the article.

When I called to ask Hunter what he wanted to write for the first issue of *Scanlan's*, he sent me the *Playboy* reject, with peanut butter stains on the manuscript, and the following message:

Dear Warren,

Here's the Killy piece. I have a clean copy around here somewhere--right here in this goddamn room, for that matter--but I've been looking for the bastard for two days and two nights and I can't find it.

Meanwhile, this half-ass copy should be enough for you to makes some kind of initial judgment. I've had so many different comments on it that I've lost track. Some people dig it for the word-action; others hate it for the style and tone. The editors of Playboy really despised it: Their edit/memos ranged from "This is a good

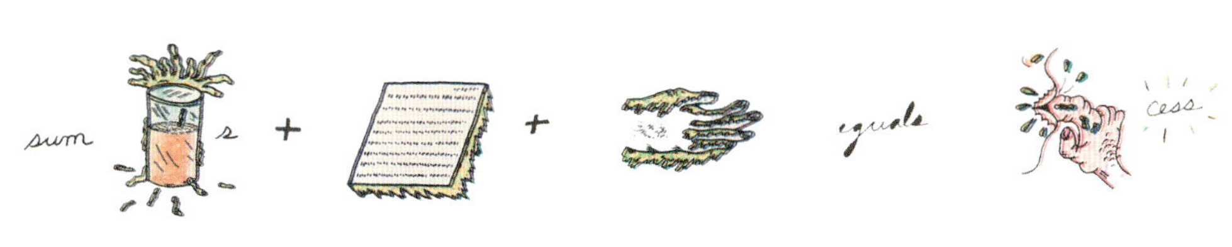

THE TEMPTATIONS OF JEAN-CLAUDE KILLY

by Hunter S. Thompson

Art by Jim Nutt

Hunter's debut article in Scanlan's *was an attack on professional sports mercantilism in his profile of skier Jean-Claude Killy. The article was rejected by* Playboy, *which had considered it harmful to its paid advertising. Thompson sent it to* Scanlan's, *which printed it--with Hunter's letter to Hinckle attacking* Playboy's *hypocrisy.*

Art by Jim Nutt

Hunter hated the artwork for his Killy article. Hinckle loved it. The old friends fought.

Esquire piece" to "Thompson's ugly, stupid arrogance is an insult to everything we stand for" and "This is our last adventure with H. Thompson; from now on we'll read his prose in book-form, or not at all... "

The Playboy editor who assigned the piece--despite my assurance that it would never see print (in Playboy)--confirmed my ho-ho phone assumption that I am now on Playboy's blacklist. His own comment was, "I don't really like the piece, but that's not the point--which is that N. Mailer shouldn't be the only writer who can get away with saying what he really thinks..."

He's a decent sort and I don't want to blow his gig any worse than I already have. He told me, for instance, that Hefner has been trying for 5 years to get Chevrolet to advertise in "the book." I knew, from the start, that the whole thing was a terrible bummer. On my first night in Chicago I was drinking with one of the Chevy people when he was suddenly joined by his old friend, Vince Tajiri, Playboy's picture editor, who had dropped by the hotel to invite Killy's PR team over to "Hef's House" for a swimming party...which didn't include me. No room in the pool for a writer assigned by Tajiri's magazine to write a long profile on the person they really wanted on the scene that night--for photos--J.-C. Killy, who didn't show up.

So all I missed, as it turned out, was a few hours in the company of assholes. But the point is that nobody knew, when they told me that my services wouldn't be needed for the rest of the night, that Killy wasn't going to grace the scene they were setting up. Tajiri didn't know me from a dog in the manager, but he knew that I was working on assignment for Playboy... yet the cocksucker told me to get lost when he wanted to use my subject for a night of orgy promo pix... and he did it in the presence of Killy's main PR hooker, which queered my act for good.

Anyway, I trust you see what I mean. I've done a lot of weird shit in 10 years of free-lancing, running a lot of heavy gauntlets with no real credentials and only the grease of human decency to get me through, like conning

Sonny Liston, Ted Sorenson and the President of Peru into long exclusive interviews when under any circumstances, have I been shit on so totally as I was in the course of this Playboy/Killy thing. That whole goddam magazine is a conspiracy of anemic masturbators... scurvy fist-fuckers to the last man. Like a gang of wild whores or inmates of some terrible peg house, the editors of Playboy roam the world by telephone, trying to get everybody down in the same bad hole where they are.

Anyway, I insisted on knowing why they wouldn't print it. One memo, for instance, said: "Publication of this article would certainly cause Head Ski to drop us permanently from their ad schedule, and cost us any chance we might have with Chevrolet... " etc. Oddly enough, there was one ranking editor who wanted to publish the thing. They wouldn't tell me who he was & I wasn't really that curious, but in fairness I should say that there was one...

Ciao...

Hunter

Thompson was elated that what he called his "doomed" piece about "flackism in America" had been given new life in the new *Scanlan's*. He wrote his editor at Random House, Jim Silberman: "Hinckle sounds happy with the notion of running the whole 110 page article, along with some correspondence from *Playboy*... and since he sent me a check for $1,500 I guess I'm happy too. God only knows what kind of magazine he has in mind, but if he can drum up anything like the old, high-flying *Ramparts*, I know I look forward to reading it. As an editor, Hinckle is one of the few crazed originals to emerge from the jangled chaos of what we now have to sift through and define or explain somehow as 'the 1960's'."

That praise, if praise it was, was short-lived as Hunter was soon mad as hell at me.

I printed his letter as an introduction to his Killy piece--after all it is not often that you pick up a magazine and learn that the article you may be about to read is second hand goods, or read the rejected author's rant about the well-paid editors who rejected it as a conspiracy of "fist-fuckers" and "anemic masturbators." Hunter's letter

indicted *Playboy* and the rest of the mass-slick publications sucking on the tit of advertising as industrial whores.

I thought it made one helluva intro. Wrong, said Hunter. When I sent him the galley proofs he was all pissed off, furious, that I had run his letter in front of his article. He thought it delayed the introduction and to make things worse, to make room for the letter I had cut precious words from his text. "It seems rotten to cut the only part of the piece which partially redeems me," he wrote, "... as it stands now, in your edited version, I come off as some kind of vicious, petulant drunk who slinks off at the end, muttering garbled slurs to himself... there is also the fact that, if anyone reads it and calls me a mean, half-bright asshole for writing what I did, I'll naturally say that "Hinckle cut the sense out of it."

I called Hunter and said that there were readers who really didn't give a shit about Jean-Claude Killy but would read the article to which *Scanlan's* had afforded so much space because they would be naturally curious about why it had been rejected; anyway, I argued the piece was more delectable with the letter than without it.

Wrong! said Hunter. We kept on pissing at each other over the telephone for days. We compromised with mutual grunting. Hunter wrote a shorter ending to replace the original bush that I had trimmed down, and he agreed with a final fuck-you to leave the letter at the front. "I'll never see a dime from *Playboy* again anyway," he said. "Go ahead and fuck them, and fuck you too."

Hunter's letter yelled to the rooftops how advertising controlled the content (and very existence) of publications--there was of course an element of self-serving on my part as *Scanlan's*, which did not have at that moment the commercial temptations of *Playboy*, announced in the premiere issue that contained Hunter's Killy piece that it would neither seek nor accept advertising except on its own arbitrary terms.

Our bitch fight over the article had the benefit of Hunter adding new copy and he good-naturedly sent me this insert--"for the beginning or end of the Killy piece... the quote, as I have it, is attributed to one Billy Lee Burroughs... but if memory serves, I think it comes from the writings of K. Marx." There was not a subeditor at an English tabloid who could have so succinctly summed up the whole point of the article: "No eunuch flatters his own noise more shamefully nor seeks to stimulate his jaded appetite, in order to gain some favor, than does the eunuch of industry."

On the hard rock of such fuck-you conversations are editorial friendships built.

[SCANLAN'S AND THE BIRTH OF GONZO]

> *Gonzo journalism is a style of reporting based on William Faulkner's idea that the best fiction is far more true than any kind of journalism--and the best journalism is 'more true' than fiction--or vice versa--but that both "fiction" and "journalism" are artificial categories and that both forms, at their best, are only two different means to the same ends.* --Hunter S. Thompson

I got to bed about an hour after the bars shut in San Francisco, so it must have been around 3:30 in the morning when the phone rang. I didn't bother with the now-who-the-hell-is-calling-in-the middle-of-the-night bit because odds were it was Hunter. It was. "Goddamnit," he said, "*Scanlan's* has to cover the Derby. It's important." The Derby. The Kentucky Derby was running on Saturday, and this was, what, Wednesday. What's the hurry.

Hunter was still high-fiving it from the praise for his devastating profile of Killy. The next day I Fed-Ex'd plane tickets and money to Woody Creek. "With expenses, anything is possible," Hunter always said.

The few days before the Derby were spent trying to find an artist to go to Louisville. Hunter wanted Pat Oliphant, the Pulitzer Prize-winning editorial cartoonist for the *Denver Post*. Hunter called Oliphant at 2:30am. Oliphant didn't appreciate the wake-up call and said he couldn't make the trip on such short notice. But he was a good sport about it, telling Hunter he might be able to do some drawings from watching the Derby on television. Hunter then suggested English cartoonist Ronald Searle; I said we'd never get him to Kentucky from England in time, if we could get him at all. Then, I thought of Ralph Steadman. I was a subscriber to *Private Eye*, the sharp, bitchy London political bi-monthly where Steadman drew vicious sketches. I loved his stuff and *Scanlan's* published a Steadman political cartoon in its first issue, a reject that the *New York Times* had turned down as not its cup of tea. *Scanlan's* well-connected art editor, J.C. Suares, a collector of Rolls Royces and an heir of sorts to the Egyptian Coca Cola franchise, fortuitously found Steadman on Long Island where he was visiting while looking for work in America, and

Photos: Wayne Ewing

HUNTER SCANLAN'S LOOK-SEE: *Hunter perusing the fourth issue of* Scanlan's, *which featured his first ever collaboration with artist Ralph Steadman, "The Kentucky Derby is Decadent and Depraved." (From Wayne Ewing's "Animals, Whores & Dialogue: Breakfast With Hunter, Vol. II.")*

off he went to a blind date at the Derby. The artist Steadman had never heard of Hunter S. Thompson and the writer Thompson had never heard of Ralph Steadman the artist.

After the deed, a stoned and hung-over Thompson miraculously made it from Louisville to Manhattan, where we locked him down for five days in a room in the Royalton Hotel, just up 44th Street from the *Scanlan's* office in an abandoned ballroom above an Irish bar a block from Times Square. The Royalton in 1970 did not possess the chic lobby it has today. In fact it was a dump. The air conditioning was less than perfect and it was hot, New York make-you-crazy hot, and Hunter spent most of his time soaking in an ice-filled bathtub prowling though his Derby notebook, pulling out pages for publication. Harvey Cohen, *Scanlan's* copy boy and general troubleshooter, kept him supplied with cigarettes, Heinekens, and Chivas. When production slowed, Harvey would seize the time and rip pages out of Hunter's notebook and run with them dripping wet down the street to the office. (On Thompson and Steadman's subsequent *Scanlan's* assignment to cover the America' Cup races, Cohen and I were drinking in the bar downstairs from the office. I thought it would be a capital idea to call in a bomb threat on Hunter's plane to Newport, which was at that moment preparing to take off from La Guardia. We flipped a coin to see who would do the foul deed and Harvey lost and went to the payphone to make the call. Things got so crazy afterward that the next time I saw Hunter I had forgotten about the bomb threat and never got to ask him if his plane was held up, a question I will forever regret not posturing.) Donald Goddard, *Scanlan's* managing editor, a former *New York Times* subeditor and a very proper Englishman with whom Hunter unexpectedly bonded, did first read while simultaneously on the phone to the NYPD trying to retrieve Hunter's wallet which had been stolen while he was watching a Knicks-Lakers game in a sports bar on Third Avenue. Hunter wanted it back, goddammit.

The multi-tasking Goddard managed to retrieve Hunter's wallet and sort out Hunter's dried-out pages. He put to one side Hunter's musings on extraterrestrial beings and other interesting subjects which as tragedy would have it are now lost to history. He isolated the pages about the Derby and arranged them in a semblance of chronological order and put them on the mojo. The mojo was a primitive facsimile machine resembling a high school band drum that had been sat on by the Fat Lady. It had a land line to the San Francisco office, where the layout and production work was done.

Scanlan's San Francisco office was on the garden floor of the magnificently restored Pacific Street firehouse of my mentor Howard Gossage. I assembled Hunter's copy off the mojo and walked down Pacific Street to Columbus Avenue and went straight to the Tosca where I sat solo in one of the big red booths and assembled and then reassembled the text, more Lego than Scrabble. Editing Hunter was like picking up the pieces of a jigsaw puzzle that had been dropped on the floor and trying to put them back together without having the benefit of the picture on the cover of the puzzle box. After many cappuccinos (the Tosca's signature "cappuccino" was a steamed blend of hot chocolate and brandy) I wrote bracketed small caps headlines for each section (in the style that is used in this book) and gave them with a grin to the typesetter. When Steadman's sketches arrived the next morning in the overnight mail I knew we had a game-changer. The Derby article--which is reprinted with Steadman's drawings in Book Two of this volume--tells its own story, which ends with the artist being maced by the writer, which thus begat gonzo.

Gonzo journalism is the unedifying concept of the reporter as the proactive part of the story with proportionate emphasis on the imaginative and comic as the real. The underlying idea is hardly new--the canon of English literature going back to Daniel Defoe unabashedly mixes fact with fiction, and then there is Laurence Sterne's "Tristam Shandy" where the narrator gets his dick squished in the falling window pane. The narrator as hero and (usually) likeable fuck-up is as familiar as Huck Finn--more contemporarily, Hunter admired the mileage in Nelson Algren's "Walk On The Wild Side" and identified with Algren's hero-heel, Dove Linkhorn. *Scanlan's* version of the genre, powered by Hunter's pills, activated a dormant volcano in the geography of contemporary journalism. "We had come there to watch the real beasts perform," Thompson wrote of the Derby. He work-shopped a phrase--the "whiskey gentry"--to describe the sporting mob which he nailed in a manner that rivaled Mencken's depictions of Bible-thumping preachers cooking souls like chicken wings in a frying pan. Hunter's Derby fan was Everyman for the spectator-hooligan--"a pretentious mix of booze, failed dreams and a terminal identity crisis; the inevitable result of too much inbreeding in a closed and ignorant culture." Anyone who has witnessed an English soccer match or an on-court pro basketball riot can attest to this cultural truth. What distinguished the Kentucky Derby piece from

the earlier 50s and 60s first-person New Journalism pioneered by Terry Southern and perfected by Tom Wolfe was Hunter's hallucinatory stimulant-fueled novelistic attention, on a sporting assignment, given not to the horses but to the outdoor loony bin of boozed-up burgher spectators. It was the first look through the other end of the binoculars usually trained on the four-footed beasts. Thompson and Steadman became as wasted as the mob of fans and a peculiar sort of truth, if not rough beauty, came out of the experience. *In vino veritas* rarely had a better literary work-out.

The advent of Gonzo did for pharmacological journalism what Macaulay did for the Whigs. It presented a new way of seeing and expressing political realities--Hunter's proverbial hog was in the tunnel. This was a savage break from what, at the time, was the prevailing cautious corporate journalism bragged on as "objective" journalism. (Hunter once said the only truly objective journalism he knew of was what was recorded on the surveillance camera in the Woody Creek fast food store.) Gonzo re-invented for a generation

---

*I wrote a tribute to Hunter in *The Nation* (March 21, 2005) which touched on the origins of gonzo and provoked a letter-to-the-editor response from Niles Southern, the son of the great comic writer (Dr. Strangelove) Terry Southern. He wrote a letter to *The Nation* in which he amplified on the origins of gonzo pre-dating the Thompson-Steadman implosion in Kentucky. I reprint it here for those who have a sufficient interest in the topic:

> "Warren Hinckle's grand tribute to Hunter S Thompson defines "gonzo journalism" (where the reporter becomes "the active part of the story") as growing "out of a 1970 assignment I gave Thompson" for his *Ramparts*-esque *Scanlan's Monthly*. Thank God (and Mr. Hinckle) for having the chutzpah and foresight to let Hunter loose on the Kentucky Derby, where he met up with Ralph Steadman. But such editorial prescience--fostering a modern author's exorcising of American hypocrisies--dates back further. Tom Wolfe, in "The New Journalism," writes about an assignment that the late David Newman of *Esquire* gave my father, Terry Southern, in 1962:
>
> "It was the first example I noticed of a form of journalism in which the writer starts out to do a feature assignment ('Go to Mississippi and see what happens when five hundred pubescent baton twirlers meet in earnest competition') and ends up writing a curious form of autobiography ... The supposed subject ... becomes incidental."
>
> Professor William McKeen, chair of the University of Florida journalism department and editor of "Literary Journalism," writes, "In many ways this story, Terry's "Twirling at Ole Miss," provides a model for Hunter Thompson to follow later in the decade."
>
> Perhaps the term "gonzo journalism" must indeed be reserved for the drugs, guns, politics and iron-in-the-soul agit-prop of HST, and the "new journalism" kicked off by Terry and carried on by writers like George Plimpton, Norman Mailer, Gay Talese, John Updike, Truman Capote, Molly Ivins, P.J. O'Rourke, Michael Herr, Mark Singer, Barbara Ehrenreich and Tom Wolfe, will be reinvented by today's outraged writers and (more important) tomorrow's media makers.
>
> While my father set out to "blast smugness and complacency," I think Thompson became that impulse. As the neocon (job) band wagon tolls along, the two of them must be shaking their heads with increasing incredulity."
>
> Niles Southern
> Boulder, Colo.

of restless readers and more importantly, a new generation of writers-to-be, the magic of the frontier journalism of Mark Twain, the You Are There journalism of the personal and the fantastic; it showed that journalism in America could at once be fun-loving and zestful while at the same time truth-telling, and yes, telling truth to power. Cirrhosis of the liver was an occupational disease of great reporters of the past but today the occupational disease of the Fourth Estate is carpal tunnel syndrome and the difference is evident in the vitality of the press.

"Fear and Loathing" became a part of the American lexicon. As Hunter would say, this was no small matter. Even Thompson's detractors must allow that gonzo put a lovely scar on the face of American journalism that a good many readers, many millions of them, found counterintuitively attractive.

Hunter later pitched the Derby story to his agent Lynn Nesbit as a movie--"The strange and heart-warming story of a wild-haired English artist and a crazed expatriate Southern journalist hurled into the maw of the heinous Kentucky Derby spectacle. Indeed. Their hopes, their fears, and their final dissolution--against this awful background." Louisville was not much of a Bethlehem, but there, slouching, and hung-over, gonzo was indeed born.

For those who care, there are two macing incidents in "The Kentucky Derby Is Decadent and Depraved." The way Thompson told it late one night on the telephone, Steadman had arrived dazed on the Saturday morning of the Derby to be picked up by Hunter in his rented convertible. The author said he had driven but two miles and barely said hello to the Englishman before he put his fiendish scheme into action. He braked the convertible, took out a can of Mace and blasted Steadman square in the face and threw him out on the highway without his pencils. "You make it to the Derby and we'll have a story going," Thompson said he said. He said he merged the two macing incidents into one at the end of the story for better dramatic effect. Steadman's account of course differs with Hunter's recollection of this drug-fueled odyssey where remembrance is not a credible currency. Ralph insisted he was maced only at the end of the story, not twice as Hunter insisted.

Regardless, Steadman sans pencils did make his way to the Derby. He caught up with Thompson and gave him a rap on the head and with borrowed lipstick and eyebrow pencil produced hallucinatory

sketches for the original "Fear and Loathing" article, which became the Koran of gonzo.

Hunter was his own most severe critic--he was in the old *New York World's* slogan "perpetually unsatisfied." After the Derby article was published he wrote me: "I wish there'd been time to do it better. With another week I might have honed it down to a finer, meatier edge. but in fact we were lucky to get anything at all... I arrived in NY in a state of crazed angst, far gone in pill stupor and barely able to think, much less write ... I wish I could have written a better Derby piece."

Hunter's letters to his editors were, typically, first a machine gun round of bitching, words that could sting like scorpions, threatening to rip your lungs out with his bare hands, that sort of thing. Then a letter would morph from insults into insights--bright new story ideas and practical suggestions for the health of the publication. Thompson wrote suggesting wild and crazy things for *Scanlan's* to build circulation, like developing a subscriber base of weapons freaks around his considerable persona of Raoul Duke. And where, he demanded, was the promotional material for the new *Scanlan's*? He hadn't seen any. "Where is your head? If I were you I'd send out notices promising a freshly cut human ear to every charter subscriber... then announce to the *New York Times* that you've hired an army of speed freaks to go out and get the ears. That will get people thinking... and a massive mail response, too. You should burst on the publishing world like a wolverine with a head full of Sandoz acid."

["A KING-BITCH DOG FUCKER OF AN IDEA"]

Wayne Gretzky said he skates to where the puck is going to be, not to where it was. Hunter scored so spectacularly with the Kentucky Derby article that the rolled-back odometer was exposed in the used car lot of journalism. His friend Bill Cardoso wrote Hunter to declare the Derby piece was pure "gonzo." Tom Wolfe wrote him, "...the two funniest articles of all time--J.C. Killy and The Derby in *Scanlan's*--You are The Boss! Not the sheriff, maybe, but you are The Boss."

Hunter said of the accolades for the Derby article: "It was like falling down an elevator shaft and landing in a pool of mermaids." The glorious tintinnabulation of approval set him to thinking big. He faxed me with a proposal to expand the "beat them like a

gong" approach to the trashing of all of America's most cherished institutions:

"... I thought I'd pass on a suggestion that one of my enemies laid on me today: "Why don't you just travel around the country and shit on everything?" he shouted. "Just go from New York to California and write your venomous bullshit about everything that people respect!" Which sounds like a nice idea--a series of Kentucky Derby-style articles (with Steadman) on things like the Super Bowl, Times Sq. on New Year's eve, Mardi Gras, the Masters (golf) Tournament, the America's Cup, Christmas Day with the Chicago Police, Grand National Rodeo in Denver ... rape them all, quite systematically and then we could see it as a book: "American Dreams ..." Ah yes, I can hear them weeping already ... where will the fuckers show up next? Where indeed? Ponder it, & send words... "

I called Hunter the next day. I wanted Thompson and Steadman to go to Australia to record the Great Kangaroo Slaughter then apace by bloody Ausssies. However this idea was a very appealing and democratic thing to do, to trash everything. We talked it through in a Goddammit-heavy conversation and decided to go for the gold. Hunter had several immediate venues in mind--the American Legion convention in Portland, Organized Labor at their big Labor Day picnic in Detroit, and the America's Cup Races in Newport. Hunter had particulars:

"As for the American Legion orgy in Portland, I like it but the question of access worries me. They'd have to be stone crazy to give two obvious freaks like me & Steadman the run of that thing, Particularly since I just shaved my head--and the visual contrast between me & Steadman is so mind-blowing that we would surely be taken for a pair of screeching faggots. God only knows how those pigs in Portland would react to us...we would need the heaviest of clearance & credentials to survive that ordeal--maybe something completely phony, like maybe if we had some elegant credentials that said we were both field representatives of the "Friends of The Earth." That would confuse the fuckers completely (and I am, by the way, a newly ordained Minister & on any ID forms I prefer to be listed as the Rev. Thompson.) Anyway, I think it would be a nasty waste of time for us

to go up to Portland & watch the whole thing from a distance...on the other hand, the calendar gives us a break here. Labor Day is Sept. 7, so we could conceivably try the Legion gig in Portland & then--if that failed--we could dash across to Detroit for the UAW picnic. Or perhaps try to do both ... Jesus, what a horror! But in theory it would work... perhaps a hit & run job on the Legion, then a more serious look at the Labor act in Detroit. And then, Yes, in a terrible frenzy of work.... On to Newport & the America's Cup, half-clad & vomiting on 500-yr-old lawns.

We at last settled on the blue-blooded America's Cup races in Newport as more easily accessible through amphibious assault. Thompson was ready for sport. As usual he worked through the night at his trusty IBM Selectric pounding out letters about the project. He wrote Steadman: "Prepare yourself: I suspect we have struck a very weird & maybe-rich vein ... I think this Rape-Series is a king-bitch dog-fucker of an idea. We could go almost anywhere & turn out a series of articles so weird & frightful as to stagger every mind in journalism."

He wrote me the mechanics of covering the story: "I've lined up a 50-foot yacht, I think ... the boat belongs to an ex-Aspen ski instructor & freak-drifter; he charters it in the Caribbean in the winter, and in Connecticut in the summer ... and I think he'd get a hoot out of participating in *Scanlan's* America's Cup coverage. We could seize the boat for expenses, then rent out space to selected members of the Freak Press--sail right into the midst of the Newport fleet, flying the red & black flags of anarchy & revolution, launching mace canisters off the bowsprit & hire the Grateful Dead to perform on the foredeck. Old Newport hands would break down & start vomiting at the sight of this fiendish vessel full of crazies. Paint a lurid fist on the balloon jib & a motorcycle hanging in the dingy rack. It would be a rotten outrage, but if we called it the *Scanlan's* Press Boat I suspect it might prove out to be a good investment. Or at least a very weird trip... "

The weird trip turned out to be *Scanlan's* itself.

Hunter wanted to write a column for *Scanlan's* on *weaponry*, a word he always italicized. The first column was a throat-clearing denunciation of the *Police Chief*, the monthly bible of law enforcement, on the grounds that it had no balls, weapons-wise. "As Chief Magistrate of Woody Creek, my legal credentials are unimpeachable. I am also a member of the PBA, the NRA & the Aspen Racing Association. These are important." He then re-considered and decided that he shouldn't use his name but should write under the cover of his nom-de plume, Raoul Duke. Hunter thought this prudent to maintain his "good standing" with the cops while he ran for sheriff in Aspen. Secrecy was, of course, of the essence. He wrote, "No doubt the FBI would visit you very soon after the first column appeared, so you'd have to protect my identity if at all possible. I decided to use my well-worn pseudonym, Raoul Duke, so as not to blow my cover with the *Police Chief* & all the various agencies, supply houses, etc. that I've written to, asking for information and weapons. If I signed this piece or any other with my right name, they would soon have me blacklisted at every corner of the Police Establishment. But now, since I've already established myself with the *Police Chief*, I suspect the rest will be easy. We could actually order police weapons, and test them, then publish the results. We could buy a fucking pepper fog machine & test it in Golden Gate Park at a Shriners Picnic."

My job was to pay him and pay for the weapons he ordered. He sent me a copy of his opening gambit:

July 28, 1970

Gen, Ordinance Equip. Corp. P.O. Box 11211

Freeport Road

Pittsburgh, PA

Gentlemen:

Please send me all details on your CHEMICAL MACE MK-V non-lethal weapon. In my present position as Chief Magistrate of this small hamlet we could only afford two or three, depending on the cost--which is also why we don't have any official stationary or letterheads. But as I am now a candidate for the office of County Sheriff I

soon expect to have a much larger budget at my disposal. In the meantime I want to learn as much about the technical aspects of the new urban-style police work as I can.

So my question for now is, What is the unit price for one MK-V weapon and enough reloads to test it properly? Maybe half a dozen?

From my own pov, I just as soon come east and rave on TV almost anytime between now & Sept--if only because I could justify the trip for various other reasons. But September and October will be busy months here, and after that I wouldn't be doing any traveling until maybe late November--depending on the outcome of the local election.

Sincerely,

Hunter S. Thompson

Chief Magistrate

Woody Creek, Colorado

Raoul Duke advanced to American legend as Hunter's alter ego in "Fear and Loathing in Las Vegas" and as "Uncle Duke" in Doonesbury. Hunter took great umbrage that Garry Trudeau had appropriated Raoul Duke and kidnapped Hunter's own persona to create a... comic strip character! He called, persistantly, to propose new legal theories on how he could sue Trudeau. He did not want to hear no for an answer. My counsel to my outraged friend was that his best recourse was not in the courts but to use his own considerable talents as an artist to draw his own Trudeau character to savage that nervy cartoonist and demand that Trudeau's syndicate give him equal time. But Hunter would not give up on what he called "the legal option" and had his old friend, the gonzo attorney John Clancy, rummage

---

SCANLAN'S *AND THE WEED CULTURE:* Scanlan's *was the first magazine of general circulation to popularize the Weed Culture, publishing How-To features on importing pot from Mexico and, at Hunter's suggestion, assigning his friend the novelist George Kimball to write about the hemp harvest in River City. Underground biker-pot-violence artist S. Clay Wilson, the fiendish creator of the "Checkered Demon" comic books, was introduced to a national audience with his stunning drawings illustrating Kimball's story of madness and violence in the Kansas hemp and meth underground.* Scanlan's *reported redneck attacks--"Hunting Hippies"--on New Mexico communes. Such cultural softie stuff was of course balanced by Hunter writing as Raoul Duke extolling the simple joys of firing guns.*

S. CLAY WILSON'S "KANSAS," 1970.

RUBY THE DYKE AND
HER SIX PERVERTED
SISTERS STOMP THE FAGS.
© S. CLAY WILSON
Beverly
"DORIS"
I WISH I HAD ONE
GAY LIB
BEER
WORKS

THE GILDED
Lily
BAR
COCK TAILS
TREE FROG BEER
TREE FROG BEER
N.D.

deep into the basement of English common law for a rationale--what recourse would the author of "Beowulf" have if some Middle Ages woodblock cartoonist tried to make money off "Beowulf"?

Hunter came up with Raoul Duke as an alias by combining Raúl Castro and John Wayne's nickname "The Duke." Now that Raoul Duke had a column in *Scanlan's* Hunter felt compelled to give him a full fledged *curriculum vitae*. These biographical details have been lost to all but the some 150,000 *Scanlan's* readers of the time. Raoul Duke, "well known weapons advisor and consultant to Hunter S. Thompson, candidate for Sheriff in Aspen, Colorado," is speaking:

"I used to be a cop--a police chief, for that matter, in a small city just east of Los Angeles. And before that I was a boss detective in Nevada--and before that a beat cop in Oakland. Weapons are my business. You name it and I know it: guns, bombs, gas, fire, knives and everything else. Damn few people in the world know more about weaponry than I do. I'm an expert on demolition, ballistics, blades, motors, animals--anything capable of causing damage to man, beast or structure. This is my profession, my bag, my trade, my thing ... my evil specialty."

Raoul Duke personified Hunter's love affair with guns. Raoul wrote: "The reason for this nation's dismal failure on the Indo-Chinese peninsula lies not in our weapons technology, but in a

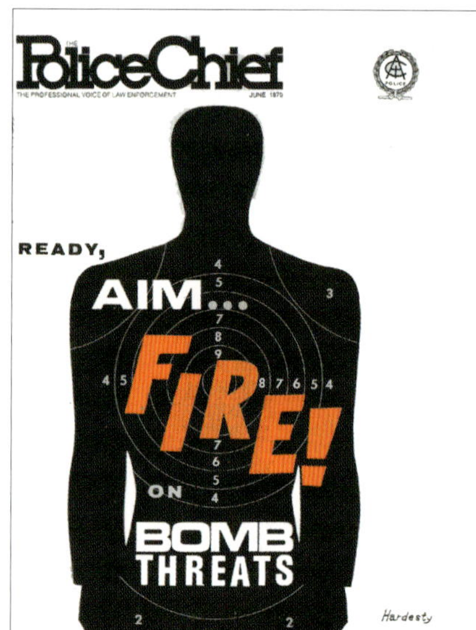

Universal Press Syndicate ©

Hunter, writing as Raoul Duke, reviewed The Police Chief, *the bible of law enforcement, in* Scanlan's, *which developed the Duke persona made famous as "Uncle Duke" in Garry Trudeau's* Doonsbury *syndicated comic strip. Hunter was furious at the cartoonist for making a cartoon out of him.*

failure of will. Yes. Our GIs are doomed in Vietnam, Cambodia, Laos, Thailand, Burma, etc. for the same inane reason that our law enforcement agents are doomed in Los Angeles, New York and Chicago. They have been shackled, for years, by cowardly faggots and spies." Turning his attention to his prey, he said, the *Police Chief* had joined the conspiracy of cowards--it had censored its ads, no longer running ads for serious weaponry, replacing them with ads for "Fag tools! Breathalyzers, "paralyzers," gas masks, sirens, funny little car radios with voice scramblers ... but no ATTACK WEAPONS!!!"

Raoul Duke had little good to say about the *Police Chief*. Once respected, it had " turned to cheap jelly." "One night in Oak., about a dozen years ago, I actually got my rocks off from reading the advertisements... I have to admit such a thing, but it's true." But no more. The Duke concluded that the *Police Chief* no longer ran ads for weapons such as the "Nutcracker Flail" because "they're afraid of hurting their image. They want to be LOVED. In this critical hour we don't need love, we need WEAPONS," such as the Nutcracker Flail--"a combination club and pincers about three feet long that can cripple almost anybody. It works like a huge pair of pliers: the officer first flails the living shit out of anybody he can reach... and then, when a suspect falls, he swiftly applies the "nutcracker" action, gripping the victim's neck, extremities or genitals with the powerful pincers at the "reaching" end of the tool, then squeezing until all resistance ceases. Believe me, our city streets would be a lot safer if every beat cop carried a Nutcracker Flail." He said the *Police Chief* should at least accept advertisements for The Growler--"a mobile sound unit that emits such unholy shrieks and roars that every human being within a radius of ten city blocks is paralyzed with unbearable pain; they collapse in their tracks and curl up like worms, losing all control of their bowels and bleeding from the ears."

Hunter was, once again, a man ahead of his time. The fictional persona of a raving-right-wing-law-enforcement man he created for Raoul Duke is more than suggestive of Stephen Colbert's character as a right wing television host on Comedy Central's "The Colbert Report."

The publication of Raoul Duke's review of the *Police Chief* magazine put Hunter into hyperdrive. He believed his monthly feature on weaponry might provide an expanded circulation base for the magazine. He had thought it through in exacting detail. He wrote

me: "The nation is full of potential bomb-throwers & snipers who know nothing about the technical aspects of their chosen Trades. I think we should help these people, and I can think of no better way than to capitalize on my newfound conduits into the official Police Establishment. We can drive the fuckers crazy by discussing the pros & cons of all their newest weapons--small but important things like the fact that Army Surplus gas masks are no good against the new improved CS. And addresses of companies, which make the new masks, so freaks, can rip them off.

"Given the rude temper of the times, I daresay this is a stroke of fucking genius. We can create, with Raoul Duke, a virtual clearinghouse for information on all forms of violence. Answer all questions, dispense strange advice of all sorts ... and meanwhile keep a fine tap on the *Police Chief* & other cop books, in order to expose everything they come up with. Also things like "How to Seize a Floating Rib, How to Choke a Vicious Dog"... & other small items like "Why Slash Tires When It's Easier to Cut off the Inner Tube Stems." Hunter saw a way for *Scanlan's* to make real money: "Jesus, the possibilities are massive & totally open-ended. Every freak in the nation would buy the magazine to keep posted on the newest weaponry... how to neutralize it, steal it, use it, etc. I see a vast market for this kind of information, and I see no reason why we can't dispense it quite legally."

Raoul Duke announced that in "*Scanlan's* next authoritative weapons report" he would discuss the bomb manual, "The Militant's Formulary," also Orient East's famous "Fighters' Catalogue," chock full of specialty items.

Before he could submit his next column, *Scanlan's* had been arrested in Canada.

[THIS IS WHY NEWSPAPERS ARE DYING:]

Scanlan's masthead read, Publisher: The Late Howard Gossage. This was more than a tribute to a dead friend. *Scanlan's* was the first publication to adopt the philosophy of publishing that Gossage had preached, Cassandra-like, to the deaf ears of publishers. His thoughts are particularly apt now when newspapers are falling like autumn leaves.

Gossage was a maverick advertising genius who hated advertising. He was always biting the hand of the industry that fed him. "He treated advertising as if it were radioactive waste," said Jeff Goodby,

"ON APPROXIMATELY THIS SPOT, MILES ARCHER, PARTNER OF SAM SPADE, WAS DONE IN BY BRIGID O'SHAUGHNESSY." Plaque on Burritt Alley, near "Maltese Falcon" author Dashiell Hammet's Post Street apartment in San Francisco.

a student of Gossage and a contemporary San Francisco ad man whose agency created the 'Got Milk?" campaign. Gossage scolded his advertising clients that they were responsible for the piss-poor state of the media by rewarding mediocre publications with advertising. He was admiringly referred to by the natives as the Socrates of San Francisco. He worked out of his magnificently restored firehouse on Pacific Street where bold-faced names from Tom Wolfe to Terry Thomas came to call. Everything Gossage did was first class--he had a restaurant face that could reduce a maître d' to tears and he ate, flew, wrote, talked, and traveled first class. He believed that a man should be comfortable when engaged in the necessary business of saving the world. In his spare time he was a genius scout. Tom Wolfe credits Gossage with the finding, promulgating, promoting, and virtually inventing Marshall McLuhan. When McLuhan heard that, he said to Gossage, that if Howard didn't mind, he preferred the word "discovered" to the word "invented." Gossage's Delphic reply was: "Marshall, we don't know who discovered water, but it certainly wasn't a goldfish."

Gossage died, of leukemia, tragically young at 60, in 1969, a few months before the first issue of *Scanlan's*.

The ad-man marqué left something behind when he left the planet. It was a memorial to another dead one, Miles Archer, the partner of Sam Spade in "The Maltese Falcon," who met a treacherous end on Burritt Alley above the Stockton Street tunnel in San Francisco. The memorial was in the form of a plaque in homage to the dead--and being done by Gossage, it was a very handsome sign indeed. We were sitting around Howard's firehouse office one afternoon, sipping Paddy's whiskey, the Irish Whiskey Distillers numbering among Gossage's clients, when somehow the subject of Sam Spade came up. Gossage lit up like an electric eel on a bungee cord. "Some-some-something has to be done for Miles Archer, the sap. Dashiel Hammett never gave him a decent goodbye," Gossage stammered. The result was your classic historic plaque, like the one in the High Sierra marking the spot the cannibals in the Donner Party ate their people. It read:

"On approximately this spot, Miles Archer, Partner of Sam Spade, was done in by Brigid O'Shaughnessy."

The monument had hardly been delivered from the engravers when Gossage up and died. I was more than a little depressed by that, and bothered with the collapsing of *Ramparts* and launching *Scanlan's* and such, and it was left in a corner of *Scanlan's* San Francisco office, on the garden ground floor of Gossage's Pacific Street Firehouse, next to the bed of *Scanlan's* pet rabbit (who had replaced *Ramparts'* monkey, Henry Luce). The rabbit distinguished itself by gobbling up the electric cords of all the office machines.

One day Hunter was on the premises and when he noticed the plaque standing in a corner, free of its box, I told him the story. "Let's put the fucking thing up," Hunter said. And so we did, after more than a few drinks at the Tunnel Top bar down the street from Burritt Alley, a real place where Hammett had Brigid shoot Miles Archer. Things did not go well that night, in terms of getting the plaque to stick to the wall--Hunter was on the lookout for the cops because what we were up to was of course illegal. The next night we came back and, with the assistance of the Nibbi Brothers, who are well known in construction in San Francisco, completed the task at 3am. Hunter gave the secured plaque a little kiss. "That Brigid," he said, "goddamit."

Photo courtesy of the Estate of Howard Gossage

ACE PILOT: Warren Hinckle's mentor, maverick advertising man Howard Luck Gossage, posing as a World War I flying ace in a 1967 ad for client Rover Motor Cars, promoting the use of "safety harnesses."

[*On the Passing of Another Newspaper*]

"WHAT GOOD IS FREEDOM OF THE PRESS IF THERE ISN'T ONE?"

—A. J. LIEBLING

TODAY, Friday January 24, 1964, is a sad day: another newspaper has died. "I wouldn't weep about a shoe factory or a branch-line railroad shutting down", Heywood Broun once wrote, "but newspapers are different".

Well, it's happened before and I'm afraid it'll happen again, soon. But this newspaper was quite different. The New York Times, Western Edition represented a genuine effort to publish a national newspaper and get it to you before breakfast the same day. (A paper isn't quite the same thing if you get it four days late; a morning paper isn't at *all* the same thing if you get it after breakfast.)

90,000 OTHER DEAD

More than that, the New York Times is unique in our nation; there is nothing like it for either authority or sheer volume of information. If "All the news that's fit to print" isn't always as fit to read as one might wish, that's a small beef. Part of the Times's inestimable value is that, in a time when most papers are scared stiff of boring somebody, they have dared to be dull in the interest of thoroughness.

But that, as of today, is all gone, at least as a living part of my daily life. So while we are mourning the death of the New York Times in the West I hope you won't mind if I shed a few tears over my own corpse before I start the inquest. For I, as a Times reader, have died too, along with the other 89,999.

EPITAPH NICELY WORDED

The inquest then. The worst of it is I didn't even know I was sick. Just last week I paid the bill for the next month's Times. And then the following day I learned that there wasn't going to be any next month. It was a very nicely worded notice, regrets and all that sort of thing; and did anybody know of jobs for all the reporters, printers, stenos, punch card operators, etc.? Sadly, decently solicitous.

I know it's a nasty thing to lose a job in a dwindling industry; still, there are other jobs. But what about us, the 90,000 readers? What we've lost is irreplaceable: the peculiar community of a great newspaper and its readers. Why didn't somebody ask us before they threw us away, before it was too late? Maybe some of us out of 90,000 could have thought of something if the facts had been squarely presented. Was it money? (It was money.) How much? (Didn't say.) How much more would a subscription have had to cost to make up the difference? I would have been willing to pay it.

COULD HAVE ASKED

As a matter of fact I got my chance, after a fashion, the next morning. A mimeographed insert in Saturday's paper said that if enough of us showed interest the New York Edition would be delivered the *same day* for around $7.00 a month. I accepted with alacrity.

It was only after the wonder of it wore off that I asked myself why, if they could offer me the Eastern Edition at twice the price the day after, then why the hell hadn't they filled me in on the facts and offered me the Western Edition on the same terms the month before, or whenever it was they were weighing the decision? They could have at least asked. I'm a reader, I'm the one they put the paper out for; readers are the only reason for a newspaper's existence, aren't they?

...THAN A BILLY GOAT

Before we get into that, let me say that I have the greatest admiration for the Times's brave try, and the greatest sympathy for them now.

If I am critical, it is of an industry-wide system that has no more real notion of where its basic responsibility lies than a billy goat. It is my belief that it simply would never occur to a big publisher to take the readership into his confidence about whether a paper should live or die.

Perhaps publishers feel that they are conducting a private enterprise, and that such things are properly private. This I feel to be a highly dubious assumption. Freedom Of The Press must imply the public interest, otherwise why bother to guarantee it? If not for the citizenry, for whom is it guaranteed? The publisher? Then why circulate a newspaper? Just run off one bold, fearless copy for him to regard fearlessly. No, I think the Founding Fathers must have had the Freedom Of The Reader in mind, too. Maybe that's *all* they had in mind.

BUBBLE GUM CUSTOMERS

As it stands, though, the subscribers to a paper have less voice as to its conduct or policies than do the customers of a given brand of toothpaste, or hair oil, or bubble gum. And for a pretty obvious reason: whereas the customer's money means everything to a product's economy, the subscriber's money has very little financial significance to a newspaper compared to advertising revenue. That's why we can buy a 25¢ paper for 10¢. Some bargain! To get it, the reader has traded away the economic power to keep our newspapers alive. With the rise in production costs in the face of inadequate advertising revenue they are dying like flies—even though they have huge circulations.

You see, if a paper is losing money on each copy it sells (because it doesn't have enough ads), then the more readers it has the worse off it is. Isn't that ridiculous? If it's unlucky enough to have 800,000 readers, like the late New York Mirror, it loses so much money on each of them it has to fold up.

ADVERTISING CHANCY BULWARK

It seems quite wrong to me that a newspaper should go under while its readers still want it; what is a newspaper for if not for them? And yet, over half of our big dailies have shut down in the past generation, leaving monopolies in their wake. Only four major cities still have competing morning papers.

What to do about it? Well, two things seem to be evident: 1) On the record, advertising seems a mighty chancy economic bulwark for a free press; 2) Newspapers ought to belong to their readers.

PROPOSAL:

Since our press needs to be subsidized to survive, why don't the readers do it? Actually, it's not a matter of subsidy as much as paying for value received. Who says a paper should cost a dime? Why not a quarter? Why not 50¢? Surely a newspaper is worth more than a pack of cigarettes.

Unless we are willing to pay for the freedom of *our* press, the Constitutional guarantee isn't worth a damn. We will continue to have less and less press to be free.

But before we can do anything to help, some paper has got to give us a chance to be something more than circulation figures. Do you suppose one will?

Howard Gossage
451 Pacific
San Francisco

Gossage's point of view about publishing seems particularly resonant for today's daily newspaper crisis. The advertising man paid out of his pocket for the ad above when the New York Times folded its western edition in 1964. He argued that the Times should have asked its subscribers permission to fold the paper--perhaps the reader would have been willing to pay more to keep it alive.

Scanlan's gobbled whole Gossage's unorthodox publishing ideas-- in a way we were his posthumous Petri dish: no cut-rate subscriptions through mass mailings, make it good and charge what the sucker is worth, let the reader pay his way, don't be seduced by advertising. *Scanlan's* spurned paid advertising (and impishly charged $1 a word for letters to the editor to encourage brevity) but paid creative small advertising firms for ads we thought were neat. We vowed to make it on circulation alone with the reader paying the freight.

Howard Luck Gossage believed that the reader lost his/her effective freedom of the press when advertising subsidized the cost of the publication beyond what the reader paid--thus publishers came to care more about the interests of advertisers than subscribers.

Scanlan's therefore charged a premium price for subscriptions and newsstand copies with the goal of making it financially on what the readers were willing to pay. When I told Hunter our publishing plan he told me that this was a plum insane thing to do. I patiently pointed out to him that it was not as crazy as it sounded--a new national magazine such as *Scanlan's*, and a radical magazine at that, had no realistic chance of getting national advertising in its first years, so why not be a little perverse and pay to print ads it liked--the Gospel According to Gossage was that people don't read advertising, they read what interests them, and sometimes it's an ad--and rattle the martini glasses along Madison Avenue? Hunter still said I was crazy.

Scanlan's passed 150,000 paid circulation in its first six months. Our break-even point was 180,000. Whether this experiment in publishing economics would have been successful remains unknown because the magazine went out of business after the Mounties arrested it in Canada. But the Gossage/*Scanlan's* approach to publishing is especially resonant today when daily newspapers are withering and dying as the weed of the Internet blights the stalk of print advertising.

Gossage once paid out of his pocket for an ad in the *New York Times* protesting the *Times* folding its then-Western Edition in 1964. The ad was headlined: "WHAT GOOD IS FREEDOM OF THE PRESS IF THERE ISN'T ONE?" Gossage's ad credited the saying to the legendary press critic A. J. Liebling. But Liebling didn't say that. Gossage just made it up, and attributed it to Liebling. I asked him why he had done that and Howard said that it sounded more interesting coming from

Liebling, and since Liebling was dead he figured he wouldn't mind; besides, it was something Liebling would have said.

The point Gossage argued in his ad was that the *Times* should have asked its subscribers permission to fold the paper--perhaps the readers would have been willing to pay more to keep it alive?

Gossage wrote: "You see, if a paper is losing money on each copy it sells (because it doesn't have enough ads), then the more readers it has the worse off it is. Isn't that ridiculous?"

The way Gossage saw it, advertising did not exist in the form that we know it much before the First World War, and did not exist in much any form at all before the 19th century. But before advertising, there were newspapers and magazines in the 19th and early 20th centuries that were very much as we know them today--except of course that the pages were filled with writing, instead of the paid hustle of advertising. Since they had almost no other source of revenue, the publications of that time lived or died on reader's penny spent, and charged an honest price; if a publication cost four cents a copy to produce, you can bet the publication charged at least five cents for it, and hoped like hell that what the paper had to say was interesting enough that enough people would pony up their nickels. It is no coincidence that the great muckraking magazines of American legend flourished under these game conditions.

If this was publishing's state of nature, advertising was its original sin. With the growth of consumer advertising early in the 20th century, publishers found themselves in the sudden happy situation of getting income from both ends, and they enjoyed that mightily, as one will gravy. At a point uncertain in time but no later than the flapper days of the post World War I period, publishers took the fatal bite from the apple. Faced with rising costs, most publishers decided not to risk losing circulation by raising the price per copy accordingly. This decision was dictated by elemental greed, not charity toward the penny-pinching reader; the way publishers figured it, they could get more money from advertisers the more readers they had, so what the hell, why antagonize the customers when the advertisers were footing the bill?

"Well," said Gossage, with his unique stammer--which bore an uncanny resemblance to Hunter's mumble--"That tore it." The day a reader paid five cents for a publication that cost six cents to produce was the day that he lost his "economic freedom of the press."

Publishers soon became so hooked on the nectar of advertising that they could not do without it and, the first junkies, took to junk mail, discovering that they could "buy" readers, i.e., build up circulation, simply by lowering the subscription price, making it a loss leader while getting a handsome return from the advertisers.

This was all right while it lasted but readers have paid dearly for this free ride. For one thing, Gossage said, they suffered the ultimate indignity that Western society can bestow upon its members: They became consumers. Howard's favorite illustration of the utter madness of publishing economics was that a newspaper or magazine was the only consumer product, from bubble gum to bras, where the selling price had no relation to the actual cost of production. It costs less, for instance, to have a magazine delivered at home than it does to buy it in the store; try that with milk.

When Gossage began preaching this Apocalypse, in the early 60s, a veritable armada of mass circulation magazines was going down with their circulations intact--*Life*, *Look*, *Colliers*, the *Saturday Evening Post*, venerable names all. The mass slicks lost their advertising to the new demon of television. That was the story of last century. In the first two decades of the new century daily newspapers as once here-forever as the *Rocky Mountain News* and the *Seattle Post Intellingencer* are folding like bad poker hands. Yes, the Internet had sucked up their advertising and there were other brutal economic factors, but at bottom line Gossage was right: if readers weren't paying their way for the publication they read, then its survival was no longer in their hands.

Scanlan's wasn't around long enough to prove or disprove Gossage's publishing theories. But one of his idealistic enthusiasms did get put to a practical test.

The genius that scout Gossage had adopted after McLuhan was Leopold Kohr, the philospher of smallness. Professor Kohr theorized that when things--corporations and governments alike--got too big they did not function well, if at all, and concluded that the ideal form of government was the city-state. Gossage put Kohr's theory to the fire and the experiment crashed and burned on the Lilliputian island of Anguilla in the Lesser Antilles. The Anguilla experiment provided one of the great examples of unintended consequences in the annals of San Francisco journalism, a story so similar to the Peter Sellers

Scanlan's

Volume One Number Eight | October 1970 | Price: $1.00

GUERRILLA WAR IN THE USA.

ALL POWER TO THE PEOPLE

EMORY

Australia 90 cents
Brazil 5000 cruzeiro
England 10s
France 5.55 F
Germany 3.63 DM
India 7.5 rupees
Ireland 8s 5d
Israel 3.5 Pounds
Italy 620 L
Japan Yen 360
Mexico 12½ pesos
Sweden 6.75 Krs

LOST COVER: This was the original cover for the Guerrilla War issue by Black Panther artist Emory Douglas. When publication was delayed several months after the press run was seized in Canada, the cover was replaced with an all-type cover.

MILITANT ART: Scanlan's *pointed out that this was the type of widespread agit-art in the ghetto that White America never saw. Hinckle said he chose this Emory Douglas poster because it pushed back against the black-on-black ghetto violence that emerged in the 70s.*

Scanlan's

Volume One Number Eight | January 1971 | Price: $1.00

SUPPRESSED ISSUE:

GUERRILLA WAR IN THE USA.

Australia .90 cents
Brazil 5000 cruzeiro
England 8s 6d
France 5.55 F
Germany 3.63 DM
India 7.5 rupees
Ireland 8s 5d
Israel 3.5 Pounds
Italy 620 L
Japan Yen 360
Mexico 12 1/2 pesos
Sweden 5.1 Krs

ARRESTED: This issue was printed in Canada when American printers refused, and then confiscated by Mounties from trucks heading to the U.S. border. The Nixon White House was involved in the seizure, which put Scanlan's out of business. There are but a few copies surviving.

1970

24 Apr. New York, N.Y. Officials closed Grover Cleveland High School in Queens following a firebombing in cafeteria.

24 Apr. Baltimore, Md. Four or more men approached a police car and fired shots into it. One officer was killed. The other was in critical condition.

24 Apr. Garrett County, Md. The Cherry Creek Bridge, located at the western end of Deep Creek State Park, was damaged by a dynamite explosion, causing officials to close the bridge.

24 Apr. Baton Rouge, La. The windows and walls of the Capitol building were damaged by explosives.

25 Apr. New York, N.Y. An Army and Air Force recruiting office was racked by the explosion of a homemade pipe bomb. The building sustained heavy damage.

25 Apr. Washington, D.C. A bomb mailed from Seattle, Wash., to the White House was detected and deactivated.

25 Apr. Philadelphia, Pa. Two Molotov cocktails were thrown into College Hall at the University of Pennsylvania.

25 Apr. New York, N.Y. An Army and Air Force recruiting office on the 2nd floor of a Harlem office building was damaged by a dynamite explosion.

25 Apr. E. Lansing, Mich. Three separate explosions shattered plate glass doors of three East Lansing banks. Damage was estimated at $1000.

26 Apr. Alton Park, Tenn. Firebombs damaged the Project Supermarket.

26 Apr. Baton Rouge, La. A bomb explosion caused heavy damage at the Baton Rouge Country Club on the outskirts of town moments before another explosion at the Louisiana Senate Building.

26 Apr. Baton Rouge, La. A bomb exploded in the Senate Chambers of the Louisiana State Capitol. The entire front area of the Senate Chamber was in shambles from the explosion; marble was ripped from the walls, a hole was knocked in the ceiling and another in the floor and electronic gear was demolished. An estimated 20 to 30 sticks of dynamite had been placed in the Speaker's alcove at the front of the chamber. Estimates of damage range from $250,000 to $500,000.

26 Apr. Robbinsdale, Minn. Bomb explosion occurred outside the front door of Local Selective Service Board Number 51.

26 Apr. East Lansing, Mich. Three small banks were bombed. They sustained slight damage.

26 Apr. Washington, D.C. President Nixon received a bomb in the mail. It had been sent from Seattle and was found before it detonated.

27 Apr. East Los Angeles, Calif. The Bank of America branch in East Los Angeles was damaged by arson. Damage was estimated at $25,000.

27 Apr. Washington, D.C. Two bombs were sent by mail to the Selective Service. Neither detonated.

27 Apr. New Haven, Conn. The Yale Law School library sustained considerable damage from arson.

27 Apr. Evanston, Ill. The Department of Linguistics Building at Northwestern University was the target of arsonists. Damage was estimated at $15,000.

27 Apr. Evanston, Ill. A stink bomb caused $7000 in damages to the new library building on the Northwestern University campus.

27 Apr. Fullerton, Calif. Seven sticks of dynamite were found in a men's restroom in the Science Building at Cal State, Fullerton.

27 Apr. Tucson, Ariz. A bridge on South Park near Valencia Road was damaged by the explosion of a dynamite bomb.

27 Apr. Ames, Iowa. An explosive device was found in the garage of State Judge John McKinney.

27–29 Apr. River Rouge, Mich. The city was placed under curfew following a series of firebombings and looting incidents.

28 Apr. Iowa City, Iowa. An explosive device detonated on a street and caused an estimated $20,000 damage to 12 business establishments.

28 Apr. New York, N.Y. An off-duty policeman was attacked by men wielding knives and a machete. The policeman was injured, as were two civilians.

28 Apr. Berkeley, Calif. A tear gas canister was set off inside Luther Junior High School, forcing evacuation of the school.

28 Apr. St. Louis, Mo. Two firebombs caused $250 worth of damage to the Bridgeton Terrace City Hall.

1970

29 Apr. Seattle, Wash. Xavier Hall on the Seattle University campus was firebombed causing an estimated $1000 damage.

30 Apr. New York, N.Y. A homemade pipe bomb was found in a brown canvas bag in front of the Harlem Police Station.

30 Apr. East Lansing, Mich. A firebomb exploded on a window ledge of the First National Bank.

1 May. Champaign, Ill. A firebomb exploded at the Carson Pirie Scott Co. store, killing one person. Damage was minor.

1 May. Detroit, Mich. The police recruiting office was firebombed. Damage was not reported.

1 May. Corvallis, Ore. Two firebombs were thrown at the Oregon State University ROTC Building, damaging its interior.

1 May. New Haven, Conn. A bomb explosion occurred in ROTC building on the Yale campus. No serious injuries were reported.

1 May. Greencastle, Ind. An explosion and fire damaged the ROTC office and library at DePauw University.

1 May. Geneva, N.Y. A firebomb destroyed the ROTC office at Hobart College.

1 May. College Park, Md. Firebombs caused extensive fire damage to the ROTC building and related equipment at the University of Maryland.

1 May. East Lansing, Mich. The Michigan State University ROTC building was firebombed and damaged.

1 May. Aliquippa, Pa. A police cruiser was stoned by a group of 50 youths.

2 May. Princeton, N.J. The Armory at Princeton University, which houses ROTC facilities, was firebombed.

2 May. West DePere, Wis. Firebombs were thrown at the indoor ROTC rifle range at St. Norbert College.

2 May. Kent, Ohio. Firebombs were thrown at the Army ROTC building on the Kent State University campus, destroying the building. Other buildings on the campus suffered fire damage.

2 May. New York, N.Y. A U.S. Armed Forces recruiting booth at 600 West 168th St. was heavily damaged by a firebomb.

2 May. Tucson, Ariz. An explosion, probably dynamite, went off at the main entrance to Sunnyside High School, damaging the administrative area, counselor offices, library, and foyer. Estimated damage was $5000. No injuries were reported.

2 May. Seattle, Wash. A firebomb consisting of a gallon jug of gasoline caused an estimated $750 damage to the second-floor classrooms of Thompson Hall on the University of Washington campus.

2 May. Carbondale, Ill. Three policemen were injured when a Molotov cocktail was thrown from a dormitory window of Southern Illinois University.

3 May. River Forest, Ill. A firebomb exploded in the university administration building, causing $100,000 worth of damage. No injuries were reported.

3 May. Milwaukee, Wis. Two buildings on the Marquette University campus were heavily damaged by firebombs.

3 May. New Paltz, N.Y. The administration building at New Paltz State College sustained moderate damage from arson.

3 May. Seattle, Wash. Two explosions, one-half hour apart, completely destroyed two telephone booths.

3 May. New Brunswick, N.J. A firebomb damaged the ROTC building at Rutgers University.

4 May. Berkeley, Calif. Firebombs were thrown at a heating plant adjacent to the ROTC building at University of California, Berkeley, causing minor damage to the building. An ROTC vehicle burned.

4 May. Chapel Hill, N.C. A plastic bomb damaged the ROTC office at the University of North Carolina.

4 May. Madison, Wis. The ROTC building and the home of a military instructor were firebombed at the University of Wisconsin.

4 May. Madison, Wis. Students stood by and cheered as a supermarket was destroyed by arsonists.

4 May. Norman, Okla. Bricks were thrown in the window of the Selective Service Office and the building was then firebombed.

HOW SCARY WAS THIS? The center section of the suppressed Scanlan's issue on Guerrilla War in the U.S. was 32 pages of agate type documenting bombing and terror incidents, organized by symbols indicating the target (school, government office, business, et cetera) and the means of assault (bomb, arson, Molotov cocktail, sniper rifle, et cetera.) Hunter S. Thompson helped hand paste the tiny symbols on the pages.

classic 50s movie "The Mouse That Roared" that it hints of the copy book, although this time the real thing happened.

The *San Francisco Chronicle* at that time was under the buccaneering editorship of the wooden-legged Scott Newhall, a buddy of Gossage who was to became a close friend of mine. Scott was front-page gung ho for the idea of Anguilla declaring its independence from Great Britain as an example of the independent city-state that Newhall wished San Francisco would become. The *Chronicle* hastened to the just cause of Anguilla's succession in 1967. Copy boys overstruck Spanish doubloons on a coin press in the *Chronicle* basement with the words "Anguilla Liberty Dollar" while Gossage manufactured deluxe Anguilla passports and designed a lovely Anguillan flag: two sexy mermaids on a field of blue. The Ad-Man placed a full page ad in the *New York Times* to sell Newhall's Anguilla Liberty Dollars to coin collectors and thereby finance the new country so it could remain small and free from the blight of tourist hotel development. The headline on the ad read: "IS IT 'SILLY' THAT ANGUILLA DOES NOT WANT TO BECOME A NATION OF BUS BOYS?"

Alas, that was precisely what Anguilla wanted to become, only not so small. The founding fathers of the declared Republic flirted with casino developers and other schemers from free-love colonies to miracle-cancer cure clinics. The spurned British overseers of the ugly duckling island smelled organized crime moving into their domain and the *Chronicle*-sponsored far-away city-state was invaded by the English who landed paratroopers in 1969 to take charge. Anguilla today is no longer small, more a neon-less Vegas strip in the far Caribbean of hotels and resorts and the employer of many busboys.

Just before he died, Gossage wrote an article for *The Atlantic* about dying. It was titled "Anytime Is Better Than Right Now." The same could be said of applying his ideas in real time. Gossage died in December of 1969 as *Scanlan's* first issue was being put together and he would never know that the publication that put his publishing theories to the test would be lassoed by the Royal Canadian Mounties before the test results were in.

[CANADIAN POLICE SEIZE MAGAZINE]

—*Washington Post headline, December 13, 1970*

Ramparts took heavy incoming from the Johnson administration, but the Nixon White House went all in on *Scanlan's*. We knew that LBJ had sicced the IRS on *Ramparts* shareholders while the CIA assembled a task force of covert specialists who infiltrated fifth columnists into the magazine. But in terms of governmental retaliation for editorial trouble-making, Richard Nixon made Lyndon Johnson look like a pussy.

Hunter was possessed of a maniacal contempt for Richard Nixon and he found his soulmate in *Scanlan's* which had become such a serious hemorrhoidical pain to Nixon that he assigned the White House canary John Dean to research ways to rid him of our pesky existence.

Scanlan's managed to cause trouble far out of proportion to its circulation and its youth. The cover of the issue with Hunter's Kentucky Derby piece was a sketch of Nixon's face being punched in by a huge fist with the headline "Impeach Nixon." This was arguably a tad early in the Nixon impeachment process, but it was said first in *Scanlan's*. We printed what we described as a "purloined" memo from the Office of Vice President Spiro Agnew studying ways to suspend the next presidential election on national security grounds and otherwise waive the Bill of Rights. The Vice President called a press conference to claim the letter was a fabrication; we pushed that envelope by responding with full page newspaper ads in the *New York Times* and *Washington Post* daring the White House to prove us wrong. Under the headline "Nixon and The Bums;" *Scanlan's* published a photograph of New York hard hat labor leaders having tea with the president at the White House—we

The Montreal Star

Canada's Greatest Newspaper

FOUNDED IN 1869

FRIDAY, DECEMBER 18, 1970

Scanlan's: an act of suppression

THE harassment of Scanlan's is as bewildering, and alarming to us, as it must be to the magazine's editors. Scanlan's was first denied publication in its home base, the United States, because members of the Amalgamated Lithographers Union refused to print it. This inspired the reminder that Benjamin Franklin, America's most famous printer, once said that if printers printed only what they agreed with, "an end would thereby be put to free writing, and the world would afterwards have nothing to read but what happened to be the opinion of printers."

The Canadian press was suspicious.

pointed out, with a lack of subtly, that the labor honchos making nice with Nixon were suspected of, or under federal investigation for, criminal activities, or had been previously convicted of same.

For touching on the ticklish subject of Tricky Dick's longtime shoulder-brushing with organized crime, the magazine was, literally, put out of business by the White House. Nothing of this sort had happened in America since the government went after the bankers and paper mills of the muckraking journals at the turn of the 20th century and succeeded in silencing them.

Strange things began to happen to *Scanlan's*.

The strangest of all was when the press run of the Guerrilla Warfare issue--printed in Canada after American printers' unions in five states refused to print it--was arrested and confiscated by the Canadian authorities as the trucks carrying *Scanlan's* neared the U.S. border. Our Canadian bindery was also raided and the workers roughed up. The *Montreal Star* quoted a homeboy police inspector saying that the raid involved "a good deal of cooperation" with the White House.

Nixon was one mean hombre--Hunter said the man had the unique ability to make his enemies seem honorable. In the nirvana state of thinking that just because we had a few bucks in our pockets, we imagined *Scanlan's* would be free and clear to expose the mob connections of the president without getting whacked. Which was, in retrospect, stupid. The Nixon administration made a blood sport of going after the press--it sued the *New York Times* to stop it from publishing the Pentagon Papers, and when the *Washington Post* began bothering them with pesky little stories about Watergate it tried to cripple the paper financially by attempting to revoke the licenses of its TV stations. And always on standby with his motor running there was G. Gordon Liddy who bragged that if ordered to kill columnist Jack Anderson he would be an obedient soldier of the state. Liddy, his Watergate jail time served, was to be seen on television advertisements on the Fox news channel selling solid gold bullion bars.

Nixon's life was lived in the shadow of felony. A friendly biographer, Earl Mazo, tried to put a happy face on his subject's life-long association with the mobbed-up world by arguing that when Nixon worked as a kid as a carnie for a crooked wheel-of-chance operation in Southern California, he barked only for the "legal front of the concession," not for the backroom where the rubes were being cheated at poker. When *Scanlan's* began looking into Nixon's organized crime

Famed jailhouse lawyer Israel Schwartzberg was Scanlan's *Ombudsman and reviewed books on the Mafia. He died of a heart attack in Canada in 1970 while attempting to get 200,000 copies of Scanlan's released from a police impound.*

hookups we were working with the brilliant Ken Kelley's short-lived yuppie magazine *SunDance* (Kelley, a Detroit lad, was once the Minister of Information of the White Panther Party--when he heard that, Sidney Zion wanted to know if White Panthers were anything like Black Panthers, to which he had an aversion). The good work of unearthing Nixon-mob connections later fell to *Newsday*, which revealed that all of Nixon's real estate deals, bloody including the Florida White House, were mob-mortgaged or otherwise mob-financed.

The snarky president had kinky relationships with (reference Francis Ford Coppola's "The Godfather") the Havana gambling mafia in the 50s, and Nixon's on-going socializing with mobsters unnerved both the Secret Service and Nixon's whackadoodle Chief of Staff, General Alexander Haig, who in the bunker days of the Watergate White House, ordered the Army's Criminal Investigation Command to probe his boss's ties to organized crime. After Nixon had bailed out of the Oval Office, an Army CIC investigator told the *Washington Star* that his investigation uncovered "strong indications of a history of Nixon connections with money from organized crime." So *Scanlan's* was right and little good it did us. *Newsday*'s investigative team were all audited by the IRS for its efforts. But *Newsday* didn't prematurely put "Impeach Nixon" on its cover, as *Scanlan's* had, so we got, one supposes, our just desserts.

The *Montreal Star* found the seizure and destruction of *Scanlan's* (the Mounties kindly stored the remainder of the captured press run in a warehouse with a leaky roof and when we finally got access to

the copies they were wet like toilet paper after the flush) very, very fishy and blamed Washington for the dirty deed.

Hunter had an abiding interest in this. The IRS was hounding him; he had just lost his campaign for sheriff in Aspen in a close vote in a three-way race in which he got triangulated; and in the chaos over the Guerrilla Warfare issue he hadn't received the money that *Scanlan's* owed him for a new article on the suspicious shooting of a prominent Chicano journalist, Ruben Salazar, by L.A. Law enforcement, and miscellaneous expenses from the doomed gonzo assault on the America's Cup Races. And now his meal ticket, *Scanlan's* had been arrested in Canada! He wrote his friend and editor Jim Silberman at Random House and sent me a copy of the letter to emphasize his dire situation that my dire situation had put him in: "Tonight I called Warren Hinckle and demanded at least some part of the $5290 that *Scanlan's* owes me ... and he was of course sympathetic, explaining that everything would be OK in a few days when the current issue of *Scanlan's* comes across the border from Quebec in a fleet of black trucks. In other words, my ability to pay the IRS depends on Hinckle's ability to smuggle 100,000 sabotage-bomb manuals past U.S. Customs in huge trucks.

"I've seen that issue. I helped them put it together in SF & as a matter of fact I have two articles in it (one is the lead piece) and I know Nixon won't want it let loose in the U.S. One of the worst items it contains, in fact, is a two-page ad for the Aspen Wallposter, half of which is a full page color photo of Nixon with blood drooling out of his mouth, a Wallposter cover that we couldn't get printed anywhere in Colorado. Horrible, horrible..."

Hunter had premonitions, a sense of forboding about *Scanlan's*, vague fears that something could go terribly wrong. Of course he had similar worries about *Ramparts*, flying too close to the sun, that sort of thing. And of course, he was right. Usually, Hunter wrote for publications where he was the crazy man who pushed the limits of the permissible and the possible. Now he was heavily invested in a magazine that itself pushed the boundaries.

Sidney and I had our (paranoid? I thought) suspicions and were both shocked and elated--Voltaire said when you hear the news, wait for the sacrament of confirmation--to discover the details of Nixon's plotting against *Scanlan's* with the publication, years later, of White House attorney John Dean's memoir, "Blind Ambition." Dean complained that the first task he was assigned as White House counsel

was "to get" a "shit-ass" magazine called *Scanlan's*, and was specifically ordered to sic the IRS on us. We offered the White House a perfect opportunity to zap us when Zion, a former U.S. Attorney and combative lawyer, decided we should sue the lithographer's union over the printers' refusal to print the Guerrilla Warfare edition, which some printers declared to be un-American. (The wisdom of Benjamin Franklin comes to mind noting that if printers decided what should be printed, only what printers wanted to read would be in print.)

That sounded like a good idea at the time and *Scanlan's* sued the bastards, all right. Then printers' unions across the country in serium refused to accept the job at their plants. After two months of lawsuits and agonizing delays that cost us dearly--the Guerrilla Warfare issue was originally dated October 1970, and finally a few copies came out in bastardized form dated January 1971--we howsoever unwisely contracted to print the issue in Canada. The subsequent seizure under Canadian martial law destroyed our credit line and *Scanlan's* went out of the business it had been in for barely a year. The filly was too bitchy to stay in the race. Not to suggest an analogy, but Addison and Steele's *Spectator* in the 18th century published for little more than a year. The point might be ventured that how long a periodical survives is not as important as what it did during the period it was alive.

During the ordeal of attempting to get our seized press run out of Canada, *Scanlan's* Ombudsman, Israel Schwartzberg, an unrepentant career criminal and expert jailhouse lawyer, died of a heart attack in Montreal while trying to save the magazine. Go make a movie.

After *Scanlan's* went under, I remained in touch with Hunter through his favored methods of communication, frantic faxes and pre-dawn telephone conversations, and occasional evenings at Elaine's in New York and field trips to Irish bars when he came to San Francisco. Hunter and I re-bonded in the Great Game when he enlisted with the O'Farrell team as Night Manager and we thereafter proceeded to commit the sin of daily journalism together at the *Examiner*.

A HISTORIE

GONZO ADVENTURES & MISCHANCES IN THE CARNEGIE HALL OF SEX IN AMERICA, A HISTORIE ENTWINING LIKE RATS IN A MAZE HUNTER S. THOMPSON, THE MITCHELL BROTHERS, THE EDITOR OF THIS BOOK, THE DANCERS OF DOOM, A RED SHARK CONVERTIBLE, MARILYN CHAMBERS, DIANNE FEINSTEIN, A TOPLESS CARAVAN TO ASPEN & JOHNNY DEPP

Shakespeare's Globe Theatre was located just around the corner from The Cardinal's Hat bawdy house in the whorehouse district of Elizabethan London. The Puritans who wanted to shutter Shakespeare saw no difference in the activities on either of the premises. That was in the 16th century and time went by. Maybe not. On the cusp of the 21st century, Dianne Feinstein--then mayor of San Francisco, now the senior United States Senator from California and former chair of the Senate Intelligence Committee and retired prude--declared holy war on the Mitchell Brothers O'Farrell Theatre. Her puritanical premise was that the activities there, such as lap dancing, were not different in kind from heat-generating activities in any other whorehouse in the famously Red Light City of St. Francis, and deserved the stern attention of the law.

The O'Farrell and its proprietors, Jim and Artie Mitchell, play such a prominent role in Hunter's life that the reader may indulge us a moment here to describe the geography of the battlefield. The O'Farrell is on the flank of the city's Tenderloin but just blocks from City Hall, a proximity that may have sparked then-Mayor Feinstein's melt-down over the lap dancing, daily flashlight-driven intimacies in the Kopenhagen Lounge and the nude dancers snatching tips with the folds of their labia on the set of New York Live! (OPENS AT TWO! The neon billboard promised.)

The O'Farrell Theatre occupies a two-story corner building painted roof to sidewalk with wildlife murals. Polished bronze double doors on the ground floor enter the terrain of a mellow Hades where low cannabis fog blurs the interior neon splendor into a vista straight out of Little Nemo in Slumberland; something of the kind must have been in Byron's mind's eye when he conjured "a marble palace of sherbet and sodomy." The second floor is protected turf where the customers--mostly lusting valley rednecks and Asian tourists with

cameras dangling from their necks like lollipops--may not tread. It is only accessible by a buzzer pressed by trusted attendants, which allows entry to the long steps climbing up beside walls hand-painted by infamous cartoon artists--Robert Crumb, Spain Rodriguez, Dan O'Neill--denizens all of the O'Farrell, the Pantheon to underground cartoonists. The second floor is where the girls undress to dress to undress on stage, eat their lunches and paint their nails in their waiting time between gigs on stage. Occasionally a dog, usually it would be my Basset Hound, would sniff through the dressing rooms and steal an exotic dancer's lunch or gobble a tampax from the garbage. And there, for five glorious years in the late 1980s, Hunter S. Thompson presided as the Night Manager.

On this sacred turf across from the dressing/undressing quarters are the accounting offices, film editing rooms, a fridge and snack area--and the Big Office, which was occupied principally by Jim and Artie, an oversized pool table, and, on Mondays, for the weekly game of high-stakes low ball poker, a professional poker table; it was an office-poolroom and office-card room.

From the ceiling hung fish netting fresh with the scent of the sea from the Mitchell Brothers' big fishing boat. In the Big Office, during the last part of the last century, artists high and low, starving cartoonists alongside million-dollar-a-portrait artists, shared the cup that cheers with fishermen, ace garage mechanics, and swinging San Francisco politicians who entered, under cover of darkness, to plot local politics.

It was a great salon. This zoo of counter culture heroes included Abbie Hoffman, Black Panthers founder Huey Newton, and radical feminists and sexologists Margo St. James and writer Susie Bright. The O'Farrell at the time of which I write was a citadel of sex under siege by Calvinistic city officials led by their Goody Two Shoes mayor, a Savonarola with a big black silk bow around her neck. (Perhaps I am a tad too hard on the blue nose side of Dianne's roseate personality; Alex Cockburn wrote in *Counterpunch* that the late Herb Caen told him that the former mayor's spouse confided that in their marital bliss she was a sexual volcano.)

The besieged O'Farrell was, to Hunter, the penultimate attractive nuisance. Thompson's affection for the outlaw Mitchell brothers was in its way predictable. They embodied all his contradictions. He was a loner who loved company, they were pornographers who married their dancers and raised large families. As Hunter had

Hunter's San Francisco doctor, Dr. Skip Dossett, on his annual vacation to Thailand.

bonded with the outlaw Hells Angels, he bonded with the renegade Mitchells. Hunter all his life had paddled upstream against the conventions of society and journalism-as-usual. The Brothers fought the mob and the law to protect their constitutonal right to porn (they sued for copyright infringement of illegal copies and won--bringing you the FBI copyright notice you see before every film) as Hunter fought the narcs to defend his recreation and his liberty. Theirs was a primal pairing; Hunter and the Brothers became joined at the hip, the perfect fit in a perfect storm.

How this most improbable--and for all that has been published about Hunter's escapades it remains little-known--alliance came to be is a sidebar to his American epic; in the precision of the cliché, a

story in itself. Like Hunter's riding with the Hells Angels, no period in his adventurous life so intensely embodies the Gonzo ethos of living your story more than the story of The Night Manager.

Hunter S. Thompson as Night Manager for the Brothers was perfect casting. Hunter was already a star, and if he wanted to dip his toe into the uncalm waters of the O'Farrell he was welcome to take a dip--as Louie B. Mayer said of Ester Williams, "Wet, she's a star. Dry, she ain't." Thus a new star was born backstage at the O'Farrell.

The Night Manager's perch was beyond the dressing rooms, past the showers and the little plastic tables where the girls ate their brown bag lunches, up into the dark high above backstage, down unsteady steps illuminated with the type of tiny lights marking the escape route from an airliner, up again onto an elevated platform overlooking Stage No. 1, New York Live!

Hunter sat like royalty on a high director's chair with a glass of Chivas in one hand and a dainty cigarette holder in the other. He perched next to the spotlights playing down on the strippers below. Hunter was both learning the business and monitoring the action. He high-fived the girls and was generous with career advice during his nightly march through the undressing rooms to his position next to the announcer cueing the ladies and playing their strip routine music. (After he broke a leg doing an indelicate back flip off the bar at the Tosca, Hunter sat on his high chair with his leg up in a Titanic cast and the girls passing by would sign the plaster with the respect of the faithful touching a holy water fount at Fatima.) While the dancers waited for the cue to go downstairs and strip, he would discuss pro basketball with them. At times Hunter would dutifully take a turn working the spotlight, careful to keep the beam on the delicate maneuvers onstage. On a given night he had trouble keeping a spot on the girl. "Just pretend it's your tongue," Artie Mitchell told him.

At times the Night Manager would exit his aerie to prowl the second floor reception area. John Carlson, the manager of Monaco Labs, the Bay Area's all-purpose professional film lab, one afternoon was in the O'Farrell office after fixing a projector problem and was having a drink with Jim Mitchell when a piece of humanity crawled out from under the pool table. "Is it dark yet?" the Night Manager asked. Carlson replied that it was still light out. "Good, I don't have

to go back to work yet," Hunter said and returned to repose under the table.

One evening he was mistaken for a prowler and jumped from behind by Dr. Donald R. Dossett, the O'Farrell's house physician. Dr. Skip, as he is called for his high school nickname, is a long-haired handsome devil, part American Indian although no one is sure which part, a gynecologist and genius General Practitioner with an uncanny diagnostic intuition about what ails his patients, who are half clinic-poor, half wealthy-degenerate. Dr. Skip was one of the last doctors in San Francisco to make house calls, and many of his house calls were at the O'Farrell, where he brought his black bag into the dressing rooms and fixed the girls wherever it hurt. The good doctor also has a black belt in karate. On the evening in question Dr. Skip came up the stairs and saw a tall man kicking and swearing at the locked office door. The good doctor, having no previous introduction to the newly-arrived Night Manager, took him for a random lunatic who had somehow escaped upstairs from the audience of drooling men in the paid seats below. He tip-toed up from behind and hoisted Hunter in the air and twirled him like a baton and dumped him without ceremony on the floor. He used the vernacular what-the-fuck-do-you-think-you-are-doing? form of salutation. "The door's not open!" Hunter said, somewhat unnecessarily. Hunter was not his usually combative self but was chastised and polite and dutifully trekked away. It was only later that Dr. Dossett learned he had tried to beat up on Hunter S. Thompson.

Dr. Skip lives on a two-story houseboat built in the shape of an owl and he takes a five week vacation to Thailand each year where he rides elephants and organizes a pick-up band to play the clubs. He does one hell of an Elvis impersonation. The doctor is also a mariner with two boats on the San Francisco Bay. One of his boats blew up near his Sausalito dock and he swam through the fiery waters to rescue his passengers. He was rewarded for his heroics with a bad back and now takes ballroom dancing classes as a cure and has more wannabe girlfriends than Nero had fiddles.

It was a nice day for a sail and Dr. Skip was out with the Brothers in his Boston Whaler for a toot around the bay. Up ahead a U.S. nuclear submarine had surfaced. Artie Mitchell who was at the helm of Skip's whaler at the time got a terrible gleam in his eye when he saw the submarine. He increased speed and steered right for it. Skip warned that the Navy would take them for terrorists or something

and shoot them out of the water if they didn't change course. Artie went faster. He would not slow down. Jim Mitchell seemed transfixed by the coming encounter, eyes staring at the sub from under his baseball cap. An officer on the sub's deck hailed the approaching craft from a microphone, "Whaler! Stand Down!" Artie held his course. "Whaler! Stand Down! We will fire!" Artie increased speed as sailors came on deck to man the guns. Dr. Skip grabbed the rudder and steered hard left. Both Brothers booed. They called him chicken.

The Brothers came from good fruit tramp stock. Their father was an Oakie who became a Sacramento riverboat gambler and taught his boys a trick or two about cards and the way life can twist you around. When you run into a wall, he told them, never try to run around it, go up and over it. His only forward position was in-your-face. These were lessons Jim Mitchell never forgot. He and his younger brother Artie grew up the hard way in the tough Delta port town of Antioch where guns were trumps. Jim was right there in the face of any kid messing with Artie. He was always trying to protect his mercurial little brother, even on the rainy night Artie died when Jim's bullet ricocheted the wrong way in an Oakie-style intervention gone awry. Life can twist you around.

Artie was always the wilder of the two--a San Francisco prosecutor once told a jury Jim was the type of guy who would dutifully go out and put quarters in his parking meter every hour; Artie would run it on red and break the glass and give the finger to the meter maid who came by to ticket his car. Artie had fallen foul to drugs and guns in a big way before his death in 1991. Dr. Skip was called as a witness for the prosecution at Jim Mitchell's murder trial in Marin County. This was one of many prosecutorial mistakes made by the Marin County DA, who was unable to resist overcharging a San Francisco pornographer with killing his pornographer brother amidst the sylvan hot tubs of Marin. Mitchell was charged with First Degree murder when the facts of the case pointed to an intervention gone horribly wrong. The prosecutor clearly hadn't done his homework in calling Dr. Skip, or he would have known about Skip's close friendship with both brothers. One especially hilarious night, Artie had talked Skip into putting a dog collar around his neck and was leading him around by the leash. Instead of affirming the prosecutor's

---

OVERLEAF: "The Night Manager" by Ralph Steadman (courtesy of the estate of James Mitchell.)

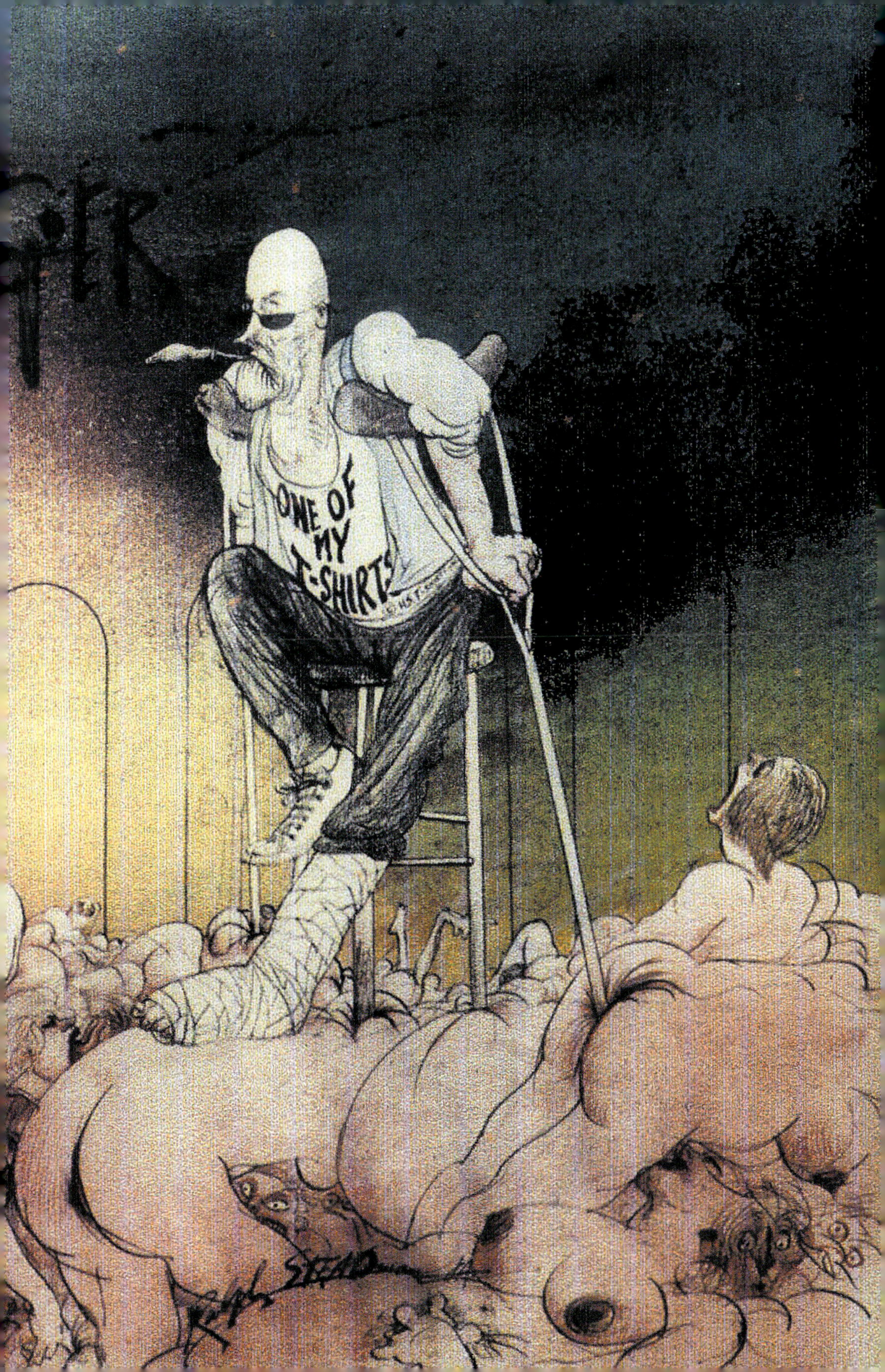
ONE OF MY T-SHIRTS

AT THE OFFICE

The Night Manager and his Bosses,
Artie and Jim Mitchell
The O'Farrell Theatre, 1985

PHOTOGRAPHS BY MATTHEW NAYTHONS

Artie Mitchell

Jimmy Mitchell and Hunter at the bar at Tosca.

The Mitchell Brothers at work.

Jim Mitchell, Hunter and cartoonist Dan O'Neill in front of San Francisco City Hall during a break in one of the many O'Farrell vice trials.

thesis that Jim had premeditatedly killed his brother for money, he testified to Artie's increasing descent into an alcoholic and drugged haze, how Artie had taken guns and shot up his girlfriend's coffee table and the roof of the O'Farrell, thrown pool balls at the heads of his friends, and warned that he'd shoot dead anyone who came to take his guns away. This bolstered the defense case, which was that Jim went to Artie's house that fateful, rainy Marin night to attempt to rescue him before he really hurt someone, or hurt himself.

A sparky court jester in the O'Farrell's *commedia dell'arte* was Dan O'Neill, a cartoonist-provocateur who had been fired from his job drawing the successfully syndicated Odd Bodkins comic strip in the *Chronicle* for secreting Morse Code recruiting messages for the IRA in the panels. When O'Neill heard the news he brought a chain saw to the paper and demanded to see my editor, Scott Newhall, who had a wooden leg. O'Neill said he was going to cut it off. Newhall was announced as not in the office so O'Neill sawed off the leg of the desk of the editorial receptionist instead.

O'Neill was the Admiral of an Irish Navy commissioned by Jim Mitchell to foul up Queen Elizabeth's 1983 visit to San Francisco. The Navy consisted of three rowboats pulled by the Brothers' fishing trawler. The rowboats were loaded with rotting herring and closely followed by a humungous flock of seagulls that O'Neill had hoped would crap on the royal yacht as it passed under the Golden Gate Bridge. This was all so simply lovely for the headline-happy British tabs: 'SAN FRANCISCO PORN LORDS ATTEMPT TO SINK BRITANNIA.' An Irish FBI agent later told O'Neill, "We were to protect the Queen from guns and bombs but nobody said anything about birdshit."

During the 1984 Democratic Convention in San Francisco--Hunter, who rarely missed a National Political Convention, was of course there--the second floor of the O'Farrell was turned into a combined City Room and boozy summer camp for cartoonists covering the convention. The *Chronicle* editor, Bill German, had succumbed to the siren of my entreaties to do something different from the percolator drip-drip of pedestrian political reporting by allowing the underground comics gang to have their way with Democratic orthodoxy. He sagely stopped short of letting my baker's dozen of lunatics armed with lethal crayons inside the asylum of the *Chronicle* building. "Find somewhere else for them to draw," German suggested equably.

That somewhere else was The O'Farrell. Jim Mitchell was famous for his unbridled generosity and nothing was too good for the artists-in-residence--strawberries the size of little watermelons, chocolate truffles to die for and wine flowing as from the fountains of Babylon were at the ready in his pool room-office across the hall from the girls' undressing room. Somehow--in the cramped office space between the regulation pool table and under the well-used fisherman's net which drooped precariously low from the ceiling--Jim had set up several artists' drawing boards. These facilities proved insufficient for the abundance of artists, who spilled over into the dressing rooms where they sat under the makeup tables with drawing pads on their knees while the naked girls above primped. The cartoonists were of San Francisco's then-underground elite--Victor Moscoso, Crumb, Spain Rodriguez, Ted Richards, S. Clay Wilson, Bob Crabb, Gary Hallgren and Phil Frank, collectively known as the "Wild Dogs Loose In The Street." Dan O'Neill whipped them like a galley slave chief. "Get busy boys, listen up, 25 minutes to deadline!"

Word of the nocturnal editorial goings-on at the city's most notorious sex emporium somehow leaked to convention delegates and in the waning hours of the convention that gave the world the Murine-eyed Walter Mondale as their party's candidate, credentialed Democrats, including those of the senatorial rank, flocked to the O'Farrell's ersatz editorial room to party with the cartoonists and the dancers. Harry Moss, a photographer and freelance writer, recalled a sour moment interrupting Hunter when he was playing pool. He took a picture of Hunter (p. 150) and asked him what new projects he was working on and said he wanted to write about it. Hunter regarded this as Grand Theft Auto. "I'm the Night Manager here. I'm trying to manage people," Hunter replied crossly. He asked Moss who he was interviewing him for and Moss said he was with the "*San Francisco Review of Books.*" Moss said Hunter then "picked up his pool stick and chased me out of the room saying, "*San Francisco Review of Books*? That's bogus. Get the hell out of here. Bogus!" The spurned freelancer got his feelings hurt and called Hunter "A real asshole."

"Pool Room-Press Room Reporter" by Dan O'Neill, as pictured in the San Francisco Chronicle.

As a party surprise for slumming Democrats, Tosca owner Jeannette Etheredge leapt like a gazelle atop the office pool table and did the can-can. "She has good legs," said connoisseur Mitchell. The *Chronicle*'s Bill German wrote O'Neill a nice note remarking how pleased he was with the cartoon coverage. Jim Mitchell didn't even get a thank you.

Although the boys from Antioch became very big indeed in the business of porn--they pioneered "art" porn movies and VHS mass distribution porn and made a fortune--theirs remained a family business. Most of the lads working for them were school buddies of the Brothers from Antioch. Hunter deeply respected the male bonding of the management, replete with fishing trips, golf games, poker tournaments and indoor target practice with pellet guns in the O'Farrell office. Hunter was proud to be taken into the family, secret handshakes and all, and to be considered a brother. Hunter's "Road Manager" was Jeff Armstrong, the general manager of the O'Farrell, who had attended the same Antioch high school as the Mitchells.

[A MEMO TO HUNTER:]

November 16, 1991
TO: HST
FROM: HINCKLE
RE: PER YR. REQUEST, THIS
CONCISE CULTURAL & POLITICAL
HISTORY OF THE MITCHELL BROTHERS.

Hunter:

I assume you are still calling your book about the O'Farrell "Polo Is My Life"? What the fuck, why not? So OK, here's the background story on the O'Farrell and the Feinstein Wars that you've been bugging me for... sorry it took so long but a lot of low flying geese had to get out the kitchen before I could get down to it & there is of course the incidental fact that I'm not your fucking researcher... but this is a matter of honor and an ACT OF BARTER, and here is my half of the deal; your half is the piece you will give me for the first issue of the Argonaut *... FYI a bunch of clips are attached about police raids, Marilyn Chambers et cetera ...*

If you want more on the Frisco underground cultural shit, goose Ron Turner at Last Gasp... you've met him often at the O'Farrell, he's the suspender-wearing big guy with a long white beard and is a dangerous Santa Claus who started off printing dirty comic books and published the original R. Crumb stuff and the weird biker bang-bang opiate drawings of S. Clay Wilson--all the stuff you like.

Just so we are clear: You owe me on this one, and you will either send me both your little fingers and your right thumb, or you will deliver that piece you promised for the first issue of the new Argonaut *which I hope to get out next year, so hurry. Barter is a serious matter, redeemable only by delivery or death. Mitchell memo follows:*

Yours in Christ Jesus,
Warren

Backstory: The cultural and political wars known as The Sixties created upheavals in American society subject to the analogy of seismic disorders. From one of the fissures in the culture emerged Artie and Jim Mitchell, soon to be known as "The Brothers" of San Francisco legend. The Brothers took refuge in the Army from the hard knocks of redneck existence in the tough Sacramento River Delta port town of Antioch where they grew up. When Jim got out of the Army in 1966, he took a film history course at a community college that gave him a new view of the world--looking at it through a lens. He transferred to San Francisco State (then a college in the fog of western Frisco, now endowed with the more proper title "University") and took film classes where he learned the scut work of making movies, skills he then deployed in the drug and lifestyle boot camp of the Haight-Ashbury. This was at height of the Hippie experiment, before the big burn out, and he began making short films starring willing Hippie lasses in itsy-bitsy bikinis without much of the bitsy. These films were shown in storefronts and hippie venues and money changed hands, which brought Jim to the *Santa Maria!* type conclusion that money could be made while you were having fun. Artie joined him when he got out of the Army and by 1969 the Brothers were

producing ten-and twelve-minute soft porn "loops" starring girls topless and soon enough bottomless.

Jim was a master of hillbilly charm and a consummate negotiator with a winner's feel for the pulse of a deal. He finessed the then very under-financed Brothers into possession of a cavernous abandoned Pontiac dealership cum auto-repair garage in the Tenderloin and christened it grandly The O'Farrell Street Theatre.

The new venue became the sandbox for the San Francisco counterculture--there were the increasingly sophisticated short-reel films shot by the Brothers, and midnight song and dance revues by the pioneering all-women comedy troupe the Nickelettes, impromptu poetry raves until dawn and cartoonists camping out and scribbling away for free eats and free drinks and free sex. Artists began their Great Hang Out at the O'Farrell shortly after it opened on the 4th of July 1969. As the porn film money rolled in the Brothers were quick to spread the wealth and became the Medicis of underground art. The naughty comic strips drawn under the O'Farrell big tent would become known as the R. Crumb school of underground comics, a madrassa for truants which rudely injected in the bone marrow of the culture the sixteen tons of bad road of Zap Comix, Mr. Natural, Fritz

Ivory Snow Girl Marilyn Chambers displaying her product identification.

Text continues on page 151

The Mitchell Brothers plastered this "Wild Dogs" poster in every City Hall bathroom after San Francisco police arrested Marilyn Chambers--and then arrested writer Warren Hinckle for criticizing the O'Farrell bust. Poster artists include Dan O'Neill, Robert Crumb and Victor Moscoso. Then-San Francisco Mayor Dianne Feinstein is depicted sheltering the vice squad under her skirts. Hinckle is the reporter with the eye patch at bottom left being beat up by the cops.

Marilyn Chambers being taken away from the O'Farrell by the SFPD, in this R. Crumb version of one of the most famous raids in San Francisco's sordid history. Published in the San Francisco Chronicle *in 1985 above Hinckle's column calling the cops, in Mencken's phrase, "A bunch of donkeys led by jackasses." More than thirty San Francisco cops showed up to take a naked Chambers to jail.*

Photo: Layla Lyne-Winkler

Note the endorsement, bottom right, " 'The Carnegie Hall of Public Sex in America,' Hunter S. Thompson, The Night Manager."

Photo: Tamben Armstrong

(Top) Hunter in evening jacket with Maria Kahn and Jeff Armstrong, his Road Manager. (Bottom) Hunter, Jeff Armstrong and Johnny Depp at the O'Farrell.

Photo: Charlie Benton

Photo: Linda Corso

Marilyn Chambers at the O'Farrell Theatre with Hinckle's basset hound, Melman, in 2003.

MY "INFORMED" SOURCE, UNCLE BENNY, LIVES IN THE ALLEY BEHIND THE FAIRMONT..
O.K. BEN.. SHOOT..
WELL.. I PUT ON MY FAVORITE DISGUISE.. THE OLD PAPER BAG ROUTINE..
..I WAS CLOSE TO THE CANDIDATE, LIKE YOU SAID, TO LEARN THE GOOD STUFF.. SUDDENLY THIS BOZO GUARD YELLS..
GRAB THAT PAPER BAG!!
I FREAKED. I RAN..
..HOW WAS I TO KNOW HIS LUNCH HAD BEEN CAUGHT BY A BURST OF ORATORY?
..AND YOU RAN ALL THE WAY HERE WITHOUT STOPPING? WOW..
..I'M SUPPOSED TO PAY YOU 5 FISHHEADS FOR THAT STORY..?
AT LEAST!! AT MY AGE I GET PAID FOR RUNNING.
..IT COST ME 10 FISHHEADS AND A WET RAT..
O'NEILL 84

LOOSE in the STREETS
-O'NEILL-
-MOSCOSO-
-CRABMAN-
-CRUMB-

AS THE WORLD BURNS
EVERYBODY LOOK!!..
I'M GONNA JUMP OFF THE GOLDEN GATE BRIDGE!
MEANWHILE AT THE WHITE HOUSE, THE PRESIDENT WONDERS..
..SHOULD I EVEN BOTHER TO CAMPAIGN THIS YEAR?..
$400,000 BUYS A LOT OF POTATO SALAD..
..OR IT COULD PUT 40 KIDS THROUGH U.C.L.A.
BUT WHAT DO WE GET?..
© CRABMAN '84

© MOSCOSO

20,000 OF HIS MOST INTIMATE FRIENDS
OH WHAT A NIGHT!!
OH WHAT A GUY!
HEY, WE GOT WILLIE!
©1984 by R. CRUMB

Art by Dan O'Neill, Victor Moscoso, Crabman, Robert Crumb.

THE "HINCKLE/O'NEILL REPORT," San Francisco Chronicle, *May 1985.*
The cartoonists sat under the O'Farrell dancer's undressing tables.

(Top) "Admiral" Dan O'Neill's account of the war at sea.
(Bottom) The Irish Navy and seagull auxillery approaching the Queen's ship.

ILLUSTRATED AND UNCENSORED

IN THIS ISSUE:
BARBARA EHRENREICH
DANIEL ELLSBERG
EDUARDO GALEANO
NORMAN MAILER
NAT HENTOFF
ROBERT CRUMB
LAWRENCE FERLINGHETTI
JULES FEIFFER
RALPH STEADMAN
MARGO ST. JAMES

SAN FRANCISCO, CALIFORNIA
JUNETEENTH, 1999

ESTABLISHED 1991 IN THE GULF WAR
VOLUME II NUMBER I
WHOLE NUMBER THREE
*Replated Edition
NOT FOR PROFIT
$2 Outside Bay Area

Warren Hinckle
Editor & Publisher

...a plot wherein
the numbers try the cause,
which is not tomb and
continent to hide the slain...
—Hamlet, XX, IV, III

U.S. SELLS STAGGERING $8.3 BILLION IN ARMS TO NON-DEMOCRATIC COUNTRIES [P. 5]

NATO'S BOMBING A COSTLY FOLLY; TARGETING CIVILIANS WOUNDS U.S., DEEPENING QUAGMIRE IN BALKANS

BRINGING THE WAR HOME. ◆ By Winston Smith

NOT ALL VOICES AGAINST AN AIR WAR OF CARNAGE WERE SILENT

BY REGIS DEBRAY

A Letter To The President

Paris. *LeMonde*

On my return from Macedonia, Serbia and Kosovo, I consider it my duty to deliver to you an impression of mine: I fear, Mr.President, that we may be going the wrong way. You are a practical person. You do not value the intellectuals who fill our columns with grandiloquent and peremptory generalizations. That is good: for neither do I. So I shall stick to the facts. Everybody has his own facts, you will tell me. Those facts that I've been able to observe during a short sojourn - a week in Serbia (Belgrade, Novi Sad, Nis, Vramje), of which four days in Kosovo (from Pristina to Prej, from Pritzren to Podujevo) - do

BY LARS-ERIK NELSON

The Trouble Is Just Beginning

Washington. *Daily News*

The KLA will make Slobo seem like a walk in the park.

It is a lawless land where the scores to settle are many, and this morning's friend could easily prove to be this afternoon's enemy.

You won't have trouble with the Serbs; they're going home, says Lawrence Korb, a former assistant secretary of defense now at the Council on Foreign Relations. It's the KLA you have to worry about. It wants the whole thing.

The whole thing is an independent Kosovo, not autonomy as a part of Serbia, as the current peace agreement now

BY BARBARA EHRENREICH

Violence Is The Victor

New York. *The Nation*

The mission of mercy morphs into ever-escalating mayhem, as we send out an air force to do an angel's job.

Here's a paradigmatic image of the Nato effort to-date, thanks to Fox TV News.

A US transport helicopter lands somewhere in Albania and a Marine, in full combat gear, leaps out. Assuming the ritual half-crouching position, he duly points his automatic weapon in various directions, although there is no one around, not even a shrub. His form is admirable, his mien menacing. And his mission, according to the voice over? He has come to build houses for the Kosovar refugees.

BY VAJIN DIMITRIJEU

The Collateral Damage: Democracy

Belgrade. *WP Reporting*

NATO's bombing campaign represents the failure of Western policy. The real solution in the Balkans is democracy, but with one night's bombing, ten years' work developing civil society has been all but wiped out.

NATO's air offensive against Yugoslavia has not simply "degraded" military installations. It has also taken its toll in human lives and is progressively destroying the economic infrastructure of our impoverished country. In the long run, however, the biggest collateral damage is likely to be to the prospects for democracy in Serbia.

Serbia's human rights community regards NATO's

BY NORMAN MAILER

Albright, Combat, Sex and Reality

Brooklyn. *Washington Post*

Milosevic grew up an orphan. And his wife's mother might as well have been the protagonist in a Greek tragedy. A Yugoslav partisan, she was captured by the Nazis, tortured, surrendered crucial information, was released, and then was executed by the leader of her partisan group, who happened to be her father.

It is obviously a family history to push beyond the measure of just about all of us. Our good Hillary was heard to remark to Larry King that the Milosevic's were looking to turn their inner tragedies out upon the Kosovars.

This about expresses the depth of our comprehension of what we have been up to in Kosovo. What may be more to the point is not Milosevic's personal pain, nor his wife's, but the identity he acquired as a young Communist in a Yugoslav regime at odds with Stalin.

The Return of War News

"Congratulations on ending another war: What do you plan for an encore?" wrote Michael Kennedy a War News correspondent from New York who missed his deadline for this re-edition of a collective newspaper first published during the gulf war. This edition was first printed before the bombing ended and was replated to keep abreast of the puss. We will continue publishing on a bi-monthly basis until all nationalist overkill ends. Wish us luck to stop.

BY BILJANA SRBIJANOVIC

Belgrade Diary

With the first bomb I lost all my earnings, from several jobs, to which I had stubbornly clung so that I could live here. Following the first explosion, my American ad agency shut, my university faculty closed down, the theatres went dark, and the newspaper for which I had been writing lost its independence. With the second explosion went my freedom of movement and of expression. With the third, my desire to live here started to fade. Then the war started, on March 24.

The first day The 10-year rule of a tyrant who treats his people like a rabble has tragic consequences: three wars, hundreds of thousands dead, millions of refugees and exiles. There can be no doubt that Slobodan Milosevic will go down in history as a criminal. But the people of this sad country will not enter history only as the victims of his machinations. The destructive power of the bombs, the trails of refugees, the mass hysteria, the constant anxiety and the panicky courage

"NATO'S AIR RAIDS HAVE BROUGHT ABOUT IN ONE DAY WHAT MILOSEVIC HAS BEEN AFTER FOR YEARS."

are terrible. But at least as terrible is the absence of self-awareness on the part of the citizens; despite the electoral fraud, despite the terror and the total destruction of the economy, they have kept this man in power for a decade.

Nato's air raids have brought about in one day what Milosevic has been after for years: the independent media have been silenced; all civil rights have been suspended; the opposition fell apart out of fear of the consquences of opposition; the large number of corpses piling up here for years got bigger. But the struggle by the opposition or independent individuals or movements was not strong enough to overthrow a corrupt regime. There are no good or bad nations, but there are good and terrible governments.

Did I write enough, speak loudly enough, should and could I have been able to do more? I ought to have done much more. And what about those who didn't even do that? Those who called out the name of the president with erotic passion, who slobbered over his photographs as if they were icons, who were obedient and tame victims, but also brutal hangmen? Right now we need self-knowledge and Serbian denazification.

See DIARY Pg 8

The Mitchell Brothers published one million copies of War News, *a standard-sized newspaper, to oppose the first Gulf War in 1991. Robert Crumb drew the masthead and Warren Hinckle was the Editor. Contributors, in addition to Hunter S. Thompson, included Art Spiegelman, Margo St. James, Jules Feiffer, Barbara Ehrenreich, Nat Hentoff, Lawrence Ferlinghetti, Ron Turner, Winston Smith, Noam Chomsky, Ralph Steadman, and Norman Mailer.*

Art by Winston Smith

War News *art by Winston Smith took aim at the first Gulf War.*

HOME MOVIES

Stills from "The Crazy Never Die," the Bros. Mitchell unfinished film on Hunter S. Thompson

KODAK SAFETY FILM 5063
WRONG WAY
→32 →32A
→07 →07
→15 →15A
→05 →05A
→05 →05B
→67 →67A
→62 →62A
→64 →64A
→64 →64B
→68 →68A

Photo: Harry Moss

Hunter with his long-suffering editor, Maria Kahn, in the O'Farrell's office-pool room in May 1985. An old Mitchell Brothers fishing boat net hung from the ceiling. (Note the "Wild Dogs" poster ridiculing Dianne Feinstein for raiding the O'Farrell prominent on the wall, right.)

the Cat, and Keep On Truckin.' Ron Turner, the publisher of this book, was among the original post-hippie O'Farrell cave dwellers. He manned the popcorn stand at the midnight shows--where everything was a nickel; admission, soft drinks, popcorn, all a nickel. Turner began printing dirty comic books and christened his publishing company Last Gasp in the spirit of the era. He eventually become a major publisher of lavishly printed coffee table books of outsider art of the Robert Williams-stripe. Today, Last Gasp and the O'Farrell Street Theatre are about the only surviving institutions of 60s San Francisco.

The Brother's began making millions from epic porn films with Marilyn Chambers and "Behind the Green Door" but with the dawning of the age of VCRs, big screen porn began to lose its big buck allure. Then Artie had a magnificent brain freeze--Why not live acts at the O'Farrell, in the grand tradition of the Barbary Coast burlesque? Why not indeed. The less-than-subtle Barbary Coast of old went for donkey sex, but the new O'Farrell pioneered the more civilized indoor sport of lap dancing. The daring and inventiveness of live acts on the multiple stages--one set was built as a giant shower room--brought out the Anthony Comstock in then-Mayor Dianne Feinstein. The Convent of the Sacred Heart High School-bred Feinstein was about as hang loose as an Easter Island statue. Her mayoralty was firm on primness--women working in the mayor's office were expected to wear dresses, no pants; as a city Supervisor she had tinkered with ordinances attempting to regulate the commerce of sex in the famous sea port city, even unto suggesting that all the city's sex emporiums be relocated into a single Red Light zone confined to the largely black Bayview District. (The girl was actually taken aback when the residents didn't cozy up to her idea.)

The Wars: If Dianne hadn't fallen into a career in politics--her predecessor, Mayor George Moscone, was assassinated along with gay supervisor Harvey Milk by ex-supervisor Dan White in 1978--she would have had an excellent future as a disinfector of public telephones. Feinstein empowered the vice squad of the SFPD as a sort of screwball-comedy Papal Swiss Guard with the sworn duty of putting the Brothers out of business. The O'Farrell was raided the way the Allies bombed Dresden. The Brothers' legal beagles, led by prominent New York attorney Michael Kennedy and Bay Area civil rights attorney Thomas Steele, worked full-time fighting off copyright VHS infringements from the mafia and daily vice squad intrusions on their premises. All of the Mitchell Brothers prostitution busts--there were literally hundreds in the 70s and 80s--were thrown out of court. The few that resulted in convictions were reversed on appeal. That did not deter Feinstein's finest from doing the stupid over and over again, continuing to hit on the O'Farrell with metronomic regularity. The assaults were regularly led by the flashlight-yielding vice squad lieutenant Dennis Martel, who put paid to the flashlight prowess of the SFPD, crawling about the O'Farrell's back stairwells carrying a long black flashlight and sending flashlight-carrying cops into the O'Farrell's darkened Kopenhagen Lounge, which already had a surfeit of flashlights--undressed ladies cavorted about in the altogether while customers sat on overstuffed sofas carrying red flashlights which they used to illuminate their endearing young charms.

The trials became so frequent that sometimes there were two in one week. The same old ending was the anticlimactic dismissal of the "prostitution" charges against the O'Farrell. These repetitive legal performances left Mayor Feinstein open to the quip that defines insanity as doing the same thing over and over and expecting different results. The proceedings jammed the city's criminal courtrooms and became a real pain in the ass to the city's judiciary. Many of

The San Francisco Examiner *featured a day at home with the Mitchell family in its Sunday magazine in 1987: The Mitchell Brothers (Artie standing, Jim sitting) with their children at a family breakfast. Kids left to right: Meta, Caleb, Jasmine, Justin, Jeniffer, Rafe and Aaron.*

the O'Farrell dancers occupied their daytime hours by coming to the courtroom in solidarity, just a bit curious to see why what they had done at night was criminal by day. The trials took on aspects of a Circus Maximus. Some spectators thought the whole thing such a hoot they brought their lunches into the courtroom. (You will no doubt, Hunter, recall that afternoon when you went to City Hall dressed for court in your usual garb of tee shirt and Bermudas, with giant tumblers of Wild Turkey on the rocks in your hands like six-guns, and you charged through the courtroom double doors to deliver a spontaneous speech demanding "a motherfucking speedy trial" for your friends the Brothers. Artie Mitchell begged you to please stay away from the courthouse.)

Marilyn's Arrest: The pus came to the pimple with the Marilyn Chambers bust in 1985 when she was dragged as naked as Venus from her tub off the O'Farrell stage by a phalanx of police during a valedictory one-woman show; a total of ten cops escorted her to her dressing room to ascertain that she didn't

conceal a weapon in some bodily orifice, and more than 30 officers were eventually on the scene when backup was called because her bodyguard carried a gun. "One of those cops had the nerve to ask me, 'You don't wear any underwear?' " she said when she got out of the Hall of Justice at 3am.

I was a one-eye witness to all this when Jim Mitchell rousted me from the sleep of the just and said You Better Get Down Here, this is really a Scene. This was the scene: Jim's white Mercedes 500 SEL was parked in an alley across from the Hall of Justice. Rocky Davidson, a cousin of the "Brothers" who grew up with them in Antioch and an indispensible man in the O'Farrell operation, was pawing through the Gucci briefcase belonging to the muscleman from Vegas who was Ms. Chambers' bodyguard. "There's nothing in here but cash," he said disappointedly. The cops were holding him for lacking a gun permit and Marilyn had already suffered an overlong detention in the lockup as cops and sheriff deputies had lined up to have their own private Polaroids taken with her. She had refused to leave without him. "Wait a minute," said Rocky, "I think I found it." He pulled a little blue card out of the briefcase like a plum from a pudding. Leaves of cash fluttered all over the Mercedes back seat. Rocky took the card and went across the alley to Barrish Bail Bonds with the permit, which gave the bodyguard the way out of jail.

Marilyn came out wearing about twenty blue foxes which had been glued together into a full length coat. The bodyguard, one Bobby D'Apice, followed her wearing a designer Italian dark suit and enough gold to start a pawn shop. "They kill her, they have to kill me too," he told me. Jim Mitchell was sitting at the wheel of the Mercedes, scratching his head underneath his Irish hunting cap. Deep into the historicity of the moment, he sighed, "The Ivory Snow Girl arrested for prostitution in San Francisco. It's awesome." Ms. Chambers, before taking the career step up to porn movies, had been a model and the upper

class white-girl-next-door beautiful innocence of her face had landed her on a gazillion boxes of Ivory Snow ("99 and 44/100 Per Cent Pure") as the rotogravure face of purity--a blond mom holding a baby. When her night job was revealed, Ivory Snow pulled millions of boxes off supermarket shelves. They made haste to destroy them without the public relations benefit of shipping the discarded soap off to the third world. Yes, The Ivory Snow Girl had indeed been arrested for soliciting prostitution. The gravamen of the charge was that she had bounced her boobs, free, against the head of some bald guy in the O'Farrell audience. That charge was later dismissed in court.

The Brothers were civic-minded chaps, always good for a go at the Comstocks of the San Francisco political establishment--they campaigned against legislation proposed at the Board of Supervisors to black out the neon nipples in Carol Doda's huge topless sign on Broadway, and were always at the inventive ready to salute the flag of free expression. Thus Mayor Feinstein did not get through her Blitz of the O'Farrell without taking incoming. The O'Farrell marquee boasted: "Want A Good Time? Call Dianne" followed by the mayor's unlisted home telephone number. Each time the sign went up she changed her number, and the next day a new marquee would go up and with it the new number. Tit for tat.

Porn Movies, the story: The old-line black and white one-reeler bachelor party blue movies had begun to show their age during the 70s' apex of American sexual exhibitionism. The Brothers were inspired with a big screen idea: a full feature, story-driven epic of unabandoned lust--"A porn 'Gone With The Wind'," was how Jim Mitchell explained his concept. This pearl of an idea was to soon enough jump through the movie screen into exhibitors' throats and pocketbooks as "Behind The Green Door." Their flick managed to include many, if not most, of the sexual fantasies of every American interviewed by Kinsey.

The advantages of making realistic adult porn at the dawn of the "Deep Throat" era--"Deep Throat" was single-mindedly focused on a narrow topic which made it, well, shallow in comparison to the sexually Rabelaisian, hilarious over-the-top erotica of "Behind The Green Door"--was that the production costs were ridiculously low and the artistic values, while equally low, were inexpensive to produce as ready and willing amateurs proved quite ready to get naked on the big screen either just for the fun of it or in the hope of becoming mature porn stars who could be discovered and command real bucks. The disadvantage was that film bootleggers abounded. The keen mob nose that smelled quick untraceable cash was high in the wind and it was common to have your movie crudely copied or a film negative outright stolen, at times at gunpoint, and then fearlessly exhibited in rival movie theaters without a dime paid to the creators who wouldn't bother to call the cops, who were loath to protect porn in the first place.

It was into this marketplace with its shades of Prohibition rum-running and the wild, lawless West that Jeff Armstrong was dispatched to New York as a foot soldier in the porn battles. His assignment was to protect The Brothers' product and bring home the cash to San Francisco. Jeff described the scene: "There were some really bizarre conferences in New York where all the parties to the dispute were packing--the exhibitor, us filmmakers, the pimp boyfriend of the star demanding the negative of the film because he owned her and in his mind that made the movie his property. Weapons made everyone in the room sort of equal and Jim and Art would sometimes fly in from San Francisco dressed for the part of hippie entrepreneurs packing guns--a derby cap for Jim, and Art wearing a top hat. That in some weird way sometimes tipped the balance in our favor because they thought we were really crazy and who knew what we might do."

The Legal Struggles: When the Brothers went to war against the mob's pirating of O'Farrell classics, including "Behind The Green Door," they were swimming upstream against the flow of the law. The mob took comfort in the then-prevailing conceit that the law would not allow pornography the dignity of copyright (of course what was considered "porn" in the 70s would now be shelved by Showtime as not sexy enough.) Municipalitites with vigilante tendencies would raid porn movies as a divine right and such busts were upheld in lower courts on the ancient legalism of 'unclean hands'--the law would not enforce an illegal contract such as a gambling debt, or lend its majesty to the cause of pornography. The mob of course took this as a big green light. Many porn filmmakers didn't even put their real names on their movies, screened them fast for as much money as they could milk and ran for cover.

Who Figured: The Brothers succeeded in changing the law governing adult porn and made it legitimate. They took their gambler-father's advice--when you hit a wall, don't try and run around it, go up and over--and did the unexpected thing by taking the legal high road. They aggressively defended their rights to films then widely considered pornographic, suing for copyright infringement in every jurisdiction where some mook had bootlegged a copy. Makers of pornographic movies had never before militantly defended their legal rights and Jim Mitchell, for his stubborn constitutional battles, earned the nickname in his rough trade as the Rocky of the First Amendment.

The Brothers also defended their turf by four-walling many films--"four-walling" in Hollywood-speak is where a producer rents the entire movie house, cuts out the distributor middle men and bags the ticket money directly. The Brothers posted armed sentinels to guard the box-office proceeds and protect the film negative from thieves. In Southern California where their movies did, excuse the phrase, box office

business, they leased movie theaters long-term and sometimes bought them outright. There was a prolonged dustup in the city of Santa Ana where a zealot DA continuously busted the Mitchell Brothers' movie house there. The extended legal proceedings fell down the rabbit hole into what became one of California's longest civil lawsuits over obscenity, lasting eleven years. The Mitchells kept winning the cases and the Santa Ana City Council eventually tired of financing their DA's losing actions and cut off his funding. Then Savings and Loan moneybags and Moral Majority fanatic Charles Keating jumped into the breach as a white knight, ponying up the money for the city to continue pursuing the Evil Empire of the Brothers. When Keating's own S&L Evil Empire collapsed and he was headed for jail, the city council gave up. To rid themselves of the legal burdens of a decade of Brother-bashing, Santa Ana wrote a $260,000 check to the Mitchell Brothers as a peace offering. Artie Mitchell literally laughed all the way to the bank to deposit the check.

After hundreds of court battles and many millions in legal fees, the income from their porn epics--"Behind the Green Door," "The Resurrection of Eve," "Sodom and Gomorrah," and others less memorable--had gone largely to pay the legal costs of protecting them. The Mitchell Brothers were lawyer-poor. The altruistic boys from Antioch were however successful in at last proving that Marilyn Chambers had the same copyright protection as Mickey Mouse. When you rent a movie and are annoyed by the FBI warning at the front of the flick, that is the copyright notice courtesy of law made by the Mitchell Brothers.

After I sent him this historie, Hunter faxed a thanks for the memo on his friends, The Brothers, and said that now he was going to start writing the Night Manager book, real soon.

He never wrote it.

Jeff Armstrong, the general manager of the O'Farrell, was otherwise ungainfully occupied as Hunter's San Francisco "Road Manager." Jeff's charge was to deal with the unscripted hysteria of Thompson's frequent visits to the Bay Area to give lectures for which he was, unfailingly, always late.

"It was challenging. It was a brutal deal." Here was the routine:

"Everything was on a top secret basis. First, there was a fax giving the time to pick him up at the airport and the flight number. That always changed, because Hunter usually missed at least two planes on the way to San Francisco. At the last minute Deborah Fuller, Hunter's saintly assistant at Owl Farm, would call with the code name of the hotel where Hunter was booked, because Hunter would more often than not cancel the original reservation.

Then came the airport run--"always an adventure." The Road Manager stocked the company 560SEL with beer, drugs, whiskey, vodka and ice--"always lots of ice, Hunter really liked his ice." After the airport there were several unscheduled stops--"usually Hunter had to pick up drugs from some guy he knew on Nob Hill"--and then the hotel checking-in ordeal--"not pretty."

Then it was into the room and Hunter on the phone to Room Service--"amazing ordering, four shrimp cocktails, a chocolate cake, eight Heinekens, a bottle of Absolut, a bottle of Chivas, and his IBM Selectric--"Where is my fucking typewriter?"--and slam goes the phone."

"From the moment of arrival it was constant questing--you quest to get supplies, get the drugs, then you start questing all over again." The night usually ended about 5am and Hunter would roll out around 2pm for lunch with a friend, usually Armstrong and Jeannette Etheredge, and it was usually abalone at Al Falchi's Waterfront Restaurant--"Hunter loved his abalone."

Then more stops for more drinks and it was off to the lecture. "One night we're in Berkeley, at Zellerbach Hall, and it's 10pm and Hunter's speech is scheduled 8pm, two hours late, and the audience is just coming down from all the drugs they took to get high for Hunter. The mood is surly, turning ugly, and Hunter walks on stage with a tall chimney glass filled with Chivas and the ice. He smiles kind of sheepishly and lights up a joint and and tells everyone to light

up, they won't dare to bust you, and the crowd loves it and gets all riotous and crazy."

Not every airport pickup was the same. Not all.

"I get to the airport and park the Mercedes. It's fully stocked, locked and loaded, but this night we never use the Mercedes. The plane from Denver he's supposed to be on he's not on but there's another one right away in an hour, at midnight. I go to the bar for a drink and walk back to the gate and there's this guy waiting there who's wearing a baseball cap pulled down over his eyes. The last plane is late and after a while he pulls the cap up and asks me if I'm waiting for Hunter. I say I am. My name's Jeff. I'm the Road Manager. "I'm waiting for him too," he says. "My name is Johnny Depp."

"Johnny Depp says there's a limo waiting outside that was sent by Hunter's publisher. There's a girl in the car, hired by the publisher to mind Hunter. Johnny says he brought a care bag for Hunter, things he would need. It's in the car with the girl.

"Hunter piles off the plane and now we're in the limo--forget the Mercedes, that sits overnight in the airport garage--and we're in the limo going up 101 to the city. The minder's in the front seat. We all have a Chivas and Hunter rolls up a joint from the bag.

"The girl in the front sticks her head over the driver's seat and says, "Excuse me, you can't smoke in here."

"Hunter does this thing with his eyes and says to me, "You are going to take care of this, you are the Road Manager."

"Yes, I am," I say.

"I tell the driver to pull over to the side of the highway and stop the car. I tell the girl, "You have to get out of the car. Now. You have to get out of the car." Everybody nods that she has to get out of the car.

"It's now one in the morning and she's on the side of the 101 around Candlestick. She's like, she can't believe it. She's out on the side of the highway in the dark. I tell her we'll send her a cab.

"Go," Hunter tells the driver.

"Well done," he says and the limo takes off.

"We all have a big laugh and Hunter lights another joint then says, "We must go back. We can't leave her there." The Southern Gentleman.

"We back up the limo and let her in. She's kind of in shock and doesn't say a word. We drop her at Sam Jordan's on Third Street in Butchertown and I go in and tell them to call her a cab and watch out for her.

"The limo drops us at the St. Francis where Hunter is booked and Hunter tells the driver to go back and get her if she hasn't got a cab, but by no means bring her here.

"Hunter goes to the desk and registers in a phony name and throws down a credit card. The desk girl says it's no good. He pulls out another one, but that's no good, too. Johnny Depp steps up and puts down his credit card.The girl reads the name and pulls back and says, "Are you really Johnny Depp?"

"Johnny pulls the visor of the cap up over his eyes and signs the card slip and gives her a smile. I think she's fainting on the spot.

"Hunter says, "Fuck this place, let's go to the O'Farrell and gives his bag to a bellboy to dump upstairs in the room. We don't want the limo we had any more, it's used, and Johnny gets one in front of the hotel and we go to the O'Farrell and take some pictures and have drinks and smokes and shoot some pool and the driver of the new limo waits outside on Johnny's credit card till about 5am when Hunter decides it's time to get some sleep."

I asked Jeff if there were any events that stand out during his four years as Road Manager? Well, Jeff says, there was the Dancers of Doom. And then there was the kidnapping in Sacramento.

The Dancers of Doom. One remembers them well. This was on election eve of the presidential election of 1985. Mondale, whom Hunter had dubbed The Murine Man, v. Reagan. Hunter was scheduled to give a lecture and analyze the returns as they came in that night at The Stone, a nightclub on Broadway.

Hunter was staying at the Miyako in a penthouse suite. The Road Manager was in the hotel bar with Hunter and Jim Mitchell. Hunter had become enraptured of a band of Samoan dancers who played huge heraldic drums as some among them pinwheeled the stage chanting. The dancers had set up camp in the bar and Hunter was deep into negotiations with them, he desperately wanted Dancers of Doom with him onstage at The Stone. "Just a half an hour," he kept repeating. "Just a half an hour of your time." A price was named, one thousand dollars American. Jim Mitchell reached into his jacket pocket and pulled out ten crisp C-notes, fruits of the loom of porn.

That night Hunter stuck with The Dancers of Doom like the stamp to the envelope. I was along for the ride because Hunter and I had planned to spot check some Frisco precincts that election evening, earnest plans which the siren call of the Dancers of Doom derailed. He was scheduled to speak at 9pm. At precisely 10:45pm Hunter and the Dancers of Doom walked on stage at The Stone. The audience was by then drunk and mean. They had paid cash money to hear Hunter call the election state by state but by now the election was over, Reagan--very much not the hometown fave--had won and the crowd couldn't hear a thing Hunter said over the frantic drumming of the Dancers of Doom. There were catcalls and boos from the crowd and bottles of Bud began hailing down on the stage. At that show of disrespect one of the Dancers of Doom put down his drum and jumped off the stage in hot pursuit. The evening had turned black and savage and the riot began. Those of us on stage with Hunter beat a retreat through an uncertain and dark back passageway. Some Dancers of Doom remained on the stage beating their drums while the other Samoans leapt into the audience and began beating the shit out of the customers.

There was the immediate matter of Hunter's purse for the evening; his guarantee of four grand appeared in peril. "The box office!" Hunter said. "Let's find the cash box and get out with what we can get." The box office was a low-ceilinged poop deck behind The Stone's marquee over Broadway which was still neon-promising "Hunter S. Thompson's View of The Election at 9 PM TONIGHT" in huge letters. The little room was harsh with olfactory hints of urine past and vomit present. A bent twig of a man with a nose barely as wide as his pony tail squatted on dirty canvas bags stuffed ungainly with greenbacks and refused to surrender them to the featured speaker of the evening.

Sometime during the conversation a revolver went off and dead plaster thumped down from the ceiling. Police sirens wailed in the distance. "FLEE," Hunter said, and we took what we could carry, exiting backwards through the front door like the Dillinger gang and piled into a Mitchell Brothers limo purring at the curb with Jim's cousin Rocky ready at the wheel. We left the loot locked in the car and walked into the Tosca and Hunter told Jeannette we had just come from a night at the opera.

The kidnapping in Sacramento. The Road Manager recalled it as one of those spur of the moment things. Hunter was living in a fabulous-view Sausalito apartment appointed with a genuine tiki bar--and there, he decided, he would secrete the girlfriend of a Woody Creek buddy name of Luckett. She had apparently run away to Sacramento where she was living with another guy. Hunter wished to redress this grievance for his friend. The idea was to get her out of Sacramento by all means possible and get her to Sausalito where she could sit at the tiki bar with Hunter and understand her mistaken ways. This maneuver brought out what the noted California historian Kevin Starr has called the "Soldier of Fortune" side of Hunter's multi-faceted personality.

The Road Manager received an urgent call in the early morning from Hunter, which meant that he had not gone to sleep that night. "Stock up the Mercedes, after lunch we have to kidnap somebody in Sacramento," the Night Manager told his Road Manager. The posse in the Mercedes made it to Sacramento in record time and explained to the woman's bewildered boyfriend that for reasons of national security they must accompany her to San Francisco so Hunter could "interview her for a book."

Jeff said Hunter excelled in charm that day and convinced the woman that this was something she would want to do.

The Mercedes had barely reached Davis when Hunter, who was scanning a police radio, learned that the boyfriend had, after sufficient reflection, called the cops on them. They veered off the freeway and took country back roads most of the way towards San Francisco with all eyes out for the CHP. Once safely in Sausalito, the woman in question succumbed to Hunter's tiki bar charms and consented after a pleasant day or so, to return to Aspen to have a chit-chat with Hunter's buddy.

"Hunter said to me, 'All's well that ends well'," the Road Manager said.

[THE WRITER IS ARRESTED]

Hunter and I seemed destined to keep becoming involved in beefs where we were on the same side--in the 60s with *Ramparts* and Wallposters, in the 70s with *Scanlan's* and gonzo-birthing madness, in the 80s with the Mitchell Brothers, and in the 90s when Hunter made himself art director of the Frisco Gold Rush-era magazine I had

resurrected, the *Argonaut* ... we seemed to be always in the trenches, fighting for, or against, something, godammit.

Hunter found it hilarious when I was arrested by the Frisco cops after making fun of them for needing thirty boys in blue to get Marilyn Chambers naked off the stage of the O'Farrell. That happened one foggy February afternoon in 1985 when I snuck out the side door of the *Chronicle*, where I was then gainfully employed as an opinion fulminator, and was shirt-sleeved on my way down to the newspaper bar on the corner when two uniformed San Francisco policemen stopped me. Both had mustaches. Both had walkie-talkies. Both had guns. "You Hinckle?" the short cop asked.

I reckoned that I was. "When you are fat and wear an eyepatch there is nowhere to hide," I wrote in the *Chronicle* the next day, reporting on my arrest.

"You got any warrants out 'n you?" asked the other cop. His face was as emotive as the backside of a postage stamp. I said I didn't drive, the eyepatch thing and all, and I didn't remember being arrested, certainly not recently,unless of course they were, ha! figuring on arresting me. They were.

"I think you got warrants," said the cop who was talking into a little black microphone on his shoulder. I said I'd be down at the bar if they needed me. They said I was going nowhere. The little box on the cop's shoulder squawked something. "You have to come with us," he said.

I pleaded to go upstairs to my office. If I have warrants how am I going to pay them if I don't have my wallet? One played nice cop. "OK, we'll let you go get your coat and your wallet." In the elevator I mentioned, casually, that it was a funny thing that I had just finished writing a column saying the police chief should be fired for sending thirty cops into the Mitchell Brothers to arrest one naked woman. The cops declined comment.

We walked into the *Chronicle* city room which looked like the set for the old Lou Grant TV series. The last time I saw blue uniforms with guns inside a newspaper was in the fabulous 50s newspaper noir thriller "Deadline USA" which I had seen at least a dozen times when I was a teenager. Gangsters disguised as cops dragged a stoolie out of the office of Humphrey Bogart, who played the editor of *The Day*, a dying newspaper with two days to live before it was sold but was spending its last breath of ink going after the bad guys. The faux cops took the stoolie out a back door above the pressroom

THE WRITER IS ARRESTED: Hinckle making news in 1985 by being busted by San Francisco's finest in the Chronicle *city room.*

and he tried to escape by inching hand-by-hand across the pipes over the roaring presses and the mob boys in blue machine-gunned the stoolie and he fell into the presses and got all squished up. It was a great movie and convinced me that I should go into the newspaper business.

While I was putting on my coat I hollered "Cameras! Get a camera! I'm being arrested." The cops called me a sonnabitch and dragged me by the arms down the hallway to the elevator and the *Chronicle* got a nice picture of me for the next morning's paper. A police car with the light twinkling on the roof was waiting outside. The two cops shoved me in the back seat and got in and there was another cop driving and that made three policemen sent to take me away. Hell, I was small potatoes compared to Marilyn Chambers' thirty cops. Now the cops had got me for razzing them; tit for tat, as the Irish say. Fair is fair.

The computer at the Hall of Justice sure enough coughed up a warrant for $178--for the crime of walking my dog without a leash. A busybody patrolman had come up to me in a park on a cold dawn years before and written a ticket for my basset hound being off leash. I righteously tore up the ticket and let the confetti go sodden in the morning fog. But the cops had said warrants, emphasizing the plural. What else was there? "You're in for a 215 MPC," the booking sergeant said. What was that? He looked it up in a fat little book with a leather cover. "That's a lewd charge. Lewd and lascivious in public,"

(Top) THREE A.M.: Hunter at the IBM Selectric writing his column at the San Francisco Examiner. *(Bottom) R. Crumb's newspaper rack card when Hinckle moved from the* Chronicle *to the* Examiner *in 1985, bringing Hunter aboard with him. Crumb fans kept stealing the cardboard rack cards from the newspaper stands and the* Examiner *had to print extra copies.*

Hunter's arrival at Will Hearst's San Francisco Examiner *provoked this 1987 cover by* California *magazine. Left to right: Associate Editor Warren Hinckle with his basset hound, Bentley, Editor Larry Kramer, Publisher William Randolph Hearst III and Columnist Thompson.*

FEAR AND TREMBLIN at the EXAMINER

WILD TURK

CAMPAIGN TRAIL

"In Rio Vista, a small riverside town about an hour's drive east of San Francisco, I met an elderly Chinese woman who claimed to be the former mistress of Richard Nixon. She lived on a houseboat that was moored in a slough near Antioch, she said, and the ex-president had often visited her there when he came to California.

"Sometimes he came in a helicopter," she said, "with a bunch of Secret Service agents. They would sit on the dock and drink long-neck Budwiesers while we went below decks and played cards. That's all he wanted to do. People said he drank too much gin, but I never saw him that way. We did it for 13 years and nobody ever found out."

"Nixon & The Whale Woman"
Hunter S. Thompson, The *Examiner*, October 21, 1985

HST on

RONALD REAGAN

"It [politics] is an evil trade, on most days, and nobody smart will defend it . . . except maybe Ronald Reagan, who seems dumber than three mules. But he is, after all, the president. He can drop bombs on any town in the world and have anybody who bothers him arrested."

TED KENNEDY

"He could soar with the condors and crawl with the wildest of swine—but when the deal went down he was simply a bad driver. There are people in Washington who will tell you that Ted Kennedy would be president of the United States today if he'd ever learned to drive."

ED MEESE

"Meese is so crooked that he is said by Washington gossips to require the help of three legal assistants to screw his pants on every morning."

ON GARY HART

"He has a very Calvinist sense of humor, and 15 years in the shadow of Warren Beatty have not been healthy for him. When it comes to "womanizing" in Washington, Hart is an amateur. Four generations of Kennedys have roamed naked and crazy like satyrs on Capitol Hill, and Wilbur Mills wallowed and howled like a rhino in the Tidal Pool with a mainline stripper from Boston named Fanne Fox."

OLIVER NORTH

" 'The Colonel,' as they call him, is like one of those Doberman guard dogs that Hermann Goering used to have, and when people stared at the beast they would look at each other and say, 'Thank God that dog can't talk.' "

HST. ON LOCATION IN GRENADA

he said grinning. "Hey, that's the same charge Marilyn Chambers was booked on."

The cops had hacked into their own computer to out smart-ass me. This meant war. One week later the *Chronicle* plopped onto doorsteps with the front page taken up by a huge photograph of Chief of Police Con Murphy trying to hide from the camera's unforgiving eye in his party boat that was moored illegally at Fisherman's Wharf. The large headline above the photo read: THE FLOATING POLICE CHIEF.

In the column underneath the photo I reported unkindly that not only was the chief's boat parked illegally--only commercial fishing boats could moor at Fisherman's Wharf--but it was outfitted rather splendidly with parts traceable to the flourishing and unpoliced hot goods market on the San Francisco waterfront. The chief was later somewhat unceremoniously removed from his duties; tit for tat.

In the aftermath I bonded with the Brothers--we had been after all in the trenches together. My daughters both had their high school after-graduation parties at the O'Farrell and Artie Mitchell fell in love with my then-80 year old Irish mother and said he wanted to marry her, or at least date; she tweaked his nose and called him a rapscallion.

[NEWSPAPER DAYS]

When I was pinched for my dog I was writing a column for the *Chronicle* but soon thereafter crossed the journalistic Rubicon to the Hearst *Examiner*. This was at the urging of Will Hearst, the newspaper scion, who wanted to remake the afternoon San Francisco broadsheet in the tradition of his wildman grandfather, William Randolph Hearst, who virtually invented the modern American newspaper when he took over the sleepy post-Gold Rush *Examiner* in 1867 and turned it yellow and painted the town red. At the new Hearst *Examiner*, where I wore an editor's hat, I urged Hunter to join the party, and join he did. Will understood immediately the wisdom of Hunter being simultaneously the O'Farrell Night Manager and an *Examiner* columnist; Hearst the Younger's editorial philosophy was, as was his grandfather's, to indulge the eccentricities and extra curricular escapades of his star writers. Hunter did little to disappoint.

This was the first time Hunter had to meet a regular newspaper deadline since he worked for the old Dow Jones *National Observer* in the early 60s. Despite all predictions to the contrary and with some

cliffhangers and significant collatoral damage to hotel rooms, Hunter never missed a deadline in three years of writing for the *Examiner*, from 1985 to 1988. Not that he took any joy in the company of newspaper people: "I have spent half my life trying to get away from journalism, but I am still mired in it--a low trade and a habit worse than heroin, a strange seedy world of misfits and drunkards and failures. A group photo of the ten top journalists in America on any given day would be a monument to human ugliness," he wrote in an introduction to a collection of 100 of his *Examiner* columns published in 1988 under the title "Generation of Swine." He produced a column the madness of which had not been seen in a daily newspaper since Ambrose Bierce's misanthropic tirades in the old Hearst *Examiner* in the 19th century. Hunter's novelistic talents were as evident as his political acumen and he freely mixed the paints on his palette between fact and fantasy. When he ventured to the Mitchell Brothers' beloved Sacramento river Delta in pursuit of an errant whale, he reported discovering an ancient mistress of his nemesis Richard Nixon who lived on a houseboat on a slough in the Mitchell hometown of Antioch: "We did it for 13 years and nobody ever found out," Hunter wrote that she told him.

Hunter was enthusiastic about his return to the newspaper game. He expressed his enthusiasm in his signature way, pouring boiling water out the publisher's office window onto the heads of striking printers below. He shot a television commercial for the paper with video of him taking Will Hearst to a shooting range and sending off a few rounds. He liked the action around the paper and urged Ralph Steadman to join the party at the *Examiner*:

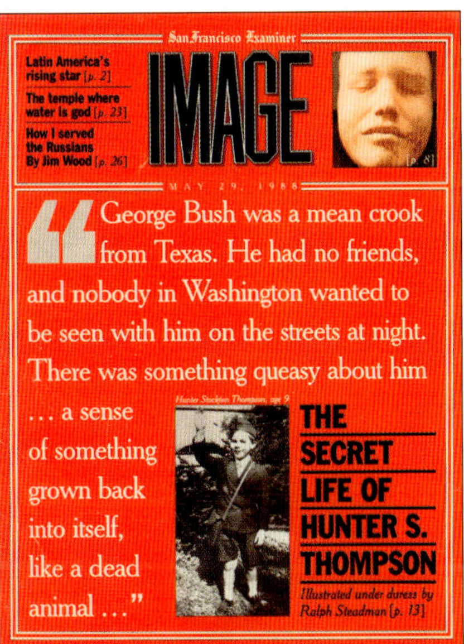

"The Night Manager is running a bit behind schedule at this point, because of my weakness for journalism. In addition to all my other jobs, titles and responsibilities, I am now a sort of new-syndicated columnist for the San Francisco *Examiner*, the once-proud flagship of what was known as "The Hearst Empire." Young Will, the heir, has decided

to make it "a thinking man's newspaper for the 80s," and of course I am out on the point.

"Why not? We have Warren on the night shift, whipping the police at all times, and I suspect there is life in the project ... which means, of course, that you will have to fill in one of the "Artists in Residence" slots, a high-powered four-week gig that will cause you to move to San Francisco and actually work for a living for a while. You will be sent out on routine assignments like an ordinary journalist and your work will be treated like offal, but I think you can overcome it and perhaps do some unusual work.

"Let's look at Groundhog Day for your opening shot. We will get you a flat in the Avenues, my old neighborhood, and your first assignment will probably be the trial of Charles C. Ng, an alleged mass sex slayer from Calaveras County who will soon be deported from Canada to stand trial here in Fat City ... or maybe in some rural jurisdiction where they will treat us like decent people when we roll into town like the Joad brothers.

"You will have to trust me on this one, Ralph. I know it sounds strange, but in fact it may even be sane."

For his new columnist job he drafted his sweetie and long-enduring editorial assistant as his on-the-road editor. Maria Kahn traveled with Hunter to Key West, Denver, Vegas, Chicago, L.A. and obscure points north and south to keep his fingers on the Selectric and fixed his weekly copy en route to the next madness. In one of his first columns Hunter told the story of taking Maria at midnight to a tattoo parlor because he needed something to write about.

The column, printed below, is a piece of wonderful madness that shortens the breath to consider that it was printed in a Hearst newspaper. For Hunter lovers and J-school students of the gonzo style, this is Coke Classic Thompson. The other reason for printing this column is that Hunter didn't tell the whole story. The column is remarkable, as much for what Hunter wrote as for what he didn't include--which tells a lot about Hunter, the Southern Gentleman. First Hunter's column, then the parts of the story, in Maria's words, that he left out:

I dropped Maria off in front of the tattoo parlor just before midnight. There was no place to park on the street, so I sent her inside and found a place on the sidewalk, in front of a house with no lights.

Why Not? I figured. Black car, dark sidewalk, nothing but cranked Chinese teen-agers on the street ... and we did, in fact, need the story. The week had been too long and fast for wise and considered reflection. I had lectured for something like 166 straight hours on morals and manners and politics, in addtion to drugs and violence. I had been awake for too long.

We had located the Picture Machine Tattoo Parlor in the Yellow Pages, only an hour before it closed. It was time to get the story.

Fortunately, it was only a few blocks away from the hotel, on the corner of Third and Geary, in the same lonely doorway as Suicide Prevention, Inc. The whole front of the building was shrouded by thick steel accordian screens, like the ones they have in Beirut.

The suicide clinic was closed, but Maria rang the bell to the tattoo parlor and then disappeared inside.

By the time I got there, she was already staring dolefully at a small white card from the Key and Cohn Dermatology Clinic. It said, "Tattoo Removals by Laser Surgery," prices and fees upon request. Another card, which the tattoo man had given her, said, "Do not pick scab ... I will not therefore be held responsible for any tattoo after you leave my premises. thank you."

The proprieter was a giant Swiss named Mark, whose arms and shoulders looked like something out of a Fabulous Furry Freak Brothers cartoon. He had knives and snakes and scorpions and skulls full of Hell's Angels slogans: Live Fast, Die Hard ... Live to Ride, Ride to Kill ... I Should Have Killed You Yesterday ... I'd Rather See My Sister in a Whorehouse than See My Brother on a Jap Bike ...

There were many other options, displayed all over the walls and ranging from dainty four-color florals to monstrous full-body murals depicting scenes like The Rape of Nanking and six-legged gorgons eating fire and gnawing the skulls of their enemies.

"Eagles and panthers," he said. "Those are still the most popular ... But, you see, ladies get more flowers and stuff. The guys get the eagles and panthers." The man seemed nervous. He had wanted to close by midight, but now he saw shadows in his life. It is not good business, on the dark end of Geary Boulevard at two minutes to midnight on Saturday, to entertain two strangers with glittering eyes and no apparent motive.

"We need something fast," I told him. "I have a deadline at noon tomorrow. How long will it take to put a tattoo on this woman?"

He eyed me warily, then took another long look at Maria. "Where do you want it?" he asked.

"Never mind that," I shouted. "We'll put it on her back." I scanned the walls for a suitable design, but most of the good ones required too much time. Some took two or three minutes, but others needed eight to ten hours.

"What about that panther?" I said finally, pointing to a raging black beast about the size of a volleyball. It was large, but the lines were not complex. It was mainly a matter of black ink and blood, from the sting of the hideous needle.

Maria stretched out on the gurney and I pulled her sweater up, to expose both shoulder blades. The unhappy Swiss took a long time cleaning his high-powered electric needle in a pan full of alcohol and ether. It hummed and whined like a huge dentist's drill, and then he plunged it into her flesh.

Sunday morning is calm on Geary Boulevard. A huge orange sign that says storage is the only living thing on the horizon. After that it is only The Avenues, a bleak vista of fogbound caves stretching all the way out to the beach. Strange vans in the driveways and huge motorcylces chained to the fireplugs.

I understand The Avenues. I know them like the veins in my neck. I can drive at top speed all the way to the Beach Boy cafe in fog so think that even the streetcars can't operate. There were nights, in the old days, when we drove big bikes in tight packs through the park, like a thundering herd of wild pigs. We would scream and drink whiskey and light our joints with Zippos as we zoomed through the darkness like rats, leaning crazily into the long curves around the lakes and the Polo Field ... just a gang of nice guys and athletes, out for a ride in the weather.

But things are different now. I am living in a penthouse suite in the Miyako with wraparound balconies and a deep ginzu bathtub, looking down through long black binoculars on the alleys and rooftops of Japantown. I have egg rolls from room service and a new black Camaro in the hotel parking lot.

They know me here. When I came back last night I saw the hotel bell captain standing out in the middle of Post Street in a sleazy black kimono, jabbering blankly at oncoming traffic ... so I stomped on the gas and swerved left at him, just to test the basic reflexes. He leaped back and cursed me as I veered off into the hotel parking lot. Maria ran quickly inside, taking the satchel of otter furs, along with the records and evidence from our recent burglary trial.

"Did you have fun?" asked the bell captain, as he opened the driver-side door for me.

"Are you crazy?" I said. "I have a serious deadline to meet. We've been at the tattoo parlor all night. It was the only way to do it.

"What?" he said. "You got yourself tattooed?"

"Oh no," I told him. "Not me." I pointed to Maria, who was already far into the lobby. "She's the one who got the tattoo," I said. "A huge black and red panther between her shoulder blades."

He nodded slowly, but I could see that his face was tense. "What do you mean?" he said. "You made that poor girl get tattooed? Just for a newspaper story?

"It was the right thing to do," I said. We had no choice. We are, after all, professionals."

The Tattoo's Tale

Maria talking: "As usual, it was the Saturday night deadline with nothing to write about. We were staying at the Miyako. All the ideas sounded flat and Hunter was pacing and I said I always had an interest in getting a tattoo."

Maria Kahn in the mid-80s was Hunter's real life Girl Friday with Rosalind Russell's sense of style and humor. She kept Hunter together through some monstruous adventures and kept getting coherent copy out of him on deadline time. This was considered by Hunter-watchers to have been a superhuman feat of editing and managing. "Fifty-two consecutive deadlines met," she said with the easy pride of the miracle worker.

Maria is now Maria Kahn Baier, a civic leader in Phoenix with two girls. She was elected to the city council and then appointed by the governor of Arizona as the czarina of ecology and water use in the dry state. In 1985 she was battling the severe drought of deadlines with Hunter. That was when, she said, she suggested the idea of getting a tattoo. She said that Hunter looked weirdly at her and said, "You've got to be kidding, why?"

"I told him that I could never remember which side Hinckle wore his eye patch on and I wanted to get a tattoo on that side of my body, so when I saw you I could see if you had switched it by comparing to my tattoo.

"You probably forgot this but we met you for a drink before we went to the tattoo parlor. You had the patch on the left side, and in the car I told Hunter that was where I was going to get it. It was just about midnight when we got to the Picture Machine Tattoo Parlor and Mark the tattoo man--he was huge and said he was Swiss but he sounded more like a Saudi--was really nice. I first said I wanted to get

an X put on my hand and he advised against that. He said you might not be so happy with it when you get older and it's better to put it in a placed where you can't see it. Boy was he right.

"We decided on a black panther because it was kind of a solid block and that could be done quickly. I said to put a panther on my left shoulder blade.

"Then Hunter said, 'I can't let you do this by yourself.'

Hunter then got a tattoo on his right shoulder blade. "The plan was, the next time we saw you we'd show you our tattoos and see which panther was on the side you had the patch on, and we'd trap you if you were switching sides. We were laughing like crazy at the insanity of it."

"Hunter said to me, 'This is really gonzo journalism, getting a hideous needle and ink stuck in you for the story.' "

This was the gentleman in Hunter coming out--he wouldn't let just Maria mutilate her body so he could get a column. So he mutilated his body too. But he didn't tell that part in the column. It made a better story if he sounded mean and callous, like the total crazy man that was his persona.

I asked Maria how much of what Hunter wrote was true, and how much was made up. How many parts were left out?

Hints of a formula: Maria put on her editor's cap and said that about 25 to 30 per cent of what Hunter wrote in a piece was absolutely true--some was patently false and simply made up--and the rest was in the middle. "Hunter would say, 'Let them prove me wrong.' "

"There's a certain amount of things that should be subject to interpretation," said Hunter's favorite editor.

The Night Manager/Columnist had no job conflicts and regularly used his misadventures with the O'Farrell gang as cannon fodder for the column, to wit:

> "Hinckle and his animal had arrived about sundown, traveling nervous and semi-incognito in a white Mercedes sedan with the Mitchell Brothers and a woman from Oakland who said she was looking for work, and also that her husband wanted to stab me in the head if he ever got the chance. The woman from Oakland was no stranger to me, or to anyone else in the hotel. She had been prowling the hallways for days, spooking the maids and scrawling pentagrams on my door. A few months earlier she had

> lent me her husband's motorcycle, and he went wild with rage...
>
> "It was madness, but I felt I could handle it more or less by myself until she turned up at the hotel that afternoon in the same car with Hinckle and the infamous Mitchell Brothers. They sent her away for a while, but soon she was pounding savagely on the door, a wronged woman out of control.
>
> "We all cowered stupidly as the hammering on the door continued. Hinckle feigned sleep and Jim Mitchell called his wife on the phone. Artie jabbered nervously about his girlfriend, the Young Republican porn star, Missy Manners and politics and morals in in her native Utah. The dog started barking.
>
> "Work was impossible... and these addled cretins have the gall to complain about my deadlines."

The remarkable run of consistent deadline copy was due to the singular fact that Hunter never had an editor quite like Maria--an editor who would immerse herself in the madness, get in the pool and get wet, too--yet managed a skillful distance from the unreality to edit the story: A true gonzo editor.

Maria quit the column when she heard that Will Hearst was talking to Terry McDonell, a veteran magazine editor and a good friend of both Will and Hunter, about becoming an *Examiner* editor and overseeing projects including Hunter's column. McDonell had been a managing editor at *Rolling Stone* and *Newsweek* and knew well that dark game. Ms. Kahn was incensed that anyone could think a New York pro could do a better job, even if he was Hunter's friend, of handling Hunter than she had so she quit. She said Will called her and asked her to come back, that it was all a misunderstanding. Hunter pleaded with her like a Carthusian monk for the return of his beads, but she would have none of it. This college English major had become as battle-scarred-seasoned as a Marine on Guadalcanal and was a professional, good goddammit, and she was out of there.

Hunter could not hear the tick-tock of the clock of weekly deadlines without her. Soon after Maria took a hike, Hunter stopped writing the column.

The year before Artie's death Hunter got into trouble in his hometown. There was a bit of typical insanity involving an intrusive woman in his hot tub and the police who arrived searched the Owl Farm compound and Hunter ended up being charged by the Aspen DA, who had been sore itching to get Hunter on something, anything, for years, with felony possession and use of drugs. The Aspen establishment had, finally, turned against the Great Nuisance that was Hunter. This time they were really out to get him. The charges were based on evidence--thin even by television crime lab standards--that had been unearthed during an outrageous 14-hour search of Hunter's disorganized casa--some of the exhibits found dated back to the glory days of Aspen in the ripe 60s, fermented weed found in a crack in the floorboards, that sort of stuff. Hunter's friends were outraged and began organizing to take out a protest ad in the *New York Times*. The Mitchell Brothers, to the rescue, took another tack. Taking off from San Francisco in a caravan headed by a big red Chevy convertible with a buffalo head on the hood--they had decided to give Hunter the car as a present for his services as Night Manager--they headed east accompanied by two vans and an entourage of O'Farrell dancers. Along the highways through Nevada and Utah they kept picking-up Thompson-supporting freaks.

The Brothers arrived the afternoon before Hunter's arraignment and cruised the streets of Aspen with dancers, topless in the back of the Big Red, standing and waving to the locals. They hit every bar in the pricey ski resort and bought several rounds of drinks for the house in each one. They announced they were the vanguard of a mob of freaks who were coming to Aspen for the trial to support their counterculture hero Hunter S. Thompson. Then they formally visited the Sheriff and the District Attorney to discuss the logistics for handling such a large gathering of Thompson fanatics for the trial and politely introduced the girls who were every bit the perfect topless ladies.

The next week all charges against Thompson were dropped. The Brothers had grossed out the Aspen Establishment, which shuddered to envision the human clutter and portable toilets and bra burning and commercial ruin from a new Woodstock of Thompson fans camping out in town during the trial.

The Aspen caper was the Brothers' last good deed together. When they got home, Artie began a scary descent into drugs and guns and booze. The bros began arguing. Artie was bored and sensed himself somehow out of place, the O'Farrell was more or less on autopilot without any new movies on the horizon and Jim's creative energy was going into *War News*, an antiwar newspaper he started to protest the Gulf War in 1991. Jim had taken a lease on a defunct nightclub on lower Broadway and was retrofitting it with a Times Square-type neon tickertape running news bulletins and installing computer terminals amid the cocktail tables--an alcoholic city room for *War News*. The newspaper would be produced while the paying public watched and drank. The cartoonists would have their own stage and draw on demand for money from the crowd; a Left Bank in North Beach. Fine, Artie said to Jim, you give me the O'Farrell and you can have *War News*.

Artie began packing everywhere he went. He shot up the O'Farrell ceiling and left a message on the answering machine of Jim's wife Lisa, a former O'Farrell dancer, that she'd better stay away from the front window because he was going to come over and shoot up Jim's house. The dancers were scared and came to Jim and said that if Artie walked in the theater the way he was they would call the cops and have him arrested. Artie began vowing that he would not be taken alive; a call to the police would mean gunfire for sure.

The night it happened, on February 27, 1991, Jim and his cousin Rocky drove to Artie's house in Marin County armed with guns, ropes and a straightjacket. The logic was to be armed better than Artie. The plan was to get the drop on Artie and tie him up and take him to a cabin in Tahoe and dry him out and beat the shit out of him and talk some sense into him. It was raining heavy and the house was dark. They figured Artie had already left for the city. Jim stayed there just in case while Rocky drove down the hill to a shopping center to call The O'Farrell to warn that the gun-toting Artie might be on his way and to station guys by the door to tackle him. Jim kicked Artie's front door in frustration and to his surprise it opened. He went into the dark house and shot at the ceiling with his rifle, the way Artie had done at their theater. A crack of light appeared under a door down the hall and Artie came toward him in the dark saying I'm going to get you motherfucker with what looked like a gun in his hand but it was a Heineken bottle. Jim didn't remember what happened next but it appeared he tried to wing Artie and a ricochet bullet went off

the wall and into his brain. When Rocky came back up the hill there was a sea of cop cars but it wasn't just another raid on the O'Farrell.

When Hunter heard the horrible news he immediately responded with sympathy for the devil and some explicit suggestions for how to handle the press. He sat down at his Selectric and rattled off this fax to Jeff Armstrong:

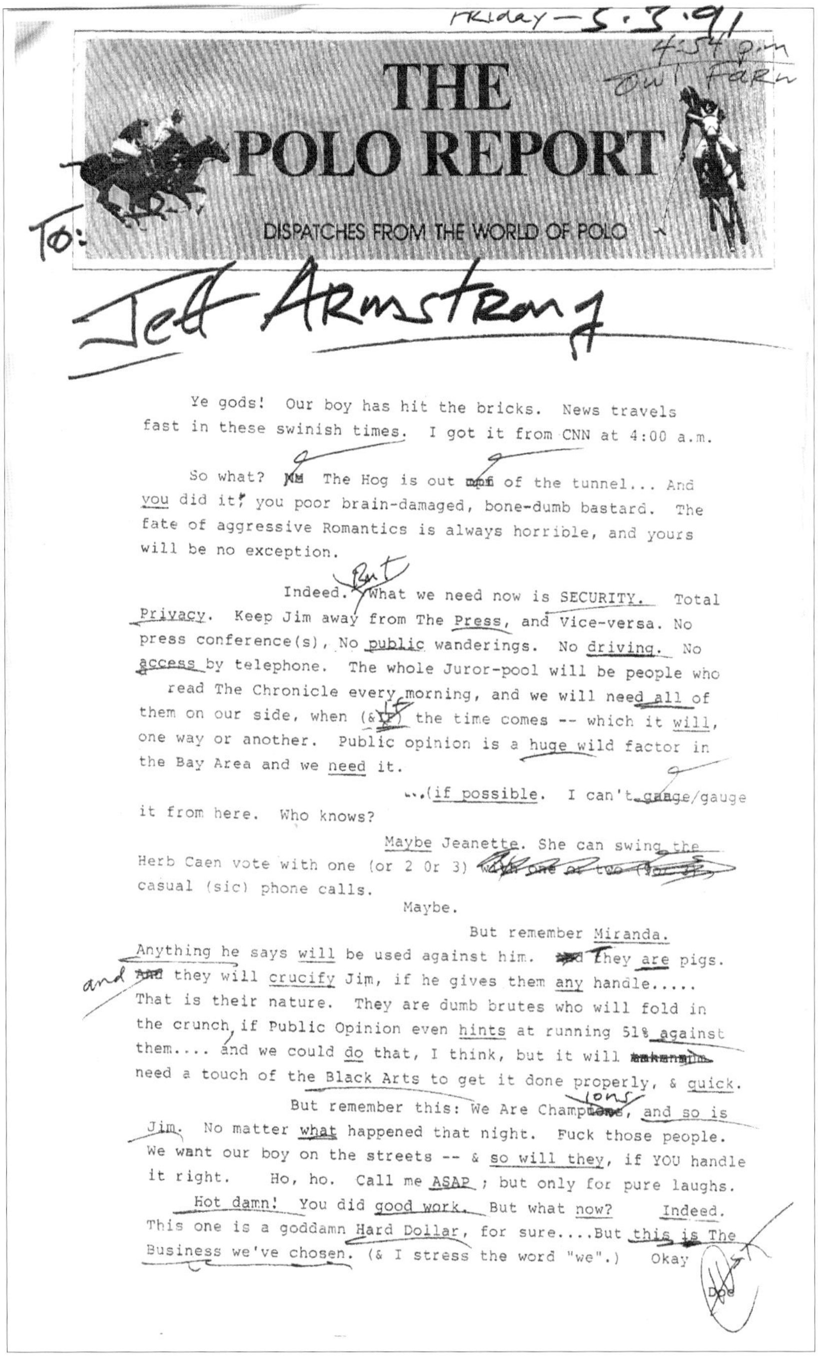

Friday — 5.3.91
4:54 pm
Owl Farm

THE POLO REPORT

DISPATCHES FROM THE WORLD OF POLO

To: Jeff Armstrong

Ye gods! Our boy has hit the bricks. News travels fast in these swinish times. I got it from CNN at 4:00 a.m.

So what? The Hog is out of the tunnel... And you did it, you poor brain-damaged, bone-dumb bastard. The fate of aggressive Romantics is always horrible, and yours will be no exception.

Indeed. But what we need now is SECURITY. Total Privacy. Keep Jim away from The Press, and Vice-versa. No press conference(s), No public wanderings. No driving. No access by telephone. The whole Juror-pool will be people who read The Chronicle every morning, and we will need all of them on our side, when (& if) the time comes -- which it will, one way or another. Public opinion is a huge wild factor in the Bay Area and we need it.

...(if possible. I can't gauge it from here. Who knows?

Maybe Jeanette. She can swing the Herb Caen vote with one (or 2 Or 3) casual (sic) phone calls.

Maybe.

But remember Miranda. Anything he says will be used against him. They are pigs. and they will crucify Jim, if he gives them any handle..... That is their nature. They are dumb brutes who will fold in the crunch, if Public Opinion even hints at running 51% against them.... and we could do that, I think, but it will need a touch of the Black Arts to get it done properly, & quick.

But remember this: We Are Champions, and so is Jim. No matter what happened that night. Fuck those people. We want our boy on the streets -- & so will they, if YOU handle it right. Ho, ho. Call me ASAP ; but only for pure laughs. Hot damn! You did good work. But what now? Indeed. This one is a goddamn Hard Dollar, for sure....But this is The Business we've chosen. (& I stress the word "we".) Okay

Doc

Just about the last thing Jim Mitchell did before he died, in 2007, of a heart attack at a youthful 63, was to do something in memory of Hunter's death. Cause some trouble. This was in the dimly lit back room of Original Joe's in the Tenderloin, where the horseshoe-shaped red booths suggested the bleary eyelids of giant tarantulas. There was the man with a Santa Claus beard, Ron Turner, also a queer fellow sporting a retro Lenin-beard, Jack Davis, the San Francisco political ballbuster, and this writer, and yes, there was a dog and a couple of girls.

The question was what would be sufficiently Hunter-esque. Mitchell had this brain-freeze--Paris Hilton was at the time in jail in L.A. and Davis, through his political connects, should get our San Francisco sheriff, Mike Hennessey, who had been sheriff for more years than Wyatt Earp was alive, to talk the L.A. sheriff into installing a 24/7 video feed in Hilton's cell, which, the leg bone connected to the shin bone, could be hooked up through Mayor Gavin Newsom's wired connections with the Internet big shots; the resulting reality-tv show of Paris peeing in her cell would benefit both the SF and LA jails. The quality of prisoner care was something that Mitchell had taken an interest in during his three years in the durance vile of San Quentin after the Artie tragedy. Mitchell argued that Paris Hilton's cooperation would be an automatic because she had got religion in the hoosegow and would want to do this good thing.

This was beautiful. A fine idea on a foggy afternoon. Davis called Hennessey with said announced intent and Hennessey ducked the call. Rebuffed, Davis then rang up the Mayor who took the call immediately, possibly because Davis had been prominent in the political gossip columns as desperately seeking a candidate to run against Newsom. Davis told Gavin there was this great, err... idea, and he put his good friend, Jim Mitchell, that prominent pornographer and convicted killer, on the wire to 'splain it. Mitchell got on the phone with the Mayor and indeed explained it with an incisive Oakie logic that made it all sound rather reasonable. I got on the line with Gavin before he hung up. "It sure sounds like you guys are having a good time," he said wistfully. The next day Mitchell said to me, "Was that really the Mayor? I thought I was talking to some lawyer from Boston."

Mitchell was not to be dissuaded from cooking up something in Hunter's honor. Jim was a whistling teakettle of ideas and often the next idea would be percolating in his head before the first one got all

the way out of his mouth. The man was so bubbly-smart he needed a cop to direct the flow of traffic in his brain. He settled on reviving the anti-war newspaper *War News*, which the Brothers had launched to protest the first Gulf War, to expose the California prison system. In Hunter's memory. Mitchell believed with the faith of a man who eats a Bible for breakfast that Hunter would want *War News* to declare California--the first prison state! Even The Terminator himself, Governor Schwarzenegger, had genuflected to the political and financial clout of the prison guards' mafia and its law enforcement lobby so more laws kept being passed to put more people in prison and build more prisons to house them and pay more guards to mind them. The concept was to publish *War News* in the tradition of Hunter's Wallposters--to present a graphic of a new license plate: California. The Prison State. It was off to the races. Before you could say Jack Sprat artists Spain Rodriguez and Jay Kinney were summoned to the office of the O'Farrell and the elves of mischief went to work hammering out the new California license plate.

Jim was looking at a proof of it the day he died. It was of course rejected by the California Department of Motor Vehicles. This was his epitaph for Hunter:

Art by Jay Kinney & Spain Rodriguez

The raids on the O'Farrell, which were a siren call to Hunter, came during a Comstockian period in San Francisco history that began in the late 60s with the City Fathers harassing the hippies and arresting the topless; the raids ended with the swan song of Feinstein's drip-dry mayoralty. These pages are in many ways a rough draft of aspects of the contemporary history of San Francisco and when that history is written, if it is written well, it will say of the Mitchell Brothers that they returned to the city its 49er can-do spirit

that made a metropolis out of a village, a village that blossomed into a Pacific city state before the unfortunate intrusion of the transcontinental railroad in 1879 which disconnected the Paris of the Pacific from its magnificent isolation. The pioneers of the city included a generous helping of college-educated 19th century peaceniks who were drawn to the polyglot frontier of San Francisco as much by the lack of Civil War violence in California as the lure of gold. But gold afforded money aplenty for both gilt and art and 19th century San Francisco became a citadel of conspicuous consumption where there was always money for artists. A century later, the hicks from Antioch had money--porn money, so it was--to give to artists, in their weapon of choice, cartoonists, those roadside bandits of the art world who were one with the Oakie outlaw mentality. Contemporary San Franciscans since the time of Bill Graham and Jann Wenner were into making money off indigenous artists; the Mitchells were into giving them money.

The O'Farrell of the Hunter years was a parallel universe, a Camelot of a kinky kind, with the Brothers as the blood royal of the San Francisco underground culture. They were the sponsors and financiers of a generation of artists who changed in immeasureable ways the world of pop art and its little sister, fashion. They fought monumental First Amendment battles and restored the city's Barbary Coast of legend to the present tense imperfect. The biggest knight-errant of all, Hunter S. Thompson, came to fight on their side and together they returned San Francisco, for a brief inglorious period last century, to its perversely splendorous past.

[WHO KILLED HUNTER S. THOMPSON?]

> *"One of my greatest shames as a journalist is that I still don't know who killed Jack Kennedy."* -Hunter

S.J. Perelman said that a dirty mind never sleeps. News of Hunter's death via a .45 in the mouth hit the Internet with the smack of a wet fish in the face. The overnight reaction on the web was that someone other than Hunter had killed Hunter. That brought up the considerable question of, if not him, whom? Which was it?--the CIA, assassins on George Bush's payroll, a covetous neighbor, the Knights of Malta? As days, then weeks, passed, this instant-action reaction continued to boil on the conspiracy stove and Hunter's hard-core

fans clung to each new theory with the desperation of winos overboard clinging to a life raft full of Night Train. Who Killed Hunter? websites sprang up. John Clancy, one of Hunter's oldest friends, took to them as a form of resuscitation of his buddy. Clancy inundated me with e-mails of the latest rumors about the less than transparent facts of Hunter's leaving the planet. The lawyer in Clancy believed there was a reasonable doubt as to whether his friend killed himself and he proffered many-splendored conspiratorial questions about Hunter's death, questions of the dog-that-didn't-bark-in-the-night type:

> "Twinkle: *Rolling Stone* just overnighted the 3/24/05 issue on Hunter. Brinkley has a piece on the last day. Pick it up. He says that Anita on the phone with HST heard a "strange clicking sound" and Juan, "in another room, heard the loud thud and thought it was a book falling to the ground.
>
> I know enough about pistols to tell you the sound of a .45 being fired simply cannot be confused with the sound of a book falling to the ground. A book falling from a height would make a sound like "crack" but a thud is not a shot."

He monitored the conspiracy websites like a hawk to pounce on what he considered to be examples of substantive conspiracy-think:

> "Mack White sums up the questions well: Thompson's family says he was not depressed, nor was he in enough pain to kill himself. In fact, by all reports, he was quite happy. He was talking on the phone to his wife Anita, getting ready to work on his ESPN column, when he decided it would be wise to kill himself?--so he could go out (we are told) while 'still at the top of his form,' even though this would mean not finishing his column or his expose on 9/11 (potentially the most important thing he would ever write) ?

Clancy was as gonzo a lawyer as Hunter a journalist. He represented several Oakland Raider players in contract negotiations and would party with the team post-game until the dawn and from those experiences wrote "The Laughing Quarterback," an uproarious, amazingly still-unpublished, novel about the intrigues of NFL football. He channeled his friend Hunter in many ways, including the tradition of using a rifle to shoot down the family Christmas tree

Photo: Wayne Ewing

HUNTER'S LAST ARTICLE: *In 2001, Hunter embarked on a four-year crusade to free Lisl Auman who, bizarrely, was the only person in Colorado history to be convicted of a murder --of a police officer--while she was in police custody. Hunter enlisted the aid of songwriter Warren Zevon, who sang "Lawyers, Guns and Money" with Hunter at a Free Lisl rally Hunter organized on the steps of the state captial.* (ABOVE) *Hunter dragooned Sean Penn and Johnny Depp to support her cause, and went uptown and convinced* Vanity Fair *to join the campaign--and twisted* Vanity Fair *editor Graydon Carter's arm to assign Ralph Steadman to illustrate his article.* (BELOW) *Two months after Hunter died, the Colorado Supreme Court ordered Lisl Auman's release from jail.*

Art by Ralph Steadman

(although I have never heard of Hunter doing such), which Clancy did with seasoned regularity to the distress of his Alta Street neighbors when he lived for many years atop Telegraph Hill in San Francisco. He also shared Hunter's affection for conspiratorial explanations of tragic events, as in this e-mail:

> "Twinkle: There was a theory about Chappaquiddick that Ted Kennedy was told the girl was being killed to keep him on the political sidelines. And that if he told that story his wife and kids would be killed. Juan and Anita could have been told something like that, eh?"

The irony is that Hunter would have been the first to embrace--indeed advance--one, or more, of the conspiracy theories that rose like so many weather balloons after his death.

That even politically centrist bloggers dipped their toes howsoever daintily into the tantalizing question of whether Hunter had been, possibly, murdered had quite a bit to do with the fact that in the years immediately preceding his death Hunter had laid a trail of conspiracy bread crumbs--more than hints, outright predictions--that he might be "suicided." The internet frenzy following Hunter's demise was fueled by the energetic digging into old files and the frantic thumbing of yellowed newspaper clippings by the conspiracy commentariat (most bloggers are at least lower-case conspiracy minded). Hardly anyone, naturally, agreed with anyone else--turf protection is more important than flood insurance to bloggers. There quickly evolved several distinct, although at times overlapping, answers to the declarative question, "Who Killed Hunter S. Thompson?"

The consensus conclusion: In the language of conspiracy-speak, was that Hunter was, as he himself had suggested, "suicided"--which translates in simple English to he was murdered in a way to make it look like suicide.

In the months after his death Hunter had good company in the Who Killed Whom? Conspiracy derby. The earnest inquiry into "Who Killed Hunter S. Thompson" was joined at the hip with questions about two other author-deaths simultaneously busying the chat rooms. Number One was "Who Killed Gary Webb?" Webb was a *San Jose Mercury News* reporter who wrote an explosive series of articles in 1996--which were upon publication almost immediately

trashed by his own paper under the weight of Establishment peer criticism outraged over Webb's reportorial conclusion--that there was a nexus of the CIA, the Nicaraguan Contras and crack cocaine in big city ghettoes, notably in Watts. Webb was then shamefully dumped by his newspaper and later found dead in his one-bedroom Sacramento apartment where he had fled to lick his wounds and write a book, "Dark Alliance" published in 1998, which is a classic of left wing investigative reporting and was adapted into the movie "Kill the Messenger" in 2014.

Number Two was "Who Killed J. H. Hatfield?" Hatfield was another writer found dead in his apartment of an apparent drug overdose. Hatfield's book, "Fortunate Son," was about George W. Bush's headier days playing in the Elysian fields of cocaine. The Internet buzz was that the Bushies had a posse of skilled assassins out to "suicide" journos who wrote that which the administration Did Not Wish To Hear. At the top of that list was Hunter S. Thompson who told one and all that he was working on a story that would do to George W. Bush what Katrina did to New Orleans.

The widespread speculation that Hunter was murdered was not a stretch too far for the opinion of the average American. "The American people," as the talking heads on the cable channels refer to us, are generous and friendly with a help-thy-neighbor ethic rooted deep as a redwood tree in the national character. The flip side is that we are as a people suspicious of the intentions, and competence, of both local and federal government and thus susceptible to rumor which, after all, is only an alloy of truth. One website maintained a running count of the deaths of journalists and scientists who had been on the Bush enemies list.

Hunter himself put the "suicided" rumors into motion like kick-starting a Harley hog by telling Canadian journalist William Roberts, the night before he died, that he was afraid he'd be "suicided" for the article he was writing that would solidify the questions about whether the World Trade Center towers went down only from the jets commandeered by terrorists armed only with box cutters--or with a little help from explosives lining the buildings from within.

Owl Farm in the early Oughts became a pilgram's stop for foreign journalists looking for some Yank to stir the pot. When Thompson told a Brit interviewer that the collapse of the Twin Towers had to be partly an inside job and the Brit expressed incredulity, Hunter

admonished him that he'd been right before about terrible things--many, many times.

The Canadian, Roberts, wrote in the February 26 *Toronto Globe and Mail*:

> "Hunter telephoned me on February 19th, the night before his death. He sounded scared. It wasn't always easy to understand what he said, particularly over the phone when he mumbled, yet there was something he really wanted you to understand.... He'd been working on a story about the World Trade Center attacks and had stumbled across what he felt was hard evidence showing the towers had been brought down not by the airplanes that flew into them but by explosive charges set off in their foundations. Now he thought someone was out to stop him publishing it: "They're gonna make it look like a suicide," he said."

Hunter discussed his developing conspiracy theory about 9/11 during a radio interview in March of 2003: "Now, do you believe that, that a bunch of Arabs jumped up from some kind of a campfire and fucking mountains and snuck into this country and hijacked those planes and did that by themselves?" The interviewer asked if Hunter was saying that there might be some American agency that gave aid or comfort to the 9/11 flyboys. Hunter: "Uhh, this is tricky territory, but yeah, that's what I'm getting at... I can't sit here and jerk up documents like Joe McCarthy, there's no proof of that. But I'm sure there is. And the idea that we're getting the whole story through the media, or from the president, is absurd on its face because you never do, for one thing. And there's too many unanswered questions and loose ends and uh, let's see, well, lies!"

Hunter, in another interview, about the possibility of being suicided: "I think a lot of people in this country agree with me (about 9/11.) A lot more never say anything. We'll see what happens to me if I get my head cut off in the next week by--it's always unknown ... (inaudible) Strangers who commit suicide right afterward. No witnesses. They have a new kind of crime."

We never found out, with any definition or satisfaction, who killed John F. Kennedy--except that it darn sure wasn't Lee Harvey Oswald, all by himself. There is, alas, no longer such an unbending mystery about the death of Hunter S. Thompson, although the

mysterious aspects of it will no doubt grow in legend over time. John Clancy--who died a biblical forty days after his best friend Hunter's ashes were rocketed into the pure Colorado air--remained suspicious until the end.

The last word Hunter typed on his IBM Selectric was "counselor." Clancy was certain that Hunter was beginning a letter to him that would have given a clue about his death. A few days before Clancy himself died in a ridiculous car crash--he was rushing to get home on time and trying to take the wax paper off a McDonald's burger with his teeth when he lost control of his car and hit a tree--he called me to talk about yet another acoustical expert's analysis of the last sounds recorded from Hunter's kitchen. Clancy theorized there might have been another person mysteriously in the room when Hunter shot himself.

"Doubt is strength," said Clancy.

["THIS IS THE BUSINESS WE HAVE CHOSEN"]

Hunter once said that in the opinion writing business you get flogged for being right and flogged for being wrong--but it doesn't hurt as much when you're right. He was, almost alone in his contemporaries among political prognisticators, right about George W. Bush from the get-go.

Let us witness his now-eerily prescient ESPN "sports" columns--mind this was at the time of an almost eerie journalistic somnolescence when the Washington press corps kept its head safely in the sand. Do these stinging--haunting in retrospect--words sound like the burnt out case some have tried to make of Hunter? Read and weep at the loss of the writer:

The Day After: "We are At War now--with somebody--and we will stay at war with that strange and mysterious Enemy for the rest of our lives. It will be a Religious War, a sort of Christian Jihad, fueled by religious hatred and led by merciless fanatics on both sides. It will be guerrilla warfare on a global scale, with no front lines and no identifiable enemy ... "This is going to be a very expensive war, and Victory is not guaranteed--for anyone, and certainly not for a baffled little creep like George W. Bush. All he knows is that his father started the war a long time ago, and that he, the goofy child President, has been

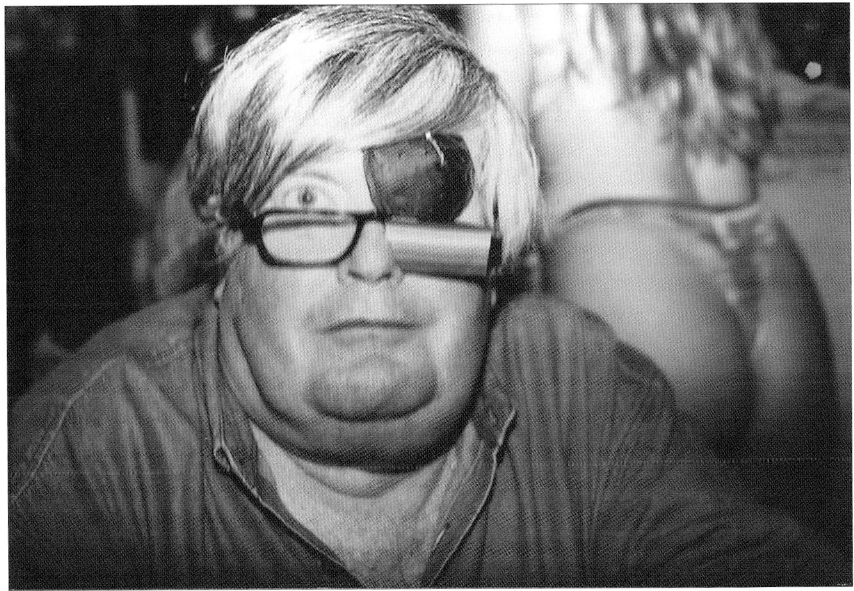

Warren Hinckle in San Francisco, sent to Hunter for his Aspen Wallposter.

> *"But for Christ's sake, don't send anything slick or straight; we need photos that will make people puke and howl for their lawyers."*
> *-- Hunter sent a letter to Hinckle asking him to send a photograph to use in his publication,* The Aspen Wallposter.

chosen by Fate and the global Oil industry to finish it off... he can clamp down Hard on Everybody, no matter where they live or why... "

Sept. 12, 2001: "There was one exact moment, in fact, when I knew for sure that Al Gore would never be President... that was when the whole Bush family suddenly appeared on TV and openly scoffed at the idea of Gore winning Florida. Here was the whole bloody family laughing & hooting & sneering at the dumbness of the whole world... the old man was the real tip-off. The leer on his face was almost frightening. It was like looking into the eyes of a tall hyena with a living sheep in its mouth. The sheep's fate was sealed, and so was Al Gore's."

Feb. 3, 2003: "We are turning into a nation of fear, fear of poverty, fear of random terrorism, fear of getting down-sized or fired because of the plunging economy, fear of getting evicted for bad debts, or suddenly getting locked up in a military detention camp on vague charges of being a Terrorist sympathizer."

April 10, 2003: "What the hell is going on here? How could this once-proud nation have changed so much, so drastically, in only a little more than two years? In what seems like the blink of an eye,

this George Bush has brought us from a prosperous nation at peace to a broke nation at war."

Sept.9, 2003: "Why are we seeing George Bush on TV every two hours for nine or ten times a day, like some kind of mutated Mr. Rogers clone? Something is dangerously wrong in any country where a monumentally-Failed backwoods politician can scare our national TV networks so totally they will give him anything he wants."

Oct. 14, 2003: "I take no pleasure in being Right in my dark predictions about the fate of our military intervention in the heart of the Muslim world. It is immensely depressing to me. Nobody likes to be betting against the home team."

On Abu Ghraib: "These horrifying digital snapshots of the American dream in action on foreign soil are worse than anything even I could have expected. I have been in this business a long time and I have seen many staggering things, but this one is over the line. Now I am really ashamed to carry an American passport."

You can't say Hunter didn't warn us about what might be coming. He began fixating on his death and his ashes-in-the-sky burial back in the 70s in the BBC goof-off movie he made with Ralph Steadman. He often wrote about thoughts of suicide. In the introduction to "The Great Shark Hunt," written when he was on the cusp of 40, he commented on the temptations of doing himself in. "I have already lived and finished the life I planned to live (13 years longer, in fact) and everything from now on will be A New Life, a different thing..."

And now we know. The historian Douglas Brinkley, Hunter's good friend, the editor of his collected letters and his official biographer, found and published in *Rolling Stone* a document that, he concluded, put paid to the question and addressed Who Killed Hunter S. Thompson? It was Hunter's note, written four days before his death to his wife Anita, appropriately scrawled with the felt tip pen that identified his midnight faxes. It was headed "Football Season Is Over" and Hunter drew a smiley face on the bottom of the page. His words:

"The Football Season Is Over. No More Games. No More Bombs. No More Walking. No More Fun. No More Swimming. 67. That is 17 years past 50. 17 more than I needed or wanted. Boring. I am always bitchy. No Fun--for anybody. 67. You are getting Greedy. Act your old age. Relax--This won't hurt."

Like JFK, Hunter had been in continual pain most of his life. It began with an early swimming injury and in his last years Hunter had been in acute pain from a troublesome back operation, and then a broken leg. The pain did in his ability to function as athletically as he had all his life. He was humiliated, totally bummed in New Orleans when he found he would have to resort to a wheelchair to ascend to a party upstairs in a hotel. This was not for Hunter. He had told Steadman maybe a thousand times that he would kill himself, and he proved good to his word. Like the late boulevardier Lucius Beebe, another good man of style and excess, he left the party when it was still good.

Was this the end of Hunter S. Thompson? I think not. His friend Tim Ferris said, "Now more movies about him are going to be made, the legend is going to grow, and young people will hear the call--Hunter will become to journalism what Che was to revolution." As Elvis Presley's longtime manager said after his death: This was a good career move for Elvis.

Vladimir Nabokov said the future was the obsolete in reverse. Hunter Thompson was out there on the Edge where the two collide, like trees falling unseen in the forest. Many people feel these vibes, but Thompson visualized them and made them real. He knew the hog was in the tunnel. He saw the alligator in the toilet that few others saw but only recognize when it inevitably comes from behind and bites you.

In his first book, the classic "Hell's Angels: the Strange and Terrible Saga of the Outlaw Motorcycle Gangs" Thompson wrote that the Angels had

> "... the same kind of anarchic, para-legal sense of conviction that brought the armed wrath of the Establishment down on the Wobblies, the same feeling of constant warfare with an unjust world. The Wobblies were losers, and so are the Angels... and if every loser in this country today rode a motorcycle the whole highway system would have to be modified."
>
> "There is an important difference between the words "loser" and "outlaw." One is passive and the other is active, and the main reason the Angels are such good copy is that they are acting out the day-dreams of millions of losers who

don't wear any defiant insignia and who don't know how to be outlaws."

Hunter understood the Angels because he himself was an outlaw--stylistically and politically--and his outlaw's perspective put him in the catbird seat to interpret and document the decline of the American Dream. And despite the tsk-tsk sensibilities of the gloomy-Gus hacks wearing the white sheets of literary critics and those holier than thou J-school types, America has always loved its outlaws.

He was an outlaw who could write with the wit and fancy of Twain and the moralism of the later Tolstoy. Tom Wolfe called this outlaw, whose weapon of choice was an IBM Selectric, "The century's greatest comic writer in the English language." Outlaws live, and die, on The Edge. Thompson defined The Edge in "Hell's Angels" in a way that could be his epitaph:

"The Edge ... There is no honest way to explain it because the only people who really know where it is are the ones who have gone over."

Hunter touched a nerve ending in the frayed American psyche. His death had the impact on two generations--from baby boomers to Generation X--that the deaths of John Lennon and Jerry Garcia did. Hunter will always be there, like a phantom limb, reminding us of the daring things we never dared to do. The story of Hunter S. Thompson is that of the axe entering the forest--the curious trees said, "Look, the handle is one of us."

[THE SHARPENING OF THE PENCIL DICKS]

After Hunter's death the naysayers and Hunter-haters popped their heads above their professional gopher holes to say he had been a burnt out case. There was more than an element of jealousy in these late-blooming critiques. Hunter had dared to do creatively what his critics could not do, or did not have the balls to try. While he was alive you didn't hear too much of this sort of carping--the man might come and run a motorized lawn mower through your daughter's graduation party--but it has since become a cliché among the smart set to harrumph that Hunter Thompson's work had declined in his last years. And much was made in hack post-mortems on Hunter of the bio-fact that one of Hunter's first articles for the *National Journal* was to go to Idaho and write about the suicide of his idol Ernest Hemingway.

The record is contrary to that bitchy view. Hunter was actually writing sharply, and even more politically, in the last few years as he ever had. In the three years before his death he put on full battle gear and launched a successful campaign to free a wrongfully imprisoned young woman, Lisl Auman, who was serving a life sentence for a murder she didn't commit. "In all my experience with courts & crimes & the downright bad behavior by the Law & the Sometimes criminal cops who enforce it, this is the worst & most reprehensible miscarriage of "Justice" I've ever encountered--and that covers a lot of rotten things, including a few close calls of my own," Hunter wrote.

Let us not further belabor these whiners. Hunter gave the finger to such critics in "Hell's Angels" thus--"There are literary critics who insist that Ernest Hemingway was a tortured queer and that Mark Twain was haunted to the end of his days by a penchant for interracial buggery. It's a good way to stir up a tempest in the academic quarterlies, but it won't change a word of what either man wrote, nor alter the impact of their work on the world they were writing about."

No more need be said.

BOOK TWO

The Kentucky Derby Is Decadent and Depraved

HUNTER S. THOMPSON
&
RALPH STEADMAN

The original "The Kentucky Derby Is Decadent and Depraved"
was published in Scanlan's Monthly, *Issue Number Four, June 1970.*
Back copies of Scanlan's *are hard to come by these days*
(it didn't last long enough to get collected in most libraries.)

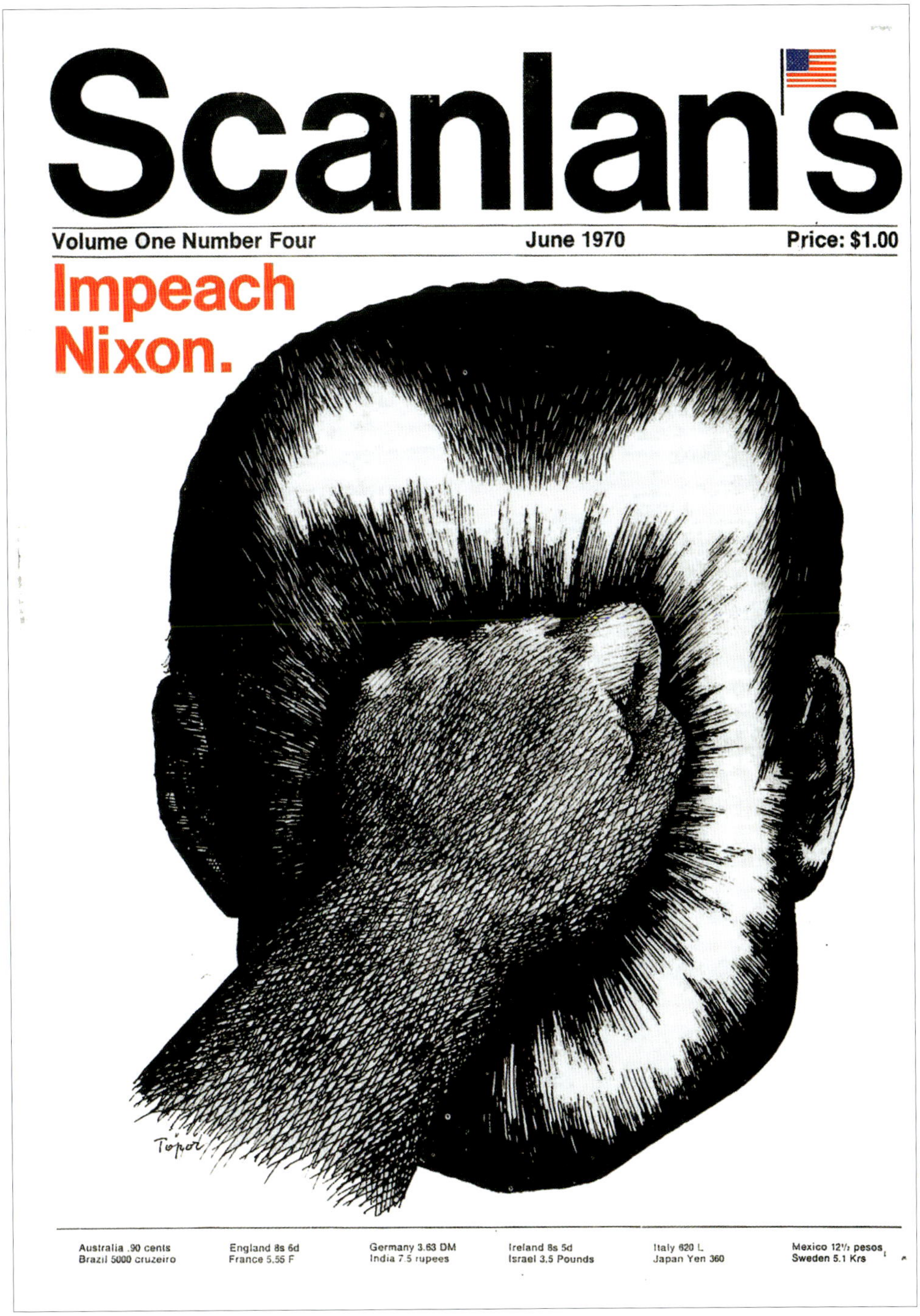

Scanlan's

Volume One Number Four June 1970 Price: $1.00

Impeach Nixon.

Topor

Australia .90 cents Brazil 5000 cruzeiro England 8s 6d France 5.55 F Germany 3.63 DM India 7.5 rupees Ireland 8s 5d Israel 3.5 Pounds Italy 620 L Japan Yen 360 Mexico 12½ pesos Sweden 5.1 Krs

The Scanlan's *issue with Thompson's Kentucky Derby article.*

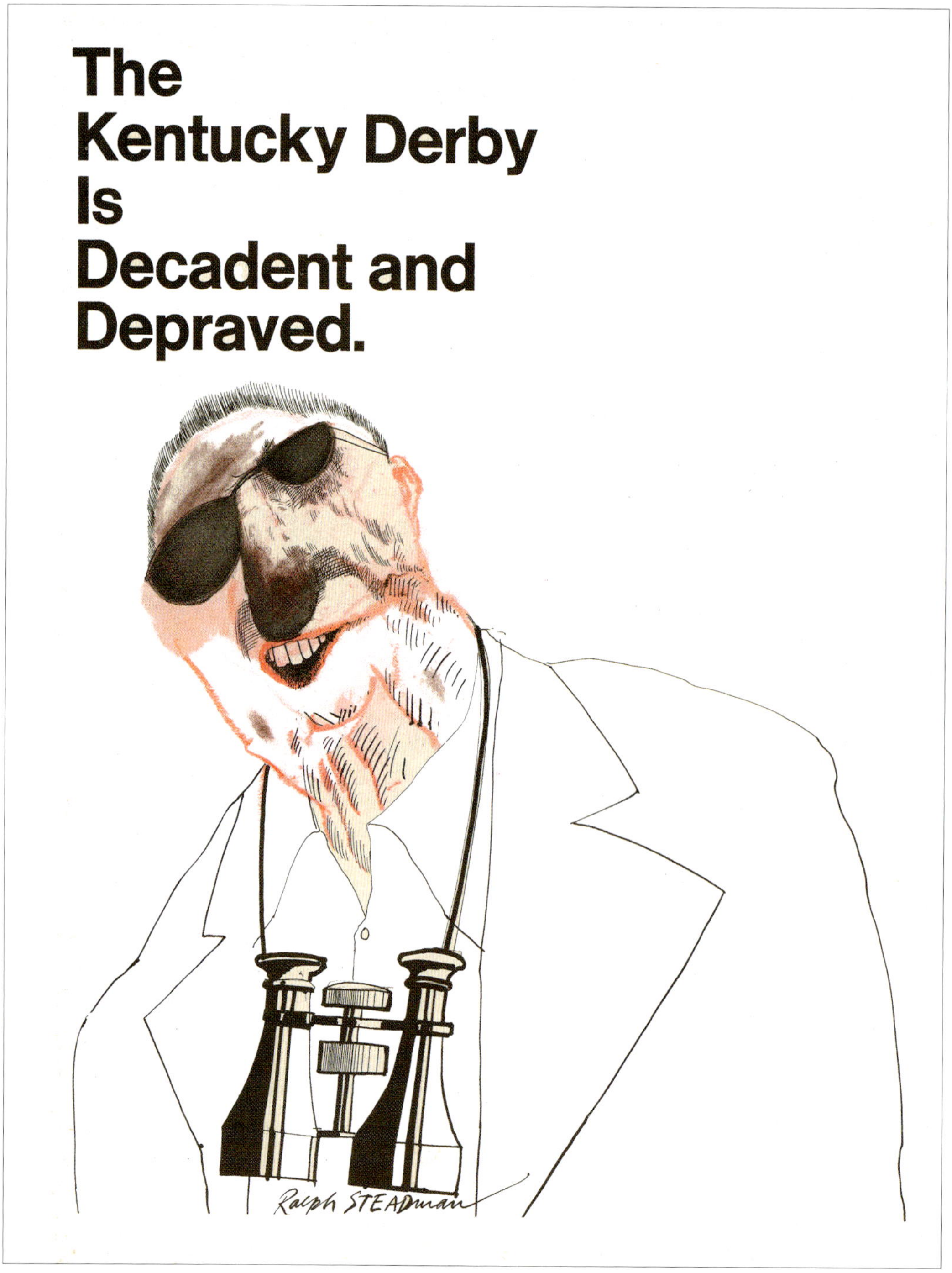

The Kentucky Derby Is Decadent and Depraved.

Ralph STEADman

Written under duress by Hunter S. Thompson

Sketched with eyebrow pencil and lipstick by Ralph Steadman

The original two-page spread layout in Scanlan's Monthly.

I got off the plane around midnight and no one spoke as I crossed the dark runway to the terminal. The air was thick and hot, like wandering into a steam bath. Inside, people hugged each other and shook hands ... big grins and a whoop here and there: "By God! You old *bastard*! *Good* to see you, boy! *Damn* good ... and I *mean* it!" In the air-conditioned lounge I met a man from Houston who said his name was something or other--"but just call me Jimbo"--and he was here to get it on. "I'm ready for *anything*, by God! Anything at all. Yeah, what are you drinkin'?" I ordered a Margarita with ice, but he wouldn't hear of it: "Naw, naw ... what the hell kind of drink is that for Kentucky Derby time? What's *wrong* with you, boy." He grinned and winked at the bartender. "Goddam, we gotta educate this boy. Get him some good *whiskey* ... "

I shrugged. "Okay, a double Old Fitz on ice." Jimbo nodded his approval.

"Look." He tapped me on the arm to make sure I was listening. "I know this Derby crowd, I come here every year, and let me tell you one thing I've learned--this is no town to be giving people the impression you're some kind of faggot. Not in public, anyway. Shit, they'll roll you in a minute, knock you in the head and take every goddam cent you have."

I thanked him and fitted a Marlboro into my cigarette holder. "Say," he said, "you look like you might be in the horse business ... am I right?"

"No," I said. "I'm a photographer."

"Oh yeah?" He eyed my ragged leather bag with new interest. "Is that what you got there--cameras? Who you work for?"

"Playboy," I said.

He laughed. "Well, goddam! What are you gonna take pictures of--nekkid horses? Haw! I guess you'll be workin' pretty hard when they run the Kentucky Oaks. That's a race just for fillies." He was laughing wildly. "Hell yes! And they'll all be nekkid too!"

I shook my head and said nothing; just stared at him for a moment, trying to look grim. "There's going to be trouble," I said. "My assignment is to take pictures of the riot."

"What riot?"

I hesitated, twirling the ice in my drink. "At the track. On Derby Day. The Black Panthers." I stared at him again. "Don't you read the newspapers?"

The grin on his face had collapsed. "What the *hell* are you talkin' about?"

"Well ... maybe I shouldn't be telling you ..." I shrugged. "But hell, everybody else seems to know. The cops and the National Guard have been getting ready for six weeks. They have 20,000 troops on alert at Fort Knox. They've warned us--all the press and photographers--to wear helmets and special vests like flak jackets. We were told to expect shooting ... "

"No!" he shouted; his hands flew up and hovered momentarily between us, as if to ward off the words he was hearing. Then he whacked his fist on the bar. "Those sons of bitches! God Almighty! The Kentucky Derby!" He kept shaking his head. "No! *Jesus*! That's almost too bad to believe!" Now he seemed to be sagging on the stool, and when he looked up his eyes were misty. "Why? Why *here*? Don't they respect *anything*?"

I shrugged again. "It's not just the Panthers. The FBI says busloads of white crazies are coming in from all over the country--to mix with the crowd and attack all at once, from every direction. They'll be dressed like everybody else. You know--coats and ties and all that. But when the trouble starts ... well, that's why the cops are so worried."

He sat for a moment, looking hurt and confused and not quite able to digest all this terrible news. Then he cried out: "Oh ... Jesus! What in the name of God is happening in this country? Where can you get away from it?"

"Not here," I said, picking up my bag. "Thanks for the drink ... and good luck."

He grabbed my arm, urging me to have another, but I said I was overdue at the Press Club and hustled off to get my act together for the awful spectacle. At the airport newsstand I picked up a *Courier-Journal* and scanned the front page headlines: "Nixon Sends GI's into Cambodia to Hit Reds" ... "B-52's Raid, Then 2,000 GI's Advance 20 Miles" ... "4,000 U.S. Troops Deployed Near Yale as Tension Grows Over Panther Protest." At the bottom of the page was a photo of Diane Crump, soon to become the first woman jockey ever to ride in the Kentucky Derby. The photographer had snapped her "stopping in the barn area to fondle her mount, Fathom." The rest of the paper was spotted with ugly war news and stories of "student unrest." There was no mention of any protest action at a small Ohio school called Kent State.

I went to the Hertz desk to pick up my car, but the moon-faced young swinger in charge said they didn't have any. "You can't rent one anywhere," he assured me. "Our Derby reservations have been booked for six weeks." I explained that my agent had confirmed a white Chrysler convertible for me that very afternoon but he shook his head. "Maybe we'll have a cancellation. Where are you staying?"

I shrugged. "Where's the Texas crowd staying? I want to be with my people."

He sighed. "My friend, you're in trouble. This town is flat *full*. Always is, for the Derby."

I leaned closer to him, half-whispering: "Look, I'm from Playboy. How would you like a job?"

He backed off quickly. "What? Come on, now. What kind of a job?"

"Never mind," I said. "You just blew it." I swept my bag off the counter and went to find a cab. The bag is a valuable prop in this kind of work; mine has a lot of baggage tags on it--SF, LA, NY, Lima, Rome, Bangkok, that sort of thing--and the most prominent tag of all is a very official, plastic-coated thing that says "Photog. Playboy Mag." I bought it from a pimp in Vail, Colorado, and he told me how to use it. "Never mention Playboy until you're sure they've seen this thing first," he said. "Then, when you see them notice it, that's the time to strike. They'll go belly up ever time. This thing is magic, I tell you. Pure magic."

Well ... maybe so. I'd used it on the poor geek in the bar, and now humming along in a Yellow Cab toward town, I felt a little guilty about jangling the poor bugger's brains with that evil fantasy. But

what the hell? Anybody who wanders around the world saying, "Yes, I'm from Texas," deserves whatever happens to him. And he had, after all, come here once again to make a nineteenth-century ass of himself in the midst of some jaded, atavistic freakout with nothing to recommend it except a very saleable "tradition." Early in our chat, Jimbo had told me that he hadn't missed a Derby since 1954. "The little lady won't come anymore," he said. "She just grits her teeth and turns me loose for this one. And when I say 'loose' I do mean *loose*! I toss ten-dollar bills around like they were goin' outa style! Horses, whiskey, women ... shit, there's women in this town that'll do *anything* for money."

Why not? Money is a good thing to have in these twisted times. Even Richard Nixon is hungry for it. Only a few days before the Derby he said, "If I had any money I'd invest it in the stock market." And the market, meanwhile, continued its grim slide.

[WAITING FOR STEADMAN]

The next day was heavy. With 30 hours to post time I had no press credentials and--according to the sports editor of the Louisville Courier-Journal--no hope at all of getting any. Worse, I needed two sets; one for myself and another for Ralph Steadman, the English illustrator who was coming from London to do some Derby drawings. All I knew about him was that this was his first visit to the United States. And the more I pondered that fact, the more it gave me fear. Would he bear up under the heinous culture shock of being lifted out of London and plunged into a drunken mob scene at the Kentucky Derby? There was no way of knowing. Hopefully, he would arrive at least a day or so ahead, and give himself time to get acclimated. Maybe a few hours of peaceful sightseeing in the Bluegrass country around Lexington. My plan was to pick him up at the airport in the huge Pontiac Ballbuster I'd rented from a used-car salesman name Colonel Quick, then whisk him off to some peaceful setting to remind him of England.

Colonel Quick had solved the car problem, and money (four times the normal rate) had bought two rooms in a scumbox on the outskirts of town. The only other kink was the task of convincing the moguls at Churchill Downs that Scanlan's was such a prestigious sporting journal that common sense compelled them to give us two sets of the best press tickets. This was not easily done. My first call

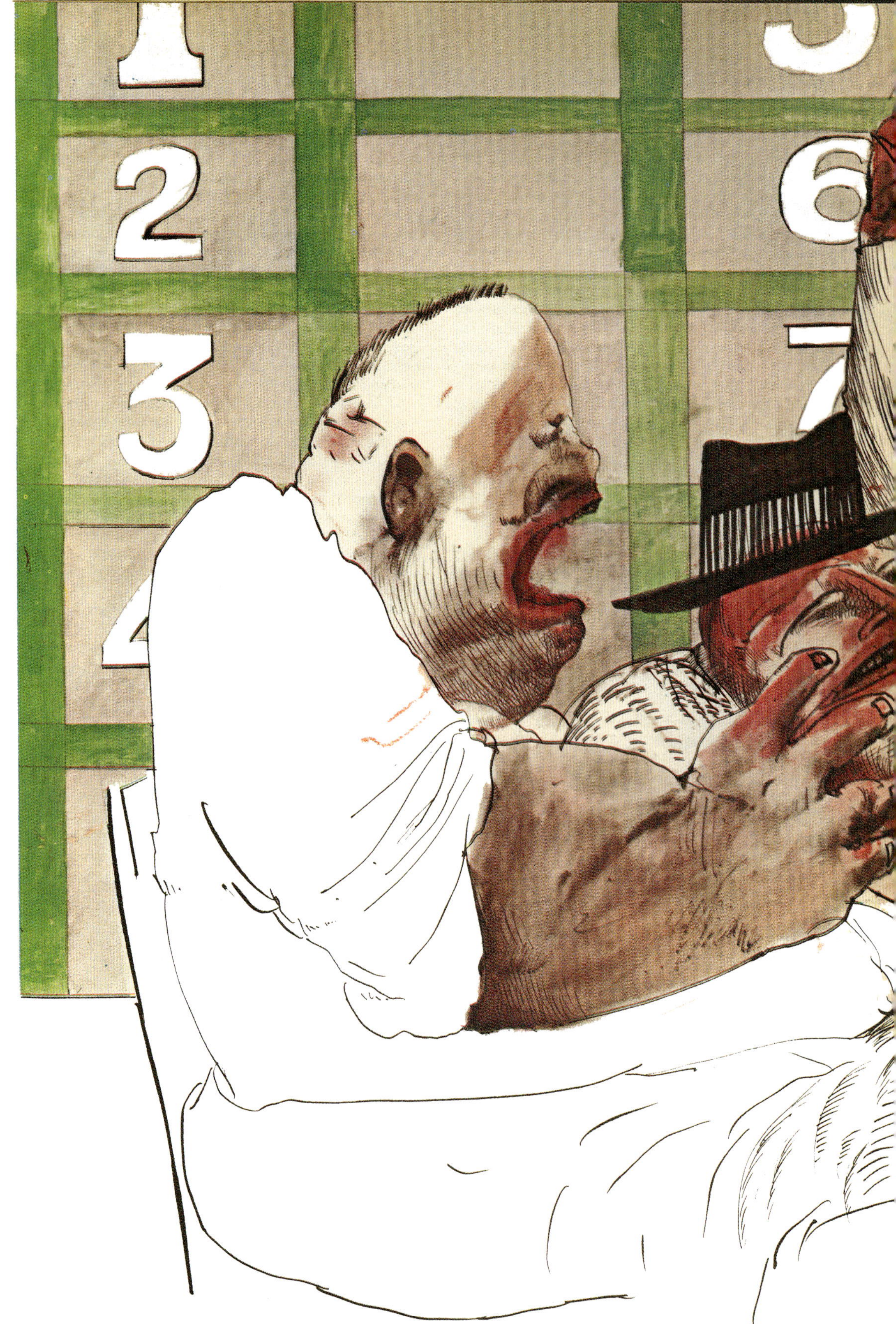
1
2
3
6

9
10
Ralph STEADMAN

to the publicity office resulted in total failure. The press handler was shocked at the idea that anyone would be stupid enough to apply for press credentials two days before the Derby. "Hell, you can't be serious," he said. "The deadline was two months ago. The press box is full; there's no more room ... and what the hell is Scanlan's Monthly anyway?"

I uttered a painful groan. "Didn't the London office call you? They're flying an artist over to do the paintings. Steadman. He's Irish. I think. Very famous over there. Yes. I just got in from the Coast. The San Francisco office told me we were all set."

He seemed interested, and even sympathetic, but there was nothing he could do. I flattered him with more gibberish, and finally he offered a compromise: he could get us two passes to the clubhouse grounds.

"That sounds a little weird," I said. "It's unacceptable. We must have access to everything. *All of it*. The spectacle, the people, the pageantry and certainly the race. You don't think we came all this way to watch the damn thing on television, do you? One way or another we'll get inside. Maybe we'll have to bribe a guard--or even Mace somebody." (I had picked up a spray can of Mace in a downtown drugstore for $5.98 and suddenly, in the midst of that phone talk, I was struck by the hideous possibilities of using it out at the track. Macing ushers at the narrow gates to the clubhouse inner sanctum, then slipping quickly inside, firing a huge load of Mace into the governor's box, just as the race starts. Or Macing helpless drunks in the clubhouse restroom, for their own good ...)

By noon on Friday I was still without press credentials and still unable to locate Steadman. For all I knew he'd changed his mind and gone back to London. Finally, after giving up on Steadman and trying unsuccessfully to reach my man in the press office, I decided my only hope for credentials was to go out to the track and confront the man in person, with no warning--demanding only one pass now, instead of two, and talking very fast with a strange lilt in my voice, like a man trying hard to control some inner frenzy. On the way out, I stopped at the motel desk to cash a check. Then, as a useless afterthought, I asked if by any wild chance Mr. Steadman had checked in.

The lady on the desk was about fifty years old and very peculiar-looking; when I mentioned Steadman's name she nodded, without looking up from whatever she was writing, and said in a low voice, "You bet he did." Then she favored me with a big smile.

I shook my head. "I'm supposed to be working with him, but I don't even know what he looks like. Now, goddammit, I'll have to find him in that mob at the track."

She chuckled. "You won't have any trouble finding him. You could pick that man out of any crowd."

"Why?" I asked. "What's wrong with him? What does he look like?"

"Well ... " she said, still grinning, "he's the funniest looking thing I've seen in a long time. He has this ... ah ... this *growth* all over his face. As a matter of fact it's all over his *head*." She nodded. "You'll know him when you see him; don't worry about that."

Great creeping Jesus, I thought. That screws the press credentials. I had a vision of some nerve-rattling geek all covered with matted hair and string-warts showing up in the press office and demanding Scanlan's press packet. Well ... what the hell? We could always load up on acid and spend the day roaming around the grounds with big sketch pads, laughing hysterically at the natives and swilling mint juleps so the cops wouldn't think we're abnormal. Perhaps even make the act pay: set up an easel with a big sign saying, "Let a Foreign Artist Paint Your Portrait, $10 Each. Do It NOW!"

[A HUGE OUTDOOR LOONY BIN]

I took the expressway out to the track, driving very fast and jumping the monster car back and forth between lanes, driving with a beer in one hand and my mind so muddled that I almost crushed a Volkswagen full of nuns when I swerved to catch the right exit. There was a slim chance, I thought, that I might be able to catch the ugly Britisher before he checked in.

But Steadman was already in the press box when I got there, a bearded young Englishman wearing a tweed coat and HAF sunglasses. There was nothing particularly odd about him. No facial veins or clumps of bristly warts. I told him about the motel woman's description and he seemed puzzled. "Don't let it bother you," I said. "Just keep in mind for the next few days that we're in Louisville, Kentucky. Not London. Not even New York. This is a weird place. You're lucky that mental defective at the motel didn't jerk a pistol out of the cash register and blow a big hole in you." I laughed, but he looked worried.

"Just pretend you're visiting a huge outdoor loony bin," I said. "If the inmates get out of control we'll soak them down with Mace." I showed him the can of "Chemical Billy," resisting the urge to fire it across the room at a rat-faced man typing diligently in the Associated Press section. We were standing at the bar, sipping the management's scotch and congratulating each other on our sudden, unexplained luck in picking up two sets of fine press credentials. The lady at the desk had been very friendly to him, he said. "I just told her my name and she gave me the whole works."

By midafternoon we had everything under control. We had seats looking down on the finish line, color TV and a free bar in the press room, and a selection of passes that would take us anywhere from the clubhouse roof to the jockey room. The only thing we lacked was unlimited access to the clubhouse inner sanctum in sections "F&G"

… and I felt we needed that, to see the whiskey gentry in action. The governor, a swinish neo-Nazi hack named Louie Nunn, would be in "G," Barry Goldwater would be in a box in "G" where we could rest and sip juleps, soak up a bit of atmosphere and the Derby's special vibrations.

The bars and dining rooms are also in "F&G," and the clubhouse bars on Derby Day are a very special kind of scene. Along with the politicians, society belles and local captains of commerce, every half-mad dingbat who ever had any pretensions to anything within five hundred miles of Louisville will show up there to get strutting drunk and slap a lot of backs and generally make himself obvious. The Paddock bar is probably the best place in the track to sit and watch faces. Nobody minds being stared at; that's what they're in there for. Some people spend most of their time in the Paddock; they can hunker down at one of the many wooden tables, lean back in a comfortable chair and watch the ever-changing odds flash up and down on the big tote board outside the window. Black waiters in white serving jackets move through the crowd with trays of drinks, while the experts ponder their racing forms and the hunch bettors

pick lucky numbers or scan the lineup for right-sounding names. There is a constant flow of traffic to and from the pari-mutuel windows outside in the wooden corridors. Then, as post time nears, the crowd thins out as people go back to their boxes.

Clearly, we were going to have to figure out some way to spend more time in the clubhouse tomorrow. But the "walkaround" press passes to F&G were only good for thirty minutes at a time, presumably to allow the newspaper types to rush in and out for photos or quick interviews, but to prevent drifters like Steadman and me from spending all day in the clubhouse, harassing the gentry and rifling an odd handbag or two while cruising around the boxes. Or Macing the governor. The time limit was no problem on Friday, but on Derby Day the walkaround passes would be in heavy demand. And since it took about 10 minutes to get from the press box to the Paddock, and 10 more minutes to get back, that didn't leave much time for serious people-watching. And unlike most of the others in the press box, we didn't give a hoot in hell what was happening on the track. We had come there to watch the *real* beasts perform.

[VIEW FROM THOMPSON'S HEAD]

Later Friday afternoon, we went out on the balcony of the press box and I tried to describe the difference between what we had seen today and what would be happening tomorrow. This was the first time I'd been to a Derby in 10 years, but before that, when I lived in Louisville, I used to go every year. Now, looking down from the press box, I pointed to the huge grassy meadow enclosed by the track. "That whole thing," I said, "will be jammed with people; fifty thousand or so, and most of them staggering drunk. It's a fantastic scene--thousands of people fainting, crying, copulating, trampling each other and fighting with broken whiskey bottles. We'll have to spend some time out there, but it's hard to move around, too many bodies."

"Is it safe out there?" Will we *ever* come back?"

"Sure," I said. "We'll just have to be careful not to step on anybody's stomach and start a fight." I shrugged. "Hell, this clubhouse scene right below us will be almost as bad as the infield. Thousands of raving, stumbling drunks, getting angrier and angrier as they lose more and more money. By midafternoon they'll be guzzling mint juleps with both hands and vomitting on each other between races.

The whole place will be jammed with bodies, shoulder to shoulder. It's hard to move around. The aisles will be slick with vomit; people falling down and grabbing at your legs to keep from being stomped. Drunks pissing on themselves in the betting lines. Dropping handfuls of money and fighting to stoop over and pick it up."

He looked so nervous that I laughed. "I'm just kidding," I said. "Don't worry. At the first hint of trouble I'll start Macing everybody I can reach."

He had done a few good sketches but so far we hadn't seen that special kind of face that I felt we would need for the lead drawing. It was a face I'd seen a thousand times at every Derby I'd ever been to. I saw it, in my head, as the mask of the whiskey gentry--a pretentious mix of booze, failed dreams and a terminal identity crisis; the inevitable result of too much inbreeding in a closed and ignorant culture. One of the key genetic rules in breeding dogs, horses or any other kind of thoroughbred is that close inbreeding tends to magnify the weak points in a bloodline as well as the strong points. In horse breeding, for instance, there is a definite risk in breeding two fast horses who are both a little crazy. The offspring will likely be very fast and also very crazy. So the trick in breeding thoroughbreds is to retain the good traits and filter out the bad. But the breeding of humans is not so wisely supervised, particularly in a narrow Southern society where the closest kind of inbreeding is not only stylish and acceptable, but far more convenient--to the parents--than setting their offspring free to find their own mates, for their own reasons and in their own ways. ("Goddam, did you hear about Smitty's daughter? She went crazy in Boston last week and married a nigger!")

So the face I was trying to find in Churchill Downs that weekend was a symbol, in my own mind, of the whole doomed atavistic culture that makes the Kentucky Derby what it is.

On our way back to the motel after Friday's races I warned Steadman about some of the other problems we'd have to cope with. Neither of us had brought any strange illegal drugs, so we would have to get by on booze. "You should keep in mind," I said, "that almost everybody you talk to from now on will be drunk. People who seem very pleasant at first might suddenly swing at you for no reason at all." He nodded, staring straight ahead. He seemed to be getting a little numb and I tried to cheer him up by inviting him to dinner that night, with my brother.

["WHAT MACE?"]

Back at the motel we talked for awhile about America, the South, England, just relaxing a bit before dinner. There was no way either of us could have known, at the time, that it would be the last normal conversation we would have. From that point on, the weekend became a vicious, drunken nightmare. We both went completely to pieces. The main problem was my prior attachment to Louisville, which naturally led to meetings with old friends, relatives, etc., many of whom were in the process of falling apart, going mad, plotting divorces, cracking up under the strain of terrible debts or recovering from bad accidents. Right in the middle of the whole frenzied Derby action, a member of my own family had to be institutionalized. This added a certain amount of strain to the situation, and since poor Steadman had no choice but to take whatever came his way, he was subjected to shock after shock.

Another problem was his habit of sketching people he met in the various social situations I dragged him into, then giving them the sketches. The results were always unfortunate. I warned him several times about letting the subjects see his foul renderings, but for some perverse reason he kept doing it. Consequently, he was regarded with fear and loathing by nearly everyone who'd seen or even heard about his work. He couldn't understand it. "It's sort of a joke," he kept saying. "Why, in England it's quite normal. People don't take offense. They understand that I'm just putting them on a bit."

"Fuck England," I said. "This is Middle America. These people regard what you're doing to them as a brutal, bilious insult. Look what happened last night. I thought my brother was going to tear your head off."

Steadman shook his head sadly. "But I liked him. He struck me as a very decent, straightforward sort."

"Look, Ralph," I said. "Let's not kid ourselves. That was a very horrible drawing you gave him. It was the face of a monster. It got on his nerves very badly." I shrugged. "Why in hell do you think we left the restaurant so fast?"

"I thought it was because of the Mace," he said.

"What Mace?"

He grinned. "When you shot it at the headwaiter, don't you remember?"

"Hell, that was nothing," I said. "I missed him ... and we were leaving, anyway."

"But it got all over us," he said. "The room was full of that damn gas. Your brother was sneezing and his wife was crying. My eyes hurt for two hours. I couldn't see to draw when we got back to the motel."

"That's right," I said."The stuff got on her leg, didn't it?"

"She was angry," he said.

"Yeah ... well, okay ... let's just figure we fucked up about equally on that one," I said. "But from now on let's try to be careful when we're around people I know. You won't sketch them and I won't Mace them. We'll just try to relax and get drunk."

"Right," he said. "We'll go native."

[DERBY MORNING]

It was Saturday morning, the day of the Big Race, and we were having breakfast in a plastic hamburger palace called the Ptomaine Village. Our rooms were just across the road in the Brown Suburban Hotel. They had a dining room, but the food was so bad that we couldn't handle it anymore. The waitresses seemed to be suffering from shin splints; they moved around very slowly, moaning and cursing the "darkies" in the kitchen.

Steadman liked the Ptomaine place because it had fish and chips. I preferred the "French toast," which was really pancake batter, fried to the proper thickness and then chopped out with a sort of cookie cutter to resemble pieces of toast.

Beyond drink and lack of sleep, our only real problem at that point was the question of access to the clubhouse. Finally, we decided just to go ahead and steal two passes, if necessary, rather than miss that part of the action. This was the last coherent decision we were able to make for the next 48 hours. From that point on--almost from the very moment we started out to the track--we lost all control of events and spent the rest of the weekend churning around in a sea of drunken horrors. My notes and recollections from Derby Day are somewhat scrambled.

But now, looking at the big red notebook I carried all through that scene, I see more or less what happened. The book itself is somewhat mangled and bent; some of the pages are torn, others are shriveled and stained by what appears to be whiskey, but taken as

a whole, with sporadic memory flashes, the notes seem to tell the story. To wit:

[UNSCRAMBLING DERBY DAY-I]
Steadman Is Worried About Fire

Rain all nite until dawn. No sleep. Christ, here we go, a nightmare of mud and madness ... Drunks in the mud. Drowning, fighting for shelter ... But no. By noon the sun burns--perfect day, not even humid.

Steadman is now worried about fire. Somebody told him about the clubhouse catching on fire two years ago. Could it happen again? Horrible. Trapped in the press box. Holocaust. A hundred thousand people fighting to get out. Drunks screaming in the flames and the mud, crazed horses running wild. Blind in the smoke. Grandstand collapsing into the flames with us on the roof. Poor Ralph is about to crack. Drinking heavily, into the Haig.

Out to the track in a cab, avoid that terrible parking in people's front yards, $25 each, toothless old men on the street with big signs: **Park Here**, flagging cars in the yard. "That's fine, boy, never mind the tulips." Wild hair on his head, straight up like a clump of reeds.

Sidewalks full of people all moving in the same direction, towards Churchill Downs. Kids hauling coolers and blankets, teenyboppers in tight pink shorts, many blacks ... black dudes in white felt hats with leopard-skin bands, cops waving traffic along.

The mob was thick for many blocks around the track; very slow going in the crowd, very hot. On the way to the press box elevator, just inside the clubhouse, we came on a row of soldiers all carrying long white riot sticks. About two platoons, with helmets. A man walking next to us said they were waiting for the governor and his party. Steadman eyed them nervously. "Why do they have those clubs?"

"Black Panthers," I said. Then I remembered good old "Jimbo" at the airport and I wondered what he was thinking right now. Probably very nervous; the place was teeming with cops and soldiers. We pressed on through the crowd, through many gates, past the paddock where the jockeys bring the horses out and parade around for a while before each race so the bettors can get a good look. Five million dollars will be bet today. Many winners, more losers. What the hell. The press gate was jammed up with people trying to get

in, shouting at the guards, waving strange press badges: Chicago Sporting Times, Pittsburgh Police Athletic League ... they were all turned away. "Move on, fella, make way for the working press." We shoved through the crowd and into the elevator, then quickly up to the free bar. Why not? Get it on. Very hot today, not feeling well, must be this rotten climate. The press box was cool and airy, plenty of room to walk around and balcony seats for watching the race or looking down at the crowd. We got a betting sheet and went outside.

[UNSCRAMBLING D-DAY II]
Clubhouse/Paddock Bar

Pink faces with a stylish Southern sag, old Ivy styles, seersucker coats and buttondown collars. "Mayblossom Senility" (Steadman's phrase) ... burnt out early or maybe just not much to burn in the first place. Not much energy in the faces, not much *curiosity*. Suffering in silence, nowhere to go after thirty in this life, just hang on and humor the children. Let the young enjoy themselves while they can. Why not? The grim reaper comes early in this league ... banshees on the lawn at night, screaming out there beside that little iron nigger in jockey clothes. Maybe he's the one who's screaming. Bad DT's and too many snarls at the bridge club. Going down with the stock market. Oh Jesus, the kid has wrecked the new car, wrapped it around that big stone pillar at the bottom of the driveway. Broken leg? Twisted eye? Send him off to Yale, they can cure anything up there.

Yale? Did you see today's paper? New Haven is under siege. Yale is swarming with Black Panthers ... I tell you, Colonel, the world has gone mad, stone mad. Why, they tell me a goddam woman jockey might ride in the Derby today.

I left Steadman sketching in the Paddock bar and went off to place our bets on the sixth race. When I came back he was staring intently at a group of young men around a table not far away. "Jesus, look at the corruption in that face!" he whispered. "Look at the madness, the fear, the greed!" I looked, then quickly turned my back on the table he was drawing. The face he'd picked out to draw was the face of an old friend of mine, a prep school football star in the good old days with a sleek red Chevy convertible and a very quick hand, it was said, with the snaps of a 32 B brassiere. They called him "Cat Man."

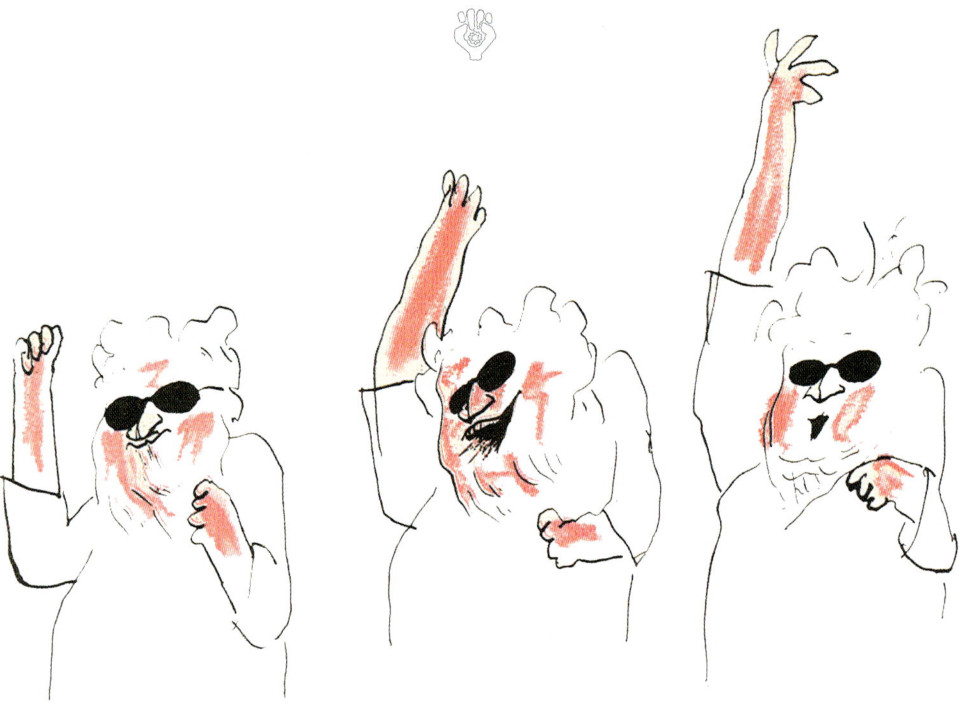

But now, a dozen years later, I wouldn't have recognized him anywhere but here, where I should have expected to find him, in the Paddock bar on Derby Day ... fat slanted eyes and a pimp's smile, blue silk suit and his friends looking like crooked bank tellers on a binge ...

Steadman wanted to see some Kentucky Colonels, but he wasn't sure what they looked like. I told him to go back to the clubhouse men's rooms and look for men in white linen suits vomitting in the urinals. "They'll usually have large brown whiskey stains on the front of their suits," I said, "But watch the shoes, that's the tip-off. Most of them manage to avoid vomitting on their own clothes, but they never miss their shoes."

In a box not far from ours was Colonel Anna Friedman Goldman, *Chairman and Keeper of the Great Seal of the Honorable Order of Kentucky Colonels.* Not all the 76 million or so Kentucky Colonels could make it to the Derby this year, but many had kept the faith, and several days prior to the Derby they gathered for their annual dinner at the Seelbach Hotel.

The Derby, the actual race, was scheduled for late afternoon, and as the magic hour approached I suggested to Steadman that we should probably spend some time in the infield, that boiling sea of people across the track from the clubhouse. He seemed a little nervous about it, but since none of the awful things I'd warned

him about had happened so far--no race riots, firestorms or savage drunken attacks--he shrugged and said, "Right, let's do it."

To get there we had to pass through many gates, each one a step down in status, then through a tunnel under the track. Emerging from the tunnel was such a culture shock that it took us a while to adjust. "God almighty!" Steadman muttered. "This is a ... Jesus!" He plunged ahead with his tiny camera, stepping over bodies, and I followed, trying to take notes.

[UNSCRAMBLINGD D-DAY III]
The Infield

Total chaos, no way to see the race, not even the track ... nobody cares. Big lines at the outdoor betting windows, then stand back to watch winning numbers flash on the big board, like a giant bingo game.

Old blacks arguing about bets; "Hold on there, I'll handle this" (waving pint of whiskey, fistful of dollar bills); girl riding piggyback, T-shirt says, "Stolen from Fort Lauderdale Jail." Thousands of teenagers, group singing "Let the Sun Shine In," ten soldiers guarding the American flag and a huge fat drunk wearing a blue football jersey (No. 80) reeling around with quart of beer in hand.

No booze sold out here, too dangerous … no bathrooms either. Muscle Beach … Woodstock … many cops with riot sticks, but no sign of a riot. Far across the track the clubhouse looks like a postcard from the Kentucky Derby.

[UNSCRAMBLING D-DAY IV]
"My Old Kentucky Home"

We went back to the clubhouse to watch the big race. When the crowd stood to face the flag and sing "My Old Kentucky Home," Steadman faced the crowd and sketched frantically. Somewhere up in the boxes a voice screeched, "Turn around, you hairy freak!" The race itself was only two minutes long, and even from our super-status seats and using 12-power glasses, there was no way to see what was really happening. Later, watching a TV rerun in the press box, we saw what happened to our horses. Holy Land, Ralph's choice, stumbled and lost his jockey in the final turn. Mine, Silent Screen, had the lead coming into the stretch, but faded to fifth at the finish. The winner was a 16-1 shot named Dust Commander.

Moments after the race was over, the crowd surged wildly for the exits, rushing for cabs and busses. The next day's Courier told of violence in the parking lot; people were punched and trampled, pockets were picked, children lost, bottles hurled. But we missed all this, having retired to the press box for a bit of post-race drinking. By this time we were both half-crazy from too much whiskey, sun fatigue, culture shock, lack of sleep and general dissolution. We hung around the press box long enough to watch a mass interview with the winning owner, a dapper little man named Lehmann who said he had just flown into Louisville that morning from Nepal, where he'd "bagged a record tiger." The sportswriters murmured their admiration and a waiter filled Lehmann's glass with Chivas Regal. He had just won $127,000 with a horse that cost him $6,500 two years ago. His occupation, he said, was "retired contractor." And then he added, with a big grin, "I just retired."

The rest of the day blurs into madness. The rest of that night too. And all the next day and night. Such horrible things occurred that I can't bring myself even to think about them now, much less put them down in print. Steadman was lucky to get out of Louisville without serious injuries, and I was lucky to get out at all. One of my clearest memories of that vicious time is Ralph being attacked

by one of my old friends in the billiard room of the Pendennis Club in downtown Louisville on Saturday night. The man had ripped his own shirt open to the waist before deciding that Ralph wasn't after his wife. No blows were struck, but the emotional effects were massive. Then, as a sort of final horror, Steadman put his fiendish pen to work and tried to patch things up by doing a little sketch of the girl he'd been accused of hustling. That finished us in the Pedennis.

[GETTING OUT OF TOWN]

Sometime around 10:30 Monday morning I was awakened by a scratching sound at my door. I leaned out of bed and pulled the curtain back just far enough to see Steadman outside. "What the fuck do you want?" I shouted.

"What about having breakfast?" he said.

I lunged out of bed and tried to open the door, but it caught on the night-chain and banged shut again. I couldn't cope with the chain! The thing wouldn't come out of the track--so I ripped it out of the wall with a vicious jerk on the door. Ralph didn't blink. "Bad luck," he muttered.

I could barely see him. My eyes were swollen almost shut and the sudden burst of sunlight through the door left me stunned and helpless like a sick mole. Steadman was mumbling about sickness and terrible heat; I fell back on the bed and tried to focus on him as he moved around the room in a very distracted way for a few moments, then suddenly darted over to the beer bucket and seized a Colt .45. "Christ," I said. "You're getting out of control."

He nodded and ripped the cap off, taking a long drink. "You know, this is really awful," he said finally. "I must get out of this place ..." he shook his head nervously. "The plane leaves at 3:30, but I don't know if I'll make it."

I barely heard him. My eyes had finally opened enough for me to focus on the mirror across the room and I was stunned at the shock of recognition. For a confused instant I thought that Ralph had brought somebody with him--a model for that one special face we'd been looking for. There he was, by God--a puffy, drink-ravaged, disease-ridden caricature ... like an awful cartoon version of an old snapshot in some once-proud mother's family photo album. It was the face we'd been looking for--and it was, of course, my own. Horrible, horrible ...

3
6
The Kentucky Derby 1970
Ralph STEADMAN

FINISH

"Maybe I should sleep a while longer," I said. "Why don't you go on over to the Ptomaine Village place and eat some of those rotten fish and chips? Then come back and get me around noon. I feel too near death to hit the streets at this hour."

He shook his head. "No ... no ... I think I'll go back upstairs and work on those drawings for a while." He leaned down to fetch two more cans out of the beer bucket. "I tried to work earlier," he said, "but my hands keep trembling ... It's teddible, teddible."

"You've got to stop this drinking," I said.

He nodded. "I know. This is no good, no good at all. But for some reason I think it makes me feel better ..."

"Not for long," I said. "You'll probably collapse into some kind of hysterical DT's tonight--probably just about the time you get off the plane at Kennedy. They'll zip you up in a straightjacket and drag you down to the Tombs, then beat you on the kidneys with big sticks until you straighten out."

He shrugged and wandered out, pulling the door shut behind him. I went back to bed for another hour or so, and later--after the daily grapefruit juice run to the Nite Owl Food Mart--we drove once again to the Ptomaine Village for a fine lunch of dough and butcher's offal, fried in heavy grease.

By this time Ralph wouldn't order coffee; he kept asking for more water. "It's the only thing they have that's fit for human consumption," he explained. Then, with an hour or so to kill before he had to catch the plane, we spread his drawings out on the table and pondered them for a while, wondering if he'd caught the proper spirit of the thing ... but we couldn't make up our minds. His hands were shaking so badly that he had trouble holding the paper, and my vision was so blurred that I could barely see what he'd drawn. "Shit," I said. "We both look worse than anything you've drawn here."

He smiled. "You know--I've been thinking about that," he said. "We came down here to see this teddible scene: people all pissed out of their minds and vomitting on themselves and all that ... and now, you know what? It's us ..."

* * *

Huge Pontiac Ballbuster blowing through traffic on the expressway. The journalist is driving, ignoring his passenger who is now nearly naked after taking off most of his clothing, which he holds out the window, trying to wind-wash the Mace out of it. His eyes are bright red and his face and chest are soaked with the beer he's been

using to rinse the awful chemical off his flesh. The front of his woolen trousers is soaked with vomit; his body is racked with fits of coughing and wild choking sobs. The journalist rams the big car through traffic and into a spot in front of the terminal, then he reaches over to open the door on the passenger's side and shoves the Englishman out, snarling: "Bug off, you worthless faggot! You twisted pigfucker! [Crazed laughter.] If I weren't sick I'd kick your ass all the way to Bowling Green--you scumsucking foreign geek. Mace is too good for you ... We can do without your kind in Kentucky."

Hunter Thompson has gone home to rest in Aspen, Colorado, where he edits the Aspen Wallposter and is threatening to become a candidate for sheriff of that community. He wrote the book, The Hell's Angels.

Ralph Steadman has gone home to rest in London, where he is cartoonist-in-residence for the satirical-politcal journal Private Eye. He has published 15 books of stories suitable for children and illustrated an edition of Alice in Wonderland *which is not.*

The Author as seen by The Illustrator.

BOOK THREE

Adventures With Hunter

JOHN G. CLANCY   BILL CARDOSO   DENNIS P. EICHHORN
ROGER BLACK   JERRY BROWN   BEN FONG-TORRES
PAUL KRASSNER   TIMOTHY FERRIS   WILLIAM RANDOLPH HEARST III
TERRY McDONELL   MARTIN F. NOLAN   WILLIAM KENNEDY
CHRISTOPHER FELVER   PHIL BRONSTEIN   BARBARA WOHL-LUTTRINGER
JOHN R. MACARTHUR   JACK THIBEAU   MICHAEL STEPANIAN
EUGENE "DR. HIP" SCHOENFELD   MATTHEW NAYTHONS   WAYNE EWING
DEBORAH FULLER (WITH SHOTGUN ART)
JOHN WALSH (WITH SHOTGUN GOLF)
JEFF GOODBY   RALPH STEADMAN   JONAH RASKIN   TOM WOLFE
GARRY TRUDEAU   JONATHAN SHAW   JOHNNY DEPP   WAVY GRAVY
STEPHEN R. PROCTOR

NEWS RELEASE

AIR PROVING GROUND COMMAND
EGLIN AIR FORCE BASE, FLORIDA

OFFICE OF INFORMATION SERVICES
Telephone 26111 - 26222

Eglin AFB, Florida (November 8, 1957)-S/Sgt. Manmountain Dense, a novice Air Policeman, was severely injured here today when a wine bottle exploded inside the AP gatehouse at the west entrance to the base. Dense was incoherent for several hours after the disaster, but managed to make a statement which led investigators to believe the bottle was hurled from a speeding car which approached the gatehouse on the wrong side of the road, coming from the general direction of the Separation Center.

Further investigation revealed that, only minutes before the incident at the gatehouse, a reportedly "fanatical" airman had received his separation papers and was rumored to have set out in the direction of the gatehouse at a high speed in a muffler-less car with no brakes. An immediate search was begun for Hunter S. Thompson, one-time sports editor of the base newspaper and well-known "morale problem." Thompson was known to have a sometimes overpowering affinity for wine and was described by a recent arrival in the base sanatorium as "just the type of bastard who would do a thing like that."

An apparently uncontrollable iconoclast, Thompson was discharged today after one of the most hectic and unusual Air Force careers in recent history. Accordingly to Captain Munnington Third, who was relieved of his duties as base classification officer yesterday and admitted to the neuropsychological section of the base hospital, Thompson was "totally unclassifiable" and "one of the most savage and unnatural airmen I've ever come up against.

"I'll never understand how he got this discharge," Third went on to say. "I almost had a stroke yesterday when I heard he was being given an honorable discharge. It's terrifying."

And then Third sank into a delirium.

Hunter wrote this press release to celebrate his decamping the Air Force in 1957.

A Master Of Tools

JOHN G. CLANCY

Twinckle: Here is the Hunter piece. If you don't publish it I will physically assault you and this e-mail is sent as written evidence of my criminal intent. Tell me what you think. Yeah, I know it's too long but so what? At your prices you can't bitch. Besides, the ending line is yours.

Best, Clanski -- March 13, 2005, Durango, Colorado.

Hunter S. Thompson first entered my life during Christmas vaca-tion in 1957 when I entered the apartment at 120 Morningside Drive I shared with two--down from three--other Columbia Law School students. I had been away and to my great surprise I found a tall, rangy young man standing in the doorway of one of the bedrooms. I thought I affably said, "Who the hell are you?" but he always insisted I glared at him and snapped, "WHO the FUCK are YOU?" He explained he had just gotten out of the Air Force in Florida and Jerry Hawke, one of the apartment dwellers, had been his Air Force captain and had given him permission to replace the fourth roommate we had just lost. "I'm Hunter Thompson," he said extending his hand. "I'm a writer." I held Jerry Hawke in high regard. I shook the offered hand mumbling something about that was ok with me and we immediately went around the corner for a beer. The rest, as they say, is history--47 years of it.

Incidents and conversations, adventures and confrontations, foolishness and seriousness, keep flooding into my memory. Bit by bit and piece by piece they float to the surface, forgotten and buried

for years. They come now because of Hunter's death. This is not the time to corral them and relate them, though. It would not do Hunter justice to try and lay them out hurriedly or in 47 years of chronological order without the time for focused reflection, without the time for dredging and doing whatever it will take to bring them all back. Doing this requires that I relive a lot of my own life in order to bring back his; something I have no interest in doing while I'm still living it as hard as I can.

Hunter and I rarely talked about the past, about things we had done and seen. We were always too busy with the present and the future. At Hunter's memorial in Aspen on March 5, 2005, Ralph Steadman and I kept coming up with new stories every time we ran into each other, stories either he or I had forgotten until the other recounted them. Warren Hinckle and I had the same experience. There was so much that went on for so long and so much that was telescoped into such intense and sustained periods like the 60s, now so long ago. New incidents keep popping up into my mind on a daily basis. Maybe someday I'll get them all out. A few need telling now to show the quality of the man Hunter was and to illuminate the man we lost.

When I met him, Hunter was 19, had never been to college, and knew no one in New York except Jerry Hawke who told great stories of his exploits and accomplishments as a journalist at Eglin Air Force Base in Florida. We were a studious lot in the apartment and, surprisingly, looking back, Hunter fit right in. Indeed, for the semester he lived with us I made my best grades, finishing right near the top of my class; Jerry was first in his class. Roger Hawke, Jerry's brother, was the third roommate. We would eat and then sit around the dining room table with Hunter and talk. He was going to be a great writer, he told us, mentioning Hemingway and Faulkner in the same sentence; he supposed he'd have to be a journalist to support himself in the meantime, though he feared journalism might develop bad writing habits. "Hemingway did it, so I guess it will work out, but I don't like the idea of doing it," I recall him grumbling.

Then there were the occasional Friday and Saturday nights of free time and the down time after exams. Hunter and I were the drinkers in the group and inevitably we would find ourselves having a few beers around the corner or at the West End Bar or in the Village. He fit right in with my classmate friends who found him interesting and enjoyed his company. Hunter asked a lot of questions about the

law and politics and how the system worked and ventured his own opinions readily. He was earnest and serious like the students we were. And compared to later years, he was restrained in his behavior, even when drinking.

There were exceptions. My best friend, Don Engle, was a tall blonde lad from Florida whom I'd met at the Jersey Shore. Looking back, he was my Hunter before Hunter--I'd met Don one night when he offered me a ride in a convertible with no top in a pouring rainstorm, a car that only had one gear--second. Everything was funny to him; he would do damn near anything, was smart as a whip, attracted girls like a magnet, was good with his fists in a jam, and totally fearless.

In the winter of 1957-1958, Don was in the Navy flying from Newfoundland out to the Azores and beyond as part of an early warning military system called the Dew Line. He planned to come to New York to work when he finished. When he blew into town in mid-winter to stay with us for a few days on leave he had a bottle of absinthe from the Azores, something that was illegal in the U.S., apparently because it contained wormwood, which caused brain damage. Well, it was about five degrees outside and not much warmer in the apartment when the three of us started on the absinthe. "This is like drinking liquid fire," Hunter exclaimed. "This is the best damn thing I ever drank," I agreed. Don unsuccessfully tried to light a glass of it on fire so we could drink it while it was burning. You could feel the stuff go all the way down into your stomach and the cold was almost immediately forgotten.

One thing led to another, as it so often does, and, taking the bottle, we piled into Hunter's old car and went down to the Village where we finished the bottle and bar hopped. I remember these tall, loud, funny southern guys getting on famously, ridiculing each others heritage. Hunter told Don that he had to be "white trash" because Florida was settled by the flotsam and jetsam and losers 86'd from every state north of it and Don derided Hunter as the decadent descendent of cruel and sexually-insane slave holders. They laughed and made fun of me as a northerner who grew up in an Irish ghetto in New York City who could know nothing of American ways as they did. I was a fucking ignorant immigrant and they were not.

It was as good an evening as I have ever had and at the end of a long and hilarious night I found myself somehow at the wheel of Hunter's car confronting one of New York's finest, whose hand was

firmly clamped down on my left arm through the window of the stopped car as he informed me in no uncertain terms that the death penalty would be too good for me. I was, he seemed to be saying, driving the wrong way on one of those short, narrow village one-way streets. He would see to it, he thundered, that I would be taken to the Tombs, a notorious Manhattan jail. "Oh shit," I said to him. "Everybody gets confused on these damn streets down here, hey, it's only a block long and I was only doing about 10 mph." "GET OUT!" he shouted, and told me I was a goner. Then I became aware that the two tall guys were out of the car and around on my side shouting things like, "This is a mistake, he wasn't driving. It's my car, he's a student, I'm a Navy pilot on leave defending our country, I'm defending your right to make chickenshit stops like this, I'm in the service just like you are ... I'm a writer and it's my car not his, arrest me, not him ... I'm guilty, I told him to go up this street" and the like. With that Hunter reached into the car and grabbed an exam paper of mine he had on the dashboard for some reason and handed it to the cop saying, "See, here's the proof, he's a student, he had an exam, he's tired, we just got lost down here in this goddamned rabbit warren, this will ruin him, he'll never get to be a lawyer, you just can't do this. Arrest me instead." Don chimed in, "Arrest me too, you'll get two of us for one of him." I was amazed to feel the cop release my arm and to watch him throw back his head and laugh heartily, a real belly-laugh. "What a pack of fucking jamokes you guys are," he said. "Get the fuck out of here right now." We did.

I remember all of this so clearly because it was the only time the three of us were together. It was the last time I ever saw Don. His next flight disappeared somewhere up there over the cold North Atlantic and was never found.

Hunter and I decided that summer when the lease was up we would share a one-bedroom basement apartment at 57 Perry Street in the Village. I worked at night as a teamster on the docks and he worked during the day as a copy boy at *Time* magazine. There was one bed that we actually used in shifts and an alcove area built out from the wall that served as a place to sleep on blankets if the bed was occupied. We rarely saw each other during the week--we each went to work before the other came home--but when I came home around 11am or so on Saturday morning after a few beers with my fellow workers--it was our Friday night--we would often start up what he called the Fun Machine and I would be expected to pitch

right in without having had any sleep. Hey, that was all right with me. Sometimes we would drive to the Jersey Shore but most of the time we ran around the Village drinking and smoking, listening to jazz, and chasing girls while we argued loudly about politics, literature, and the future. Or we sat in the coffeehouse around the corner doing the same thing, or reading. Or we went our separate ways. Hunter had a peculiar loping kind of gait, he walked funny just like I did, people told us. Whenever he felt like it, it seemed, he would emit an unearthly deafening howl and bang his hand down on things, like the bar. This occasionally led to trouble in bars but he was good with his fists like Don and we covered each other pretty well.

I was seeing a girl down the street from our apartment on Perry Street. She lived on the second floor of a four-story apartment house. She and I would wrestle around in her bedroom a couple of times a month and I mean wrestle because we never did do much more. One night she started laughing and said, "While I'm fighting you off in here your roommate has been sleeping with my roommate in her bed down the hall. He's coming over the roof and down the fire escape into her window and leaving the same way back to the roof."

"How long has this been going on?" I asked.

"About six weeks," she said.

I was astounded. Here was a guy I got down with most weekends, lived with, ate with, drank with, shot the shit with about everything, past, present, and future and he had never crowed about this feat, let alone mentioned it. This was a guy, I figured, who really kept his mouth shut. This was a guy with a sense of honor.

One afternoon we came up with the idea to barbecue steaks in the apartment. We put charcoal pieces on top of a metal tray set on the concrete floor. We propped up the grill from the oven with bricks and fired it up with lighter fluid. We were funneling most of the smoke out of the kitchen window but it was pretty smoky in the place. I was turning the steaks over when we heard Sam the superintendent shouting in the hallway outside that there was a fire in the building. Sam was a black man who shouted when he spoke and we had learned his strict rules for his kids and the serious consequences of violating them because he shouted them into the interior courtyard into which the only windows in this dungeon opened. Hunter and Gene McGarr, a fellow *Time* copy boy and running buddy--a lifelong friend to both of us--went out the door into the hallway and shut it tightly behind them. Gene, another tall, big guy, who is now a

very successful voice-over in movies and television, had a very smooth persuasive manner of speaking. I remember the conversation I heard through the door as I waited for the steaks to be done so I could shovel the burning charcoal into the sink to destroy the evidence. Sam shouted, "You have a FIRE in there, I'm going in there to handle it. You dumb city boys don't know how to do ANYTHING. This is MY building. You boys are going to burn it down. People will DIE." Hunter and McGarr told him there had been a little problem with burning some lamb shanks in the oven, it had been taken care of, that there were women in there who were not fully dressed who would leave if Sam embarrassed them by going in and catching them in that state, this would just ruin all the work they had done to get them there. They told Sam that surely he remembered being young and chasing girls before he was married. The fire was out, they assured him, there was no danger. Sam grumbled inaudibly, said he understood and shouted that we were GOOD BOYS and he wouldn't spoil our party. If he had come in we surely would have been evicted after he saw the glowing charcoal on the kitchen floor.

Hunter used to monitor classes with each of his Morningside Drive apartment mates and later would say he went to school at Columbia, a statement that was literally true. I used to rib Hunter about being a typical southern bigot. One day he went with me to hear Thurgood Marshall speak at the Law School. Marshall was then the chief attorney for the N.A.A.C.P. and in the forefront of the civil rights movement. After a rousing civil rights talk in a small classroom he challenged the audience to ask him some tough questions. "Come on," he said, "ask me some tough questions, ones I haven't heard before, some real hard ones. Come on, you're supposed to be so smart." Hands went up and I noticed Hunter's had gone up immediately as if by involuntary reflex, and that he pulled it down using his other arm like Peter Sellers in "Dr. Strangelove." As we were walking out I asked him what he was going to ask Marshall. "I was going to ask him," he replied, "what it was like being a nigger."

I went to San Francisco in the summer of 1959 to work for a federal judge. Hunter met Sandy in the Village and moved with her to Big Sur sometime in 1960 or 1961. I was in the Army stationed at Fort Ord in Monterey, about an hour's drive north. Instead of making the long drive to Berkeley where my girlfriend lived, I would drive down to Big Sur on weekends where my girlfriend would join me most of the time. We eventually fixed up our own place in an old chicken house that adjoined a place where Joan Baez was living, on property then known as Slate's Hot Springs, which later became the Esalen Institute. Hunter and Sandy lived on the adjoining property owned by the grandmother of Dennis Murphy, whose book "The Sergeant," won the National Book Award in the late 1950s. We'd read it in the Village and liked it a lot. On the back cover there had been a picture of the Big Sur house where the author lived. Hunter and Sandy were in a little upstairs guesthouse, or servants quarters, next to the house right on the edge of a cliff that dropped 300 feet or so straight down to rocks fronting the ocean. The Big House, as we called it, was a three-story wonder with spectacular views of the coast, mountains, and ocean.

The mountains come down to the ocean along the coast there and it is dramatically beautiful country. We made our own beer, which we traded for abalone and venison, and there were always gallon jugs of cheap Safeway white wine that I would bring down from Monterey. Sitting in the sun on a Sunday afternoon on the deck looking over the ocean, listening to Miles Davis' "Sketches in Spain," drinking and eating, it was paradisiacal. Soaking in the big hot spring tubs built out from the middle of a cliff about 50 feet above the raging surf; arguing about politics, talking about writing, and speculating on the future. These were good times.

Dennis Murphy was a screenwriter by then and spent most of his time in Hollywood but Hunter and I used to play touch football on the lawn in front of his big house when he and his Hollywood cronies like Stuart Whitman came up. The only catch to the field was that if you were going full out while you caught the ball at the western end of the field, you would keep right on going over the cliff and die. Afterwards, if we were lucky, Dennis would invite us into the Big House, or onto the oceanfront patio, to drink beer and talk. He and Hunter would talk about writing mostly and Hunter would listen intently.

One evening Hunter was driving a station wagon south to Gorda to see if we could talk the store owner there into opening up and selling us some beer. Our latest batch of homemade wasn't ready yet and, as always, the last batch was already gone. Suddenly, a deer showed up in the headlights moving left to right toward the ocean; Hunter moved left sharply into the other lane to avoid it, braking hard and stopping. Damned if the deer didn't reverse field, run back to the left and start up the steep hill running down to the road and

then reverse field again and head straight for us, running smack into the front of the car. Hunter moved the car to the side of the road, we got out, determined the deer was dead, and threw it in the back. Then we noticed a little deer on the side of the road having trouble walking on a front leg. I picked it up and put it in the back seat.

We hung the dead deer from pipes in the cellar of the Big House and butchered it. Then we put a splint on the little deer's leg. Well satisfied with our work we were sitting having a beer on the grass the next morning next to a little contained area we built for the deer. It had taken milk from a baby bottle, was hobbling around, and seemed to be coming along well. Alan Watts, a well-known guru on Zen Buddhism, who had published a number of books and had a large following, walked up with some companions and examined the deer. In a deep and resonant voice, he pontificated that "this deer needs some of nature's herbs if it is to heal." He proceeded to gather up various shoots of plants he cut up with a knife and mixed together. Then he hand fed them to the little deer saying some incomprehensible phrases that sounded, perhaps, Tibetan. "Mumbo, jumbo," Hunter called them. And the deer lay down to sleep.

A few hours later while we were still sitting there, the deer suddenly staggered to its feet, uttered forlorn cries, twitched spasmodically and fell over dead. Hunter leapt into the air, his face dark and angry. "That fucker, that crackpot, that filthy guru, that rotten cocksucker!" he shouted. "Nobody should ever believe anything that charlatan ever says about anything. He killed the deer, he murdered it, that rotten prick. Let's see if we can find some hemlock and give him an organic treat."

When I mustered out of the Army, my girlfriend, Judith Spector, and I got married in Pacific Grove before heading to San Francisco where I had a job. We had our reception on the patio of the Big House. She had asked Hunter to wear a tie. When we drove in we found a goat tethered to a post on the lawn. It was wearing a tie. Hunter never showed up. I understood completely--like Sam, Hunter had his rules. He'd rather forego free food and drink at a friend's wedding than compromise his principles.

Hunter and Sandy moved to San Francisco after being evicted from the Big Sur property after Hunter had an article published in *Rogue* magazine that called his landlady a "scumlord." He and I had season tickets to the 49er games at Kezar Stadium, played basketball together in a schoolyard near his apartment, went to boxing matches

at Kezar Pavilion, and continued to drink beer, discuss, and argue. We did the things good friends do, like helping each other move our possessions and furniture, lending each other money--I had a steady paycheck and from time to time Hunter would get a decent-sized check--and trying out ideas and thoughts on one another.

One late afternoon at an apartment he had near the Presidio, David Pierce, then the Mayor of Richmond, and I were sitting with Hunter. We had been to a 49er game and drinking beer heavily. Suddenly, for no apparent reason, Hunter jumped out of his chair, grabbed a shotgun from under the couch and ran to the back door. After opening the door, he screamed, and fired the shotgun into the air--it sounded like both barrels at once. Then he ran back into the room and put the shotgun back under the couch, sat down and picked up his beer. We forgot about this quickly enough and when the loud knock on the door came Hunter acted surprised it was a cop. The cop was alone and acted angry. He said they had received a complaint at the station house about guns being discharged and what the hell was going on. Hunter said he could look around all he wanted, we were just mourning the 49er loss and invited him in, never denying that guns had been fired. Pierce told the officer that he was the Mayor of Richmond--I could hear the "Yeah sure, next you'll tell me you're really Charles Lindbergh" in the cop's mind--and that Hunter was going to be a famous writer and would he please not do anything that could wreck his career. I just sat there. Next thing I knew the cop pointed at me and said, "You take that gun off the wall, you take it off the wall by lifting it off the hook it's on and you keep it pointed the way it's pointed, you don't point it any other place and you don't point it at me because if you do I'll shoot you." I looked behind me and saw a little plastic toy pistol hanging from a hook. I did exactly as he said and he took it, examined it, and handed it back to me. "Another complaint and you're all arrested, including you, Mr. Mayor," he said and turned to go. "Good luck with your writing," the cop said to Hunter, over his shoulder. "I tried to do some of that, it's a lot harder than it looks."

When the 49ers were playing at home, we would meet at his Parnassus Street apartment just above the football stadium before noon on Sunday. We kept the tickets there. After a beer or so we would walk down to the stadium. One Sunday, the day of a much discussed and anticipated titanic contest with the Green Bay Packers, I went over to his place and there was nobody home. I waited

and waited and became angry. At least he could have called me, I thought. Then, just before game time he roared up and got out of his car slowly. "I'm sorry," he said. "I just couldn't get here any sooner. The Hells Angels stomped the shit out of me last night when they found out they weren't going to get any royalties out of the book." He pointed to his face. I could see his nose had been pushed in--broken it turned out--and welts on his forehead and face. He walked gingerly into the house, got the tickets and we walked to the game, arriving in our seats only a couple of minutes after the kickoff. I was impressed that Hunter could drive himself to the game and thanked him. He just grunted. And he did not act injured at all. Indeed, we were greatly impressed by the Packer fullback, Jimmy Taylor, who fought, scratched, churned, and drove with every inch of his energy for every inch of ground. So much so that the rabid 49er fans around us got on our case for praising the enemy. We would later admire Pete Banaszak for the same relentless toughness as he drove for those crucial short yards late in the game in the darkening gloom of the Oakland Coliseum.

We would watch the football games intently--at Kezar Stadium you could see the players up close unlike at the cavernous Polo Grounds and Yankee Stadium. Kezar was like a big high school football stadium and when the fog would creep over the west rim of the stadium late in the afternoon--which it did with some frequency--the crowd would cheer. It was the best place either of us had ever watched or played football in. Our discussions were deadly serious and focused--the game plan, the upcoming play, the defense for it, the play called, what should have been called, the particular players, etc. And Hunter would help me years later when I was trying to develop strategies for David Meggyesy at the football players union.

I have never had better conversations about football with anyone and I wasn't surprised at all when he gave Nixon--a man he hated--credit for good football knowledge after discussing the subject with him. At halftime or during a timeout, Hunter would whip out the latest business he wanted to discuss. It was at Kezar that I read the Hells Angels piece published in *The Nation* in 1965 and the proposed book contract from Random House. It was there we lined out strategy and tactics. It seemed perfectly normal to do these things in the midst of thousands of screaming, drinking football fans. It was the perfect office.

Hunter and Sandy, with baby Juan, moved to Aspen, Colorado, and then to Woody Creek, just north of Aspen, sometime in late 1966 or early 1967 but he was always coming to town to help launch, ride on and write about the Rocket Ship 60s as it thrust into the air from the Bay Area. We were at Raiders games, rock concerts, and club performances; *Scanlan's* and *City of San Francisco* magazines and Warren Hinckle's bars; *Rolling Stone*, and its bar, Jerry's; and Jann Wenner's house; as well as meetings, protests, and marches against the Vietnam War. We were involved with, and hung out with--and serious meetings were indistinguishable from hanging out a lot of the time--the political activists, the Raiders players, the musicians, the writers, with all and anyone, it seemed, who was involved with making things happen in that intense time. As Hunter said in "Fear & Loathing In Las Vegas," "[I was] absolutely certain that no matter which way I went I would come to a place where people were just as high and wild as I was: No doubt about that . . . There was madness in any direction, at any hour. If not across the Bay, then up the Golden Gate or down 101 to Los Altos or La Honda . . . You could strike sparks anywhere."

When he was in San Francisco for *Rolling Stone* he would usually hole up out at the beach at the Seal Rock Inn. When he came into town it was like the lunatic parade from J.P. Donleavy's "The Ginger Man," a book we both loved. He would appear at the head of a line of people who would all dance around trying to impress, emulate, or compete with him. It seemed like everyone he was with would try and get his attention, to try and be the most favored one. One afternoon Hunter showed up at my office with a couple of six packs. He said that Jann Wenner was going to hold back some $11,000 from the $15,000 final payment due for delivery of "Fear & Loathing On The Campaign Trial," money that would be held until there was a final settlement of Hunter's expenses on the road doing the articles on the McGovern-Nixon campaign. We called Alan Rinzler over there and he said he had been instructed to withhold the amount. I told him I had instructed Hunter to withhold the final chapter.

After we hung up, Hunter looked me in the eye and said, "This calls for the application of Gonzo Law. I have some ideas. Call Rinzler and tell him we'll take $12,500, they can hold $2,500 the cheap, conniving, thieving bastards. I'll do the rest." I called Rinzler and told him to get Jann to cut a check to Hunter for $12,500 and withhold $2,500, not $11,000, that this was a reasonable compromise. He said

he would ask Jann. When Hunter got over there, as he explained it to me right afterwards at Babe's Monte Carlo--a marvelous old bar on the Barbary Coast around the corner from my office--"I let Rinzler read the last chapter. He said it was classic, that he loved it. I grabbed it out of his hand and told him there were a lot of things I loved but couldn't have. $12,500 was the price, I told him, cheap for something he really loved. When he said he couldn't do that I grabbed the telephone on his desk, yanked it out of the wall, and threw it through his window down into the street, smashing the glass. I told him that was impossible too, that a lot of things were impossible, including the possibility of *Rolling Stone* publishing my book. Then I turned and tried to get out of his office but the door was one of those goddamned sliding kind and I couldn't figure how it worked so I just kicked it down." Rinzler was on the phone to me right after Hunter stormed out telling me there had been violence and mayhem and could I please calm Hunter down as they had to have that last chapter. I told him I thought I could if he sent a check for $12,500 right over to Babe's. When Hunter cashed it in the morning I would deliver him the final chapter. Hunter had a big smile on his face when the check walked in the door.

Another time at Babe's, Hunter leans over to me and says quietly, "Jesus, John, I took some acid last week while I was driving from Palo Alto to La Honda to see Kesey and things got so distorted I just pulled off the road and I had the thought I should turn myself in to the police. Jesus, John, we need to look at acid carefully. Any drug that makes you want to turn yourself in is a dangerous drug."

One late afternoon we were sitting at a big round table in the lounge of the bar at the Oakland Hilton after a Raider victory. With us was Lydia Pense, the great lead singer of the group Cold Blood, and assorted players and their wives and girlfriends who had stopped there on the way to the traditional Raiders gathering after a home game where food and drink was provided by Al Davis. Sitting at a table next to us was Curt Gowdy, a broadcaster known nationally, a Wyoming boy originally. Hunter went over and introduced himself to Gowdy who, unlike Al Davis, didn't have the faintest idea who he was. Hunter told our group that Lydia was just a great singer, a soul singer and a rock and roll singer. Some of the black women started ribbing Lydia about being a white soul singer, expressing some disbelief in her abilities. Lydia, all 4'10" of her, got right up on the table and belted out a version of a spiritual, "To Be Free," that just took the

roof off the place as she grew taller and taller right before our eyes. There was wild applause. A few minutes later a waiter came over and said we'd have to cut that stuff out, that Mr. Gowdy had complained. Hunter jumped up and shouted, "Gowdy, you pigfucker, you Wyoming sheepfucker. You are a world class swine." With that we all got up and left. Outside as we stood in the parking lot one of the black women grabbed my arm to keep from falling down with laughter. It seemed her cousin, who was on welfare, had signed for the check using some kind of welfare card that looked like a credit card.

Warren Hinckle and Hunter and I were the only three people in the Pyramid bar on the corner of Jackson and Kearny streets in San Francisco one late afternoon. The owner and bartender was Bill Pappas, a fellow I knew fairly well. After Pappas served us a round of drinks I suddenly heard Warren say, "Bill, you bastard. You shortchanged me $5." I watched Pappas do a double take and start counting on his fingers. "Damn it, Warren, you're right" he said. "I'm sorry, I guess you guys bought me too many drinks." With that he slid a $5 bill across the bar to Warren saying, "I hope you don't think I tried to jew you out of this." Warren took the bill and started tearing it into little pieces. Hunter made a growling sound and reached into his airline bag on the floor. Warren put the torn up money into the whipped cream on his Irish coffee and threw the drink in Pappas' face shouting, "Have some jewish coffee you thief!" At the same instant Hunter rose up from rummaging in his bag and sprayed mace into Pappas' face shouting, "Here's some instant justice you swine." As Pappas staggered around behind the bar waving his arms and groaning, his face and the front of his shirt covered with whipped cream and little pieces of green paper money, we made a hasty exit. On the way out, not to be outdone, I managed to get the metal cover off a fireplug hose connection outside--usually they are firmly attached with a chain--and threw it through the window. Hunter was revving the car up out front with Warren in the back. He reached over to the passenger side front, grabbed my shirt front, and yanked me partway into the car shouting, "We must FLEE!" As he gunned the engine and took off like a shot up Kearney street toward Broadway I was struggling to get all the way in with one heel dragging on the ground shooting off a train of sparks from a metal heel cleat. "It's all your fault, John, everything was just fine until you broke the window," Hunter shouted. Warren, laughing uproariously in the back, yelled, "He's right, it's all your fault." The next time I had the courage to return to the Pyramid, Bill

Photo: Deborah Fuller

(Above) John Clancy's wife, Judy, bringing new peacocks and peahens to Hunter at Owl Farm, 1998. (Below) Clancy (left) and Warren Hinckle at film director Francis Ford Coppola's City of San Francisco magazine in 1976, where Hinckle was editor and Clancy was the libel attorney.

Pappas shook his head at me and then started laughing. "I should have turned you all in," he said. "But you know I could never do that." The window, he said, had been covered by his insurance.

I went to Aspen from San Francisco a fair amount over the years. I had projects in Colorado and would fly over from Denver to discuss his campaign for sheriff. After one weekend where I skied all day and stayed up all night with Hunter, I found myself at lunch on Monday at the Petroleum Club in Denver being told by colleagues I looked great, tanned and all, and asked did I have a good weekend. I nodded, smiled, and was terse--"great snow"--hoping my eyes weren't visibly spinning and saving what was left of my voice for when I needed it.

One snowy evening I arrived at the Woody Creek house with a case of beer and found the stereo blasting through an open front door. Hunter was drinking with Gene Johnson, a friend from town. After many drinks I heard Hunter say it was time for some work and watched as he carried a shoebox full of marijuana outside and put it up on the roof by the front door with a plastic cover over it that he took from the record player. "I'll show you I am a Master of Tools," Hunter shouted and began wrestling an old couch in the living room out the door, a couch he had threatened to get rid of several times, a couch I had referred to as his "semen-stained" couch. We helped him get it out the door and into the front yard about 20 yards from the house. Then he handed Gene a rifle and told him it was loaded with tracer bullets and positioned him between the couch and the road. "Fire, when I tell you," he said, pointing the gun in Gene's arms toward the hills behind the house. Then he disappeared around the back and shortly reappeared staggering under the weight of a bucket filled with liquid which he emptied over the couch. He moved back and threw a match onto the couch. A huge fireball some 40-50 feet high exploded into the snowy night. "Fire!" he yelled and Gene began shooting tracer bullets through the tops of the flames, arcs of light that went on into the hills. I was standing in the snow reflecting that the sight was quite beautiful when he came over to me, looked me right in the eyes and said, "You see, I am a Master of Tools." Just then he seemed to jump while pointing to the roof-- "Look," he shouted. I did. In the light of the fire it looked like there was a thousand pounds of pot growing in a bush out of the roof--the plastic record player cover had some kind of a magnifying effect and the heavily falling snow hadn't stuck to it. "Jesus," Hunter shouted. "We'll go to prison for life!" He immediately took it down and ran around to the back

of the house with it. "My God," he said calmly when he reappeared without it. "We're supposed to be Professionals. There's no room in the Big Game of Life for mistakes like that. We should be ashamed of ourselves."

One day in 1971, at Woody Creek, Hunter asked me to read a manuscript because he wanted my opinion, something he did not do often. It turned out to be "Fear & Loathing In Las Vegas," which he said he hoped would be published by *Rolling Stone*, perhaps in two separate issues. He pointed me up to an old abandoned cabin behind his place up on a hill that had a car seat in it. I sat there looking out from time to time over the beautiful valley while I read and made notes. It was a remarkable experience--I laughed out loud, I was amazed and impressed by the scenes and the dialogue, and I just loved the two main characters, Raoul Duke and Dr. Gonzo. The piece was long and intense and when I finally finished I was exhausted.

"Well," he said when I staggered down just before dusk.

"You hit the white light," I replied. This was our code for the very best writing, coming from a pun about the light at the end of Gatsby's dock.

"Why should I fuck with children," I said, "they're too small."

He laughed and shouted, "It's a fucking masterpiece!" We shook hands and beamed at each other. I had some minor points from my notes, most of which he rejected--for example, I thought he should take out the Back Door Beauty scene with the waitress in the diner in North Las Vegas. After a few beers we got into the future, as was our way, and I told him the piece might change his life completely, that he might become identified with Raoul Duke and seen as a drug-crazed version of Sebastian Dangerfield in "The Ginger Man." Maybe he would have trouble finding work, I speculated, or maybe his property would be overrun with fans. Maybe he would become notorious, maybe he would become famous, maybe he would become rich, maybe all those things would happen. He laughed and said, "I'm sick and tired of being broke. I deserve money and there's nothing wrong with fame. Whatever happens it's better than now and I'll be able to handle it. Those are problems I would be glad to have. Wouldn't you be glad to have them?" I didn't reply but I shook my head in the affirmative. After all, we were broke when we met, we were broke for many years after that, and he was broke longer than I was because scratching out a living as a writer was hard--and it was hard on Sandy and Juan. George Plimpton famously once wrote words to the

effect that while people think writing is easy, it isn't, and that every word is written in the writer's own blood.

In the mid 1980s I moved to Southwest Colorado where my two daughters, Kate and Claire, were born. My wife, Judy Campbell, and I would drive up to Aspen and visit Woody Creek, about a five plus hour drive. One time--when Kate was about four--we brought up two peacocks to replace some Hunter had lost and sat in that living room where so much had gone on, watching the new peacocks adjust in the big outside wire cage built right up against the picture window; a living room where I'd heard tapes of Hunter talking to Jimmy Carter, among others, and Hunter's latest musical discoveries, invariably excellent; a living room of blazing fires and blasting music. We would often sit in the kitchen where the dedicated Deborah Fuller worked to keep Hunter's life in order for some 22 years; unenviable and trying work for which she deserves at least a Bronze Star. One time my wife Judy and I were watching a movie in his kitchen while he worked the phone. After a while he came over. "What are you watching?" he asks.

"Something about fighting against Nazis in occupied France," Judy answered.

"You can pretty much tell it will be a good movie if there are Nazis in it," Hunter said.

Once, Hunter came down to speak at Fort Lewis College in Durango. He sat on the stage in the packed auditorium with a bottle of whiskey, a cattle prod, and Dana Ivers, a good friend of Judy's, and put on a dancing bear circus act while he spoke and answered questions. It seemed like half the audience loved him and half the audience didn't.

Through the years we talked on the telephone whenever the spirit moved us, his calls usually coming near or after midnight. In our last conversation on the Friday night before the Sunday he died I called him with a specific problem, a reason we often called each other. The problem I told him was that my new pit bull puppy was eating shit and I was calling on him in his capacity as the one guy I knew who had used the phrase "shit-eating dog" so many times over the years in describing people. I read to him from a book by a Hollywood dog trainer who said the solution was to remove the dog from exposure to feces and told him that, as he knew, I could not do this because when you stepped outside my house there was nothing but feces from the peacocks, geese, ducks, guinea hens, chickens,

dogs, cats, rabbits, pigs, and cows. He listened patiently and then cut to the quick with a pointed question--"Is your dog eating its own shit?" I answered that it hadn't reached that level of degeneracy yet. We laughed. He said he was involved in "talking to a man about heavy weapons," but would call me back later that night. He didn't.

[SOME RANDOM BITS AND PIECES OF HUNTER]

At Jann Wenner's house in San Francisco, Hunter asks George Plimpton his opinion of the bet he and John Walsh made on whether black or white running backs would score the most touchdowns in a Steelers game. A black-back and a white-back had each scored one touchdown and the third and final one was scored by Franco Harris who was half-black and half-white. George is decisive, "Franco is half-black and half-Italian," he says. "Italians used to be classified by the census as colored people, so on balance Franco is black."

At a Raiders-Steelers game in a pouring rainstorm on a dark, late-winter afternoon, a titanic struggle between two great teams in a jam-packed Oakland Coliseum, Earnie Holmes, Mean Joe Green, Dwight White, and L.C. Greenwood, the best defensive front four in the game, are dug in on defense. It is late in a close game, the ball on the Raiders 30-yard line or so, right in front of us. Bob Moore, the Raiders tight end, says he made eye contact from the field with me just about then. The field is wet and the players are smeared in mud. The lights barely illuminate the scene in the pouring rain. It is primordial.

Hunter jumps up and screams at the top of his lungs, "We need a sign!" Almost immediately a four-engine bomber plane looms out of the murk and screeches right over the top of the stadium traveling West to East, right over us. Shocked and horrified fans duck involuntarily and scream in fear all around us. On the next play, Ray Guy, the great Raiders punter, runs instead of kicks on fourth down on a bad snap and gets a first down. The place goes insane. People behind us start pounding Hunter on the back in appreciation. Later Hunter wonders if it would be right to refer to the Raiders cheerleaders in print as "The Suckettes."

Sitting in Perry's in San Francisco with several people including, George Sauer, a former Jets wide receiver, and David Meggyesy, a former St. Louis Cardinals linebacker. It is after a 49er's playoff game at Candlestick Park where Bing Crosby sang "White Christmas"

Photo: Judy Clancy

Counselor John G. Clancy

and Oscar Acosta had to be taken to the emergency room after swallowing a ball of opium. Hunter leans over to me and says quietly, "The owner who lives upstairs wants us to come up and party with him. I don't think this is wise. You do a good me or I do a good you, I can't remember which it is, so would you call him as me and tell him thanks but we just can't do it?" I laughed and did it. The owner thanked Hunter profusely for calling. I told Hunter and he grinned broadly, toasting me with his glass.

Talking on the telephone. Hunter says, "What if they find out the semen on Monica Lewinski's blue dress is from O.J."

Lying on the grass with beers in our hands looking up at the stars in the darkness of a Mendocino night midway between Ukiah and Mendocino just off the old Low Gap dirt road with no lights to interfere with the view. Hunter helped me load a trailer of furniture in San Francisco and unload it at this little building in the country that a compatriot at work was letting my wife and I use. The next day Hunter helped me dig a cesspool. Out of nowhere Hunter says: "Bottomland, oh, that bottomland. If only I had gotten some bottomland. If only my people had lived on bottomland. If only I could have bought some or inherited some. Bottomland, God Damn It, Bottomland. If I had some I wouldn't be in the fix I'm in. God, what happened to me?"

In 1998, Hunter invited us to the Manhattan movie premiere of "Fear & Loathing In Las Vegas." He also pressed me into service, as he did from time to time, to help him get a book deal done with Simon & Schuster and David Rosenthal for "Rum Diary" when he found himself without an agent. Both happened in the same intense few days in New York City. I didn't like some things I heard said to him during that trip--negative, even poisonous, statements about others that seemed to me designed to fuel the dark suspicions he harbored about people and their motives. I also didn't care for an increasingly totalitarian manner he displayed at times and told him he had become a Sycophanthrist. The word amused him. I didn't care for the political jockeying, and the downright stupidity of a lot of what was going on there. On the other hand I knew it was as big-as-it-gets so I made allowances--a star-spangled movie premiere of your own book (a movie that was about you with you being played by no less a great actor than Johnny Depp) and a big-money book deal, all at the same time. And yet, I still felt a little sad. Perhaps he had created a monster and, maybe, it was consuming him.

He had once asked me in San Francisco if I knew that I had recently taken to getting mean when I drank, unlike the way I had been in the past. The way he said it was as a comment, not a judgment or a question, and I did not respond. I asked him at the Carlyle Hotel in 1998 if he was enjoying himself because it didn't seem like he was. It was said as a comment, not a judgment or a question, and he did not respond. Of course now, in the wake of his death, I think that maybe I should have, or could have, said or done more; perhaps if I'd been more in touch or in tune, maybe if I had ... This was not our relationship, though. Not at all.

We would help each other do stuff and when we hooked up, we would argue and discuss politics, literature, and football and have some fun. We almost never discussed personal matters such as wives and children, only our dogs and our personal finances. I can think now of only one instance--when Hunter became a grandfather. We each lived our own lives and did completely different things. As Hunter so often famously said, "Buy the ticket. Take the ride." And yet, I still wonder ...

Over the years people have asked me what kind of guy Hunter was. Usually I would answer that he was a good and loyal long-time friend and a great writer. I didn't add that he was also a courageous fucker who never held back and always stood up and fought. I didn't add that he was whip-smart, would argue on a dime, and kick your ass if you stood in his way. I didn't add that he believed desperately in a better America and would fight for it as hard as he could. I didn't add that he would fight in the ring with his pen for justice as a champion for people like Lisl Auman and organize and march for them. I didn't add that he was fiercely intense and could cut to the heart of a problem with blunt and pointed questions. And I didn't add that I would fight for him and alongside him at any time and at any place. I add those things now--he was all those things and more.

Yes, he did drugs and drank hard, but most of the time he was deadly serious when he worked. And he worked like hell. Hunter wrote by writing and he was always writing something--articles, columns, books, letters, faxes--planning what he would write or doing legwork or scheming for an assignment. The image or caricature of Hunter as Raoul Duke, the image from the Doonesbury panels, and his own reinforcement of this image by his public circus act should

not obscure the truth--Hunter wrote like he was using a jackhammer and his words and descriptions struck his targets and his enemies hard and sank in deep.

He was a savage and relentless observer and a formidable foe. And his energy and endurance were way beyond normal human capabilities. The Hunter Stockton Thompson I knew was no cartoon character--he was a force of nature.

Much has been made of the supposed declining quality of Hunter's writing in his last years. He once told me in the 1990s that he was writing one piece to see "just how much I can get away with." Even if the decline were true, why should a journalist and writer be expected to stay at the top of their game? So what if they decide to hang it up and coast? We know that great athletes have to hang it up when their skills diminish through aging, but we don't remember them for what they can't do then; we remember them for what they did do in their prime.

My memories of Hunter are the things he accomplished and the person he was in his prime. That he might have chosen to slack off or goof off, or capitulate to his fame is simply not for me to criticize or judge. Nor does it diminish what he achieved in his prime anymore than the later life of a Joe DiMaggio or a Jim Brown. I'll always see that tall, rangy figure leaning forward carrying the ball, spitting, cursing, and shouting with his eyes fiercely glaring at the opposing players. To me he'll always be a Jimmy Taylor and a Pete Banaszak churning for that last yard with the full intensity of his mind and body. Hunter was a great player--an All American--and I was privileged to be his teammate.

When the phone rings late at night, my first groggy thought will still be that it's that bastard Hunter and then, against my will, a grin will form in the anticipation of talking to him as I struggle to reach the phone. In the shock of his abrupt departure, I miss him greatly. And I know, too, that I will miss him for the rest of my days. All of us should be so lucky. AVE ATQUE VALE.

Note: This piece is dedicated to Warren Hinckle who made me write it.

The Origin Of Gonzo

BILL CARDOSO

Running through the hopheaded hemp fields, gruntled full back in full-body leather apron, in the homestretch; the manufactory, where the apron is scraped of resin, looming, camouflaged as a pear shed, at the gravel crossroads of South Finley, happy home of the "hand-groomed" Hav-a-Hashey Bar, when the cell phone noised, and slowed to a chug.

It was Hinckle.

"Write," he said, "about gonzo."

Okay. I was covering Richard Nixon for the *Boston Globe* during the 1968 campaign and was about to get back on the press bus somewhere in New Hampshire when the ABC TV crew roped me for an evening news sound bite. When I finally boarded the bus all the seats but one, about two thirds of the way back, were gone. There was a big raw-boned guy in the other seat. He looked unlike the rest of the pack and I quick figured him for a country editor from somewhere up there in the north country, along for the day. There were some weird people practicing journalism in those mountains during the Sixties. I made my way down the aisle and pointed to that empty seat. "NO, uh take it," the big fella said. I nodded, sat, and introduced myself.

"Hunter Thompson," he said. "*Pageant Magazine.*"

Pageant, a *Reader's Digest*-size monthly, was in its final days but tried to stay a player. Something about the name rang a bell and I asked, "You the guy who wrote the Hells Angels book?" He proved to be a very graciously-distracted hillbilly gent and a connoisseur of America obscura. We became friends and began correspondence. He

sent me some of his poetry from a magazine called *Spider* and some earlier pieces he did for the *National Observer* and I sent him some of my *Globe* pieces. He lived at Owl Farm in Woody Creek, Colorado, and I lived at The School House in Hopkinton, New Hampshire, which appealed to his imagination.

After, I was promoted to editor of the *Globe Sunday Magazine* and I hired Hunter to cover the Nixon inauguration. The piece he filed was unorthodox, to say the least--a sort of gonzo in embryo-- and though the *Globe* in those days was truly a writer's paper, it cantankered the old guard and cost me some points among the hierarchs, which I later regained by assigning ukelele-strumming falsettoed Tiny Tim, a hockey nut, to handicap the Stanley Cup. That, they loved. A wild man writing sane was fine; a sane man writing wild was adios.

Eventually, Hunter came east again to profile Jean-Claude Killy, the legendary Olympic downhill racer, for *Playboy* and we rendezvoused. He didn't care for weed in those days and I did, but he liked to drink, whereas I was cautious around the ignorant oil. Back then, old Boston vipers didn't goof their high--that came later when you moved to California. Hunter said he'd been booted the day before from a Chicago convention because he sat in Killy's chair, at Killy's booth, and impersonated the skier, yodeling pidgin French and signing autographs. Now, here we were again in the cold wild of northern New Hampshire tracking Killy at Waterville Valley. I couldn't believe Thompson's stamina and physical constitution--remember, Hunter was a pretty big guy.

Out of nowhere, Hunter started attacking his hotel room, just tearing it apart. It was a mess, demolished by brutish, unacceptable behavior. "I'm outta here," I said. "The cops are gonna be here any minute. And I'm not gonna compromise the *Globe* by being here when they come for you." The guy was a real scenery chewer. I doubted if I wanted the friendship of a violent menacing nut case.

But then, a few months later, he turned the world of journalism, as we knew it, inside out when he took an assignment from Warren Hinckle at *Scanlan's* magazine, the short-lived but authentic incubator for the birth of gonzo, and teamed with bewildered British illustrator Ralph Steadman on a piece called "The Kentucky Derby Is Decadent and Depraved." I was in awe at this pioneering accomplishment and said so in a note, telling him, "I don't know what the fuck you're doing, but you've changed everything. It's totally gonzo."

Hunter ran with it. That's how the word was coined.

Marty Nolan, my old *Globe* colleague and a friend of Hunter, believes the word "gonzo" is strictly Boston Irish patois, voiced mostly in Southie and Dorchester. Well, that's his story. I was never much on either Southie or Dot, for my mother forbade me from going there. "The Irish, you know," she confided. But I continue to maintain the word is of French Canadian origin, a corruption of gonzeau, which is itself a corruption of the old Dominican Republic dandy insider-insider baseball phrase sendero luminoso, roughly meaning, "Signify the batsman electric to take two, then hit to right, sending the spheroid beyond your grandmother's paisley shawl," when murmured by the manager in the dugout to the third base coach. That's my claim, see, and I'm sticking to it.

But what the hell do I know? For all I care it might've been called "goofo" or "goofeau," should one prefer, Journalism, for a rose is a rose ...

I quit the *Globe* when they took my magazine away after two years. They asked me what I wanted to do next, and when I said Washington, they said no. So I wound up in Las Palmas in the Canary Islands, running what was probably the only jazz club in the middle of the Atlantic Ocean, and that's where Hunter mailed me tear sheets from *Rolling Stone* of the instant classic, "Fear and Loathing in Las Vegas," another most wonderful, thigh-slapping breakthrough, deeper, darker, and wider than all that went before. "If I can write like this and get away with it," he told *Playboy*, "why should I keep trying to write like the *New York Times*?"

Indeed. Hunter understood as he raised the bar that writing was an all or nothing game. He also believed a piece is never finished. "Make them come and rip it out of your hands," he would say.

When I tired of the Canaries, I wrote to Hunter, asking if he knew of any heems state-side. He suggested I contact Bob Sherrill from *Esquire* and Karl Fleming from *Newsweek*, who were starting a weekly in Los Angeles. My wife and I paid a visit to Woody Creek on our way west. On leaving, Hunter warned me I was making a mistake moving to L.A.

"Why?" I asked.

"Because," he said, "your marriage will break up. That's what happens there."

When he came to L.A., we got together. We watched the Super Bowl from my West Hollywood home, which he called a Day of the Locust bungalow, though we had press passes for the Coliseum. One night as we passed the Angel Moroni Mormon Temple (which newcomers to L.A. are sometimes told is Al Jolson's tomb), way out on Santa Monica Boulevard, he started shrieking. "Go back! Go back! Turn Around! Make a U-turn! Hurry!"

"Why?"

"We've got to see if that old woman is still alive!"

"What woman?"

"The Mexican washerwoman you just hit at 50 miles an hour in the crosswalk in front of the Angel Moroni!"

I had heard no thump. No old woman was sticking through my windshield. Yet, he was so insistent that I knit my brows and insta-brooded myself into half believing him and turned back at the next corner just to be sure. Hunter loved to tell that one, saying it just so, laying shame, cake-walking the fine filament between goof and real, creating room for doubt, while casting me one of those sideways, tilted, sly, chuzzlewit grins. He loved a good put-on and so did I and it was always a special part of our social routine.

When my marraige broke up in L.A., Hunter and his wife Sandy generously invited me to Colorado to cool out. He put me in the cellar at Owl Farm, in a tiny room, a penitent's cell. I had to go through a trap door and down a ladder. Hunter would lower a bottle of scotch on a rope, then bolt the trap door, locking me down there until he left the house. Then Sandy would unbolt the trap door and I would climb the ladder to daylight and have a taste or two of scotch with her until it was time to go into Aspen and meet Hunter at the Hotel Jerome bar. That penitent's cell was a great way to get rid of a broken-hearted nuisance guest.

Hunter and I crossed paths in many other places over the years. Montreal. New York. Newport Beach. Sausalito. Las Vegas.

And, of course, Kinshasa, the old Leopoldville in Zaire, the old Belgian Congo for the George Foreman-Muhammad Ali fight.

None of it exists now but that's voodoo for you.

All I remember for sure is that my room at the Hotel Memling in downtown Kin, was 263 and my telephone number was 601 and that I had been there for thirty days and thirty nights as the guest of president Joe Mobuto, a man I never met.

Bill Cardoso with his love, Mary Miles Ryan.

Late one night while I was asleep someone fist-pounded my door. It was Hunter, flying high. Delivering him was a shy middle-age African in a business suit who said he had been on his way home when he came upon this mundele at the side of the road, flagging him, lost and driving deep into the bush toward the space where the Ndokes dwell. He said it was difficult getting the mundele to understand that he was in fact going away from Kinshasa, not toward it. He said he was required as a gentleman of the host county to guide the mundele out of the bush and back to the city. He declined a scotch, bowed humbly, and said good night.

Trying to be helpful, I told Hunter that I had learned a lot of Lingala, the native tongue, during my thirty days and thirty nights as a guest of old "Doc Mobutu," and that he needed to cut through the ice, tear away the fabric of formality, because time was of the essence and he was so late an arrival, the fight now being only two days away, and that I could teach him the ropes. I told him he should always address the older native population--especially the gray-haired ones, men or women--as "mundele," a term of respect meaning "venerable one." Call them that and they're putty in your hands, I confidently said.

"Mundele, huh?"

Yeah, I said, and spelled the word for him. Of course, if you want to lay it on, I told him, you can say, "M'bele mundele," which means "very nice venerable one." But don't try to remember too much for now, I said. Just say "mundele" and doors will open. You'll see. He said later that when he tried out "mundele" the next day he saw jaws drop in disbelief.

That's because you honored them, I said.

"Bullshit," he replied. "'Mundele' means white man."

Hunter understood that anything is potential story material and he worked it into the title of the piece he would, unfortunately, never write.

On the eve of the fight, Hunter, Ralph Steadman, and I were in the cocktail lounge of the Intercontinental, and I was trying to educate them about voodoo and Ndokes. How else, I asked, could Foreman get his eyebrow splashed while sparring in headgear two days before defending his title against Muhammad Ali, causing a month-long delay? And why was Foreman sparring two days before a bout? I sensed they weren't getting my drift, so I slammed my scotch tumbler on the tabletop for emphasis. The glass shattered, spraying

Hunter and Ralph with shards and scotch. Amazed, Steadman pulled out a Polaroid camera and snapped a picture of me. Then he whipped out a sketch pad and drew manically.

I remember begging Hunter to get out of the Intercontinental pool and get on the last press bus to the stadium or he'd miss the fight. But he wouldn't and he missed the fight.

Later, while packing to leave, Hunter found Steadman's Polaroid and tossed it in a duffel bag. In London, he called Jann Wenner at *Rolling Stone* and told him about the Polaroid, claiming I'd been a victim of voodoo by Ndoke. "You won't even recognize him from this picture!" he told me he said. "Make it the cover! We'll call it, 'God's Pity on the Poor Mundele Man.' I'm sending it immediately." Wenner dispatched David Felton, with whom I shared a flat in San Francisco's Mission District, to the airport. Felton picked up the Polaroid, looked at it, shook his head, and got back in his cab. As he handed the envelope to an expectant publisher, he said, "It's just a picture of Cardoso." Influenced by Felton, Wenner figured Hunter had gone gogo in the Macoco. Hunter wouldn't write. And I blew my chance to be on the cover of *Rolling Stone*. Ah, me.

And that is a little bit about the gonzo way and how Hunter Stockton Thompson found it. May he rest in peace.

Bill Cardoso: The Godfather Of Gonzo

DENNIS P. EICHHORN

WHAT is GONZO?
BY DENNIS P. EICHHORN
I MET BILL CARDOSO WHEN I LIVED IN SAN FRANCISCO.
MY FRIEND TIM CAHILL THOUGHT HIGHLY OF HIM.
'S BAR & GRILL
YOU'RE REALLY GOING TO LIKE THIS GUY, DENNY...
OPEN
THEY CALL HIM THE GODFATHER OF GONZO.
BILL AND I HIT IT OFF...HE WAS A FREELANCE WRITER OF GREAT REPUTE.
I THINK I'LL USE YOU AS A ROLE MODEL
FEEL FREE TO FALL BY MY CRIB ANYTIME!
AT THE TIME, BILL WAS ROOMING WITH DAVID FELTON IN THE MISSION DISTRICT...
CARE FOR A BALLOON OF NITROUS OXIDE?
DON'T MIND IF I DO...
BEACH BOYS
PARTY BALLOONS
NO2
JOHN MCLAUG
BESSIE SMITH
WHY DO THEY CALL YOU THE GODFATHER OF GONZO?
HAHAHA
HAHA WUUOOOOO
SWOOOOOO
I COINED THE WORD IN 1969...
WHHOOOSSSSSS
HEEEHAA
HA HAHA
HUHHH
...HUNTER THOMPSON HAD WRITTEN A GREAT PIECE ABOUT THE KENTUCKY DERBY...
MICHAEL DOUGAN

* YEARS LATER, BILL CLAIMED THAT "GONZO" COMES FROM THE FRENCH-CANADIAN "GONZEAU," WHICH MEANS "SHINING PATH."

TELL THE STORY AND GET OUT! DON'T BE AFRAID TO RE-WRITE.... THE STORIES WILL WRITE THEMSELVES AS LONG AS YOU STAY HONEST AND DON'T SELL OUT!
YES!
WRITE WHAT YOU MEAN TO SAY, AND NO COMPROMISES!
OF COURSE, IDEALLY YOU'RE ON AN EXPENSE ACCOUNT...

BILL HELPED ME AS A WRITER BY SENDING ME OUT TO DO INTERVIEWS FOR HIM.
HOW DO YOU LIKE BEING A LEGMAN?
I'VE ALWAYS BEEN MORE OF A BREAST MAN...

I MOVED NORTH TO SEATTLE AND EASED INTO JOURNALISM. YEARS WENT BY... I NEVER FORGOT THE LESSONS BILL TAUGHT ME...
WRITE IT DOWN... NOUNS AND ADVERBS... DON'T BE AFRAID...

I WAS ALWAYS ON THE LOOKOUT FOR A GOOD STORY... THEN ONE DAY...
...HUNTER S. THOMPSON ABBIE HOFFMAN AND TIM LEARY TO APPEAR AT UNIVERSITY OF WASHINGTON
SEATTLE TIMES

A FEW DAYS LATER
BILL? LISTEN, I WANT TO INTERVIEW HUNTER THOMPSON. CAN YOU HELP ME SET IT UP?
SURE...
BY THE WAY... HOW'S THE SMOKE SITUATION UP THERE?
"FROM THE DESK OF HUNTER S. THOMPSON TO: DENNIS P. EICHHORN, SEATTLE... RE: INTERVIEW... O.K. H.S.T.

ABBIE HOFFMAN HADN'T CHANGED MUCH.

TIM LEARY MADE A POOR IMPRESSION

HORAAAAAAAY
HAAAAHAAAAAAAA

ANY QUESTIONS?
YES?

UHM, DR. THOMPSON? JUST WHAT IS "GONZO"?

GONZO... HMMMM... CARDOSO... HMMM MMM... HELL

ASK EICHHORN!
WHERE'S EICHHORN?

YOU CAN ASK DENNIS P. EICHHORN WHAT GONZO IS AFTER THE SHOW. ... NEXT QUESTION?

Waiting For Copy

ROGER BLACK

When I first met Hunter, he was sitting in the dim living room of Susan and Bill Cardoso's apartment in West Hollywood in 1972. It was one of those middle houses built between an original bungalow and its guest house. There wasn't much yard left for the two emaciated Borzois who paced restlessly, like Cardoso himself, the coiner of the term "gonzo." The word came from his Cambridge, Massachusetts, "Gee" neighborhood. "It's gone, it's gonzo," he would say.

It smelled funny in that place, and Cardoso, a lanky hipster of the old school, was herding flies out through the sliding glass door. This is a good trick, which I still use. You get in one corner of the room and start windmilling your arms and wiggling your fingers, moving the flies toward an open window. It helps if you have Cardoso's long arms and lugubrious countenance with just a touch of sparkle in the eyes. He could scoop out a dozen flies in one pass.

Hunter sat on the couch, sullen, not saying much, waiting for drugs to arrive.

Later I remember him talking about Marxism, in that dry, rapid-fire voice, which resonated inside his skull, Hunter saying that the rhetoric would be around a lot longer than the movement. The dialectic of materialism. He was right, of course. The Berlin Wall came down two decades later, but the argument about class is still not settled.

Designer Roger Black

Hunter was right about many things. He had a native sense of politics, of the way people work with each other, personally and in society. He overlaid that with a terrifying talent for observation. His analyses was sprayed with cultural detail, but so acutely funny you missed the point.

The second part of "Fear and Loathing in Las Vegas" was the apex of this wild humor. I will never forget the impact it had when the first half appeared in an issue of *Rolling Stone* in November of 1971. It was the fourth anniversary issue of the magazine, still a quarter-folded tabloid, and the piece was accompanied by those Steadman drawings with the bats and the floating circles. That was the funniest thing that had ever been printed.

It seemed to sum up the exact state of mind the "counter culture" had arrived at, when, with Nixon and Vietnam, we realized that the sweet "60s" dream was an illusion. I read it through twice, and started thinking about the two weeks before Part Two would arrive.

I was in Houston, and I called the biggest newsstand in town, Big City News, and asked when they got their *Rolling Stone*. They said next Thursday morning. That beat the mail by five days. I asked what time?

They said the truck usually gets here early around 7am ...

At 6:45am that Thursday I drove my 1967 white Plymouth Fury (perfect camouflage in Houston in those days) into the parking lot of Big City News. And there, already waiting in a line by the door, were twenty other freaks. Most of them probably hadn't gotten to bed yet. Maybe Dickens had them lining up like that for an installment, but I had never seen anything like it before, or since.

It was that moment that I decided I wanted to work for *Rolling Stone*, and the next spring, I went to Los Angeles to get my first art director job at *LA Magazine*, where Cardoso was an editor. When I came to San Francisco to work for *Rolling Stone*, Hunter had already become a cultural hero, and his infrequent visits to the office were treated like a papal tour.

Stardom probably didn't hurt Hunter much, he was too honest. But the success did nothing to sate his appetite for drugs and alcohol. And by the mid-70s he had tipped over into the capricious, angry, wildcat state of mind he is remembered for. Copy became increasingly hard to get out of him.

I learned that he could be a treacherous critic of layouts, and would demand that Jann Wenner change them before he would finish a piece. Early on, I would give his stories to another designer so I didn't get trapped into waiting up all night complying with his demands, as the mojos, which we called the early version of faxes, slowly trickled in.

When the magazine moved to New York, Hunter enjoyed the visits more, staying in a big Central Park suite at the Park Lane on Jann's expense account. Harriet Frier, an early *Rolling Stone* editor, tells the Marx Brothers-like story of meeting Hunter at the hotel restaurant for lunch, Hunter's breakfast. She ordered a bloody mary, and Hunter nodded assent. The waiter said, "Two bloody marys?" And Hunter said, "Okay, two for me and one for her."

That was 1976 and Hunter was covering the presidential campaign. He didn't think much of Jimmy Carter, but Jann put him on the cover anyway and was furious that Hunter wouldn't, or couldn't, turn out an accompanying panegyric.

He put Hunter in an office near his on the 23rd floor, to keep an eye on him, and Hunter kept the place in an uproar. (One time I remember carrying a tray of sandwiches back to the art department so people wouldn't leave for lunch, and Hunter just grabbed the whole tray, went back in his office, and closed the door.)

Jann then moved him up to the business department's floor, but still no copy was delivered. I went up to find out what was going on, since everyone else was terrified of him, and he made me sit and talk about the piece. Then he reached down into a bag and produced a quart Ziploc filled with cocaine. With surprising speed, he pulled out a hunting knife and dug it into the bag. He covered the tip with coke and lunged in the general direction of my nose.

"Want some?" he asked, with that characteristically intense gleam in his eye. I could only think, "Chinatown."

Later, at Terry McDonnell's *Smart* magazine, I would be on the receiving end, waiting for copy. Faster fax machines had replaced the "mojo" Xerox Telecopier, but the trickle was drying up.

Once, I was in Aspen for the Design Conference, with Janet Waegel, the art director of *Smart*. Terry McDonell called up and asked if we would go over and see if we could get a story out of Hunter. No one answered at his house. So I called over to the Woody Creek Tavern, and they admitted he was there. I refused to go out there and beg for copy. Janet, however, who was happy to go down that road, went to the Tavern, and then followed him home. She had to be the hundredth woman who left that house screaming, running out the back door, just before a toaster or something crashed on the wall next to her head.

The last time I heard of someone making the effort to get copy out of him was by the elegant Ian Ballantine. He took me to lunch in early 1995 at the Knickerbocker Club and we ended up talking about Hunter: how great he was, how impossible he had become. Ballantine had gone back to the company he founded, Bantam Books, as a consultant to the editors. They had paid a big advance to get Hunter's coverage of the 1992 election, but so far had received not a single page.

Ballantine asked the young editor what he proposed to do, and the editor said he didn't know, maybe he'd go to Aspen and supply Hunter with a lot of drugs.

"That's the last thing you should do," said Ballantine. Instead, he flew to Aspen and checked into the Jerome Hotel. "The next morning I put on my best suit, and drove out to Woody Creek. Hunter's girlfriend came to the door, and was suitably impressed with the well-dressed gentleman, and let him in and got Hunter."

"Mr. Thompson," Ballantine said. "I am prepared to make you an offer."

Hunter looked at him intently. "For each page of manuscript you produce, I am willing to pay you an additional advance of $100 in cash." He took out his wallet and fanned out a few bills.

Hunter began to tear up the house looking for stray pages. He came up with about forty scraps, old faxes, notes, and some real writing, and Ballantine paid out the $4,000. Two weeks later he left Aspen with a raggedy manuscript, but he had the book, which they called, "Better than Sex."

Res Ipsa Loquitur

JERRY BROWN

Hunter S. Thompson took muckraking to the outer edge in the early 1970s, when he was among the first to detect the rancid odor of White House corruption. His creeds against the sitting president were overwrought and tinged with paranoia, but Nixon's resignation would vindicate his torrid animadversions. As California's secretary of state at the time, I had to yank the notary public commission of Nixon's personal lawyer. It seems he notarized a backdated deed of Nixon's papers so that the president could qualify for a charitable deduction--illegally. These were unusual times. Thompson's personal life was not as grounded as his work, but Dr. Gonzo often observed, via Dr. Johnson: "He who makes a beast of himself gets rid of the pain of being a man." In the end it seems, the pain caught up with him out at Owl Farm. Like a Chekhov story, the firearms he favored during a turbulent life figured in the manner of his untimely exit.

In recent years, Thompson has penned a column on politics and sports for ESPN's website. The current political scene horrified him--as did the Oakland Raiders--and he pined for the company of his late fellow football addict, Richard Nixon.

"Big darkness come soon," he predicted in a column last year.

Thompson's gone and so is much of the 1960s. He had the roughest of edges but such raw journalism--in some unimagined form--might be just the antidote to mendacious media interface.

Ad astra per aspera, or as Hunter would end his pieces, *Res ipsa loquitur.*

Janis Joplin Knew What She Was Doing, Too

BEN FONG-TORRES

I don't remember what day or for that matter, what year it was. All I know is that it was about 9:00 in the morning--that's because no one had shown up for work yet at the offices of *Rolling Stone* magazine. Except for this thumping bass drum beat blasting out of the large corner office usually occupied by the editor. But since the editor usually went to sleep around 9am, it had to be someone else.

I tossed my stuff into my office and made my approach. But as soon as I saw the overstuffed, four-foot-long canvas bag outside the door, with an IBM Selectric typewriter sticking out of it, I knew that the doctor was in. I walked into the room and yelled good morning at Hunter S. Thompson. The Doctor (of Divinity, he says) turned from the editor's typewriter; he looked startled at the sight of another human being--he'd apparently been by himself for quite a few hours--but recovered quickly and yelled back, "Got any good rock and roll records?" He waved his head at the four overhead speakers, as if dismissing jazz-rock fusion as noise. "Got any Stones? Dead? Anything! I need volume!" I put on the Stones, "Exiles on Main Street" for him and made my escape. Back in my own room, I had some trouble rapping out my own story, what with the distant yet immediate accompaniment of Bill Wyman's bass and Charlie Watts' drums. But in the other room, a miracle was unfolding: Hunter Thompson was meeting

a deadline, and all was well. When I go to high school press conventions or college journalism classes, the first question in the Q & A sessions afterward is, invariably, "What is Hunter Thompson really like?"

I remember responding, once, "Don't take anything Hunter says seriously. In fact, don't take anything Hunter takes." Which got the cheap laugh it deserved, but was hardly to the point. Hunter simply can't be dismissed with a one-liner. I mean, we're talking about:

Hunter, who rode with the Hells Angels, got stomped by them and lived to write about it.

Hunter, who stumbled into what has become known--and, in college circles, quite revered--as "Gonzo Journalism" by fouling up while on a story; then, reporting on his experiences, he'd give vent to all his adrenalized emotions and, in the process, tell more about the event than any objective facts or highly placed sources ever could. He titled a song that he wrote recently with Warren Zevon "You're a Whole Different Person When You're Scared," and he doesn't feel that he knows you properly until he knows that person.

Hunter, the demented, acid-eating, speedfreak journalist who went to Las Vegas with his attorney to look for "the American Dream." On assignment, of course.

Hunter, who scored a scoop on the campaign trail by interviewing George McGovern while the two stood at adjacent urinals.

Hunter, the comic strip hero in Doonesbury (he's called "Duke," as in "Raoul Duke," Thompson's alter ego) who's gone Hollywood.

Some straight bio material: Born in Louisville, Kentucky; sportswriter in Florida; worked as South American correspondent for The *National Observer*; wrote "Hell's Angels: A Strange and Terrible Saga," in 1966; moved to Colorado and ran for sheriff in Aspen as part of a movement called "The Aspen Freak Power Uprising;" wrote for *Rolling Stone*, also published in *Playboy*, *Esquire*, *The Nation*, *Scanlan's*, and *New York Times Magazine*.

Which still doesn't answer the question, "What is Hunter Thompson really like?" Which, I figure, is a polite way of saying, "Is he really as screwed up as he seems to be?"

The answer is yes and no. Yes, he can be deranged, as indicated by the gibberish that makes up much of what he writes. Even at his most berserk in print, as Tom Wolfe explained in his anthology, "The New Journalism"--"That approach seldom grates in Thompson's hands, probably because Thompson, for all his surface ferocity, usually casts

himself as a frantic loser, inept and half-psychotic, somewhat after the manner of Celine."

So, when he staggers on stage at one of his college lectures and mumbles his way through some alcoholic parody of a Hunter Thompson talk, he knows just what he's doing, much the way a Southern Comfort-swigging Janis Joplin knew just what she was doing. He may abuse himself, but he doesn't mean to hurt anyone else. He breaks rules, but then, more rules ought to be tested. And in searching for the American Dream, he paints screeching-ugly nightmare portraits of its presidents, its powers, its proles.

Yet in the end, he, too, is an American dreamer, as in the last sentence of "Fear and Loathing in Las Vegas," set in an airport somewhere in the Rocky Mountains: "I took another big hit off the amyl, and by the time I got to the bar my heart was full of joy. I felt like a monster reincarnation of Horatio Alger ... a Man on the Move, and just sick enough to be totally confident."

Blowing Deadlines With Hunter

PAUL KRASSNER

High Times **founder Tom Forcade and gonzo journalist Hunter** Thompson were both dedicated dopers and enthusiastic adventurers. Forcade phoned me on behalf of Thompson to invite me on board a rented yacht from which he wanted to cover the America's Cup yacht race in Rhode Island.

I had to turn down the invitation because I was in the middle of preparing an issue of *The Realist*. Forcade called again, and said, "Hunter is really pissed.' I said: "Well, tell him just because he doesn't believe in deadlines, I still do."

I first met Hunter in 1965--in Berkeley at a Vietnam Day Teach-In for which I emceed. When his first book, "Hell's Angels," was published in 1967, I assigned him to write a behind-the-scenes article about his promotional tour. He was having financial problems, so I paid him $200 in advance. Later, I had to extend his deadline, and I offered to send him some LSD if it would help.

"Good," he wrote back. "I've blown every deadline I've had for the past two months. All at once, I got evicted, my wife went into a lingering two-month miscarriage, and my lawyer came out from San Francisco and flipped out so badly that two sheriff's deputies took him one Saturday night 200 miles across mountains to the state loony bin ... As for acid, thanks, but I'm suddenly OK."

Paul Krassner

Soon after, another letter arrived, asking, "Can I get any leeway on the July first delivery date? ... In the meantime, you can send me some acid to help me level out. And I'll send you a dozen just-born marijuana weeds. You can plant them in Central Park."

As it turned out, he bungled his book tour by appearing as either a blathering drunk or an insane mumbler. He walked off his first TV show when the interviewer said, "Tell me, Hunter, what do you think of the Hells Angels?" Who could blame him? But at least he was honorable with me.

In October, he wrote, "There's no avoiding the fact that I blew this one completely. I'm sending you $200 of the $1,900 I now show as book-profit on the hardcover edition ... With [Lyndon] Johnson as president, I feel on the verge of a serious freakout but if I ever get over that hump I'll write a good article for you. In the meantime, we're at least even on the money. This check is good. I've sworn off money articles a/o December, so maybe I'll level it out then. If not, I might run for the Senate or send off for a Carcano [the rifle ostensibly used to kill President Kennedy]."

Instead, thirty-eight years later, Hunter pointed a handgun at himself.

When Lee Quarnstrom was executive editor at *Hustler*, he wanted to interview Thompson. "Hunter wanted $5,000 for the interview," he told me. He said, "Get Larry Flynt to kick in some of his money." I said, "Well, we don't pay for Q & As." So he called me back and he said, "OK, I'll do the interview for nothing, if Hustler will fly us both to Bora Bora and you can conduct the interview on a veranda as we sip mai-tais and watch the sun set into the Pacific."

Art Kunkin, publisher of the *L.A. Free Press*, told me, "Hunter wanted me to put him up at the Chateau Marmont, and I wouldn't do it, and he threatened to kill me. He was pissed at me for not having the kind of budget to do that."

In 1970, I assigned three stoners who were running for sheriff --Stew Albert in Berkeley; George Kimball in Lawrence, Kansas; and Hunter Thompson in Aspen, Colorado--to write about their experiences in *The Realist*. Albert and Kimball came through, but nothing from Thompson. I sent him a follow-up note, and he finally replied:

"Yeah, your letter got thru & found me in the middle of writing almost exactly the piece you asked for--but I've already agreed to give it to *Rolling Stone*. Jann asked about a month ago ... "

As a writer, I could understand. As an editor, I was frustrated. Like other editors, though, I was willing to tolerate Hunter's irresponsibility in the hope of presenting his talent.

Several years ago, at a memorial for Allen Ginsberg, Hunter was supposed to make an appearance but he didn't show up; Johnny Depp, who played him in the movie version of "Fear and Loathing in Las Vegas," did. I told the audience I was disappointed because I was hoping to present Depp, Thompson, and Bill Murray (who played him in "Where the Buffalo Roam") all together, and then I would say, "Will the real Hunter Thompson please fall down."

Fear & Loathing

TIMOTHY FERRIS

Hunter's writing is, first of all, extremely funny, he ranks among the finest American humorists of all time.

It is also, like all real humor, essentially serious. At its center resides a howling vortex of outrage and pain, which Hunter has managed to transmute into works of lasting value. These works have the additional virtues of being factually reliable, so long as he intends them to be.

Hunter is a meticulous reporter who wasn't joking when he told an audience at The Strand in Redondo Beach, "I am the most accurate journalist you'll ever read." Over the thirty years that we've been friends he has corrected my grammar and word usage more often, and more accurately, than I have corrected his--and not just because he is customarily armed with, say, the .454 Magnum pistol with which he shot up one of his many IBM Selectric typewriters.

("That gun really is too much, unless you want to destroy a Buick at two hundred yards," he recalled, musing over the Selectric shooting episode. "The bullet went through the typewriter at such a speed that it just pierced it, like a ray of some kind. You could hardly see where it hit. So I went and got a 12-gauge Magnum shotgun and some .00 buckshot. That produced a very different shot pattern.")

He is capable of sea-anchoring an otherwise sheets-to-the-wind drinking fiesta with studious ponderings about matters ranging from whether to credit a rumor at the 1972 Democratic National Convention that George McGovern was about to offer the second spot

on his ticket to United Auto Workers President Leonard Woodcock (Hunter decided that he didn't trust it, and, as usual, was proved right) to browsing thesaurus entries for the word "force." ("They include violence, vehemence, might, rigor, impetuosity, severity, fierceness, ferocity, outrage, eruption, convulsion, violent passion ... It's scary, kind of a word picture of me.")

But then with little more that a barely perceptible signal, his words slip anchor and venture into a kind of hyperspace, where the facts shrink to a pinpoint like a cosmonaut's view of the receding Earth, and the goal shifts from factual literalness to a quest for deeper truth. Few readers can infallibly detect these points of departure, so many have raised the recurring question: How much of Hunter's accounts of his own escapades--the fast cars, furious motorcycles, big-bore firearms and powerful explosives, the beautiful women and mind-warping drugs, the frightening misadventures and reckless flirtations with imminent disaster that have made "fear and loathing" part of the language--are exaggerated? Not nearly enough for comfort. Hunter was a lifelong student of fear--and a teacher of it, too.

He titled a song that he wrote recently with Warren Zevon "You're a Whole Different Person When You're Scared," and he doesn't feel that he knows you properly until he knows that person. On various occasions he has lunged at me with an evil-looking horse syringe; brandished loaded shotguns, stun guns, and cans of Mace; and taken me on high-speed rides to remote murder sites in the dead of night--and I doubt that he found my reaction to such travails particularly interesting, since I always calmly trusted him with my life. Those whom such treatment transforms into someone more apt to arouse Hunter's infrared sensors of viperous curiosity are in for an interesting evening.

At the same time, this howling violence freak, habitually loaded with potent intoxicants and a skull full of Beethoven-grade egomania, is studious and thoughtful, courtly and caring, curiously peace-loving in his way, and unwaveringly generous. When he and I were young and broke, and I was fired from the last job I've ever held, the first thing he did was offer to send me four hundred dollars--which, although he didn't know I knew it, was all the money he had left in the bank at the time. His fundamental decency helps explain how he has managed to survive his many excesses, as does the fact that he's blessed with extraordinary reflexes. I once saw him accidentally knock a drink off a table with the back of his hand while

reaching for a ringing phone and then catch it, unspilled, with the same hand on the way down.

When we onlookers expressed astonishment at this feat, he said, "Yes, well, when we're applauding my aptitude at making rescues, we should keep in mind who causes most of the accidents in the first place."

I've never met anyone who really knew Hunter who didn't love him.

How The Doctor Rated The Game

WILLIAM RANDOLPH HEARST III

For a man who seemed to live in such a slapdash manner Hunter could be a careful writer. Most of his faxes were layered with edits and re-writes and often dotted with drawings of various import--all looking like they had been carved into the paper with a felt tip pen.

He once told me he thought Gatsby was a perfect novel and that as a student he had diagrammed its structure in entirety. Like many of Hunter's stories the most plausible were often fabricated and the most Outlandish simply fact. But there is no doubt he was widely read, with a taste, at least in our conversations, that favored the classics. His language was rich, varied, and laced with dark hilarious irony.

He was one of the most un-Buddhist shamans you will ever meet.

He could not remain still--physically or mentally. I'm not sure he could sit through a meal and I would not be in the least surprised if his closest friends confirmed that he never slept at all. At all times his company was full of projects and often people too. His copy was often late--but it was as though our project was only one of many competing for attention.

He was among the first to see that sports, politics, gambling, and media were all forms of The Game--and one should be aware of its expert practitioners as well as its frauds, road kills, fakers,

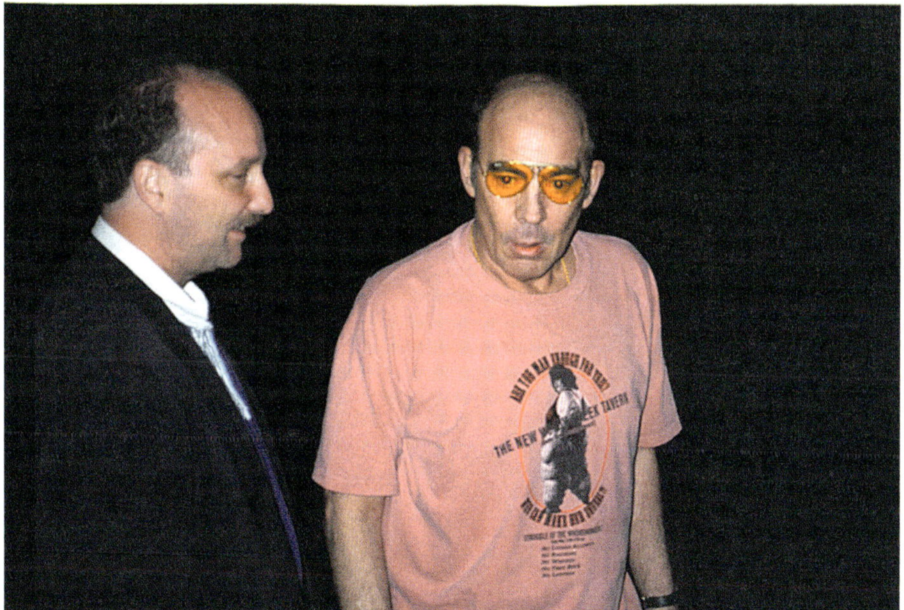

Will Hearst with Hunter at Owl Farm, 1996.

Photo: Deborah Fuller

and bankrupts. The Game has its geniuses and its evil geniuses. The Doctor rated them all.

Owing to his black bag, many assumed his Ph.D. was in pharmacology, but I believe it was more likely psychiatry. He had an instinct, less like Freud (another user), and more like Castaneda, to intuit the nodes of tension in your psyche. He could see them in the dark, across the room, and he would move closer, and hone in on them. Like "The Don," he would do this for your best interest--for the purpose of healing you--assign you a task, a challenge, a journey, a test to force you to confront fear, weakness, and illusion. Like the abbot, he would pace slowly behind you and then strike suddenly with his cane. Pay attention. He was disrespectful of all power but also unsympathetic to rubes of all stripes. His mood could swing in an eye blink. I recall a waiter at The Waterfront restaurant in San Francisco who hovered goofily by Hunter's table. The Doctor suddenly turned and said, "I wish you wouldn't stare at me."

The waiter mumbled something of a denial and then asked if "I can get you something to drink?"

"Yes, bring me a staring asshole," Hunter replied. It was time to stand and clear the silverware.

As much as anything, I will miss his writing. He had much more to say. It was a life cut short in youth. Luckily, we still have all those thousands of letters and mojo faxes. They should all be collected and donated to the Louvre. If you find one in your attic trunk, don't call Antiques Roadshow; leave it to your kids.

His novel "The Rum Diary" was a masterpiece, written at the dawn of the Sixties, and accurately anticipating all that was later to come. It should be taught in high school alongside Twain and Melville. You can delete "Catcher in the Rye" if you need to open up a slot on the reading list.

Hunter was a gifted writer, political observer, and sportsman with a huge appetite for life in every dimension. Like Mark Twain before him, he occasionally wrote for the *Examiner* and neither of them tolerated fools gleefully. We will miss his words and collect his letters.

No More Smoking

TERRY McDONELL

The outlaw journalist who loved and wrote about sports for 50 years, Hunter S. Thompson, died by suicide at age 67 at his home in Woody Creek, Colorado. Over a raucous career that began as a sports editor of the Eglin Air Force Base newspaper in Florida in 1956, Thompson wrote about sports and politics with an unpredictably personal style that changed American culture. Intrigued by the NFL, heavyweight fights, and big-game fishing, as well as presidential campaigns, Thompson ripped across a hilarious landscape of his own invention peopled with friends and admirers from Muhammad Ali, Kenny Stabler, and Jim Irsay to Bill Clinton and Johnny Depp.

His first book, "Hell's Angels," earned him the title "quintessential outlaw journalist" and an assignment to cover Nevada's Mint 400 motorcycle race for *Sports Illustrated*. This ultimately resulted in "Fear and Loathing in Las Vegas" (1971), his "gonzo" book masterpiece, which Tom Wolfe pronounced "a scorching, epochal sensation." Thompson went on to write a dozen more books, hundreds of magazine pieces, and a long-running column for ESPN.com.

Cigarette smoke in the press box is now officially retired.

Photo: Deborah Fuller

Former Sports Illustrated *editor Terry McDonell at Owl Farm.*

Hunter By Moonlight

MARTIN F. NOLAN

I knew the Doc when he was in the employ of Dow Jones. Not many of his fans know that he was a solid, straight, by-the-rules reporter before he ascended to the essence of Hunterness. It's rather like Pablo Picasso's skill at representational, almost photographic painting, before he became Picasso. Hunter wrote for the *National Observer*, a weekend version of the *Wall Street Journal*. Dow Jones killed it only to revive it in 2005 under the Journal's name.

Several excellent reporters wrote for the *Observer*, their bylines a guarantee of sharp, no-bullshit prose: James M. Perry of the *Wall Street Journal* and Robert B. Semple of the *New York Times*. But there was only one Hunter S. Thompson.

On a bus in New Hampshire in 1971, we talked about his earlier stuff. "You ever read *Rolling Stone*?," he asked.

"Yeah," I replied, "but Jesus, why is your stuff so tedious? Why do you bury the lead so laboriously?"

"Tedious?" he fairly sputtered.

"Yeah," I said. "That's the word ... " When he sent me letters later, he signed them, "Tediously yours."

After that exchange, I became his buddy, shepherd, and blocking back. One night, in the twilight of the Nixon Era, we were enjoying drinks at The Class Reunion on H Street, a favorite saloon of White House reporters. HST said he wanted to travel with the White House press to San Clemente, CA where Richard Nixon went to brood.

This was a more daunting assignment than scrubbing "Jeff Gannon," the ventriloquist's foil of the Bush II White House. I asked Hunter if his rap sheet would attract the suspicion of the Secret Service. "It's surprisingly short," he muttered.

In San Clemente, I introduced him to Nixon's press secretary, Ron Ziegler, with whom he talked about motorcycles. "That guy's weirder than his reputation!" was Ron's wide-eyed reaction. In the pressroom in Laguna Beach, Hunter engaged Nixon's rabid rabbi, Baruch Korff, in earnest conversation about the Old Testament. It was a priceless dialogue. Hunter's very presence freaked out the Haldeman-Ehrlichman gunsels, who blamed me for it. I didn't care because I couldn't get much lower on their shit list, as the "Enemies List" proved.

Hunter and I had a mutual friend, Bill Cardoso, who had been editor of the *Boston Globe Sunday Magazine*. Bill coined "gonzo," not a Summer-of-Love San Francisco phrase, but from working-class Boston, more Southie-Dorchester than Haight-Ashbury.

Cardoso, who wrote "The Maltese Sangweech," was delightfully gonzo himself. Ditto for Dave Burgin, twice editor of the *San Francisco Examiner*, another friend, whose disdain for cliches attracted Hunter. In 1985, Burgin hired Hunter at some risk while Ex higher-ups blanched and stammered. But the Doc delivered.

In our halcyon days covering Nixon's Gotterdamerung, *Boston Globe*, *Rolling Stone*, and a crew from Belgian television did not stay at the beachside hotel in Laguna Beach with the rest of the press corps. The White House arranged for our billeting some miles down the coast in South Laguna. We were in rustic cabins surrounding a swimming pool. After a few days, Hunter disappeared, I presume on a run to Tijuana. Various editors, agents, and family, everyone but his bail bondsman, called me looking for him. I could only say, while just guessing, "He'll be back."

When he returned, I was enjoying a solitary midnight swim in the pool. The Doc came sprinting out of the shrubbery. I screamed at him, "Hunter, don't! That's the shallow end!" He then swam underwater, swiftly, and gracefully. He was in amazingly good shape.

After a half-dozen laps, his familiar dome emerged, the Pacific moonlight glistening upon his elfin grin. "What's the matter, Marty?" he said. "Haven't you seen my famous running shallow dive before?" I still expect someday to see him come back running and gloriously splashing.

A Box Of Books: To Send Or Not To Send

AN EXCHANGE ON LITERARY AND POSTAL MATTERS BETWEEN HUNTER THOMPSON AND WILLIAM KENNEDY

WILLIAM KENNEDY

As is well known among modern Caribbean historians, Hunter Thompson fled from Puerto Rico in June 1960, a fugitive from prosecution on charges of public drunkenness and disorderly conduct from a fight at a beachfront bar over a check he refused to pay. He was facing a year in jail so he, his wife-to-be Sandy Conklin, and their old friend Paul Semonin, hired on as crew on a 47-foot sloop, headed for Spain. They were dumped in Bermuda with no money. Money was an ongoing problem with Hunter, who chose to live as a freelance journalist and would-be novelist, but who couldn't find a compatible employer or publisher. If 1960 wasn't the low point of his financial life, it was close.

When he left San Juan in a clandestine hurry, he left behind assorted debts, some of which I was aware of: a bill for a car rental, a bill for phone calls he denied charging to the *San Juan Star*, of which I was the managing editor. Also he was jumping bail, something like $300, perhaps $1,000, on some bail bondsman or lawyer I barely remember finding for him. In his sudden departure from San Juan he

also left his duffel bag, a box of books, and other items at my home in Isla Verde with a note: "I had no way of getting the duffel & the box to P.O.--so had to leave them here. If it's not too much trouble, could you mail the duffel bag, COD, to [Florida address] & the box to me COD to [address in Spain] ... we'll drop you a line and let you know what's happening."

He left me a list of the books in his box:

Hardcover
- Modem Spanish Course (two books)
- Basic elements of Spanish
- Ulysses
- Faulkner reader *(this was not in the box)*
- Lectures Escogidas
- Fitzgerald Reader
- A Death in the Family
- Ginger Man
- Dylan Thomas Poems
- Advertisements for Myself
- Reynard the Fox
- Last Tales
- U.S.A.
- Doctor Zhivago
- The Plague
- Proust, Rembrances, etc. (two books)
- Don Quixote
- Leaves of Grass
- Child's Christmas in Wales

Paper-back
- War with the Newts
- Heart of Darkness/Secret Sharer
- My First 2,000 Years
- Grapes of Wrath
- Fear & Trembling/Sickness Unto Death
- Green Mansions
- Huck Finn
- Portable D.H. Lawrence
- Sound & Fury
- Decameron
- Heart is a Lonely Hunter
- Dante's Inferno
- The Crack-Up
- Last Angry Man
- Immoralist
- Maggie Cassidy
- Don Quixote
- Naked & Dead
- D.H. Lawrence collected poems

Word of Hunter's departure from San Juan got around and so did his debts, which I probably commented on to someone. Word got back to him and he sent me a postcard from Bermuda in July 1960: "What is this rot about me owing you money? I knew you'd try to cheat me as soon as my back was turned. If you keep fooling with my money I'll write the police and have you arrested ... Sandy says hello. Cheers, HST."

In early August he wrote from New York that his novel "Prince Jellyfish" had bounced for the third and last time and he denied charging any phone calls to the *Star*. "I'm tired of being accused of things like that. My assaults are usually more frontal--or at least more damaging." He said he sold a tourism article on Puerto Rico to the *New York Herald Tribune* that should square him on the debt for the car rental he ran up getting it. And he added: "What is the status of my gear? Is everything still there? Don't worry about it not being paid for in Louisville. If it's cheaper send it to [Florida]. But for God's sake send it COD. I have my debts divided into 'general' and 'personal'--and I can't stand any more in the personal column. I won $50 on a quiz show last week. Missed the $600 question."

I wrote him I'd keep his belongings until he decided where I should send them. "So far I've received instructions to send all, sometimes part, to Spain, Florida and Kentucky. If I had taken any or all of your advice they would belong to the world at large. Why don't I keep them until you light somewhere? Or, if you want, I'll send them to Kentucky. But please make up your goddamn mind."

In September he was on his way to Seattle and San Francisco and he wrote: "Hang onto bags & stuff until you get further word." In October Sandy sent us a blank check to cover the mailing of the duffel bag to her in Florida by the cheapest possible method. She longed to be back on the beach in San Juan. She said she was joining Hunter in San Francisco. She wondered what it would cost to send the books to Florida, including the "coconut set," which was in the book box. "I can't really say if Hunter's fine or not," she wrote. "I don't think he really knows. San Francisco is a good city but I'm not sure just how long it can hold him." Sandy sent us a card that the duffel arrived, thanked us, and said Hunter was wandering in the Big Sur area.

I wrote Hunter my adventure in sending the duffel to Sandy. "The goddamn thing almost cost me a finger. The Post Office wouldn't accept it with a lock on it unless I attached the key. They didn't seem to care that I didn't have the key. So I had to buy a hacksaw blade,

borrow a hacksaw handle and saw the lock off; almost sawing off my thumb in the process. I mean, goddamn, Thompson. If you get to Big Sur, give my regards to Henry Miller. Ask him if he ever tried it standing up in a hammock."

In 1961 Hunter wrote from Big Sur: "We have hot sulphur baths here, every day a long soak in a big roman tub--after the touch football. Just sit in that hot water with a beer and a cigarette, peering out at the surf, co-ed bathing ... in all it's enough to give a man paws." He added: "Also--and this is vital--please send that cardboard box containing our coconut cups and my pipe rack. And if they pack easily--and they should--my packet of books. As a matter of fact, I think they were already packed. I would enclose a blank check for it, but oddly enough we are temporarily out of checks instead of money. If you feel like trusting us (me) for the blank check, send the stuff on. If not, get it ready for mailing and send it when the check arrives."

I wrote and told him that: Despite having to run a newspaper and write a novel and keep a wife and two small children happy; despite knowing what a goddamn martyr I was to conformity, I understood his condition out there in the freedom of the Big Sur sea spray ... And I added: "I know how it is to be sitting there immersed in a hot sulphur bath engaged in co-educational nooky watching, Roman style, but ... alas ... with no pipe rack. You must be frantic, wondering what to do with your pipe." I said I'd try to figure out where I put the box of books. "Did the dogs get it? Did I let the kids play with it? Did the rust get it like it gets everything else?"

I received a post card: "Dear Mr. Kennedy, Mr. Thompson is currently away on pleasure. He has asked me to write you and say that because of your last letter, he will soon be on his way to Puerto Rico to destroy your teeth with a huge bamboo splint, and ram eight coconut cups far into your small intestine. I'm sure you're aware that Mr. Thompson is a vicious, brutal ass. As far as I'm concerned, your story is a touching one. I would advise you to take up writing as a form of therapy; they say it takes your mind off your problems. (signed) Annie Jo Feen, secretary to Mr. Thompson."

Then another post card: "Still here, you pompous jap. Just returned from SF & and week of god-awful drinking ... Send my gear. I have got in a fight here & am barred from the baths. Drink is dangerous. Eros giveth and Eros Taketh away."

I wrote and told him I was ready to go through the postal tortures to get his gear to him, but that I wouldn't do it at a financial loss to myself. I said I wouldn't let his inability to pay me back "annihilate a perfectly good friendship." I said I never doubted his honesty and integrity but debts without urgency can go unattended and erode all good will. To forestall this I said I would consider taking a few of his books in payment for my cost of sending them. I also mentioned that Paul Semonin had sent $3 to the *Star* for a debt he owed, but no one could find such a debt and I was in possession of the $3. I said I was considering sending it back to Paul or maybe buying a bottle of rum with it. "Probably I'll buy the rum," I said.

Hunter wrote from Big Sur about me taking books as payment and asked for a list of my choices: " ... if you want the cream of my book crop I will say no and send money. If, however, you constrain yourself selecting only those tomes I have no use for, we can settle the thing without resorting to cash." Either way, he said, "I will see to it that our friendship is kept solvent."

He said he would tell Paul Semonin about my theft of his $3.

In October I got a card: "Send no books until further word."

Then came a note: "Send all books at once to Louisville ... You've had time to read every goddamn one of them. My novel has gone to pieces and I need a job. How about yours?"

I wrote back and told him about the two rejections of my book and my growing pessimism about ever selling it. It was viewed as too grim, too gloomy. I advised him to write an upbeat novel, but he didn't; and neither did I. I told him if he was serious I'd send the books to Louisville, "But you've been serious before, California, Spain, New York etc. Are you sure you're sure?"

In February of 1962, I wrote him again: "As for your books, your rotten goddamn books, they are crated ... They have caused me no end of grief. First the kids spilled chocolate syrup over them. Then the mold set in. Then when the rain came in that time I protected them as best I could. Finally I got the sonsabitches packaged ... then fully prepared mentally to face the Postal Tortures, I lugged the box to the car, drove halfway to the Post Office only to recall that I had no money, neither with me nor at home. So I came back and they have been sitting ... awaiting new mental preparations, availability of lucre and the propitious moment, astrologically, for shipping books over the seas."

In January of 1964, after I had moved to Albany to live and work, I had a letter from him that he had been hired by the *National Observer* to cover the west coast on a regular basis, in his own style. His novel, he said, was stagnant and Cavalier had rejected one of his old stories. He was going to be living north of San Francisco, he said, and I should come out and have a look at the coast. We hadn't communicated in some months and he said he felt he was losing track of my whereabouts. He added: "I think you still have my copies of: 1) The Hemingway Reader 2) The Fitzgerald Reader 3) The Ginger Man ... please send them at once ... Repeat, send at once, collect or any other way that is quick. Send them first-class and I'll send you a cheque for the postage." It's been almost forty-two years since then and I have looked on all my shelves for those books. They are not here. I feel certain that I sent them.

Photo: Dana Kennedy

William Kennedy, Hunter and Jeannette Etheredge at the Tosca, 1989.

Shooting Hunter In *f*8

CHRISTOPHER FELVER

Hunter S. Thompson took muckraking to the outer edge in the University in 1994. He was on a panel being interviewed by Dr. Douglas Brinkley. There was a dinner party, and over dinner I told Hunter that I'd love to make a portrait, maybe at Woody Creek.

That summer there was a Beat celebration to dedicate the Allen Ginsberg Library at Naropa College in Boulder. Since I was headed to Colorado, I thought it might be the perfect time to connect with Hunter. I'd been in touch with Brinkley about how to arrange this. This is when the mystery started. Following Brinkley's loose prescription, I called Hunter and told the answering machine I was leaving San Francisco headed for Colorado. The next day, from a piping hot phone booth in Utah, I basically left the same message. Two days later from a phone booth in Aspen, I called again.

The man himself answered: "Head to the Woody Creek Tavern and await instructions."

I knew this was the notorious "holding tank" for anyone coming to town intent on meeting with the journalist. Stories abounded about how Hunter would leave visitors at the bar for hours until their dream of connecting with him was replaced by twisted mescal visions brought on by too many margaritas dispensed by Hunter's chief of security--the bartender. I must have passed the test, because after the third drink he gave me directions to Owl Farm. Back in the sunshine, driving up the hill, I felt triumphant, having passed through the security net. I pulled in the wraparound driveway and

was immediately met by Deborah, Hunter's dear friend, who gave me the ground rules: "No pictures inside the house."

"Fine with me," I said.

Walking through the kitchen, I headed for the living room. There was a stone fireplace and firearms on the mantle and an adjacent door leading to a screened porch with a peacock basking in the warm afternoon sun. Just then, Hunter's campaign manager for his 1970 run for sheriff walked in with a big "howdy." He gave me the complete rundown on how close the contest really had been. If Hunter had won, he would have just managed the position and delegated authority to those who knew how to carry out police duties.

Hunter entered from behind a door in the kitchen/office with a mason jar in his hand, lamenting how he had dumped his motorcycle the day before and it was just too heavy to pick up. Then the steely-eyed journalist came to life: he wanted to know my qualifications and did not offer a word of encouragement. I rambled on about my convoluted years of photographic adventures and gave him a copy of my book, "The Poet Exposed," as a gift. It turned out we had a few friends in common, including Bill Cardoso, with whom he covered the Ali/Foreman fight in Africa, so right then and there Hunter decided this photographic stuff would work out between us. But of course there was "no time" since a July 4th party was looming and

Photos: Christopher Felver

the bike thing had to be taken care of. "So let's make it fast," he said, going out through the same door he had come in.

I wandered out back trying to find a dark background for the shoot. I put the camera in place on a tripod in the afternoon light and knew it was all going to be over in a flash. Sure enough, out came the gonzo journalist for the shoot, fashionably attired, clutching his omnipresent mason jar. Somehow, he slowed down long enough for me to shoot four flash-portraits and then it was, "See you later." I followed behind as Hunter got in his big late-model convertible and settled behind the wheel. Just as he was about to roar out of the driveway, he jumped out announcing, "We're missing the essentials." Two minutes later he emerged from the house smoking a freshly packed Meerschaum pipe full of sweet-burning specially-blended marijuana. With his stash secure, the Doctor bounded into the car again, giving me the high sign and adding, "Next time." He blasted out of the circular driveway as though he were in a chase scene.

Later, from a mutual friend, I found out that Hunter dug the fastest photo session in history. He called my manner, "Strictly professional, the way all photo shoots should be." If I recall the wild ride it was f8 and be there--quickly.

A Night At Hunter's

PHIL BRONSTEIN

He loved having someone else read his work out loud. We'd gone for a ride at dusk on the way over to his house, gotten lost on a dirt road and seen a gigantic deer the size of a minivan, scary big. Hunter laughed when he heard. He pointed out: that was no deer. That was an elk. But the prize for being stupid and from out-of-state was to read a story he'd written at [age] twenty-one.

It was a long, struggling, unpublished coming-of-age thing--unrequited love in lower Manhattan. I was on a bar stool halfway between the refrigerator and the kitchen counter where Hunter always sat, facing visitors or watching sports on the big screen TV.

There was a stunning young woman standing behind me the whole time I was reading. Out of the corner of my eye, I'd see her walk around past me every once in a while and share something powdery with Hunter that he kept in a tin tucked up in that famous drawer. Then she'd come back to her post, over my shoulder. Like most new people in his company, I don't think she knew exactly what she was getting.

I finished the story and looked around at her. She was staring back at me but her face was like the underside of a fish, dead white, drained of color. Her eyes rolled up in her head and she fell backwards like an ironing board, straight up and down. There was a thud, then a stunned moment of silence. Her head had missed the frige by an inch. Hunter was the first to speak: "That's why we had the kitchen carpeted."

When she came to a minute later, Hunter waved his tin from the drawer: "Honey, this is the best way to get back up!" Anita shoved him out of the way, carrying a portable oxygen machine. "This happens all the time," she said, reassuringly.

At home with Anita, Hunter was a generous and fine host; solicitous, funny, fond of sharing all the mementoes that reflected his unique role in popular culture and literature. (That giant Avedon book took up his whole living room table but there he was in it and proud about that.)

There were the loud debates and occasionally explosive nights with Don Johnson and other friends where we all ended up wearing lipstick at Hunter's insistence, but feeling OK about it (he went first). But, at home, he was not the railing, lurching, sometimes-mean prankster and raging iconoclast of legend. That dangerous Tourette's-like thing he did, that was largely for the tourists at the Woody Creek Tavern bar who came to gawk at an icon; for his public, who all wanted to get a little bit closer to something dangerous--the proximity to unpredictability that's so frightening and alluring.

Out and around, he could be the menacing Hunter, always coiled to strike. He sent cowering waiters with mild glandular problems sobbing into the night ("Hey you! I'm talking to you! Bug-eyed motherfucker! What are you staring at?")

But here in Woody Creek, he was a guy with a nice home in the mountains, a loving wife, and a big imagination, figuring out how to navigate the murkier waters of later life.

Once, he bellowed at Anita when she was helping him into the hot tub, that famous uber-male growl that had quailed generations of editors and the callow copy desk victims whose editors sent them to "take care of Hunter." But Anita bellowed right back and in a second he was easy and relaxed, soaking in warm water in the company of friends and family.

We needed him and his sensibility to help us laugh at those cultural upheavals we could never fully understand--make them funny, make them interesting, make the perpetrators pay a price for us being so fascinated with them. Hunter avenged our worst instincts and made a sometimes grey world fully Technicolor.

If we didn't understand, if we were overwhelmed by an event, or seeking meaning, he would fold it inside out for inspection, give us the full, airplane-toilet-water, blue-armed Hunter vision. No stops, no quiet moments, no sanctimony or correctness of any kind until we were done. And, when he was in his glory, we never wanted to be done with him, or have him done with us.

I Told You I Was Sick

BARBARA WOHL-LUTTRINGER

Dr. Hunter S. Thompson is sick again, languishing at L'Hermitage, "Une Hotel de grand class," in Beverly Hills. He is confronted by two Betamaxes that play snatches of the film, "Where the Buffalo Roam," which purports to depict his life. I was asked to write about the film.

Bill Murray shuffles across the room in search of answer, a cure, or at least a beer. He imitated him so well in the movie that if you catch him moving in the corner of your eye, you get the creepy crawly feeling that Hunter has been cloned. The filming is done, but he can't seem to knock it off.

Ralph Steadman is solicitously wringing his hands over the condition of his friend. Steadman's illustrations of Thompson, starting with the Kentucky Derby story in *Scanlan's* ten years before, through the Fear and Loathing expeditions, have faithfully clarified the weird and twisted visions of this Twentieth Century spokesman for the disillusioned American dreamer.

But not even the luxury of sympathetic friends seems to medicate the good doctor effectively. He is sick about this film. As far as "Where the Buffalo Roam" is concerned, Dr. Thompson discovers that he might as well have been in a monk's cell under a vow of silence--his voice has not been heard. John Kaye ("American Hot Wax") who wrote the script, and Art Linsom ("Car Wash"), who directed it, just didn't get it. There is a funereal aspect to this gathering.

Hunter then had all his hair. He was a damn good-looking man. A tall, handsome Kentuckian, he was a bit like Gary Cooper in "Saratoga Trunk," with all those camera angles up the long, long legs to the handsome features. Hunter had a touch of Southern courtliness and that rare sweetness found in some men, who--with nothing to prove-- are comfortable in their maleness. The best of macho, he could make your heart stir. There was also something Mandarin about him. His eyes and mouth were thin lines, a little pinched.

He is subdued, fatalistically accepting the brutal fact that for all the fire of his prose, he couldn't get anybody to understand a thing. The movie makes a bully out of him--this man who raged against the biggest of bullies, Richard Nixon.

Scene: Hunter, riffing all the while, jabs a hypodermic needle into the arm of a middle-aged nurse.

Scene: Hunter roughs up a black taxi driver, has him in a headlock, bending him back across the fender of his own cab.

Scene: Hunter terrorizes a youthful maimed hitchhiker by holding a pistol to his head.

Cruel and mindless scenes all. No question, there have been such scenes in his life, like his own confession of macing the headwaiter at a restaurant in Louisville. Or half drowning *Rolling Stone* publisher, Jann Wenner, in fire extinguisher foam. Oscar Acosta told the strange story of having been shot at close range by the inscrutable Dr. Thompson, his best friend. The gun was loaded with blanks, but by the time Oscar understood that, he said he could have killed Hunter. The deed would have been done and Hunter dead had the knife that Oscar habitually carried been in his back pocket. The weapon was, by some blessing, missing when Oscar made the reflexive grab for it.

But there is a difference between this energy in the buff and the boring cruelty in the film. I don't know about the head waiter, but Oscar was definitely up to it. After the fear of having come so close to killing the man he cared so much about, he was probably most annoyed because he hadn't thought of it himself. This man Thompson chooses his victims carefully, carrying them to the edge along with him. He does not prey upon the weak.

Thompson had the misfortune to be born with a relentless capacity to see the truth. Very few of us have to face it the way he does, it is as if there is some analog circuitry embedded in his brain. The truth about what has happened to America really tore his heart out. If he cannot escape it, he is going to be sick. Thompson has

tried to escape, tried to drive himself crazy with drugs, unbelievable amounts of whiskey, and heart-stopping doses of obstreperous living that could drive most of us back to scratching pictures in a quiet cave in the Pyrenees. He would do anything to destroy the terrible reality.

Movie as movie, "Buffalo" doesn't work because it shows the man attempting to drive himself crazy, and John Kaye has provided some funny lines, but the script of this soothsayer is such a debasement of the spirit of the man that it could have been written by Thompson's own beast in the night, old Dick Nixon himself.

There is a break in the wake for cocktails with John Dean. He looks like the happy kid brother of the man on television during the 1970s Watergate hearings. He is exceedingly polite and so mild mannered that you keep forgetting that this was the man who brought down the President. He, too, is concerned about the distortions in the film. He and Steadman chew over the lack of nobility in it. That's the kernel of it--it's Thompson's nobility that is missing.

A tape deck plays in the background. It is a song that was never used in the film but was written for the movie by Thompson, Steadman, and Maureen Dean--the blonde with the smile men wrote books about--who sat behind her husband at the Senate Watergate Committee.

"Mangled bodies tell no tales," Steadman sings on the tape.

In the film Hunter is accompanied by a side-kick, Oscar Lazlo, played by Peter Boyle, a bona fide knee-jerk liberal attorney who defends lost causes by either maliciously or stupidly sacrificing his clients. Lazlo is supposed to be the aforementioned Oscar Acosta.

Acosta disappeared following his own murky version of the cocaine dream in the waters off Mazatlan. The details of his end remain shadowy. He was a lonely man, a melting pot soul in an Indio body. He spoke lousy Spanish. He paid his racial debts and fought the causes of the Sixties with audacity and rage. But he deserved what he coveted most--to be ascribed the role of a whole human being without the qualifying adjective. He was always the "Chicano" writer, the "Chicano" attorney, the tawny-skinned outsider--Hunter makes him a Samoan in "Fear and Loathing"--that America has always ripped off.

At the hotel, Oscar tells us he subpoenaed all 130 judges of Los Angeles County in his defense of Corky Gonzales, who led the massive demonstrations against the Vietnam War in L.A. in 1970. Those old boys of the judiciary community would know that the antics of

the movie's Oscar Lazlo don't measure up to the kind of rash courage Oscar Acosta had.

Steadman said there was also an attempt to embody in the role a bit of the infamous and very funny San Francisco barrister, John G. Clancy. He was known as the Gertrude Stein of Telegraph Hill, a great host until his neighbors ran him off. They couldn't live with the gunfire in the early morning. But you couldn't beat him in a courtroom.

There's some action. Steadman is attacking Hunter. Hunter is lying back on the couch, his feet in the air, bicycling his legs out at Ralph. He tries so hard to forestall laughing that he nearly cracks his cigarette holder with his teeth.

This is the first sign of life all weekend. Maybe there is going to be a party yet. They are both laughing now. Ralph is hitting down at Hunter, gaining an advantage. Hunter grabs the entire Sunday *L.A. Times* next to him and hurls it into Ralph's face.

Even the sturdy Welsh satirist is floored by the formidable *Times*. He slides back across the coffee table onto a plate of fudge pudding cake heavy with vanilla sauce. Ralph sits in it, and then makes a long, slow glide across the table and down to the floor, doing a good job on the rug and his trousers all at once. With a howl he kicks the coffee table. It falls apart.

The fun stops.

They are all oooing and awwwing, perturbed by the destruction of this flimsy coffee table in a hotel where the rooms cost $225 (1970s prices) a night.

In the old days it would have been:

"Christ! Look at the thing. Just fell apart."

"Damn. Some nerve."

The table goes back together again as easily as it came apart. Someone cleans up the rug and wipes off Ralph's bum. There is no damage except to the fragile spirit of play. Somberness again prevails. The malaise comes back in full force. The truth about what has happened to America really tore his heart out.

There is a problem. Hunter has written some beginning and ending narrative for the film. Steadman, who made the credits, has finished the calligraphy, but Hunter insists that Ralph not give it to the filmmakers. Hunter does not want his name in the credits. He is adamant. "I won't be satisfied, do you hear me, Lazlo, till I can gnaw on his white skull with my very own teeth." Hunter is sick over the movie. He says it "never really got weird enough for me."

An American doctor name Gajdusek won the Nobel prize a few years ago for discovering a slow-acting virus contracted by cannibals in New Guinea who feed off the brains of their enemies. The virus lies dormant for years, and after being triggered by something like a stroke, it causes senility.

Perhaps Thompson has guessed his own medicine and after the stroke, he'd contract the virus. Just short of death, perhaps senility would be the cure for the illnesses that have plagued him all his life. The boys are bandying about what each of them would write on their tombstones. Hunter says he wants his to say: "I told you I was sick."

I wrote this for New West *magazine in 1970. They didn't print it. John Clancy told me not to take it too hard. The piece beat up on "Where The Buffalo Roam" and Clancy said some of the people who owned* New West *were investors in the movie, which bombed.* New West *later folded.*

A Night On The Town

JOHN R. MacARTHUR

I was in town on business with Lewis Lapham, then the editor of *Harper's Magazine*, and we had dropped by the Tosca Cafe in North Beach for a drink. "Baghdad by the Bay," Herb Caen's nickname for his adopted city of San Francisco, never seemed more bizarre to me than it did that night. The Tosca was packed with eccentrics bellying up to the bar, including Warren Hinckle, the legendary columnist and editor at the *San Francisco Chronicle*, whose fame in San Francisco rivaled even Hunter Thompson's at its zenith. In recent years, Thompson has penned a column on politics and sports for ESPN's website. The current political scene horrified him--as did the Oakland Raiders--and he pined for the company of his late fellow football addict, Richard Nixon.

Thompson owed much to his friend Hinckle, whom he once called "the best conceptual editor I've ever worked with." He was also one of the most noticeable conceptual editors--no one could miss Hinckle's sheer girth, distinctive eye patch, and basset hound, Bentley, which he took everywhere with him.

At the Tosca, Hinckle introduced me to Bentley, after which he guided me to a smallish, mostly unremarkable-looking man named Artie Mitchell. In my East Coast innocence, I didn't know that Mitchell and his brother Jim were the porn kings of San Francisco, just then embroiled in a feud with then Mayor Dianne Feinstein over their O'Farrell Theater sex emporium.

Unduly sensitive about her city's image when she hosted the 1984 Democratic convention, Feinstein tried to clean up the Mitchells' act--the police had gone so far as to arrest porn star Marilyn Chambers for "performing" live at the O'Farrell. Artie, drunk and self-righteous, wanted me to know that Feinstein's "harassment" was a First Amendment violation of the greatest magnitude.

Hunter Thompson was in San Francisco doing "a big piece" on the sex business for *Playboy*, so when Hinckle invited me to dinner to meet the great man, I jumped at the chance. Lapham, older and wiser, declined.

I strolled with Hinckle to Vanessi's, another classic hangout, around the corner from the Tosca. What I didn't know was that a nasty restaurant strike was tearing cuisine-obsessed San Francisco apart. I also didn't know that Thompson had invited his sources--five strippers from the O'Farrell--to join him at Vanessi's.

Socially speaking, things were awkward inside the restaurant, which was nearly empty. But they got even more awkward when Thompson suddenly announced that he needed to make an emergency run to a liquor store before it closed. Because of the restaurant strike, the usual waiters weren't around, management was tense, and I had to make small talk with a stripper, very plain and modestly attired, who was at best an uninspired conversationalist.

In Thompson's absence, Hinckle and Bentley seemed bored, but everyone was hungry and we had all ordered food on the questionable assumption that the world's most famous "outlaw" journalist would return to pick up the tab. By the time the meals were served, Thompson still hadn't reappeared, so Hinckle placed Bentley in our host's chair, and the happy hound proceeded to wolf down a blue-plate special.

Hinckle was pro-strike and therefore feared by restaurant owners, but the dog at the table was more than Vanessi's manager could tolerate. He came over and ordered Bentley to be removed. Hinckle pronounced himself and his dog's honor insulted. Things turned ugly; if Bentley couldn't sit at the table, said Hinckle, we would leave en masse, without paying. The strippers rose as one and, well, I followed.

The manager, a Chinese gentleman pushed to the limits of his patience, promptly locked the restaurant's doors from the inside and said he was calling the police. Hinckle didn't help matters by calling him a "[expletive] scab." Mention of the cops put the strippers,

instinctively feeling on the wrong side of the law, into a panic. Who was going to buy our freedom?

My previously uninspired dinner companion had an inspiration. She pulled out her checkbook and started to scribble what would have been a very large sum for a hard-working showgirl.

Then, just as suddenly as he had disappeared, Thompson was banging on the locked glass doors from the sidewalk and rescuing us with his credit card. He'd found the portable booze he needed. Then, just as quickly, he vanished into the night. His "assignment" was working at the O'Farrell Theater as the night manager (on a *Playboy* expense account, of course), and I guess he had to get back to the job.

But we weren't quite clear of Thompson's manic wake. Very much the worse for drinking, we wound up at 3am in the Mitchell Brothers' office, above the darkened theater, where Artie was amusing himself by firing a pellet gun into targets superimposed with Mayor Feinstein's face.

Urged on by the nearly incoherent Artie, I thought it politic to join in and fire a round. Only then did I realize how crazy this was; only then did I see myself playing a ridiculous cameo role in the Bay Area version of *Fear and Loathing in Las Vegas.* And I didn't feel very good; in fact, I was kind of bored. That Thompson could live like that every day--armed with real ammunition and far more potent stimulants than I could handle--was a tribute of sorts to his immense creative drive, if not his powers of self-preservation.

My favorite "new journalist," Tom Wolfe, a supposed "conservative," saw past Thompson's politics and described him as the twentieth century's "greatest comic writer in the English langauge." But I wouldn't overlook Thompson as the Enraged Journalist of the Left, who wrote the following as his epitaph for George McGovern's failed 1972 crusade for peace against Richard Nixon:

"This may be the year when we finally come face to face with ourselves; finally just lay back and say it--that we are really just a nation of 220 used car salesmen with all the money we need to buy guns, and no qualms about killing anybody else in the world who tries to make us uncomfortable."

That suits the present just fine, and there's nothing funny about it.

This piece appeared in a different form in the Providence Journal.

One Of Those Learning Experiences

JACK THIBEAU

A driving rain fell as I was leaving North Beach for Richmond early in the afternoon. Before I could depart, I was stopped by Lawrence of Arabia, an old, street mystic and prognosticator, who wore a steel ball etched with Hieroglyphics around his neck.

"You're going too fast, man."

"What does too fast mean, Lawrence?"

"Too fast means too fast!"

I thought I knew what he was trying to tell me. Like the Zen expression says, "You're getting ahead of yourself." I was getting ahead of myself. I was moving too fast. It scared me momentarily. But I sped off across the Bay in the rain anyway.

I was in the East Bay and visiting David Pierce, then the mayor of Richmond and a friend of Hunter's, when the weather worsened. David wanted me to call the Actor's Workshop to say that I couldn't get there for my performance. He advised me to make up an excuse, if need be. They'd understand, he said. I thought he just wanted me to stay for his party. After all, the show must go on.

When I started for San Francisco at about six in the evening, the weather had not improved. Sheets of cold rain slammed down on me on the freeway in Berkeley. Suddenly, while I was driving at fifty miles per hour, my rear tire blew out. The bike almost went out from

under me, but I managed to ride it down. If I'd been in the fast lane, I might have been crushed in onrushing bumper-to-bumper traffic. After I waited by the side of the freeway for a half-hour, a pick-up truck stopped. The driver helped me push my bike up a ramp into the back of his truck. Then he drove me to a gas station where I stashed the bike since the tire couldn't be fixed until the next day. I called the theater and informed them I couldn't make it, then I called David. He picked me up in his Porsche.

When I arrived at the party, a drenched rat, there was nothing left to do but forget about the accident. I felt that I had come eyeball to eyeball with disaster and disaster had blinked.

Hunter was at the party. He told me he didn't know if he was writing a book about the Hell's Angels or being absorbed into the gang. He was loaded on something. When I asked him what it was, he pulled out some pills.

"What are they?"

"I don't know. The people who gave them to me didn't know either. But they'll knock down an elephant."

"I think I'll pass."

"A wise decision. I wish I'd made the same. I don't know when I'm going to come down. Or maybe it's up. That's how drugs work. To keep you guessing, I guess."

"What else do you have?"

"Some nickel-and-dime mescaline."

"What do you mean?"

"Costs five or ten dollars to find out if it's going to work."

The bit of mescaline I ate came on slowly but it suddenly overtook me. I held on and went for the long, strong, pastel-and-phosphorescent ride. David saw what was happening and suggested that Thompson and I spend the night, but Thompson said he had to stop off at the El Adobe, the Hell's Angel bar in East Oakland, before he went home to write in the morning. He said if I wanted a ride home, I could go with him and he would drop me off afterward. I elected to join him.

"If you go with me, you'd better watch your step at the El Adobe. The Angels might not like your style."

"I'll take my chances."

"With an attitude like yours, you certainly will be."

The rain had let up, but the late-night streets were still slick. We rumbled down the hill from David's, the B.S.A rapping its powerful tattoo. At the bottom of the hill, Thompson stopped and took off his white helmet.

"Put this on."

"It's yours. You wear it."

"Do as I tell you. Put it on."

I did, and we set off.

We turned the corner onto Cutting Boulevard and headed toward the freeway, Berkeley, Oakland, and the Bay Bridge. A red light a quarter of a mile ahead had just turned green giving Thompson a chance to step up through first gear into second. We passed through the intersection at what must have been fifty miles per hour. Then he stepped up into third and kept on accelerating. I had stopped watching by now. I just held on and got into the ride. All I could hear was the awesome, awful rumble of the B.S.A.

I didn't see or hear what happened next. In his book, Hell's Angels, Thompson wrote that it was "like being shot out of a bazooka with no noise." I was told later that an unmarked, unbanked curve appeared in front of us on Cutting Boulevard. All of a sudden I was in mid-air, thrown end-over-end like a man in a tornado. And I stopped just as suddenly as I had taken off. I woke up and shock had set in and I didn't feel much pain. When I looked down, I saw that my right pants leg was ripped and that my knee was bleeding. When I picked up my leg, it fishtailed back and forth. I put my leg down. I knew it was seriously injured. I looked closely at my knee and saw the femur protruding.

I searched myself for drugs. I didn't want to have any in my possession. After all, I'd just come from the home of the mayor of Richmond.

I looked around and saw the twisted, smoking wreck of the motorcycle. Then I saw the outline of Thompson's inert body next to the wreck. I remember calling him over and over again, with no response. I thought of crawling to him, but I figured I had better stay where I was. Then I saw lights approaching from Cutting Boulevard. As they got closer, I saw that they were police flashlights.

Then I noticed Thompson on his feet, his face bloody from a gash in his scalp. He had a Buck deer-skinning knife in his hand.

"All right, you fuckers, it's about time we settled this!"

The cops drew their guns. They weren't taking chances.

"Put down your weapon, sir."

"You've been following me for weeks, haven't you?! It's about time we settled this!"

"Put down the weapon, sir, or we'll use force."

The police finally talked the knife out of Thompson's hand. Beneath the gash on his scalp proved to be a major concussion, not the first he ever had in his life.

When an ambulance arrived, paramedics splinted my leg and put me on a stretcher. They took off my helmet and laid it on my lap. As we crossed a vacant field to the ambulance, I noticed a nasty, dark dent in the white helmet, which had saved my life.

At a nearby hospital, a concussion-addled Thompson produced an expired Blue Cross card and insisted he was going to pay our hospital bills. But before the emergency room physicians could even look at his scalp wound, he disappeared. Twenty minutes later, the hospital staff received a phone call from a bowling alley down the street informing them that a man in the coffee shop was bleeding all over the place and banging on the counter demanding beer. The hospital dispatched aides to collect him.

By now I had come out of shock and was in excruciating pain. However, the doctors wouldn't give me morphine until my insurance coverage was assured. They got what they needed when I presented my seaman's documents. (Fortunately, I had registered with the Sailor's Union of the Pacific when I had shipped out a few months earlier. Registering with the union insured that I would have full medical coverage.)

After I waited for what seemed like hours they shot me full of morphine. I was "walking with the king."

I'll never forget that night's ambulance ride across the Bay Bridge to the San Francisco public health hospital. The bridge's beatific overhead orange lights and the celestial music I was hearing brought me close to what I could only describe as a near-death experience. I also consider it the end of Act One of my life.

I learned a lot from Hunter, more than a few times, but mostly the hard way. This was just one of those learning experiences.

Life Was Perfect, Life Was Real

MICHAEL STEPANIAN

I grew up with Ken Kesey and grew old with Hunter S. Thompson. They both had, along with others, a profound effect on my life. I changed from a hard-nosed New Yorker to a beautiful person. Hunter, like Mort Sahl and Lenny Bruce, loved to mess around with the law and lawyers. They even envisioned themselves as lawyers. Imagine what a better place it would be if Hunter, Mort, Lenny, and Ken were on the Supreme Court!

Hunter was a dogged fact gatherer. He understood the human condition and how things worked better than anyone. He was a brilliant cross-examiner. He could take a piece of your argument and grind on it until the true factual picture emerged. He was passionate about the Constitution. I was proud to be, along with Goldstein, Lefcourt, Haddon, and Tigar, a member of his Fourth Amendment Committee. Hunter saved the life of a young woman in Denver, Lisl Auman, who got life on a felony murder rule when she was arrested while sitting in a cop car when a skinhead killed a cop a mile away. She was convicted and would have rotted away in prison if Hunter had not become her vociferous advocate and pushed the case.

Hunter had passion and loved his family. Hunter loved sports. At the rugby tournaments in Aspen, Hunter was our mascot and in-house sports psychologist and pharmacist. Hunter had tremendous physical strength, endurance, and stamina. At 3 p.m. one afternoon he demanded that we go salmon fishing out in the ocean in my 17-foot Boston Whaler. I told him that it was crazy. The next thing,

we were blasting out under the Golden Gate beating our way through the swells to Duxbury buoy where we arrived at dusk. Miraculously, we caught an enormous salmon, which Hunter gaffed by diving over the side into the frigid water past his shoulders with the giant salmon writhing on the gaff. He then demanded that we go to Bolinas for a drink. I'm dying. This is a crazy idea. We were in real danger being out in the evening with no lights or radio. We ended up surfing the boat into the Bolinas Channel and bounded into a local bar like wet dogs. Hunter needed scotch and food. The bartender put out the word that Hunter was there and before we could bite into our burgers we found ourselves surrounded by about twenty or more locals firing questions at Hunter. After two hours we decided to leave. A couple of guys offered to drive us back to San Francisco but Hunter would have none of that and demanded we leave by boat. I told him it was crazy; it was dark and surely we were going to die. He called me a chicken-shit and jumped into the boat and proceeded to blast out of the channel with me hanging on for dear life. It was pitch black as we worked our way up the coast in a howling wind, past Stinson, past Muir Beach, through the Potato Patch, sea spray blasting over the bow, the ocean roaring. We were entering Hades! We finally got around the corner and as we blasted through the channel with the lights of the Golden Gate like a halo above us, there were tears in my eyes. Hunter was laughing, screaming, cursing. We were soaking wet but delirious.

Life was perfect. Life was real.

Photo: Deborah Fuller

Michael Stepanian (left) at Owl Farm on Super Bowl Weekend in 1999, with Hunter and Abe Hutt.

Medicating Hunter

EUGENE "DR. HIP" SCHOENFELD, M.D.

We're alive, we're alive! exclaimed Hunter Thompson as we hugged, my head in his chest. Hunter is 6'2" and I'm not yet 5'7" tall. We had first met as writers for *Rolling Stone*, when the magazine was based in San Francisco. We were both at the 1972 Republican Convention in Miami, where we witnessed something never imagined during my student years at Miami Beach High School--tear gas obscuring the full moon. I had last seen Hunter in 1977 when we watched a football game in a room at the Watergate Hotel in Washington, D.C.

Now we were both on the speakers program at a 1989 Taos, New Mexico seminar sponsored by the National Association of Criminal Defense Lawyers (NACDL). To show me he was not only alive, but still fit, Hunter did a back flip, impressing me and startling some of the lawyers milling about the conference hotel's mezzanine. My talk was about the effects of psychoactive drugs on defendants and witnesses. During that year, the sitting president of the NACDL, Alan Ellis, had also asked me to help develop a program assisting criminal defense attorneys with alcohol/drug problems of their own, a fairly common malaise of the profession.

Hunter's talk? I don't know what it concerned, nor does anyone else. Hunter was an infamous mumbler. I'm told and accept that I'm soft-spoken, but have learned to get close to the microphone when doing radio, or testifying in court. But it was often difficult to understand Hunter even when he used a microphone. It was easier if you already had the gist of what he was saying and were close enough to

read his lips, while trying to listen to his words. Remarkably, lecture bureaus sent him out on college tours more than once, despite negative reviews by students. For most people, it was enough to just see the legendary writer in the flesh. But not for some of the attorneys attending the NACDL conference: "This is an outrage," grumbled one woman in the audience. Several other attorneys got up and left. I think illuminated streaming subtitles would have helped, like those utilized by some opera companies.

The morning after Hunter's "lecture," I joined Keith Stroup, then the executive director of NACDL, in the effort to rouse Hunter in time for his flight home to Aspen. Texas attorney Gerry Goldstein had arranged a private Lear jet for the occasion. Responding to the loud incessant knocking on his hotel door, a disheveled Hunter let us in and stumbled around his room, dressing and gathering his belongings. He swallowed a large glass of Chartreuse liquor and took a huge snort from a round container of cocaine before leaving the hotel room for the airport.

Five years passed before I saw Hunter again. In 1994, he was in San Francisco on a book tour for "Better Than Sex," about Bill Clinton on the campaign trail. One day, a mutual friend, attorney Michael Stepanian, telephoned and asked if I would check on Hunter. Stepanian said Hunter had fallen and injured himself the previous night. On my way to the hotel, I heard a furious talk show host blasting Hunter for not showing up for his scheduled appearance. Hunter hobbled over to greet me when I arrived at his room. No back flips this time. An attractive woman was with him, his ex-personal assistant and ex-girlfriend, who now lived in San Francisco. Abrasions covered one side of his face. Seems he'd had a yen to commune with the seals near the Cliff House, but slipped on the rocks and was knocked out cold. I did a physical examination, including checking his blood pressure. It was elevated.

At one point, while Hunter was on the telephone, the woman told me why she'd left his employ--she couldn't stand the continual explosions set off by Hunter on his Woody Creek property.

During my visit, several reporters came and went from the hotel room. Hunter was drinking prodigious amounts of alcohol and *San Francisco Bay Guardian* editor Tim Redmond noted Hunter's use of cocaine. A woman who came to interview him for the *Chronicle* told me she was much relieved I was in the hotel room because she'd heard so many lurid stories about him. My autographed copy of "Better

Photo courtesy Eugene Schoenfeld

Eugene Schoenfeld, M.D.

Than Sex" reads, "To Gene--Thanks for the high blood pressure and the fear of massive contusion. Yr. Old friend, Hunter."

I called to check on him when he'd returned to Colorado. George Burns had just died of a brain hemorrhage some days after hitting his head in a bathtub and I wanted to be sure Hunter was all right. He assured me he was.

My last visit with Hunter was in December 2003. I was in Hawaii on the island of Oahu to attend the wedding of Terence Hallinan's son Brendan and his bride, Maira. Days earlier, Terence had been defeated for re-election after serving eight years as district attorney in San Francisco. His victorious opponent was Kamala Harris, an African-American/Asian-Indian woman. I couldn't help but think that Kamala Harris' victory was, in some part, the fruit of Terence Hallinan's civil rights activism in the 1960s. Attorney Michael Stepanian was also one of the wedding guests. Once more, he asked me to check up on our friend Hunter. He said that Hunter had broken his leg a day earlier, was in a Honolulu hospital, and would appreciate a visit.

Hunter was in Hawaii to cover the December Honolulu Marathon for his ESPN column. But he never got to watch the race. Two days before the marathon, he slipped on a slick bathroom floor in his hotel suite, fell onto his left knee, and fractured the tibia and fibula of his left lower leg.

Hunter was alternately dozing and watching football when I entered his hospital room. He had a plaster cast on his left leg, beginning at mid-thigh. We watched football until his wife, Anita, returned from making arrangements for his transfer back to the hotel where he'd had the accident. Anita was bright, attractive, and very devoted to her husband. I followed their van back to the hotel in my rental car. We had to take a circuitous route because many of the streets in Honolulu were still blocked off, due to the marathon. Two nurses and a concierge were waiting and helped Hunter into a wheelchair, which wasn't easy since he weighed about 190lbs. Moving that leg caused some awful pain, but Hunter felt better once he was back in his suite, fortified by two or three Bloody Marys. The concierge was extremely attentive--not a surprise considering that her famous guest had seriously damaged himself in her hotel. Placing a cigarette in his signature holder-filter, Hunter amused himself and a growing number of friends entering the suite by having the concierge read aloud from "The Curse of Lono," which he'd written with Ralph Steadman. This book contains outrageous characterizations of proclivities of various ethnic groups in Honolulu, but the concierge couldn't help laughing, even when her own background was defamed. Anita had me open a FedEx package which contained copies of *Playboy*'s 60th Anniversary issue, to which Hunter had contributed an article. There ensued a discussion about beauty. Anita said Hunter was also beautiful. "Don't you think?" she asked me. I replied that I'd never considered describing him that way. "Well, he's beautiful when he's typing." she said. Awwww.

After a while, three of us moved Hunter to his bed and Anita elevated the injured leg by wedging a number of pillows beneath the cast. I checked into the hotel, had supper, and returned to their suite a couple of hours later. Hunter seemed even more relaxed than earlier.

Much has been written by Hunter and others about his extravagant use of substances, but I had known him for thirty-one years and, as I told him that night, I could honestly say I had never before seen him so heavily medicated on prescribed drugs. That made him smile.

16 Alexander Avenue

MATTHEW NAYTHONS

16 Alexander Avenue, in Sausalito, was the perfect bachelor pad for a gonzo journalist looking for the complement to his Rocky Mountains: onsite parking, a romantic view of San Francisco Bay, a small deck outfitted with a saggy Nicaraguan hammock, and an authentic Tiki bar from the sixties--thatched roof, bamboo siding, rum stains, cigar burns, the whole enchilada.

I was leaving it, with some regret, to move in with my fiancé up in the hills, but I figured that I owed a fellow war correspondent a cheap, comfy little bunker in Sausalito. “Hey, Jacques,” I said to my friend the landlord, “I’ve subleased our place to Hunter Thompson.” To Jacques’ Gallic ears, those nine words were nearly as unwelcome as, “Hey, Jacques, I’ve subleased our place to Attila Le Hun.” He was reasonably upset, but in spite of Hunter’s anarchic reputation, how could a cool French ex-hippie-computer-scientist-sybarite-Existentialist with a ponytail bring himself to turn away the new Night Manager of the Mitchell Brothers’ O’Farrell Theatre and, with him, perhaps, entrée to the inner sanctum of that fabled fleshpot?

As the tenant of record, and erstwhile guarantor for the said new night manager, I played by the rules: inspection, inventory, signatures, a credit reference, and oaths, from Hunter, of good behavior. What would Jacques say if his apartment was turned into an all-night gambling den and bordello? What would the coked-up lawyer paying big rent for the upstairs unit say? Probably, “Cut me in,” but who knew?

Photo: Warren Hinckle

Hunter, Artie Mitchell, Kathleen Golden and Matthew Naythons at the tiki bar in the 16 Alexander Avenue apartment.

So one afternoon I drop in at #16 for a regular "visit" and beer, i.e. check-up. At first, all seems relatively normal--at least for Hunterland. It's 2pm--time for breakfast, and a few rounds of Cuba libre--so the night manager is tending the Tiki bar. An upturned garden hose, pressure to the max, is gushing like the Trevi fountain off the upstairs landing. A large Japanese kite, in the shape of a koi, is bobbing from the deck, attached by a long string to Artie Mitchell's deep-sea fishing rod. The Mitchell Bros and Warren Hinckle are schmoozing while Warren's basset hound, Bentley, is snoring like a guerrilla-camp generator.

But appearances, where Hunter is concerned, are generally deceptive. The boys are in possession of Artie Mitchell's very high-powered pellet pistol, they are having a shooting competition, and the dumb-looking koi is studded with "Impeach Dianne Feinstein" buttons, each featuring a Dan O'Neill/Robert Crumb/Victor Moscoso sketch of the San Francisco Mayor coyly lifting (or,

under the circumstances, koily lifting) a hoopskirt, and the goal is simple: who can knock the most Dianne buttons off the fish?

I could have chalked the whole scene up to boyish high spirits (and to 100-proof spirits) but for one small glitch. The shots are zinging directly over the roof of the house immediately downhill from us. And that house below belongs to the only neighbor I knew who, unlike Hunter, was actually licensed to carry a gun in the Golden State of California.

"Yo, guys," I say, "Do you have any fucking idea whose house you are raining pellets on?" Silence, except for more fire. "It's Nunzio Alioto's house." Nunzio was a member of the famed San Francisco Alioto political family, the owner of a major Fisherman's Wharf restaurant, and known to his neighbors as a man whose peace and domestic tranquility were not to be disturbed.

The contest, nevertheless, continued.

[WARS MAKE STRANGE CARPOOLS]

At dawn on October 25, 1983 American forces entered into combat for the first time since Viet Nam on the island of Grenada. More Scoop than Guadalcanal Diary, the invasion set the stage for a picture-perfect foreign correspondents' war--good guys, bad guys, little danger, a place to swim in late October, and cheap rum. Grenada had "gonzo" written all over it, and it was a story Hunter couldn't pass up--one that TIME had me scrambling to cover.

I arrived on D-Day+3 via a wrangled military flight from Barbados. Landing early allowed me to grab one of the last available rental cars, as well as to meet a local named Oldbrick who was hanging out by the rental agency. Oldbrick said he could find every alley and goat path on the island and navigate around military roadblocks. Since it turned out that our invading army had requisitioned all available tourist maps, he was hired on the spot.

When I asked Oldbrick how he got his nickname, he said that he was the last of his dad's twelve kids and "brick" was slang for semen in Grenada, hence "old brick." Dignified Grenadian ladies in their Sunday church finest would see us drive by and laughingly callout "Morning, Oldbrick."

What Oldbrick didn't say, however, was that he couldn't drive. Returning from an ice run in early November, he handed me a scrap of paper on which was written, "plese (sic) pay for one male billy

goat." Whether it was the goat or a tree stump, the car's radiator was kaput. And while it was worth every penny of $200 to be able to include an aggrieved goat herder's invoice with my *TIME* expenses, it also meant that I no longer had a working car. Grenada was by now crawling with journalists and rental cars were non-existent.

It was about this time that Hunter showed up in search of a hostelry with hot water. Mine had a sudden vacancy, and that's how we became neighbors at the Hotel Calabash. The Calabash featured beachfront cabanas on a tranquil bay, and a fabulous open-air restaurant/bar. Rumors were swirling around about mysterious Cuban troops living in the hills. A vehicle was needed. Hunter understood these things.

And so the next day he miraculously showed up at the hotel bar driving a giant red golf cart. At least it looked like a golf cart to me. More beach buggy than car, his rented Mini Moke weighed almost nothing, seated four, and sported an 850 cc engine with a four-speed manual transmission. It had no seatbelts, no license plates, no roll bar, but did have a very Oklahoma fringed canvas roof. It also, I soon discovered, had almost no suspension.

But hey--the best all terrain vehicle has always been rented wheels, whatever chassis sits on top of them. And since I was in need of transport, a deal was struck. Hunter would drive, and I (now familiar with the byways of Grenada) would guide. Oldbrick was assigned to the *TIME* motor pool until he showed up with a repaired *TIME* car.

As a self-proclaimed gear-head and driver's driver, I approached the Mimi Moke with utmost caution. It looked like a toy. Surely this was not a vehicle meant to slalom through corners on narrow roads perched 500-700 feet above the sea. Surely this was not a vehicle in which to perform nighttime doughnuts in front of Marine Corps 50 caliber gun positions. Surely this was not meant to go 60mph through small towns ... And then there were the goats.

Well, it did all of the above. And in spite of screeching turns that I'd swear put us on two wheels, Thompson managed to drive with sufficient skill to stay on the road 100% of the time. The tighter the corner, the bigger his smile.

OVERLEAF: Hunter driving V.S. Naipaul during the invasion of Grenada
Photo: Matthew Naythons

THE DOG ATE THE WEDDING CAKE: At the October 19th, 1985 wedding of Matthew Naythons to Kathleen Golden in San Francisco, the following happened immediately prior to this photograph. Hunter, in one rapid jerk of his arm, knocked off the top of the wedding cake before, according to tradition, it could be placed aside for the bride and groom's first anniversary meal. The cake top landed directly in front of Warren Hinckle's basset hound, Bentley. Bentley pounced on the cake and ate it. Naythons' mother, a nice Jewish lady from outside Philadelphia, observed all of the above silently before asking her son, "Tell me again why that dog is at your wedding?" (Left to Right: Matthew Naythons, Kathleen Golden, Warren Hinckle, Hunter Thompson, Bentley on the floor.)

One morning as we got ready to leave for the day, a nattily dressed Asian gentleman in a linen sports coat asked if we would be so kind as to take him into the countryside. Why not? When Hunter went to get the Moke, I introduced myself. "My name is Naipaul," he replied. "And you can call me 'Naipaul'," he added. "I believe it is rather sissified when men address one another by their first names."

"This will be interesting," I remember thinking as I climbed into the back seat.

Naipaul had no idea who his driver was, or what he was in for. And Hunter went for it--white knuckles all the way. I could see our passenger wincing at corners, and heard him moan at a sudden stop, but in spite of these racecar antics, Naipaul remained a perfectly stoical, uncomplaining fellow traveler. When Hunter braked for a noon beer, however, he turned around and whispered to me, "Does this man always drive like that?"

"Yup," I replied.

It was the beginning of a friendship. We never found any Cubans.

[THE ARM]

"Nothing impressed Thompson like the arm. It was black and clad in green fatigues. Loren Jenkins of the *Washington Post* saw it in a garbage can outside his hotel. 'My God,' he yelled, 'look at that.' It turned out to be a prosthesis, apparently planted by a prankish MP, who splattered it with ketchup for dramatic effect. 'We hung Goebbels for jokes like that,' declared Thompson. He demanded an explanation. An Army public affairs officer told him, with a straight face: 'Sir, that's our disarmament policy.' "

--from TIME *magazine's coverage of Hunter Thompson covering Ronald Reagan's ersatz invasion of Grenada in 1983.*

Hunter kept the arm. He showed it to me when I got into his car and he smiled sheepishly.

"Hunter," I recalled saying after he showed me his war trophy, "There is no fucking way you can bring an artificial arm home to the States (or even back to your hotel) as a war souvenir. This goes beyond craziness ... "

After considerable discussion, in the end we agreed that it had to go. We found a suitable pile of trash near the deposed Grenadan

leader Bishop's old HQ. He drove and I ran out and carefully put it with the rest of the detritus of war.

When we decamped Grenada, Hunter inscribed a copy of the fly page of "Curse Of The Lono" to me, with thanks for talking him out of the arm business:

The Curse of Lono

Matthew
Thanx for getting rid of that arm for me in Grenada.
Good luck.
Nov 18 '83 – St. Georges

Never Call 911

WAYNE EWING

This essay is composed of excerpts from Wayne Ewing's notes of filming Hunter's Rebelasian adventures, which are posted in their entirety on his Hunter Thompson Films website: www.HunterThompsonFilms.com.

[THE GONZO PILOT]

In the late winter of 1986 I began filming with Hunter for the first time. The idea was to make a short, entertaining pilot to prove to the right television programmer that Dr. Hunter S. Thompson could actually host his own, regular television series. We were going to call the show either the "Gonzo Tour" or "Breakfast with Hunter"-the latter title being Jack Nicholson's clever idea spoofing morning television talk shows.

These were the days before cheap, digital video. Shooting 16mm film was expensive. We planned to travel to Key West, and Hunter demanded to be paid so I found a producer in Ross Milloy of Austin, Texas who financed the deal, and I handled the filmmaking. We began shooting in Woody Creek on a snowy day. Hunter was a natural performer; he loved the camera, and the camera loved him. Hunter ad-libbed coming out onto the porch. All I told him was "pretend you're on your way to Florida" and he emerged in his shorts in the snow with all sorts of "business" to do, even ironically checking the time on his wristwatch in the end. Hunter never cared about the time and was habitually late to everything.

Once in Key West among his old friends--drug smugglers, drunks, and Jimmy Buffett--he was much less forthcoming. We all stayed in Hunter's favorite Florida motel--the Sugar Loaf Lodge on

Photo: Deborah Fuller

Filmmaker Wayne Ewing (left) shooting Hunter in Key West in 1986 for the movie "Breakfast With Hunter," which had the working title "The Gonzo Pilot." Ewing is holding the camera and assisted in the shoot by soundman John McCormick.

Sugar Loaf Key, about 15 minutes from Key West proper. His girlfriend Maria was there, along with his secretary Deborah, my girlfriend Lynn, the patient soundman John McCormick and our money man Ross. A captive, one-eyed dolphin named Sugar swam endlessly in circles in the motel lagoon while we waited for Hunter to perform for the camera each day.

After a week at the Sugar Loaf, I figured Hunter was actually in front of my camera for a total of about two hours. He never arose until well after noon, no matter what plan we made the night before. When I went to beat on his door he would mumble that he needed to take a shower. The water would go on, and it could still be heard running when I returned a half hour later. Of course, Hunter had gone back to bed ("I never turn on the hot water," he would say in defense of the ruse). After two days, the Sugar Loaf Lodge Management (who actually were rather fond of Hunter from his previous stays) threatened to kick us all out, unless one of us moved in next door to him. The loud sounds in the middle of the night--lightbulbs exploding, Maria gurgling as if she were being strangled--were upsetting the guests next door who checked out complaining bitterly. So Lynn and I moved in next door, and hoped every night that the screams were from pleasure and not pain.

The cinematic breakthrough came with the boat ride which plays throughout the credit sequence of "The Gonzo Pilot." Hunter had bought a boat on an earlier trip to Key West and he was keen to take it out of storage and race around the Keys. An old buddy of Hunter's supplied the second boat for my camera, and part of the time I would shoot boat to boat and sometimes on board with Hunter and Maria.

At one point, as you can see in the film, a school of dolphins gracefully surfaced and began to swim in formation with Hunter. "I'm back, Boys," Hunter called out.

"What did you mean by that?" I later asked him in the bar at the Sugar Loaf.

"I'm Lono and I'm back with my people," declared Hunter. (Lono was a mythical Hawaiian figure featured in "The Curse of Lono" who Ralph Steadman concluded is reincarnated as Hunter.)

After the boating sequence I figured we were on a roll, so I suggested to Hunter in the bar that we continue filming and shoot an interview to tie the whole pilot together. He agreed, and I left him with Maria and three Bloody Marys while soundman McCormick

and I lit a set in McCormack's motel room. In less than a half hour I went back to the bar to get Hunter.

"I'm feeling too dumb to do the interview," mumbled Hunter, now sipping Scotch.

"Okay. We'll just keep the set ready in McCormack's room until you are," I suggested amiably. Hunter said he'd call and retreated to his room with Maria ... for over two days, until I got the call at 3am on the third night.

"I'm ready for my interview now," the Beast said. So we all scrambled awake and shot until dawn. Not the greatest interview he ever did, but it sufficed.

Jimmy Buffett provided another high point, agreeing to be filmed in conversation with Hunter in his backyard at the beach in Key West. Years later in New York City at 3 a.m. as I was leading Hunter out of Elaine's after the premiere of "Fear & Loathing in Las Vegas" I heard a voice call out, "Your film is still the best, Wayne." I looked up to see Jimmy smiling from the back of a black SUV, and knew he was referring to the "Gonzo Pilot." For that I will forever be grateful.

But the programmers at HBO to whom we had hoped to sell the show weren't of the same opinion. Producer Milloy reported that their head of documentary programming at the time threatened to call security if he ever mentioned Hunter's name again. These were the days of Reagan and a middle-aged dope fiend was not welcome on the air waves.

The best of the Gonzo Pilot is to be found either in the credits of my film "Breakfast with Hunter" or in Alex Gibney's documentary "Gonzo" which includes the scene with Buffet that we gave him. Someday we may find the right use for the rest.

That winter of '86, I left Hunter with Maria in Key West, and returned to Aspen, not hearing anything for about a week and then he called:

"You've got to help get us out of here. I've spent all the money you gave me and have no credit cards to get a plane ticket," he pleaded. "If you will pre-pay our plane tickets home, I promise I'll pay you back the minute I'm at Owl Farm." American Express and every other credit card company known to man had long before cancelled any card in the name of Hunter S. Thompson or anything similar.

What else could I do, but pay for the tickets and hope for reimbursement from my new television star? In fact, when they returned, Hunter immediately wrote me a check, saying "Let this be a lesson to you, Wayne. Never lose your credit cards."

[MCGOVERN'S BIRTHDAY]

"Thank God you're here," said Hunter, collapsing like a rubber man into my arms at the gate of his flight arriving at Washington Dulles airport from Denver.

It was April 7, 1997, and in those pre-9/11 days, you could still get through security to meet folks as they came off the plane. As the Road Manager it was my duty to be there to greet the Rubber Man, and thankfully I was on time since he clearly could not make it any further without assistance. As he continued to go limp in my arms, I spied an empty wheelchair sitting in the boarding area. He could barely put one foot in front of the other as I dragged him into the chair.

"What happened?" I asked. "The stewardess was giving me a hard time about drinking. I decided the wise course was to take a Halcion rather than get in a fight with her," replied the Rubber Man. Keep in mind that Halcion is a cleverly named drug for the treatment of insomnia. George Bush Senior once blamed the pill for causing him to vomit on the Prime Minister of Japan at a state dinner in Tokyo and then pass out. Hunter took it regularly, but never while traveling. But this was an important trip and he dared not be delayed by armed FAA agents upon arrival. The next day was George McGovern's birthday and Hunter was expected at a lunch in George's honor and a symposium afterwards at the National Archives.

The stretch limo was waiting at the curb outside the baggage area. Unfortunately, I had found on the way to Dulles that the driver did not have much of a sense of humor, so I feared he would be the next source of trouble. Life on the road with Hunter was always the Art of the Next Fifteen Minutes; what could go wrong next?

In the limo, Hunter came around quickly from the Halcion, and its after effect kept him from fucking with the driver, although he did let loose a ton of abuse on the cell phone at his secretary Deborah when she dared to suggest that he should not have stayed up all night before getting on the plane for Washington, DC.

"Fuck You! I'll do it again and again anytime I want to," he screamed into the phone.

Hunter had agreed to stay at the Fairfax Hotel, a fashionable choice just off Dupont Circle and the home of the storied Jockey Club. Checking into a hotel was always stressful for Hunter, especially the part where they asked for his credit card, so upon arrival I walked him straight through the lobby and into their elegant bar, crowded with men and women in serious suits. Distracted by the women, Hunter gave up his credit card with surprisingly little resistance, and I went to find the Manager to make sure "Mr. Ben Franklin" (his road name that spring) would have a choice room.

The manager must have read a bit of "Fear & Loathing" and seemed to know the dangers involved in any delay so I was back in the bar in less than five minutes with the room key. The Rubber Man was gone, replaced by a suave and sophisticated "Mr. Franklin" who had already managed to pick up a thirty-something lawyeress from Nashville with great legs and a sweet accent in town for a job interview with US Securities and Exchange Commission. Thinking that this development could either make my job a whole lot easier or worse, I sat down for a drink to see how it played out.

"You look just like that crazy writer ... you know ... what's his name?" observed the Lawyeress.

"I'm not him," replied Mr. Franklin with a sly grin.

"Yes he is," I interjected, anxious to cut to the chase and get him to the room.

Hunter actually welcomed my intervention since it hooked her so thoroughly that she instantly agreed to go to the room with us, rather than being left behind in the wake of fame. Up in the room, we all got quite drunk and giddy as Hunter held court, attempting to seduce the Lawyeress into spending the night with him. I kept trying to excuse myself, but he seemed to want me to stay, fearful that she would bolt as soon as they were alone.

After a few hours of this game, the mouse finally left, insisting that she had to get ready for her job interview. Hunter and I talked for a bit about McGovern's birthday. Making a sharp appearance was most important to him, and he wanted to be ready for the event. He had marked certain passages in the campaign book to remember, and asked me to read them to him while he got in bed and soon fell asleep. It was a touching moment with The Beast, one that I had never seen

before or after. Usually I faded away while he partied on, but not on the eve of McGovern's Birthday.

The next morning I showed up at the Fairfax sharply at 8 a.m. as agreed. Apprehensively I walked down the corridor of his floor, wondering what to expect. At other times I've had to call hotel security and have the door removed from its hinges to get him up, but not today, not on McGovern's Birthday. As I rounded the corner he was already opening the door and grabbing the newspaper from the floor with a smile.

The rest of the day was smoother than a Biff from the Woody Creek Tavern (Bailey's Irish Cream with an Irish Whiskey floater). The limo driver tolerated us and everyone Hunter invited into the stretch along the way for refreshments. You can see most of the day in my "Breakfast with Hunter," movie a short preview of which is included on the www.hunterthompsonfilms.com website. The staff of the National Archives even let him smoke in a special room back stage at the symposium. For Hunter, that was a bit of true respect, and that's what he was looking for that day in Washington, DC. He was lauded by two Presidential candidates--Eugene McCarthy and George McGovern--and his old friends from the Washington press corps from Bill Greider to Jules Witcover came out to hear him speak. That night we went to the Australian Embassy where the Ambassador--a rabid non-smoker--spent the evening chasing Hunter around to stop him smoking, and we ended the night in stitches drinking at the apartment of P.J. and Tina O'Rourke.

The next day when I dismissed the serious limo driver, Hunter put a hundred dollar bill for him in an envelope with a piece of Fairfax Hotel stationery on which he wrote:

"Good Luck in Jail"

Still without a sense of humor after three days with Hunter, the driver read the note and then asked sorrowfully, "Am I going to jail?" I noted that he didn't ask "Why?"--just whether or not he was. So I replied "Not yet, but I'll let you know."

[NEVER CALL 911]

"Have you noticed how no one comes to the door unannounced since I shot Deborah?" Hunter asked with an odd sense of pride.

About a month had passed since the shooting incident at Owl Farm which was covered by over 800 news outlets worldwide. GONZO WRITER SHOOTS SECRETARY was a popular headline and essentially true, but the local press was particularly misleading with their banner HUNTER THOMPSON SHOOTS WOODY CREEK WOMAN. You'd think Hunter had done a drive-by shooting on the Woody Creek tavern, leaving some biker bleeding through her latex.

In fact, the real story was far stranger, and as the only one to witness it other than the victim and the shooter who can no longer be held accountable, I'll tell you the truth.

Hunter and I were working alone on his second book of letters, "Fear & Loathing in America," that long night into the morning. My habit was to wait until about 3 a.m. when the cops were busy processing the drunks picked up after the bars closed in Aspen and then head for my cabin up the Frying Pan River. But if the work persisted I would give up on my two beer rule as dawn approached and sleep next door in Deborah's spare bedroom for a few hours and then head home. Even though I usually left for Owl Farm in the dark I always brought my sunglasses for the possible ride up river against the sun.

At about 6:30 a.m. in this first year of the new century Hunter and I shared a smoke and I headed for Deborah's cabin about a hundred feet from the main house. The soft bed in the spare room could put anyone to sleep quickly, and I was down within minutes. Then the phone rang, waking me slightly. I heard Hunter's voice mumbling into Deborah's answering machine. His usual instructions for the day shift, I figured, slipping back into sleep and then BANG!

One gun shot followed instantly by Deborah screaming, "You shot me, you bastard!"

Rising up, I started to run out of the bedroom and then realized I was naked. The question arose in my mind whether to continue or stop to put on my pants. "Get the pants," I thought, figuring that I would not have a chance to retrieve them for some time.

Deborah was still standing in the front doorway, just beginning to bleed from multiple shotgun pellet wounds to her arms and legs. The color had drained from her face, but Hunter looked even paler as he rushed up to the door with the shotgun cradled in his arms.

He never looked sadder in all the years I knew him. Hunter truly loved Deborah. She had been with him since the early 1980's. Hunter also prided himself on being a good fire arms instructor. The idea of shooting anyone accidentally was abhorrent to him and as far as I

knew it had never happened before. (He once blew out a door frame that I was standing in with a 12 gauge, but that was on purpose and another story.) This was a true dilemma for me. "Never Call 911. Never. This means you!" was inscribed on the refrigerator at Owl Farm in his artful script, reminding me of the cardinal house rule every time I went for a beer. To call 911 would be to place all three of us "in the system" and start a legal log rolling that none of us could stop.

Looking at Deborah, I tried to assess whether she was about to go into shock. For a multiple gun shot victim she still looked pretty steady on her feet, so I figured the best strategy was to get her into my car immediately and take her directly to the Aspen Hospital. I rationalized that even if I called 911, I could get her to the emergency room faster than waiting for an ambulance. The local paparazzi were known to scan the police frequencies for celebrity fuckups just like this. No need to alert the media. I just hoped she would not bleed out too much during the ride. Dabbing at her wounds now with a towel I found no heavy, arterial bleeding.

"Can you make it to the hospital," I asked.

"I guess I'll have to, won't I, Wayne" replied Deborah sarcastically through clenched teeth. She's one tough lady. How else could she have survived twenty years with Hunter?

Leaving Hunter behind to deal with the authorities who we knew would inevitably arrive to investigate the scene, Deborah and I headed for the hospital through morning rush hour on Highway 82 (which the residents of Aspen have fought to keep as inaccessible as possible in the weird belief that traffic jams will keep out workers and tourists in cars.)

I called Sheriff Bob Braudis on his cell phone, assuming that this was not a violation of the 911 rule and that he could pave the way for me at the emergency room. Gun shot victims tend to produce many questions.

"Hunter shot Deborah," I said as soon as Bob answered. "She's alive. I'm driving her to the hospital."

Sheriff Bob loved Deborah at least as much as Hunter and I.

"That sonofabitch," Bob swore. "What happened?"

"It was an accident," I said.

"Okay, I'll see you at the ER," said Bob, hanging up.

By driving on the shoulder of the road I was able to skirt the workers waiting in their cars to serve rich people, and was proud that I made what was usually a 20 minute drive in about 10. We parked in

front of the emergency room, and Deborah said she could still walk, so I led her inside.

"What's wrong with her," asked the receptionist behind the desk where nurses were milling about on a quiet morning for an ER.

Leaning over the desk so that no one else could hear, I said softly, "She's been shot."

"GUN SHOT VICTIM," screamed the receptionist, and the whole room full of hospital workers froze.

The male nurse behind the desk picked up a RADIO microphone broadcasting to the world on the police frequency "Gun shot victim in the ER."

So the media was alerted and I might as well have called 911 in the first place. I did get Deborah to the hospital quicker than the system would have. Now, I just had a bloody car to deal with, the sheriff's deputies who were beginning to descend on Owl Farm, as well as worry about Deborah's wounds which turned out to not be so bad, all things considered. She still carries shotgun pellets in her legs as far as I know. It wasn't worth the trouble to take them out.

Hunter on the other hand faced a world of trouble. Sheriff Bob was not going to let him get away with a shooting, especially if he meant to hit Deborah.

The truth was, and I firmly believe this, that after I left Hunter at 6:30 a.m. he was about to go to bed as well and looked out towards Deborah's cabin and saw a bear around the dumpster between the two cabins. He went back into the kitchen and called Deborah's phone, leaving the message which turned out to be "do you see that bear outside your house?" Deborah heard the message, and got up to see the bear.

Meanwhile Hunter had grabbed a shot gun. He went to his side porch and shot at the ground just behind the bear to scare it off, just at the exact moment that Deborah opened her screen door.

She wasn't actually in the line of fire, but the shotgun pellets hit the open screen door frame and ricocheted into her arms and legs. Fortunately, she had not stepped outside or she would have been hit directly and more severely wounded.

In the end, Deborah refused to press charges against Hunter, all was forgiven, and I'll still never call 911. Never!

Owl Farm Album

DEBORAH FULLER

Hunter leaving Owl Farm on his BMW R75/5 headed to the Woody Creek Tavern. (1993)

Hunter at one of his many IBM Selectrics working on the manuscript of "Better Than Sex" at his Owl Farm kitchen-command post. (1994)

Hunter in the "Red Shark," a 1972 Chevy Caprice convertible, a gift from the Mitchell Brothers that they delivered to him in Woody Creek during what Hunter called the "Twisting of the Nipples" trial. (1994) (See Book Four for reporter-cartoonist R. L. Crabb's full account of the trial.)

A peacock in full preening was a normal sight at Owl Farm during the Spring peacock mating season. Predators including owls, foxes, and coyotes would frequently attack the peacocks. When Hunter needed new breeding stock for his peafowl flock he would call his old friends, John and Judy Clancy in Durango to drive up to Woody Creek to deliver new birds and visit. (1991)

A peacock and peahen at Owl Farm. (1995)

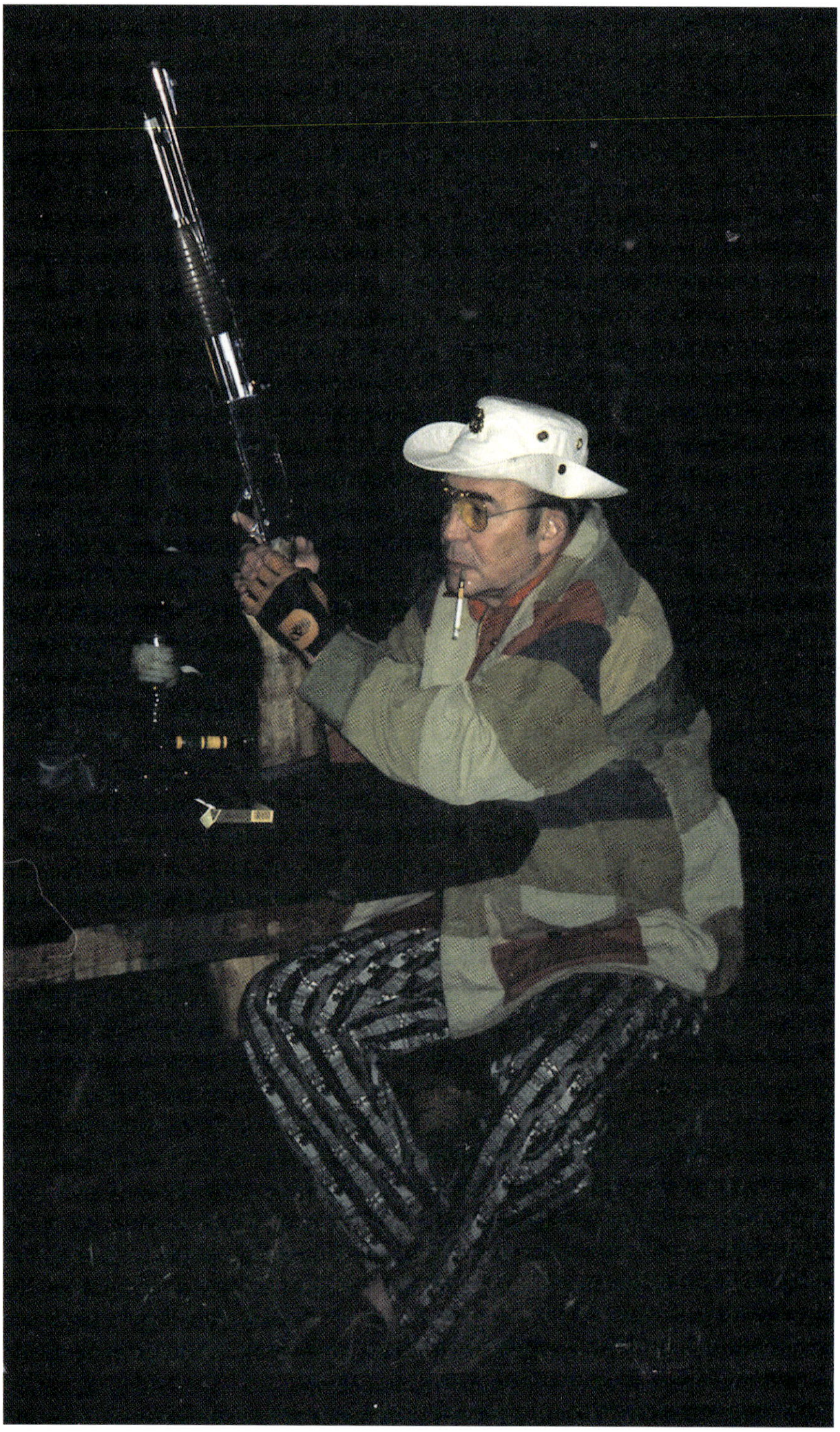

Hunter in his shooting jacket from Abercrombie and Fitch that he called the "coat of many colors," his signature Tilley Hat, and his favorite 12-gauge nickel-plated shotgun on the Owl Farm firing range. (2002)

Hunter at the Owl Farm shooting table preparing to do some celebratory shooting on his July 18th birthday. (1999)

Hunter shooting a "Thompson For Sheriff" poster one evening at Owl Farm. (1992)

Hunter with Jennifer and Juan Thompson at Owl Farm. (1997)

Ralph Steadman in Hunter's Owl Farm command-post kitchen on the 25th anniversary of "Fear & Loathing in Las Vegas." (1996)

SUPERBOWL SUNDAY: Hunter in his living room discussing strategy for Lisl Auman's defense with his friends from the National Association of Criminal Defense Lawyers: (left to right) Jerry Lefcourt, Michael Stepanian (standing), Abe Hutt, and Gerry Goldstein. (2001)

Historian Douglas Brinkley, the editor of Hunter's collected letters and his official biographer, the Paris Review's *George Plimpton, and* Sports Illustrated's *Terry McDonell working on Hunter's* Paris Review *interview. (2000)*

Shotgun Art:

Hunter began seriously working on his "Shotgun Art" technique in the 1970s. Shotgun Art was a mix-media approach which usually involved shooting a poster-sized photograph of a political or media personality or a personal friend of Hunter's, and then enhancing it with enamel spray paint and shooting it again. At times Hunter would hang paint cans over the poster-portrait and shoot the cans, letting the paint drip on the target. Here he is signing his Shotgun Art portrait of J. Edgar Hoover. (1991)

A night art shoot. Hunter working on a portrait of Ronald Reagan for his 1992 gallery show in Aspen, where he exhibited his Shotgun Art along with the works of two other artist-friends, Tom Benton and Ralph Steadman. (1992)

Hunter looking very much the mad artist working on his Marilyn Monroe art. (1991)

Hunter on his porch working on the Marilyn Monroe for his gallery show in Aspen. (1991)

Hunter working with enamel spray paint on his Shotgun Art portrait of one of his favorite writers, Ernest Hemingway. (1991)

Hunter's portrait of Hemingway. (1991)

Warren Zevon and Hunter at Owl Farm. Zevon traveled in his own bus and when he had a gig in the Aspen area he would often park his bus at Owl Farm and hang out with Hunter. In this photo Hunter slapped two Zevon posters on a board and he and the singer took turns shooting them, pouring on paint, and shooting them again. (2001)

Hunter with his old friend, the acclaimed artist Russell Chatham, at Owl Farm. (1994)

"Yesterday's Weirdness is Tomorrow's Reason Why"--Shotgun Art self-portrait. (1992)

George Plimpton in the Owl Farm kitchen for his final interview with Hunter for the Paris Review. *(2000) Plimpton died in 2003.*

Hunter As Elvis

JOHN WALSH

The first time I met Hunter was in October in 1973 at the California Street mansion of Jann Wenner, founder of *Rolling Stone* magazine, where I had just been hired to be the managing editor. Jann accurately predicted that Hunter and I would bond over sports. (It was Jann's last accurate prediction.) As I walked into the living room, Hunter was watching the Monday Night Football Buffalo Bills-Pittsburgh Steelers game. Within fifteen minutes we had devised a game of chance: Hunter would have the left side of the screen, the light jerseys, the even-numbered uniforms, and all the Caucasian players. I would have the right side of the TV, the dark jerseys, the odd numbers, and all of the non-Caucasian combatants. Add up the points scored for each of our "teams," and the loser would buy the winner a bottle of Wild Turkey, Hunter's preferred adult beverage of the day.

What we had not foreseen was that the critical points that would determine the outcome would be scored by Franco Harris. And, of course, the deciding factor was whether Franco Harris, the son of a mixed marriage, was on the Caucasian or non-Caucasian side of the ledger. Into the room walked George Plimpton, world renowned sports author of "Paper Lion," world class intellectual (Harvard), and diplomat extraordinaire. Hunter and I quickly agreed that George would make the ideal arbiter. No sooner had we posed the issue when George, as only George could, poured forth his ruling with the expertise of Hippocrates and the authority of a Supreme

Court justice. Did we get an earful of recessive genes! Hunter listened attentively and watched with bemused amazement until George declared Hunter the loser, at which time Hunter furiously grabbed a full bottle of the host's very old Wild Turkey, guzzled half of it, stole the keys to the host's white Mercedes Benz, and pulled out of the driveway, foot to the accelerator, waving the host's Wild Turkey out the window and screaming, "Vermin, Scum, Rat eaters."

What I did not know until Hunter "left the building" for good last February was that Hunter was Elvis. He was Elvis especially for young people who are looking for something new and different that's groundbreaking, passionate, and challenges authority, the system and conventional wisdom. Across the country, Hunter's literary works can easily be found in college curriculums, on high school syllabus, or in graduate studies for literature, social justice, or protest. The American education institution is embracing Hunter S. Thompson to teach students about life.

Socially, Hunter and Elvis were both style-dogs with much larger-than-life appetites for living closer to the edge than anyone you or they knew. Night Owls and American Originals, they are at their best when connecting entertainingly and emotionally to the heart of the Great American Dream Machine. Like Elvis, Hunter was bigger than the room and it wasn't just the cigarette holder and the aviator glasses. The entrance was grand-loud and stomping, sometimes physical and threatening, and usually with a laugh-out-loud gimmick; lipstick, wigs, brass knuckles, ridiculous hats, stylish scarve--after which Hunter fled to His Corner to hide for the rest of the night. And like Elvis, Hunter was a victim of his appetites, and for both the excess is a part of their legacy, sometimes obscuring their vast accomplishments and place of prominence in 20th century popular culture.

In the aftermath of Hunter's death, it was astounding the number of critical assessments of his corpus which, after acknowledging his originality and impact, observed that he had long since "lost his fastball," that his voice was "a faint echo" of the glory days, that he was "living on his literary fumes," etc. Hell, some colleagues at *Rolling Stone* in 1974 argued that Hunter was "losing his edge." So how many of our genre-defining artists keep it up over time, let alone keep their high wire act at full throttle until the very end? The challenge, beyond recognizing the obvious and the well-known works for their historical impact is to uncover the not-so-well known pieces and to

re-examine the full body of work to see if time and age may change our earlier valuation.

Certainly, there was more in Hunter before his lifestyle overtook his talent. By this time he had chosen indulgences that he sometimes could not overcome and this condition frustrated and annoyed him immensely. Still the talent was so great that it broke through in bursts, often when he was inspired by his pet causes or favorite vices. When Duke knocked Maryland out of the Final Four, his "Hey, Rube" column chronicled:

"There are many harsh lessons to be learned from the gambling experience, but the harshest one of all is the difference between having Fun and being Smart. It is the difference between Winning and Losing on most days, and the second-half of the Maryland-Duke game on Saturday was a lesson for the Fun-Loving Losers ... If Sunday is the Lord's day, then Saturday belongs to the Devil. It is the only night of the week when he gives out Free passes to the Late Show at the Too Much Fun Club ... Maryland was a special case this year and only a fool would have bet real money on them to hold a big lead for more than 33 seconds in a serious game. They curled up like worms in a bonfire."

Gems like this were a part of Hunter's last gallant run--in cyberspace of all places. He had a hard time producing them and the audience had to be on red alert for them. One of the reasons for this situation was that Hunter finally met his match in the land of dotcom. Whether it was an article, a manuscript, an insert, or a revision, Hunter forever had this weird relationship with deadlines. You could theorize that Hunter used deadlines to torture editors and he would take great pride in this observation. You could also surmise that Hunter used deadlines as motivation. Until, that is, he confronted publishing on the Internet. Before that, Hunter had the comfort of knowing that his editor would be on his case to meet the agreed upon and scheduled publishing date. There were greater forces in play to make him produce eventually--whenever that was. This frequently resulted in a jousting match to determine how far the deadline could be pushed. Procrastination was also a convenient tool in the writer's arsenal to fuel conspiracy theories. So when the inevitable "When do you need it by?" question arose early on, the stunning response was "Whenever it's ready, we'll publish it."

Hunter: Oh.

Walsh: They edit and post it whenever they get it. It would be great to post it every Monday midday and that helps regular readership. But if it gets here late, that's when it will go up.

Hunter: I'll be damned.

Walsh: It's up to you.

Hunter: What happens if you don't get it?

Walsh: We don't publish it and you don't get paid.

Hunter: Oh! That would put my addictions at risk.

Walsh: So you're saying that your addictions have become your hammer?

Hunter: Well, hot damn.

Shotgun Golf:

After a collection of the "Hey Rube" columns were published as Hunter's last living book, he continued to write in the fall and winter of 2004-2005, but a lot more infrequently, and it's interesting to note that "guns" or "suicide" frequently appeared somewhere in many columns. In fact, his final column posted February 15, 2005 probably told us what was on his mind. This is the column:

The death of professional hockey in AMERICA is a nasty omen for people with heavy investments in NHL teams. But to me, it meant little or nothing--and that's why I called Bill Murray with an idea that would change both our lives forever.

It was 3:30 on a dark Tuesday morning when I heard the phone ring on his personal line in New Jersey. "Good morning," I said to myself as I fired up a thin Cohiba. "He's bound to be wide awake and crackling at this time of day, or at least I can leave a very excited message.

My eerie hunch was right. The crazy bugger picked up on the fourth ring, and I felt my heart racing. "Hot damn," I thought. "This is how empires are built." Late? I know not late.

"Genius round the world stands hand in hand, and one shock of recognition runs the whole circle round.

HST: "Are you ready for a powerful idea? I want to ask you about golf in Japan. I understand they're building vertical driving ranges on top of each other."

Bill (sounding strangely alert): "Yes, they have them outdoors, under roofs ... "

HST: "I've seen pictures. I thought they looked like bowling alleys stacked on top of each other."

Bill: (Laughs.)

HST: "I'm working on a profoundly goofy story here. It's wonderful. I've invented a new sport. It's called Shotgun Golf. We will rule the world with this thing."

Bill: "Mmhmm."

HST: "I've called you for some consulting advice on how to launch it. We've actually already launched it. Last spring, the Sheriff and I played a game outside in the yard here. He had my Ping Beryllium 9-iron, and I had his shotgun, and about 100 yards away, we had a linoleum green and a flag set up. He was pitching toward the green. And I was standing about 10 feet away from him, with the alley-sweeper. And my objective was to blow his ball off course, like a clay pigeon."

Bill: (Laughs.)

HST: "It didn't work at first. The birdshot I was using was too small. But double-aught buck finally worked for sure. And it was fun."

Bill: (Chuckles.)

HST: "OK, I didn't want to wake you up, but I knew you'd want to be in on the ground floor of this thing."

Bill: (Silence.)

HST: "Do you want to discuss this tomorrow?"

Bill: "Sure."

HST: "Excellent."

Bill: "I think I might have a queer dream about it now, but ... " (Laughs.)

HST: "This sport has a HUGE future. Golf in America will soon come to this."

Bill: "It will bring a whole new meaning to the words Driving Range."

HST: "Especially when you stack them on top of each other. I've seen it in Japan."

Bill: "They definitely have multi-level driving ranges. Yes."

HST: (Laughs.) "How does that work? Do they have extremely high ceilings?"

Bill: "No. The roof above your tee only projects out about ten feet, and they have another range right above you. It's like they took the façade off the building. People would be hanging out of their offices."

HST: "I see. It's like one of those original Hyatt Regency Hotels. Like an atrium. In the middle of the building you could jump straight down into the lobby?"

Bill: "Exactly like that!"

HST: "It's like people driving balls from one balcony to the next."

Bill: (Laughs.) "Yes, they could."

HST: "I could be on the eighth floor and you on the sixth? Or on the fifteenth. And we'd be driving across a lake."

Bill: "They have flags out every 150 yards, every 200 yards, every 250 yards. It's just whether you are hitting it at ground level, or from five stories up."

HST: "I want to find out more about this. This definitely has a future to it."

Bill: "They have one here in the city--down at Chelsea Pier."

HST: "You must have played a lot of golf in Japan."

Bill: "Not much; I just had one really great day of golf. I worked most of the time. But I did play one beautiful golf course. They have seasonal greens, two different types of grass. It's really beautiful."

HST: "Well, I'm writing a column for ESPN.com and I want to know if you like my new golf idea. A two-man team."

Bill: "Well, with all safety in mind, yes. Two-man team? Yeah! That sounds great. I think it would create a whole new look. It would create a whole new clothing line."

HST: "Absolutely. You'll need a whole new wardrobe for this game."

Bill: "Shooting glasses and everything."

HST: "We'll obviously have to make a movie. This will mushroom or mutate--either way--into a real craze. And given the mood of this country, being that a lot of people in the mood to play golf are also in the mood to shoot something, I think it would take off like a gigantic fad."

Bill: "I think the two-man team idea would be wonderful competition and is something the Ryder Cup would pick up on."

HST: "I was talking with the Sheriff about it earlier. But in one-man competition, I'd have to compete against you, say, in both of the arts--the shooting AND the golfing. But if you do the Ryder Cup, you'd have to have the clothing line first. I'm going to write about this for ESPN tonight. I'm naming you and the Sheriff as the founding consultants."

Bill: "Sounds good."

HST: "OK, I'll call you tomorrow. And by the way, I'll see if I can twist some arms and get you an Oscar. But I want a Nobel Prize in return."

Bill: "Well, we can work together on this. This is definitely a team challenge." (Laughing.)

HST: "OK. We'll talk tomorrow."

Bill: "Good night."

So there it is. Shotgun Golf will soon take America by storm. I see it as the first truly violent leisure sport. Millions will crave it.

Shotgun Golf was invented in the ominous summer of 2004 AD, right there at the Owl Farm in Woody Creek. The first game was played between me and Sheriff Bob Braudis on the ancient Bomb & Shooting Range of the Woody Creek Rod & Gun Club. It was witnessed by many members and other invited guests and filmed for historical purposes by Dr. Thompson on Super-Beta videotape.

The game consists of one golfer, one shooter and a field judge. The purpose of the game is to shoot your opponent's high-flying golf ball out of the air with a finely-tuned, 12-gauge shotgun, thus preventing him (your opponent) from lofting a 9-iron approach shot into a distant "green" and making a "hole in one." Points are

scored by blasting your opponent's shiny new Titleist out of the air and causing his shot to fail miserably. That earns you two points.

But if you miss and your enemy holes out, he (or she) wins two points when his ball hits and stays on the green. "And after that, you trade places and equipment, and move on to round two.

My patent is still pending, and the train is leaving the station, and Murray is a Founding Consultant, along with the Sheriff, and Keith Richards, etc., etc. Invest now or forever hold your peace.

As for Bill's triumphant finish at Pebble Beach, I am almost insanely proud of him. He's an elegant athlete in the finest Murray tradition. Bill is a dangerous brute with the fastest reflexes in Hollywood, but he is suave, and that is why I trust him even more than I trust all his brothers. Yes, I say Hallelujah, praise Jesus. Where is Brian? I will need him for this golf project, if only to offset Bill's bitchiness. We will march on a road of bones.

OK. Back to business. It was Bill Murray who taught me how to mortify your opponents in any sporting contest, honest or otherwise. He taught me my humiliating PGA fadeaway shot, which has earned me a lot of money ... after that, I taught him how to swim, and then I introduced him to the shooting arts, and now he wins everything he touches. Welcome to the future of America. Welcome to Shotgun Golf.

So long and Mahalo.

Hunter.

The column about Thompson's 3:30am conversation with Murray reminded me of Hunter's comedic talents which manifested themselves at the strangest times, like when ordering room service. Hunter visited Washington in the fall of 1978 and invited me to a Sunday football feast at his Hyatt Regency hotel suite. Before the first kickoff, Hunter, the always-gracious host, ordered room service for the game. "I'd like a fifth of Chivas Regal, three six-packs of Heineken, a half-dozen bloody marys, and everything chocolate on the menu." I was the only other person in the room and informed my

host that I was on a diet that precluded sweets and alcohol. One hour later, two waiters delivered the order with looks only cameras could capture. The chocolate tray included a German chocolate cake, a vat of Breyer's chocolate ice cream, a half-dozen chocolate cupcakes, a plate of chocolate cookies, one chocolate sundae, two chocolate cream pies, and a buffet of various chocolate pastries. And of course, the requisite postprandial chocolate bonbons. Hunter was ready for some football.

The last time I saw Hunter was one week before the Super Bowl. Whenever I visited him, he would ask me to bring him sushi or some hot dogs from a roadside stand, smothered with every possible condiment in Aspen. But this time he never ate a morsel.

He had a stationary bicycle in the kitchen, which he sat on. That was his idea of exercise--pedaling slowly on the bike while holding a glass of Johnnie Walker Blue in his right hand and the ubiquitous cigarette in the left hand. Occasionally the cigarette would be replaced by a pipe and from time to time he would ask his guests if anyone was in need of a stimulant, as he pedaled away. He'd ask a guest to read from his latest book, "Hey Rube." While the guest was reading, you could see Hunter's eyes close, his head tilted to the ceiling as he thought about the words and passed judgment on each of the passages. The next step was to watch a home video of his latest book-signing in Los Angeles. On the video, Harry Dean Stanton and Benicio Del Toro read from "Hey Rube" while Hunter sat in the background with Anjelica Houston until Hugh Hefner entered the room with a posse of bunnies. Hunter's mood was quiet, reflective, proud, and he had a certain uncomfortable air of contentedness.

Next, he went to his command post with his phones and connected me to his wide swath of friends. He called Jim Irsay to get him to bond with me at the Super Bowl. He called Anita to entice her to come home for the second evening of my visit. He called his former wife, Sandy, to see if we could all get together when I visited Denver for the NBA All-Star Game. And of course he called Doug Brinkley, because he had to check in to see how his life was being organized.

Over the last couple of years there had been a decline in his health, as well as a corresponding spiritual decline. It was hardly noticeable, but you could sense it. It wasn't the full-frontal Hunter. He had visited ESPN a few years ago. It was torturous for him to get around before his hip operation, you could see the pain, his physical pain. He wasn't writing as much. When he started to write in

2000 for ESPN.com, he was doing it pretty regularly. But it declined each year, and then there was a precipitous drop, and I know that it wasn't right because he loved to write about sports. He just couldn't bring himself to do it any more. There was no foreboding at the time. But, in reflection, this was Hunter's farewell. His body was failing him, and it was difficult for him to write.

As we parted, he signed a copy of "Screwjack" for me, we made our bets on the Super Bowl, and he pulled out the latest gimmick to sell his book--a black thong with the gonzo logo and "HEY RUBE" embossed in pink. Then there was the usual hug, accompanied by an unusually tearful goodbye.

Photo: Deborah Fuller

John Walsh and Hunter at Owl Farm, 2004.

Hunter Makes A Commercial, Sort Of

JEFF GOODBY

After Will Hearst took over the *San Francisco Examiner*, he began hiring off-the-wall people as his columnists and at the top of the list was Hunter.

My company was doing the paper's advertising, featuring black and white, cinematic commercials in which Hearst went out into the world assembling his new staff. Naturally, we decided to do one with Thompson. Andy Berlin and I wrote it and--when you think about it, it was crazy--it took place at a firing range.

John Francis was directing the commercials for us and he found a range to use at the Army Presidio in San Francisco. For some reason, my partners went to the shoot that day without me. Around 11, I was at the office when I got a call from Berlin.

"Goodby, you've got to get out here and help me," he said. He wasn't being funny.

"Why? What's going on?"

"Well, you know how you always thought Hunter Thompson was crazy but probably really fun to hang out with?"

"Yeah."

"Well, the first part's true but the second part kind of isn't."

I drove out there and went into the range. On the monitors, I saw Hunter waving a .44 pistol to make a point to the crew. I headed inside just as he headed out the same door.

I can distinctly remember what he looked like. He was as tall as I am, maybe even a bit taller. His was scowling with big bushy eyebrows under an Air Force cap, and I could tell from his look that he'd probably been doing some drugs. His eyes looked right past me. "Excuse me," he said, in a Southern gentlemanly sort of way, but the way he brushed by me was not gentle. A nice-looking woman followed him, looking even more wasted. She would crop up again.

"You okay?" I asked Berlin and Hearst.

"Yeah, Hunter's been a handful, though," Will said. "I had to get the hotel security to let me into his room to get him up. Then he got into the shower and wouldn't come out. I sat on the bed for half an hour, watching TV. Finally, I went to the bathroom door. 'Hunter, this is your publisher!' I said to him. 'Get the fuck out of the shower! Now!' 'Yes sir, Mr. Hearst!' he said to me, and got out immediately. I drove him over here."

"He won't read the script," Berlin said.

"Why not?"

"And he wants real bullets in the gun, not blanks. He says he needs real bullets so that the recoil is realistic." Just then, Hunter walked up.

I introduced myself. "You want to rework the script?" I said to Hunter.

"It's terrible," he said. "I can't read that shit. You really think that's good? Who wrote it?"

These were questions I didn't think we should answer. "Let's just fix it. What part is the problem for you?"

Hunter glowered at me. "Well, the ending, for one. This line isn't funny."

"Well, what do you want to say? I think you should say something you think is funny there, something that feels good to you."

The three of us thought hard for about thirty seconds. Then Hunter brightened up.

"I want to say: 'We will chase them like rats across the tundra.'"

I didn't think it was a line Hunter could actually pull off. On the page, it might be good, but I was skeptical about saying it out loud. "Okay, let's try it."

Hunter and Hearst headed back inside. I watched from the monitor. Hunter's girlfriend was next to me, pretty cooked on something. She started flirting with me egregiously.

"You're cute. What do you do?" she said.

EDITORIAL DIRECTION: *Examiner publisher William Randolph Hearst III with Hunter at the Presidio shooting range attempting to shoot a television commercial for the* Examiner.

I told her and began to make small talk about Hunter and his predicament. Great, I thought. Hunter will come back out with a .44 and see his girlfriend hitting on me.

"I just want to give him something he's comfortable saying," I said.

"He's having fun." She shrugged and smiled warmly at him on the monitor. It was like a mom smiling at her naughty child.

The "tundra" line was actually funnier than I thought it would be, but there was no way to end the commercial after Hunter said it. It was one of those lines that stops the whole drama in its tracks, that calls too much attention to itself. We ended up trying to get a funny look out of Will and just let everyone go home.

That was when the truly disturbing thing happened.

At some point, as they were dressing Hunter for the filming, someone suggested that he borrow a high school athletic jacket that one of the female crew members had on. It was big enough for Hunter to wear, I guess, and he liked it. It had patches and pins on it. At the end of the filming, Hunter started to head off with the jacket still on his back. A guy from the crew was dispatched to retrieve it, just as Thompson was heading into his girlfriend's Saab.

"Excuse me, Hunter," the guy said. "We need to get that jacket back from you."

"They said I could keep it," Hunter said, opening the car door.

"No," the crew member said politely. "We need the jacket to do some insert shots of you firing the gun. I need it back."

"Insert shots?"

"Well, you know, something where we just see your hand and the sleeve of the jacket. We'll get someone else to be your hand."

I could see Hunter was going to cause some kind of scene over this. "So you just need the jacket for the sleeve?" he said.

"Yeah."

In one motion, Hunter took the jacket off and suddenly a jack knife appeared in his hand. He hacked at the sleeve of the jacket until it was almost cut off, then gave up and flung the whole pile at the crew guy. "Here you go!" he said, got into the car and slammed the door. His girlfriend smiled and rolled her eyes like a wife leaving a Connecticut cocktail party, then got in and they drove off.

There was a woman in tears next to me. "That was my boyfriend's jacket," she said to me. "Why did he have to do that?"

The next time I saw Hunter was at the *Examiner* Christmas party, in some mansion on Nob Hill. He had a tumbler of bourbon in his hand and a yellow smoking jacket on. He remembered me and was as nice as could be.

I asked him if he had seen the commercial.

"I thought it was great!" he beamed. "Really funny. Were you guys happy? Did you get what you needed?" Everything was forgotten, forgiven. He shook my hand, said "Well, Merry Christmas!" and walked off into the crowd.

Months later, I found myself playing pool with Artie and Jim Mitchell, the self-described "pornographers" who produced "Behind the Green Door" and "Inside Marilyn Chambers." They owned the Mitchell Brothers theater, a notorious strip joint. It was noontime and Warren Hinckle, the ex-publisher of *Ramparts* and then an editor at the *Examiner*, had taken Berlin and me up to the brothers' office, a Victorian room just down from the stage. Totally nude women walked in and out as we played pool, asking us to light their cigarettes.

After an hour of drinking and pool, Jim took us up onto a catwalk above the theater. At 1:00 in the afternoon, a half dozen men were receiving lap dances below us. They couldn't see us looking down at them. "We called Hunter 'the night manager,' " Jim said. "He used to sit up here for hours, watching the action below." And sure enough, there was a chair still up there. You could see Hunter in it, buzzed out with a cigarette in the holder, watching the futile, humorous, desperate parade below.

Thinking of that moment, I went to the Mitchell Brothers website this morning. The wallpaper behind the nude women in the pictures features Hunter's signature and then, in his own handwriting: "THE CRAZY NEVER DIE!" I could hear him saying it.

I Knew He Meant It

RALPH STEADMAN

Hunter said these words to me many years ago. "I would feel real trapped in this life if I didn't know I could commit suicide at any time." I knew he meant it. It wasn't a case of if, but when. He didn't reckon he would make it beyond 30 anyway, so he lived it all in the fast lane. There was no first, second, third, or top gear in the car--just overdrive.

He was in a hurry.

"Drive your stake into a darkened heart in a red Mercedes-Benz. The blackness hides a speeding tramp. The savage breast pretends. But never mind the nights, my love, because they never really happened anyway." So we wrote in a Beverly Hills house one drunken night. I wrote the stanzas, he wrote the chorus. "Don't write, Ralph," he said, "you'll bring shame on your family."

"Those Weird and Twisted Nights." That was the song.

On Sunday morning, I had just finished signing the 1,200 title pages for a limited-edition Taschen version of "The Curse of LONO." Hunter had signed all of them so uncharacteristically obediently, mechanically--over the month of December. I thought that was very strange. He has to be cajoled like a child to do anything like that, so I drew his portrait across the last sheet, glaring out, his two eyes in the two Os of LONO, put the cigarette holder with long Dunhill prodding upwards in his grimacing mouth, signed it with an extra flourish, and closed the last of the four boxes. The old bastard! He waited to make sure I had finished the task. Then he signed himself off.

I knew it was too good to be true. Now I will be expected to build a monstrous cannon in Woody Creek, a 100-foot-high column of steel tubes, with the big red fist on its top and his ashes placed in a firebomb in its palm.

"Two thumbs, Ralph! Don't forget the two thumbs!!" Such were his demands as he tipped at his windmills. People were fucking with his beloved Constitution and he was born to banish the geeks who were doing it. In that way he was a real live American: a pioneer, frontiersman, last of the cowboys, a conservative redneck with a huge and raging mind, taking the easy way out and mythologizing himself at the same time.

He spent a lot of his early years in rejection writing; verbatim excerpts from Hemingway, Faulkner, and Conrad, trying to imagine what it was like to write some classic text. He could be very persuasive.

As a boy he was hired by the milkman to collect bills outstanding from the citizens of Louisville, Kentucky, but he was shunned by his neighbors, and especially the literary establishment in the town, so he had a score to settle.

I had only just arrived in America in late April of 1970, and was staying with a friend in the Hamptons to decompress. I got a call from J.C. Suares, art editor of *Scanlan's*. He said: "How'd ya like to go to the Kentucky Derby with an ex-Hell's Angel who just shaved his head and cover the race? His name is Hunter S. Thompson and he wants an artist to nail the decadent, depraved faces of the local establishment who meet there. He doesn't want a photographer. He wants something weird and we've seen your work."

The managing editor, Don Goddard, had been a *New York Times* foreign editor and he thought I was naive enough to take this on. I was looking for work--so I went. Finding Hunter, or indeed anyone covering the prestigious Kentucky Derby who is not a bona fide registered journalist, was no easy matter, and trying to explain my reasons for being there was even worse, especially as I was under the impression that this was an official trip and I was an accredited press man.

Why shouldn't I think that? I assumed that *Scanlan's* was an established magazine. I had been watching someone chalk racing results on a blackboard while I sipped a beer. I was about to turn and get myself another when a voice like no other I had ever heard

cut into my thoughts and sank its teeth into my brain. It was a cross between a slurred karate chop and gritty molasses.

"Um ... er, you ... er wouldn't be from England, er, would you ... er? An artist maybe ... er ... What the ... !"

I had turned around and two fierce eyes, firmly socketed inside a bullet-shaped head, were staring at a strange growth I was nurturing on the end of my chin. "Holy shit!" he exclaimed. "They said I was looking for a matted-haired geek with string warts and I guess I've found him."

We took a beer together and sat in the press box. Somehow, he had got our accreditation and we were in. He asked me if I gambled and I said only once, in 1952. I put two shillings on Early Mist to win in the 1953 Grand National. And it did. I picked a horse but didn't bet and it won so then I picked another, backed it with a dollar, and lost. "That's why I don't gamble," I said.

"I thought you had been picked up," he replied. "Picked up?" I didn't quite understand. "Er, yes, the police here are pretty keen. They tend to take an interest in something different. The, er ... um, the beard. Not many of them around these parts. Not these days anyway."

I was beginning to take in the whole of the man's appearance, and his was a little different too. Certainly not what I was expecting. No time-worn leather, shining with old sump oil. No manic tattoo across a bare upper arm and, strangely, no hint of menace. This man had an impressive head chiseled from one piece of bone and the top part was covered down to his eyes by a floppy brimmed sunhat. His top half was draped in a loose-fitting hunting jacket of multicolored patchwork. He wore seersucker blue pants and the whole torso was pivoted on a pair of huge white Plimsolls with a fine red trim around the bulkheads. Damn near six-foot-six of solid bone and meat holding a beaten-up leather bag across his knee and a loaded cigarette holder between the arthritic fingers of his other hand.

Arthritis was to plague him all his life, as was the football knee injury that left him with one leg shorter than the other, but it never truly encumbered his physical rage or his action-packed approach to a deep respect and love of writing--and righteousness.

We found the decadent, depraved faces of Louisville by the end of the first week we spent together. They were staring at us from a mirror in the gents toilet on the infield, where the rest of the riff-raff,

who are not eligible to stand in the privileged boxes of the chosen few, spent their time at the races, just like us.

We spent many assignments together, bucking the trend, against the cheats and liars, the bagmen and the cronies; me an alien from the old country and him raging against the coming of the light. "Fuck them, Ralph," he would say, "we are not like the others."

Well, he wasn't anyway, but I was easily led. Before "Fear and Loathing in Las Vegas" we tried to cover the America's Cup yacht race in Rhode Island for *Scanlan's* (who were just about to go bust and get on to Richard Nixon's blacklist) from a three-masted schooner. There was a rock band on board for distraction, booze, and, for Hunter, whatever he was gobbling at the time. I was seasick and Hunter was fine. I asked him what he was taking and he gave me one. It was psilocybin [magic mushroom], a psychedelic hallucinogen, my first and only drug trip apart from Librium. I was the artist from England so I had a job to do.

He handed me two spray-paint canisters. "What do I do with these?"

"You're the artist, Ralph. Do what you want, but you must do it on the side of one of those multimillion-dollar yachts, moored hardly 50 yards away from where we are."

"How about 'Fuck the Pope'?" I said, now seeing in my mind red, snarling dogs attacking a musician singing at a piano dressed as a nun at a shore-bound bar.

"Are you a Catholic, Ralph?"

"No," I replied, "it's just the first thing that came to mind."

So that was the plan and we made it to the boats and I stood up in the little dinghy with the spray cans and shook them as one does. They made a clicking sound and alerted a guard. "We must flee, Ralph! There'll be pigs everywhere. We have failed." He pulled fiercely on the oars and fell backwards with legs in the air. He righted himself and started rowing again. We made it back to our boat and while I was gabbling insanely, he was writing down all the gibberish that I uttered. I was now a basket case and we had to get back to shore and flee. Hunter shot off two distress flares into the harbor and we hailed a boat just coming in. The flares set fire to one of the boats, causing an emergency fire rescue as we got to dry land. There's more and I won't go on, but I guess that was the genesis of "Fear and Loathing in Las Vegas."

Such a wild game was possible, but it needed all the genius and application of Hunter S. Thompson to make it live. He has done that and he has proved that a redneck Southern gentleman who has the fire in his belly and the indignation in his soul can make it happen.

I had the good fortune to meet one of the great originals of American literature. Maybe he is the Mark Twain of the late 20th century. Time will sort the bastard out.

I have always known that one day I would know this journey, but yesterday, I did not know that it would be today.

--February 20, 2005

The View From The Left

JONAH RASKIN

"The Kentucky Derby is Decadeant and Depraved" is the title of the article by Hunter S. Thompson that appeared in *Scanlan's Monthly* in June 1970, the start of what came to be called "gonzo journalism" that reached a crescendo in two powerful books, "Fear and Loathing in Las Vegas" and "Fear and Loathing on the Campaign Trail '72." Hunter S. Thompson was a fearless reporter who loathed the rich and the powerful, and took deadly aim at them in nearly everything that he wrote until, sadly, he committed suicide on February 20, 2005.

In many ways American journalism has not been the same since his death. He was journalism's moral compass.

Though there are some exceptions, American journalism has become in large part lapdog for the rich and the powerful. It is fawning, subservient, docile, and toothless. Much of the time, it aims to tell people who have money where to spend it and how to spend it. It is the decadent mass media of a decadent empire that stokes the egos of the wealthy, and provides distractions from the realities of war, exploitation, poverty, and disease. Were he alive today, Hunter S. Thompson would be writing articles entitled "The U.S. Is Decadent and Depraved." The contagion has spread.

Thompson saw through the phoniness, the lies, and the deceits of American politicians, and lashed out at them, especially at Richard Milhous Nixon. When Nixon died in 1994, Thompson wrote a piece entitled "He Was a Crook" in which he memorably said, "I beat him

like a mad dog with mange every time I got a chance, and I am proud of it. He was scum."

Thompson spoke and wrote for the disenfranchised, the dispossessed, the poor, the homeless, and the persecuted. At times he could be cynical and depressed, but he also had clarity of moral vision and a commitment to tell the truth. It is true that he was not an objective journalist, that he wasn't always fair and accurate. It is true, also, that he fictionalized, and that he made himself an essential part of the stories that he wrote about. That was gonzo and that was a part of the greatness and the genius of gonzo.

But gonzo was far more than just fictionalizing and making the author a principal player in the story. Gonzo meant lashing out at the American plutocrats, millionaires and Wall Street thieves who are served by newspapers and magazines such as the *New York Times* and *Vanity Fair* with their nauseating adulation of the elite. Yes, sometimes there is investigative reporting that brings an important story to light, but that is the exception. The bigger the story, the slower it takes big media to cover it. Hunter Thompson's gonzo was a karate chop to the heart of a newspaper establishment that lied year after year about war, and the military and economic invasions of countries.

Much has been made of the fact that Thompson broke the laws about drugs, including marijuana. Indeed, he never hid the fact that he smoked pot. He has also been described again and again as an "outlaw journalist," and while there is a certain cache about that metaphor especially in the counterculture, it might give a false impression of Thompson. He was largely law abiding, and for the most part he respected the rules governing journalism. When he did break the rules he knew he was doing so, deliberately and consciously with a purpose. Like Hemingway, who was one of his literary heroes, he had a personal code of honor, and a set of ethical guidelines to live his life.

One can turn to Thompson's 1967 article for the *New York Times Magazine* to see his rules about writing, his views about confidentiality, and his perceptions of the American double standard regarding alcohol use and abuse, and drug use and abuse. "To write from experience is an admission of felonious guilt," he wrote. "It is also a potential betrayal of people whose only 'crime' is the smoking of a weed that grows wild all over the world but the possession of which, in California, carries a minimum sentence of two years in prison for a second offense." Thompson belonged to a long tradition of American dissidents like Anne Hutchinson, Henry David Thoreau and Jack

London who broke the law, but who remained true to their own moral sense of right and wrong, and obeyed their own conscience. He had a moral compass and he kept on course.

Thompson inspired a generation of reporters. Some of them are still around, still writing, and still fighting the good fight with blogs and books. Thompson's in-your-face style of reporting was very popular and immensely contagious, and it caught on. Readers loved it because it was real, and because it was alive and genuine. It expressed the sense of moral outrage that readers felt. Editors went with it for a time. But that time is mostly past. To a large extent American journalism is back to its old form: covering up, concealing the bodies, and telling lies. Editors and publishers tend to want pretty pictures.

Some professors of journalism say that gonzo can't be taught. Maybe they're right; after all they have advanced degrees. Maybe gonzo is something that a writer has to find for himself or herself in much the same way that Hunter S. Thompson found it for himself--the hard way, by writing and writing and writing again. But let's pray and hope that a new generation comes along that finds inspiration in Hunter S. Thompson's fearlessness, and his loathing for the likes of politicians such as Nixon, Reagan and the Bushes. There are plenty of targets for young journalists to take aim at, and right in their own communities

When journalism professors say that gonzo can't be taught they might be missing the essential point. To borrow the old but true cliché, reporters are supposed to afflict the comfortable and comfort the afflicted. As a professor teaching media studies, I can say that Thompson's books belong on your reading lists.

In one of the stories Thompson wrote soon after the Democratic National Convention in Chicago in 1968, he describes himself in the street along with the protestors. Just a few feet away were armed National Guardsmen, city policemen, and the national news media. One of the protestors offered Thompson a joint. He looked at it, looked at the soldiers and then he took the joint and inhaled. "It seemed at the time like a thing that had to be done," he wrote. "I knew which side I was on, and to refuse that joint would have been--in my own mind--a fatal equivocation."

Thompson always knew that there were sides. He always knew, too, what side he was on: the side without the power and the money; the side that had nothing to lose and everything to win. He gave it all he could for as long as he could, and American journalism and

American reporting was better because of him. I hope students who think he's cool and hip can appreciate the fact that he fearlessly took sides.

Some of his former friends and associates from the big national magazines are hard on him today. He couldn't not stop drugging and drinking, they say. He couldn't "clean up his act." But that inability to "clean up his act" was his saving grace. It meant that he didn't go to the Kentucky Derby to celebrate with the rich and decadent. It meant that he didn't buy into the trapping of material success. Thompson never went to any of the spectacles of the rich and decadent to celebrate with them, but to record and describe their depravity. He didn't become a Yuppie, didn't applaud the gentrification of America, didn't put on a tuxedo and go to the White House on bended knees as so many other journalists did. That makes him a kind of hero.

When he committed suicide in 2005, conservative commentators used the occasion to berate him and to blame him for many of the ills of the society. Some even had the audacity to say that he wasn't a journalist. I supposed those same critics don't consider John Reed a journalist either, and never did approve of Jessica Mitford, who exposed the funeral industry, and whose pen was as sharp and as witty as Thompson's. He was a great satirist, and no one was too rich or too powerful for Thompson to satirize. We took him for granted for decades. Now that he's gone, there's a huge hole in the world of newspapers and magazines.

As Gonzo In Life As In His Work

TOM WOLFE

Hunter S. Thomspon was one of those rare writers who come as advertised.

The Addams-family eyebrows in Stephen King's book jacket photos combined with the heeby-jeeby horrors of his stories always made me think of Dracula. When I finally met Mr. King, he was in Miami playing, along with Amy Tan, in a jook-house band called the Rock Bottom Remainders. He was Sunshine itself, a laugh and a half, the very picture of innocent fun, a Count Dracula who in real life was Peter Pan. Carl Hiaasen, the genius who has written such zany antic novels as "Striptease," "Sick Puppy," and "Skinny Dip" is in person as intelligent, thoughtful, sober, courteous, even courtly, a Southern gentleman as you could ask for (and I ask for them all the time and never find them).

But the gonzo--Hunter's coinage--madness of Hunter Thompson's "Fear and Loathing in Las Vegas" and his classics such as "The Kentucky Derby is Decadent and Depraved," was what you got in the flesh too. You didn't have lunch or dinner with Hunter Thompson. You attended an event at mealtime.

I had never met Hunter when the book that established him as a literary figure, "The Hell's Angels: A Strange and Terrible Saga," was published in 1967. It was brilliant investigative journalism of the

hazardous sort, written in a style and a voice no one had ever seen or heard before. The book revealed that he had been present at a party for the Hell's Angels given by Ken Kesey and his hippie--at the time the term was not "hippie" but "acid-head"--commune, the Merry Pranksters. The party would be a key scene in a book I was writing, "The Electric Kool-Aid Acid Test." I cold-called Hunter in California, and he generously gave me not only his recollections but also the audiotapes he had recorded at that first famous alliance of the hippies and "outlaw" motorcycle gangs, a strange and terrible saga in itself, culminating in the Rolling Stones band hiring the Angels as security guards for a concert in Altamont, California, and the "security guards" beating a spectator to death with pool cues.

By way of a thank you for his help, I invited Hunter to lunch the next time he was in New York. It was one bright spring day in 1969. He proved to be one of those tall, rawboned, rangy young men with alarmingly bright eyes, who more than any other sort of human, in my experience, are prone to manic explosions. Hunter didn't so much have a conversation with you as speak in explosive salvos of words on a related subject.

We were walking along West 46th Street toward a restaurant, The Brazilian Coffee House, when we passed Goldberg Marine Supply. Hunter stopped, ducked into the store and emerged holding a tiny brown paper bag. A sixth sense probably activated by the alarming eyes and the six-inch rise and fall of his Adam's apple, told me not to ask what was inside. In the restaurant he kept it on top of the table as we ate. Finally, the fool in me became so curious, he had to go and ask, "What's in the bag, Hunter?"

"I've got something in there that would clear out this restaurant in 20 seconds," said Hunter. He began opening the bag. His eyes had rheostated up to 300 watts. "No, never mind," I said. "I believe you! Show me later!" From the bag he produced what looked like a small travel-size can of shaving foam, uncapped the top and pressed down on it. There ensued the most violently brain-piercing sound I had ever heard. It didn't clear out The Brazilian Coffee House. It froze it. The place became so quiet, you could hear an old-fashioned timer clock ticking in the kitchen. Chunks of churasco gaucho remained impaled on forks in mid-air. A bartender mixing a sidecar became a statue holding a shaker with both hands just below his chin. Hunter was slipping the little can back into the paper bag. It was a marine distress-signaling device, audible for 20 miles over water.

The next time I saw Hunter was in June of 1976 at the Aspen Design Conference in Aspen. By now Hunter had bought a large farm near Aspen where he seemed to raise mainly vicious dogs and deadly weapons, such as the .357 magnum. He publicized them constantly as a warning to those, Hells Angels presumably, who had been sending him death threats.

I invited him to dinner at a swell restaurant in Aspen and a performance at the Big Tent, where the conference was held. My soon-to-be wife, Sheila, and I gave the waitress our dinner orders. Hunter ordered two banana daiquiris and two banana splits. Once he had finished them off, he summoned the waitress, looped his forefinger in the air and said, "Do it again." Without a moment's hesitation he downed his third and fourth banana daiquiris and his third and fourth banana splits, and departed with a glass of Wild Turkey bourbon in his hand.

When we reached the tent, the flap-keepers refused to let him enter with the whiskey. A loud argument broke out. I whispered to Hunter. "Just give me the glass and I'll hold it under my jacket and give it back to you inside." That didn't interest him in the slightest. What I failed to realize was that it was not about getting into the tent or drinking whiskey ... it was the grand finale of an event, a happening aimed at turning the conventional order of things upside down. By and by we were all ejected from the premises, and Hunter couldn't have been happier. The curtain came down for the evening.

In Hunter's scheme of things, there were curtains ... and there were curtains. In the summer of 1988 I happened to be at the Edinburgh Festival in Scotland one afternoon when an agitated but otherwise dignified, silver-haired old Scotsman came up to me and said, "I understand you're a friend of the American writer Hunter Thompson."

I said yes.

"By God--your Mr. Thompson is supposed to deliver a lecture at the Festival this evening and I've just received a telephone call from him saying he's in Kennedy Airport and has run into an old friend. What's wrong with this man? He's run into an old friend? There's no possible way he can get here by this evening!"

"Sir," I said, "when you book Hunter Thompson for a lecture, you have to realize it's not actually going to be a lecture. It's an event--and I'm afraid you've just had yours."

Hunter's life, like his work, was one long barbaric yawp, to use Whitman's term, of the drug-fueled freedom from and mockery of all conventional proprieties that began in the 1960s. In that enterprise Hunter was something entirely new, something unique in our literary history. When I included an excerpt from "The Hell's Angels" in a 1973 anthology called "The New Journalism," he said he wasn't part of anybody's group. He wrote "gonzo." He was sui generis. And that he was.

Yet he was also part of a century-old tradition in American letters, the tradition of Mark Twain, Artemus Ward and Petroleum V. Nasby, comic writers who mined the human comedy of a new chapter in the history of the West, namely, the American story, and wrote in a form that was part journalism and part personal memoir admixed with powers of wild invention, and wilder rhetoric inspired by the bizarre exuberance of a young civilization. No one categorization covers this new form unless it is Hunter Thompson's own word, gonzo. If so, in the 19th century Mark Twain was king of all the gonzo-writers. In the 20th century it was Hunter Thompson, whom I would nominate as the century's greatest comic writer in the English language.

Some Nasty Karmic Shift

GARRY TRUDEAU

AND YOU MEET WITH THE MAY-OR OF TIKRIT AT 2:30...
YEAH, WHATEVER. YOU HAN-DLE IT, HONEY.
3-7

YOU SEEM OUT OF SORTS TO-DAY, BOSS.
I KNOW. IT'S LIKE SOME NAS-TY KARMIC SHIFT.
GB Trudeau

SOMETHING AMISS KARMA-WISE. BETTER CHECK MY E-MAIL...
"HUNTER S. THOMPSON DEAD AT 67..."
3-8

KA-BOOM!
UNIVERSAL PRESS SYNDICATE © 2005 G.B. Trudeau

THAT CAN'T BE RIGHT. BETTER GOOGLE IT...
GB Trudeau
www.doonesbury.com

KA-BOOM!
SIR? ARE YOU OKAY IN THERE?

SIR, WHAT'S WRONG? YOU LOOK STRICKEN.
HUNTER S. THOMPSON IS DEAD, HONEY.
3-9
UNIVERSAL PRESS SYNDICATE © 2005 G.B. Trudeau

THOMPSON? THE WRITER?
YES. HE SHOT HIM-SELF.

THAT'S... THAT'S TERRIBLE, SIR.
YES, IT IS.
GB Trudeau
www.doonesbury.com

I'VE STUMBLED INTO SOME SORT OF TRIBUTE, HAVEN'T I?
YEAH, BUT NO MEDIA, GOT IT?

YOU FELT A KINSHIP WITH MR. THOMPSON? SERIOUSLY? BUT WASN'T HE LIKE REALLY, REALLY IMMATURE?
NO! HE HAD THE BODY OF A 120-YEAR-OLD!
UNIVERSAL PRESS SYNDICATE © 2005 G.B. Trudeau

BUT WHAT ON EARTH COULD YOU HAVE HAD IN COMMON?
WELL, FOR OPENERS, POLITICS...

NO COMPARISON, SIR. HE WAS A FAILED CANDIDATE FOR SHERIFF OF ASPEN—YOU'RE THE MAYOR OF ALL AL AMOK!
3-10
www.doonesbury.com

OF COURSE, YOU SEIZED POWER.
YOU MAKE IT SOUND LIKE IT'S CHEATING.
GB Trudeau

www.doonesbury.com

YOU DON'T UNDERSTAND, HONEY—DOC WAS MY INSPIRATION! IN A WAY, I OWE HIM EVERYTHING!

IN FACT... HOLD IT...
SIR?
PIP!
3-12

SIR? **SIR!** WHERE **ARE** YOU?

JUST CHECKING FOR MY WALLET. IT'S ALL GOOD.
DON'T **DO** THAT, SIR! LEAVE A NOTE OR SOMETHING!
GBTrudeau

The Gift Of The Severed Fingers

JONATHAN SHAW

(WITH AN AFFIRMATION OF THE HORRIBLE TRUTH BY JOHNNY DEPP)

I was walking around the 26th Street flea market, waiting for the call from Johnny Depp to come through on my little Nokia cell phone. It was another late summer Sunday afternoon in the mid-1990s and I was a big shot New York City underground tattoo artist with a pocket full of cash and a fancy new cell phone, living it up, waiting for a call from my big deal movie star brother. A few years earlier I was a loser. Broke and unknown, living in a little shack in a squalid favela in Rio de Janeiro with no electricity or running water, no money, no friends, circling the drain around drug addiction and obscurity. But now I was here in the big city, running with the rich and famous. Wooo.

Johnny had called an hour earlier and told me that he and Hunter Thompson were up in Hunter's room in some fancy hotel somewhere uptown doing press or doing lines or doing some fucking legendary thing. Hunter S. Fucking Thompson! He'd always been one of my big literary heroes, ever since I'd first gobbled up Fear and Loathing in Las Vegas with a handful of good 1970s LSD as a crazed, rootless teenager running the streets of Hollywood with other wild-eyed Manson Family refugees.

JD hadn't been 'round to visit NYC for a few months, so we were overdue for a reunion. Now he was staying way the fuck uptown, way up there in the sanctified stratosphere of the 50s. Maybe it was the 60s... 70s. It all got to be a big blur up there in the high numbers for guys like me and my downtown friends and immediate neighbors, Jim Jarmusch and Iggy Pop. We rarely strayed from our sheltered little septic bunkers on the Lower East Side. Jarmusch, another card-carrying, notorious downtown hipster once told me, "I get a nosebleed whenever I gotta go up above 14th Street." That memorable phrase always came jumping into my head like a little prankster monkey when I had to go uptown.

I was nursing a psychic nosebleed, wandering around the flea market like a dark helmeted deep sea diver taking time to decompress in safe, familiar waters to keep from moving uptown too fast and getting a deadly case of the bends. I walked around in my usual afternoon stupor, not really shopping, waiting for JD's call. A familiar voice snaps me out of my spell and I look up.

"JS! What's up, buddy?"

It's just my friend, Biker Billy. 6"4' and 275 pounds of heavily tattooed muscle-bound hustle. Biker Billy was a sometimes Hells Angel hang-around who haunted the flea market like a diamond Rolex-wearing shaggy grinning lunatic pirate scourge. I'd known Billy since before he was an FXR-riding sidewalk commando. Since when he was still just a schoolboy, a button-down uptown preppy who went nuts on liquor and drugs on the downtown scene and suddenly emerged one day looking like some hung-over shabby tattooed Cossak, mercilessly reinventing himself as a cheap second-generation knockoff of guys like me.

There seems a very fine line between fear and love and respect and imitation and Biker Billy looms and lurks and hovers over me with an ass-kissing sycophantic stance as he tells me he's got something I've just fucking gotta see. I blow him off. Biker Billy's always got something you just gotta see. That's his hustle. But sometimes he really did come through--not that I'd ever give him the satisfaction of letting him know it.

"Alright, hot shot, let's see watcha got," I growled. He reached in the inside pocket of his leather jacket, looking around like a criminal. "Cut the shit," I said to counter his contrived dramatic effect. Biker Billy produced a dusty looking zip-loc bag and handed it to me

Photo: Vera Perrone Shaw

TRADING PLACES: Johnny Depp tattooing Jonathan Shaw--who among other claims to fame is Artie Shaw's son--at Fun City Tattoo in New York.

proudly. "What the fuck is this?" I spat. It looked like an old bag of dried up dog shit.

"Check it out, dude," he smirked. That same smirk was plastered on my memory banks like Puerto Rican gang graffiti on a jailhouse wall. He wore that smirk when he sat down at my desk at the tattoo shop a year earlier and unveiled a gruesome decapitated human head in a jar... so I was prepared as I cautiously opened the bag and rolled a turd-like item out onto the palm of my hand. Fuck. I was holding a petrified human finger! With a perfectly manicured fingernail. There were four more fingers in the plastic bag. Biker Billy had robbed a fucking grave or something.

"Where did this shit come from, man?" I asked casually.

"They're souvenirs some guy brought back from 'Nam, I think," he said.

"You THINK!?"

"Well, the guy I got em from told me..."

"Some guy told you..." I sneered, depreciating the goods, hopefully driving the eventual price down. Biker Billy shrugged, losing ground. "Talk about a fuckin' trick bag..."

"I'll give em to ya cheap, man," he whispered desperately.

"Whatever, dude," I said unaffected, holding the bag away from me as if it stunk. "How much you want for this shit anyway?"

"For you, JS... Fifty bucks."

"Fifty bucks?!? For THIS!? You gotta be fuckin' kidding!" I knew Billy didn't pay more than twenty, so I figured I'd just try and jew him down to thirty and let him make a ten spot for his trouble. Who else was he gonna sell a bag of somebody's severed, dried-up digits to around there? "This shit ain't for me man," I said shaking my head, handing him his bag back.

"Gimme forty," he said, refusing to take the bag.

"Uhh uhhn" I said. This was the moment of truth. "I'll give ya thirty... and ya better take it fast, Billy, before I change my fuckin' mind."

"Thirty-five," he tried. I had him.

"No way! I don't want this shit, Billy!"

"Ok ok. Gimme the thirty," he said, biting the dust as I quickly stuffed the bag of dubious origin in my pocket. I handed him thirty and walked away fast, leaving him standing him there talking to himself.

I was halfway across the lot when the Nokia rang. "What's up, fucker," that ultra famous voice crackled through the airwaves.

"Nothin' to it, man. What's up witchoo, big time?"

"Just finishing up here. You comin' up? Hunter wants to meet you."

"That makes two of us, brother. How soon?"

"Whenever you get here. We'll dangle with Hunter for a minute, then go down your way. You motorized?"

"Got a spare helmet if ya don't mind sittin' bitch for a minute. See ya in fifteen." I hung up, putting the Nokia in my pocket with my bag full of fingers as I got on the old Triumph and gave it a kick...

A dour-faced white haired porter in a red monkey-grinder's suit approached purposefully with a look of disdain as I got off my dirty black wasp, obviously about to shoo me off hotel property like an oversized shit fly. "I'm here to see Johnny Depp," I said casually, as

I planted a greasy black motorcycle boot onto their fancy-pants red carpet.

"Johhny Depp..." He mumbled. "Oh, yes, of course! Yes sir, just go right up to the desk and they'll announce you... I'll keep an eye on your... Motorcycle for you... sir..."

Instant attitude change, right before my eyes. Nice.

I glided like Fred Astaire over to the front desk.

"May I help you, sir?" A pleasant young front desk jockey in a spotless black suit said in an ear-pleasing British accent. I especially dug the 'sir' thing.

"Uhh, Johnny Depp's room?" I said.

"Oh, of course," he said, looking relieved, as if I'd suddenly solved a riddle for him. "I'll ring him up just now," he said pleasantly. "And your name, sir?"

"JS"

"Yes sir, of course," he said as he lifted the phone and called the room. After a minute, the handsome young man frowned, ever so pleasantly.

"I'm so sorry, sir. They don't appear to be answering in that room. Would you care to have a seat for a moment?"

"Can't I just go up?" I said. "He's expecting me. I just spoke to him a few minutes ago..."

"I'm sorry, sir. All visitors must be announced..."

Then I remembered. They were in Hunter's room. I told the desk guy to try Hunter Thompson's room and he did.

After a minute, same frown, same story. Shit. I staggered over to a plush white sofa and plopped my greasy old ass down in defeat. Hurry up and then fucking wait. I sat there and waited. And I waited. Every once in a while I wandered over to the front desk and the pleasant handsome young man in the spotless black suit looked up from whatever he was doing to try the room again. Same diplomatic frown. Same helpless shrug. I went back to my post and waited some more.

Half an hour later I was good and sick of waiting. I paced the lobby like a caged tiger, watching the elevator restlessly, looking at my Rolex. What if I just made a run for the elevator and went up? Fuck. I didn't even know the room number. I looked over at the pleasant young man behind the desk. He managed to smile reassuringly and shrug helplessly at the same time. He was good. British. A born diplomat. Probably gay. But he wasn't gonna give me that fucking room number. No way. Hotel policy. Shit... I shrugged back and

tried to smile, squeezing out something that probably looked more like an agonized gold-toothed rigor mortis grimace. There I was. Just another big fucking loser, a greasy old Nobody waiting in a fancy uptown hotel lobby for some hot shot fancy pants Hollywood movie star who didn't give a shit. Self-pity is a terrible, deadly malady. And I was drowning in it, going down fast. Another forty-five minutes went by. Fuck it. I was done. I walked back up to the front desk and asked the pleasant young man for an envelope and a piece of stationary. He gladly obliged.

Vindictive, I sat back down on the sofa and laid out the crisp sheet of hotel stationary on the table in front of me. Fifty-three minutes passed. Fair enough...

I got out my Mont Blanc and I wrote.

HERE'S A LITTLE SOUVENIR FROM THE LAST
ASSHOLE WHO LEFT ME WAITING FOR AN HOUR
IN A FUCKING HOTEL LOBBY.
HAVE A NICE DAY. JS

I looked around. Then I reached in my pocket and took out the dusty Ziploc bag, lowered it discreetly between my knees and opened it. Nobody around. Fuck it. I reached in the plastic bag and extracted a finger with a good-looking fingernail on it. Middle, I think. That would do the trick.

Then I remembered Hunter. A writer of his stature was certainly worthy of a finger of his very own. I popped out another one. Index. I quickly rolled the two dried digits in my hastily-scrawled note like a burrito and dropped it into the envelope. I licked the envelope somewhat distastefully, wondering vaguely about possible diseases. I stood up and looked at my watch.

Over an hour. Ample justification. I looked at the elevator. Fuck it. Now or never.

I sauntered over to the smiling, helplessly shrugging young British diplomat at the front desk. He smiled back. No turning back now.

"Something's come up, man. I gotta go," I said. "Would you please make sure this envelope gets delivered to Johnny Depp personally? Its very important."

"Of course I will, sir," the pleasant young hotel man smiled pleasantly, reassuringly, taking the grim package from my sweaty hand. I thanked him and walked quickly out of the hotel. I got back on my greasy old motorcycle and rode the fuck out of there.

I would've gladly given a thousand bucks to be a roach on the wall of that fucking hotel room when they opened that envelope!

Here's Johnny Depp's full account, in his own words:

"Me and Hunter were sitting around this big table up in his suite, telling stories and drinking absinthe and... ingesting things. We'd been sitting there for quite a while. Days maybe... Hunter always had stories and you just sorta lost track of time around him. Especially when you'd been ingesting things with him... The table was littered with all sorts of stuff. Hunter's stuff. We'd been sitting there for a long long time, ingesting Hunter's stuff... It was all pretty surreal.

There was a knock at the door. Hunter looked around and said, 'Did you order from room service, Colonel?' He always called me Colonel. I told him it was probably just my friend, JS. He said, 'Well you better go find out. I'll just stay here and keep an eye on things.'

So then I went to the door and the bellboy handed me this sort of bulky little envelope. He didn't know where it came from. So I went back over to the table and Hunter said, 'What's that you've got there?' I told him I didn't know. He looked at it and told me, 'You better open it then, Colonel' and I did. There was something in it, wrapped up in a note. From JS. These two brown clumps of... stuff fell out onto the table. I didn't know what it was.

Hunter picked one up and mumbled, 'looks like hash. Let's try it out. I've got a pipe here somewhere...' Then suddenly he goes, 'uuuh-hgghhh!!!' And drops the thing on the table... He looked pretty startled... It'd been another very weird day for us."

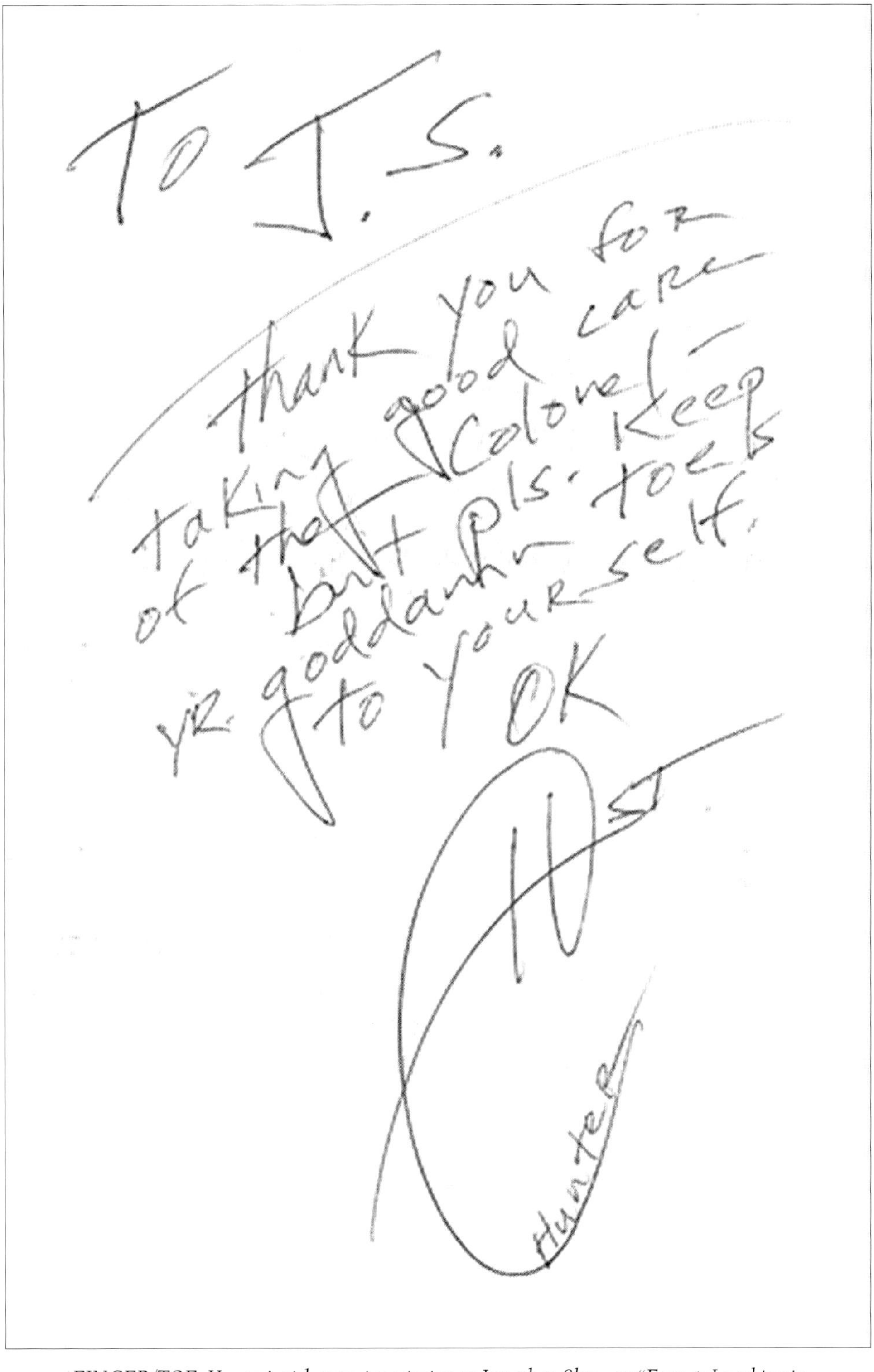

To J.S.

thank you for taking good care of the Colonel — but pls. keep yr. goddamn toes to yourself. to Y OK

HST

Hunter

FINGER/TOE: *Hunter's title page inscription to Jonathan Shaw on "Fear & Loathing in Las Vegas."*

A Haiku For The Good Doctor

WAVY GRAVY

Balance of Glory
Cuz Contentment's Not Enough
Hunter S. No More

Heir Aberrant: Thompson & H.L. Mencken As Spiritual & Stylistic Twins

STEPHEN R. PROCTOR

Fans of H.L. Mencken, the original bad boy of American journalism, argue endlessly about the details of his life and work, but few would disagree on this point: There will never be another like him.

But, the truth must be faced. There is, and has been, another Mencken. He"s the outlaw journalist of our era--Hunter S. Thompson.

Comparing the erudite Mencken to a drug-addled madman like Thompson may leave scores of Menckenites sputtering into their coffee. Blasphemy! But consider.

In the 1920s and 30s, as a reporter and columnist for Baltimore's *Evening Sun* and literary critic for New York magazines, Mencken towered over American journalism--railing at Puritans and Babbitts, thumbing his nose at Prohibition and writing outlandishly about everything from the Scopes Trial to the "imbecilities" of Roosevelt's New Deal.

Flash forward 50 years and there is Thompson, the new *enfant terrible*, with a persona to match his times. He was a prankster run amok, reveling in the culture of booze and drugs as he pursued the outrageous craft he called Gonzo Journalism everywhere the American Dream could be chronicled, from the Kentucky Derby to the presidential campaign.

Scoff if you will, but this much can"t be denied: Barely two years after Mencken's death, his ghost appeared in Thompson's fervid imaginings.

In December 1957, when Thompson was starting out as sports editor of the *Jersey Shore Herald*, he wrote a rollicking letter to a friend recounting a cynical daydream about the godforsaken town where he worked. In it, Thompson has Mencken mock the place as "enough to make a man pray for a plague of maggots."

Thompson"s two books of letters--"The Proud Highway" (1997) and "Fear and Loathing in America" (2000)--show that Mencken was much on Thompson's mind as he found his way in journalism. He devoured Mencken's collected works and began to quote and mimic him. Thompson fell under the spell of many writers as he worked to develop his own style--chiefly F. Scott Fitzgerald and Ernest Hemingway.

He was so entranced by them that, like a young painter copying a Rembrandt, Thompson typed out every word of "The Great Gatsby" and "A Farewell to Arms." The editor of his letters, Douglas Brinkley, believes Thompson's journalism was most influenced by George Orwell's "Down and Out in Paris and London," an account of slumming with low-lifers in two cities.

But a close reading of Thompson and Mencken--along with a study of his letters--makes it unequivocal: It was Mencken who inhabited Thompson's consciousness from the moment he set out in journalism.

Casual comparisons of the two writers are hardly uncommon. Book critics are fond of referring to Thompson as an acid-headed Mencken, or the like. But delving more deeply into their work shows how close Thompson comes to being Mencken reincarnate.

The underpinnings of everything Thompson came to stand for as a journalist--his commitment to "total subjectivity," his insistence on making himself a character at the heart of his stories, even aspects of his style--are found in Mencken.

By the time he set out to write his classic "Fear and Loathing on the Campaign Trail '72," Thompson had established his persona as the larger-than-life *agent provocateur* of the press corps, spewing invective and stalking his mortal enemy, Richard Nixon.

Whether contrived or spontaneous, Thompson's persona was not unlike Mencken's when he showed up in Dayton, Tenn., in 1925 to cover what he had famously dubbed "The Monkey Trial," in which teacher John T. Scopes was accused of violating state law by teaching evolution instead of the Biblical story of Genesis.

Mencken arrived in Tennessee as something of an outlaw journalist himself, having already published his scathing essay "The Sahara of the Bozart," describing the American south as "almost as sterile artistically, intellectually, culturally as the Sahara Desert."

His coverage of the Scopes Trial and its immediate aftermath provides a convenient case study of how Mencken's work inspired Thompson's Gonzo Journalism--starting with the notion of reporter-as-character. Mencken was so much a character in the Scopes trial that he would be a central figure in "Inherit the Wind," a play written about those two weeks in Tennessee, just as Thompson would be the inspiration for the character Duke in Garry Trudeau's comic strip "Doonesbury."

In fact, Mencken covered the trial for the same reason Thompson dove into the '72 presidential campaign--the chance to take on his nemesis, William Jennings Bryan. Mencken decided to go to Dayton only after learning that Bryan--the Fundamentalist preacher, presidential candidate and lawyer he had hounded throughout his career--would be there to help prosecute Scopes.

Before the trial began, Mencken had the *Evening Sun* post Scopes' bail, and he met with defense lawyers, including Clarence Darrow, to plot strategy. It was Mencken's idea to put Bryan on the stand and make him, not Scopes, the focus of the trial. On the stand, in perhaps the case's most memorable moment, Bryan rejected the idea that man is a mammal; giving Mencken the grist he needed to ridicule the aging warrior.

While he did not acknowledge it in his *Evening Sun* dispatches, revealing it only later in his memoir "Heathen Days," Mencken also thrust himself into the story the moment he arrived in Dayton. As a prank, he whispered to a town clergyman--one T.T. Martin--that Bolsheviks from Cincinnati were plotting to come to Dayton and dispatch Bryan.

His July 15 report about the ensuing flap noted only that news of the Bolshevik threat had come to Martin, who “first warned Bryan and then complained to the police. The latter were instantly agog. Guards were posted at strategic centers and watch was kept upon all strangers of sinister appearance.”

From his first dispatch, Mencken also made it clear, as it was in nearly every story he ever filed, that his approach to the Scopes trial would be what Thompson later described as a fundamental tenet of Gonzo Journalism--total subjectivity. Mencken’s first report on June 15, headlined “The Tennessee Circus,” lambasted the “Ku Klux Klergy” behind the prosecution of Scopes.

“I rejoice that they have forced the fighting, and plan to do it in the open,” he crowed. “My prediction is that when the peanut shells are swept up at last and the hot-dog men go home, millions of honest minds in this great republic, hitherto uncontaminated by the slightest doubt, will have learned to regard parts of Genesis as they now regard the history of Andrew Gump,” a well-known comic strip character of that era.

Mencken’s most famous story from the trial--a July 13 dispatch later recast as “The Hills of Zion”--displayed another trait central to Gonzo Journalism. For Mencken, and Thompson after him, the story was never the who, what, when, where, why and how of classical journalism. It was the great human carnival, the otherwise unrecorded background noise of high-profile events like the Monkey Trial or a presidential campaign.

In Dayton, Mencken found the real story on a steamy July night when he drove into the hills to take a first-hand look at a Holy Roller service unfolding in a mountain cornfield under a light strung from the branch of a towering oak tree--a scene of “barbaric grotesquerie” that spoke volumes about why Tennessee lawmakers had their hands around the throat of the “infidel Scopes.”

Thompson had begun reading Mencken in 1956, the year the 76-year-old journalist died at his home in West Baltimore. At the time, Thompson was a young airman working as sports editor of the *Command Courier*, the newspaper of Elgin Air Force Base in Florida. What he loved most about the job was his 'Spectator' column.

“Each week,” he wrote to a friend in October 1956, “I come closer and closer to libel, slander and calumny. This week’s ‘Spectator’ will raise much hell, I’m sure--but that’s just the way the ball bounces. If H.L. Mencken could do it, then so can I.”

Until his approach was cemented with the publication in 1971 of "Fear and Loathing in Las Vegas," Thompson struggled with what it meant to be a journalist. He despised much of what he read in the press. "Newspapermen have become a breed of useless hacks and gossip-mongers," he wrote to author William Kennedy.

But the truth is that in his early years, Thompson pursued a fairly traditional approach to reporting. "The only way to attempt journalism," he wrote to a friend in April, 1964, "is to assume you know nothing at the start, and then only write what you find evidence to support--along with the evidence, so neither the editor nor the reader is forced to take your word for it."

Even as he wrote those words, another thought was creeping into his mind. "Personal Journalism," he wrote to the same friend barely three weeks later, "is the wave of the future. Art is passé, and so is the *New York Times*." Over the next five years, spurred on by a magazine assignment that would turn into the career-making book, "Hell's Angels: The Strange and Terrible Saga of Outlaw Motorcycle Gangs," Thompson came to his conclusions about what that idea meant.

In a June 1971 letter to Jim Silberman, his editor at Random House, Thompson got to the bottom line: "What I'm talking about, in essence, is the mechanical Reality of Gonzo Journalism ... or Total Subjectivity, as opposed to the bogus demands of objectivity."

It is impossible to miss echoes of Mencken in the early works that put Thompson on the map as a writer, especially his 1970 piece for *Scanlan's Monthly* titled "The Kentucky Derby is Decadent and Depraved."

Thompson began that piece with a scene in the bar at the Louisville airport, where he met a visitor from Houston named "Jimbo" and let him in on a secret. Thompson said he was on assignment for *Playboy* to take pictures of a riot the Black Panthers were plotting on Derby Day.

More tellingly, Thompson's interest was not in covering the horse race. He wanted to expose the truth about the hideous scenes that unfold on Derby Day among the rabble in the infield and Kentucky Colonels in the Paddock bar--exactly the sort of "barbaric grotesquerie" Mencken set out to uncover among the Holy Rollers in Tennessee.

There would be other evidence of Mencken in Gonzo Journalism, none more striking than Thompson's use of Richard Nixon as a foil. Just as Mencken made a career out of bashing Bryan--and later Franklin D. Roosevelt--Thompson's fame grew exponentially from his bouts with Nixon.

Beyond the kinship of their reporting, Mencken and Thompson share stylistic characteristics--namely a voice defined by invective, the hallmark of which is using trademark pejoratives over and over to bludgeon their subjects. In Mencken, the politicos of the day are charlatans, mountebanks, or zanies dispensing buncombe to the booboisie. In Thompson, they are vile, treacherous, swine defiling the American Dream.

Nowhere is Mencken's presence in Thompson's work more vividly on display than in the obituaries of their life-long enemies--Mencken's "In Memoriam: WJB" and Thompson's "Chapter 666: The Death of Richard Nixon." Both open with a savage blast. Both build to a merciless final assessment. Both make a mockery of those who, following convention, found something nice to say about the departed. Even the cadence of the writing is remarkably similar.

Anyone who doubts that Mencken was Thompson's literary progenitor need only read these obituaries side by side--preferably aloud. They make the case eloquently.

None of the techniques that made these journalists famous would be acceptable today in any mainstream newspaper. But thanks largely to Mencken being reborn in Thompson, they are a mainstay of in-your-face magazines and outsider journalism.

But, as important as Mencken's influence on Thompson was, it would be unjust not to emphasize the magnitude of Thompson's creativity and talent. He took Mencken's foundation and built something that approaches performance art.

He carried the notion of reporter-as-character farther than Mencken ever did. The Derby story, for example, is built around his search for one face that displayed the consequences of decadence--a "symbol, in my own mind, of the whole doomed atavistic culture that makes the Kentucky Derby what it is." The morning after the race, Thompson stumbled out of bed in his hotel room, looked in the mirror and discovered that the face he'd been searching for was his own.

He also took Mencken's penchant for exaggeration to make a point and made the leap to combining fiction and journalism. "Gonzo," Thompson wrote, "is a style of 'reporting' based on William Faulkner's idea that the best fiction is far more true than any kind of journalism."

And, finally, Thompson added his own ideas to the mix, most importantly that readers should experience Gonzo as the writer did. He took them into the moment by dropping into his pieces passages of unfiltered notes. He even left instructions for reading Gonzo: "Read straight thru, at high speed, from start to finish, in a large room full of speakers, amplifiers & other appropriate sound equipment. There should also be a large fire in the room, preferably in an open fireplace & raging almost out of control. The mind & body must be subjected to extreme stimulus by means of drugs & music."

But Thompson, unlike Mencken, always dreamed of being something more than a journalist. In the 1960s, he set out to write the next Great American Novel, "The Rum Diary". It was never published until journalism had made him famous. Thompson's letters are infused with an undercurrent of sadness about his failure to make a mark as a novelist, a sense of regret that he never became what he declared himself to be in a 1957 letter to a girlfriend--the "new Fitzgerald."

The pity of it is that he seems never to have appreciated having become the new Mencken.

[NEVER LET THE ENEMY REST IN PEACE]

Nothing illustrates Mencken's influence on Thompson more vividly than their obituaries of lifelong enemies--William Jennings Bryan and Richard Milhous Nixon.

Begin with the sledgehammer openings:

Mencken: "Has it been duly marked by historians that William Jennings Bryan's last secular act on this globe of sin was to catch flies? A curious detail, and not without its sardonic overtones. He was the most sedulous flycatcher in American history, and in many ways the most successful. His quarry, of course, was not Musca Domestica, but Homo Neanderthalis. For forty years he tracked it with coo and bellow, up and down the rustic back ways of the Republic."

Thompson: "Richard Nixon is gone now, and I am the poorer for it. He was the real thing--a political monster straight out of Grendel and a very dangerous enemy. He could shake your hand and stab you in the back at the same time. He lied to his friends and betrayed the trust of his family. Not even Gerald Ford, the unhappy ex-president who pardoned Nixon and kept him out of prison, was immune to the evil fallout. Ford, who believes strongly in heaven and hell, has told more than one of his celebrity golf partners that "I know I"m going to hell, because I pardoned Richard Nixon."

Conclude with the brutal final assessment:

Mencken: "It was hard to believe, watching him at Dayton, that he had traveled, that he had been received in civilized societies, that he had been a high officer of state. He seemed only a poor clod like those around him, deluded by a childish theology, full of an almost pathological hatred of all learning, all human dignity, all fine and noble things. He was a peasant come home to the barnyard."

Thompson: "If the right people had been in charge of Nixon's funeral, his casket would have been launched into one of those open-sewage canals that empty into the ocean just south of Los Angeles. He was a swine of a man and a jabbering dupe of a president. Nixon was so crooked that he needed servants to help him screw his pants on every morning. Even his funeral was illegal. He was queer in the deepest way. His body should have been burned in a trash bin."

[KINSHIP OF PEJORATIVES]

Mencken and Thompson both peppered their writing with stock vocabularies of pejoratives, used mostly to bludgeon their subjects.

MENCKEN VOCABULARY	THOMPSON VOCABULARY
Buffoon	Atavistic
Buncombe	Doomed
Charlatan	Demented
Debauched	Fear & Loathing
Mountebank	Ominous
Imbecile	Perverse
Ignominious	Screed
Ignoramus	Treacherous
Poltroon	Twisted
Quackery	Venal
Swinish	Venomous
Zany	Vile

BOOK FOUR

"They Came For Blood... We Gave Them Ink"

R.L CRABB

¶*The Graphic and textural memoirs of R. L. Crabb on his encounters with The Good Doctor at the O'Farrell Theatre and civic battles to preserve the premises from the forces of rectitude...*

¶*Culminating in the untold story of The Caravan of cartoonists and dancers sent to Aspen to rescue Hunter from the iron maiden of the Colorado Establishment...*

¶*With almost 3,000 words of actual text Narrative by the Author--and not all in cartoon lettering!*

WE HAD NOTHING TO LOSE ... THE APE WAS OUTNUMBERED ANYWAY, SO WE WENT ON ABOUT OUR BUSINESS AND DID OUR BEST TO IGNORE THE HAIRY THING! IT WATCHED WITH RENEWED INTEREST BUT DIDN'T ATTEMPT TO INTERFERE.
WAS THE APE WORKING ALONE, OR WAS HE TAKING ORDERS FROM HIGHER UP? IF SO, WHOSE SIDE WAS HE ON? WAS HE DEMOCRAT OR REPUBLICAN? WAS HE REALLY A HE?!!

THE BROTHERS WENT ON TO FINISH "THE GRAFFENBERG SPOT," AN EROTIC COMEDY ABOUT A WOMAN WHO DISCOVERS THAT HER "G" SPOT WILL PRODUCE ORGASMS THAT HAVE THE SAME EFFECT AS EXPLODING WATER BALOONS! THERE WERE MANY FINE SCENES, INCLUDING ONE THAT LAMPOONED MAYOR FEINSTEIN BY PORTRAYING HER AS A NYMPHO WITH A CRAVING FOR COPS! UNLIKE STRAIGHT MOVIES OR TELEVISION, THERE WERE NO EXPLODING CARS, VIOLENT DEATHS OR RAPE SCENES...

ARTIE

JIM

I HAD ALMOST FORGOTTEN ABOUT HUNTER WHEN HE SUDDENLY APPEARED ACROSS THE ROOM HOLDING UP A CASSETTE AND BECKONING ME TO FOLLOW HIM AND JIM MITCHELL TO THE SOUND BOOTH...

JIM TURNED ON THE POWER TO THE MASSIVE SOUND SYSTEM FOR THE EMPTY THEATRE BELOW US AND WENT BACK TO THE PARTY. ONCE THE CASSETTE BEGAN TO ROLL, WE HAD TO STICK OUR HEADS THROUGH A WINDOW TO HEAR WHAT WAS ON THE MYSTERIOUS TAPE!

HUNTER TURNED TO ME AND SAID, "HEY! WHERE CAN WE FIND A TAPEDECK?" ..I THOUGHT ABOUT IT FOR A MINUTE... "THERE'S ONE IN THE NEXT ROOM, BUT WE'LL HAVE TO GET JIM TO SET IT UP FOR US." ...HE SHOULD HAVE KNOWN THAT! AFTER ALL, HE WAS THE NIGHT MANAGER!

YOU'RE PROBABLY CURIOUS AS TO WHY WE WERE MORE CONCERNED WITH HIGH POWERED STEREO SYSTEMS THAN A MENACING APE.. ALL I CAN SAY IS: WE WERE IN SAN FRANCISCO! ...IN S.F., THERE WERE GORILLAS EVERYWHERE. SOME OF THEM WERE DARK AND HAIRY... OTHERS WERE PALE AND NAKED... IT WAS TAKEN FOR GRANTED THAT YOU'D RUN INTO A FEW OF THEM AT EVERY PARTY! ...AND SPEAKING OF PARTIES, IT WAS TIME TO MAKE AN APPEARANCE AT THIS ONE...

THE PREMIERE OF THE LATEST MITCHELL BROS. SEX EPIC- "THE GRAFFENBERG SPOT!"

EVEN THEN, IT WAS HARD TO DECIPHER... IT SOUNDED LIKE PRIMAL, GUTTURAL GIBBERISH! IF IT WAS A LANGUAGE, IT HAD TO BE THE MOST PRIMITIVE EVER COMMITED TO TAPE! BUT THERE WAS AN ODD RHYTHM TO IT... MAYBE IT WAS AN EPILEPTIC RAP GROUP!!

HUNTER SEEMED PLEASED...

"WHAT DO YOU THINK?" HE ASKED.

"IT'S GOT A GOOD BEAT, BUT THE WORDS ARE HARD TO UNDERSTAND! ...I GIVE IT A FIVE..."

"UH...WHAT IS IT, ANYWAY?..."

"A FRIEND SENT IT TO ME ITS A GUY HAVING A NERVOUS BREAKDOWN IN A MENTAL INSTITUTION IN TENNESSEE!

...AND THEN I UNDERSTOOD...

THE ANTHROPOID DISEASE WAS SPREADING THROUGH OUT THE COUNTRY!

...THE GORILLAS WERE EVERYWHERE..

...EVEN IN TENNESSEE...

THE BROTHERS HAD BEEN ON MAYOR FEINSTEIN'S HIT LIST FOR YEARS...EVER SINCE SHE DISGUISED HERSELF AND WENT ON A "FACT FINDING" TOUR OF THE CITY'S STRIP JOINTS. GOODY TWO-SHOES WASN'T READY FOR SODOM AND GOMORRAH!

JIM AND ARTIE WERE UP TO THE CHALLENGE! THEY RESPONDED BY PLACING DI-FI'S PRIVATE NUMBER ON THE MARQUEE OF THE O'FARRELL! ...THAT GOT HER ATTENTION!!

SHE WAS DEALING WITH AMERICANS! ..THE KIND OF TRUE SPIRIT OF SILLINESS THAT INSPIRED ACTS LIKE THE BOSTON TEA PARTY, WITH EMPHASIS ON THE WORD PARTY!!

THIS BATTLE WOULD BE FOUGHT ON THE ELECTRONIC FRONT AS WELL AS IN THE COURTROOM! OUR WEAPONS WERE HUMOR AND SEX... YOU WANT TELEVISION COVERAGE?.. SHOW UP FOR COURT WITH TWENTY HALF NAKED LAP DANCERS CARRYING PROTEST SIGNS...

THAT CAN BE TOUGH WHEN YOU'RE IN THE FUNNY BUSINESS!

SO WE DID OUR BEST UNDER THE CIRCUMSTANCES. ARTIE AND JIM WERE HUSTLED INTO THE JUDGE'S CHAMBERS, SO THERE WAS NO TRIAL TO COVER. CRUMB, O'NEILL AND I SAT ON A BENCH IN THE HALLWAY TRYING TO MAKE SOMETHING OUT OF NOTHING!

I SENSED SOMEONE LOOKING OVER MY SHOULDER. ...WHEN I LOOKED UP I SAW A TALL MAN DRINKING SCOTCH... ...AND I KNEW THINGS WOULDN'T BE QUIET FOR LONG!

HUNTER SCOLDED THEM LIKE TARDY SCHOOLCHILDREN.. "WHAT THE HELL IS GOING ON HERE?" HE BELLOWED. "THIS IS SUPPOSED TO BE A PUBLIC TRIAL! YOU WON'T GET ANY ANSWERS OUT HERE!!"

AND THEN HUNTER ENTERED THE JUDGE'S CHAMBERS AS ONLY HE COULD, AND DEMANDED TO KNOW...

"WHAT ARE YOU PEOPLE DOING BEHIND CLOSED DOORS?!!"

IT WAS A SPECTACULAR ENTRANCE.. LIKE JOHN WAYNE ON ACID, OR MAYBE THE LONE DERANGER, A MYSTERIOUS GUNSLINGER WHO RIDES INTO TOWN SHOOTING DOWN THE WEREWOLVES WITH SILVER BULLETS!

YOU SEE... THE BEST WAY TO GET A STORY IS TO BE A PART OF IT! OVER THE YEARS, DR. THOMPSON HAS BECOME WELL-VERSED IN THE DARK WORLDS OF SEX, DRUGS, AND POLITICS!

...NOW I WAS A MEMBER OF THE GANG!!...

MAYOR FEMSWINE

THE BROTHERS WON AND THE O'FARRELL WAS SAVED! THE RIGHTS OF ALL AMERICANS WHO WISH TO FREELY WORSHIP SEX WERE UPHELD IN A COURT OF LAW! IT WAS A GROUP EFFORT THAT INCLUDED LAWYERS, ARTISTS, EROTIC DANCERS, WRITERS, AND BARRELS OF MONEY!!

BUT FOR ONE SHINING MOMENT, SOMEONE TOOK ON THE ESTABLISHMENT AND KICKED ASS!!

THEY CAME FOR BLOOD..

GONZO

...AND WE GAVE THEM INK!!

IN THE SPRING OF '86, THE MITCHELL BROTHERS HELD A PARTY IN HONOR OF EXAMINER EDITOR AND AUTHOR WARREN HINCKLE. IT WAS TO COINCIDE WITH THE AMERICAN BOOKSELLERS CONVENTION AT MOSCONE CENTER, AND THE INVITATIONS PROMISED AN APPEARANCE BY HUNTER THOMPSON. O'NEILL CALLED AND TOLD US TO COME DOWN AND BRING ALONG BOOKS TO SELL, SO KATE AND I PACKED UP THE PICK-UP AND HEADED WEST. IT WOULD BE MY LAST ENCOUNTER (FOR FIVE YEARS) WITH THE MAN KNOWN AS THE

NIGHT MANAGER

THERE'S A BALD GUY!

FEAR AN' LOATHING, DUDE!

LONO LIVES

EVERYBODY WANTS TO MEET THE PRINCE OF GONZO!

..NOBODY WANTS TO BUY BOOKS!

RAOUL DUKE?

IS THERE A DOCTOR IN THE HOUSE?

I WANNA AUTAGRAPH

WHERE IS HE?

'97

TO PASS THE TIME, KATE WAS SELLING POSTERS FOR SPAIN RODRIGUEZ. THERE WAS ONE DRAWING OF NICARAGUA THAT WAS SELLING LIKE HOTCAKES...

..GET YER RED HOT POSTERS.. ..GOIN' FAST!

THE LAST COPY WAS RESERVED FOR WRITER BOB CALLAHAN...

..I'LL PICK IT UP LATER...

NO SWEAT

MEANWHILE, THE NATIVES WERE GETTING RESTLESS! NO LONGER CONTENT WITH NAKED DANCING WOMEN, THEY HUNGERED FOR THE MAIN ATTRACTION...

COLLECTIVE GRUMBLE

SUDDENLY HUNTER LEAPED INTO THE ROOM THROUGH A HOLE IN THE WALL!
SECRET PASSAGE TO OFFICES UPSTAIRS
THE CROWD WAS VISIBLY IMPRESSED!
EVENTUALLY, THINGS SETTLED DOWN. I WAS STANDING BEHIND KATE, WHO WAS STILL SITTING AT THE TABLE, WHEN I NOTICED HUNTER STARING AT US FROM A DISTANCE... IT WAS WEIRD! I MEAN... WHY US?!!
IT WAS HARD TO TELL ANYTHING FROM HIS BODY LANGUAGE... HE APPEARED TO BE SLOUCHING, BUT HE WAS COMPLETELY STIFF AND MOTIONLESS. HE LOOKED LIKE THE CAT THAT WAS ABOUT TO POUNCE ON AN UNWARY CANARY!!
AND THAT STARE! I COULDN'T SEE HIS EYES BEHIND THOSE AMBER LENSES, BUT I COULD HEAR MENTAL GEARS SPINNING WILDLY INSIDE HIS HEAD! I COULD FEEL THE HUM AND PULSE OF PSYCHEDELIC ELECTRICITY FROM ACROSS THE ROOM... WHAT DID HE WANT?!!
HE WALKED OVER TO THE TABLE AND ASKED, "WHERE IS THE SPAIN POSTER?"
"SORRY, THEYRE ALL GONE," KATE REPLIED.
...HIS RESPONSE WAS SWIFT...
WHAT?!... NO POSTER FOR THE NIGHT MANAGER?!!
TAKE IT! ...TAKE ANYTHING!

AND THEN HE WAS OFF TO NEW ADVENTURES!
HE WAS LONO IN THE LAND OF THE INFIDELS, AND HE WAS READY TO WRESTLE!
I ONLY ENCOUNTERED HUNTER A FEW BRIEF TIMES, SO I NEVER REALLY GOT TO KNOW HIM AT ALL. HOWEVER, I DID LEARN FOUR THINGS ABOUT THE MAN. THE FIRST WAS THAT HE IS ALWAYS ON THE OFFENSE IN A CROWD! YOU COULDN'T BLAME HIM... HE WAS CONSTANTLY BEING SWARMED BY FANS...
WHEW
THE SECOND WAS WAS A GOOD SHOT WITH THE PELLET PISTOL!
IT WAS A GOOD IDEA TO STAY CLEAR FROM HIS LINE OF FIRE...
HAH!
...JUST IN CASE...
THE THIRD WAS THAT HE LIKES WHISKEY.... AND SCOTCH AND RUM AND TEQUILA ETC....
THE GUY HAS THE CONSTITUTION OF AN ELEPHANT!
YE GODS!
AND THE FOURTH WAS THAT HE IS STILL A GREAT WRITER! HUNTER HAS DANGLED OUT ON THE FRINGE FOR DECADES AND NOT ONLY MANAGED TO SURVIVE, BUT THRIVE! SOME OF THE COLUMNS HE DID FOR THE EXAMINER WERE TRUE CLASSICS!
WHO ELSE COULD WRITE A STORY ABOUT GEORGE BUSH GIVING CPR TO A DEAD CAT WHILE WANDERING PENNSYLVANIA AVENUE IN THE MIDDLE OF THE NIGHT, AND GET IT PRINTED IN A HEARST NEWSPAPER?

HUNTER WAS WORKING ON A BOOK ABOUT THE SEX BUSINESS THAT WAS CENTERED ON THE BROTHERS AND THE O'FARRELL THEATRE. THAT WAS WHY HE TOOK ON THE POSITION OF NIGHT MANAGER (ALSO THE WORKING TITLE OF THE PROJECT.) HE CALLED THE O'FARRELL "THE CARNEGIE HALL OF SEX IN AMERICA" BUT IT WAS REALLY MORE LIKE THE RINGLING BROTHERS CIRCUS! EVERY DAY, JUNKIES, PERVERTS, BUSINESSMEN AND ORIENTAL TOURISTS WOULD CROWD INTO THE DARK CORRIDORS TO OGLE PRANCING COWGIRLS, TRAPEZE ARTISTS AND WRITHING LAP DANCERS. THE PLACE WAS A GYNECOLOGIST'S DREAM!

EVEN THE OUTSIDE OF THE THEATRE WAS REMINISCENT OF A CARNIVAL SIDE SHOW! THERE WAS A SPECTACULAR MURAL OF WHALES, DOLPHIN AND OTHER AQUATIC THEMES FACING BOTH O'FARRELL AND POLK STREETS. (LATER, IT WAS REPAINTED AS A RAINFOREST.)

THERE WERE MANY WILD DAYS AND NIGHTS AT THE O'FARRELL. SOME PEOPLE FOUND IT DEGRADING, DISGUSTING AND SINFUL, BUT MOST OF THE MEN AND WOMEN I TALKED TO ENJOYED WORKING THERE. TO ME, IT WILL ALWAYS BE THE ULTIMATE BOY'S CLUBHOUSE!

IT WAS THE HEADQUARTERS OF TOTAL CHAOS AND JIM AND ARTIE MITCHELL WERE THE COMMANDING GENERALS! THE STRATEGY ROOM WAS UPSTAIRS, WHERE ELABORATE PLOTS WERE HATCHED FOR MOVIES, POLITICAL CAMPAIGNS, AND MANY OTHER PROJECTS. SOME OF THEM WERE REALIZED, WHILE OTHERS DRIFTED AWAY WITH THE SMOKE OF THOUSANDS OF CIGARETTES.

SEVERAL YEARS LATER, I ASKED JIM MITCHELL WHAT EVER BECAME OF "THE NIGHT MANAGER."

"HUNTER DECIDED THERE WASN'T ENOUGH OF A STORY," HE TOLD ME. "HE WAS WAITING FOR THE COPS TO SURROUND THE PLACE, AND IT JUST NEVER HAPPENED."

AFTER THE POSTER INCIDENT, WE PACKED IT IN AND JOINED THE PARTY UPSTAIRS, WHERE WE ENCOUNTERED A YOUNG FELLOW IN A THREE-PIECE SUIT...HE HAD A PROBLEM...

EGGSKUZE ME... BUT HAFF YOU SEEN DR. THOMPSON?...I MUZ FIND HIM... ID IZ VERY IMPORTANT...

I HAFF A BEER FOR HIM

...HE AZGED ME TO GED 'IM ONE AN' I DID! ..YOU ZEE, I **WORZHIP EVERY WORD** HE HAZ WRIDDEN... IF I COULD, I...I WOULD HAVE ASEXUAL **SEX** WITH THE MAN...

...HAVEN'T SEEN HIM...

...TRY DOWN-STAIRS...

AN HOUR LATER, I FOUND MYSELF HOLDING UP A DOORWAY...THE FELLOW IN THE SUIT HAD WARREN HINCKLE CORNERED, BUT WARREN DIDN'T SEEM TO MIND...

BABBLE BABBLE BUBBLE BURP

ZZZ

THERE WAS A COMMOTION IN THE NEXT ROOM...

?

CRASH!

GUESS WHO?...

I WOULDN'T GO IN THERE, HUNTER...

EH? WHY NOT?

THERE'S A GUY IN THERE WHO WANTS TO **FUCK YOU!**

HAH! THEY'RE EVERYWHERE!

HE GRABBED A BOTTLE OF BUSHMILLS AND DISAPPEARED INTO THE NIGHT...

HUNTER WAS RIGHT, OF COURSE, BUT IT WASN'T UNTIL THE NINETIES THAT THE **REAL** SCREWING BEGAN!

...LET'S GET BACK TO THAT STORY...

The Caravan

As Reported & Drawn
By Mr. Crabb

"Guilty" Illustration by Dan O'Neill

[OUR TRAVELS BEGIN]

In the Sierra Foothills, on a warm spring afternoon I was busy vacuumning flies off the ceiling. The neighboring horse pasture was returning to life after the sun had melted the last of the winter snow, and millions of flies were proliferating in the muddy manure soup. The flyswatter was out, unless I wanted to permanently stain the walls and ceiling with flattened flies, so the vacuum seemed to be the ideal method of dispatching the annoying little bastards.

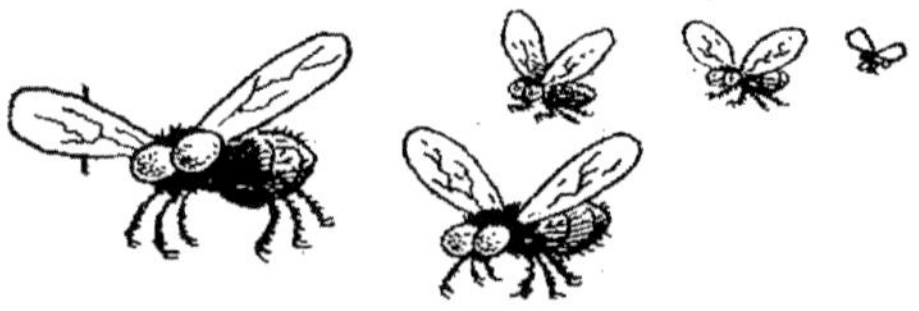

I was jumping up and down on the bed in an attempt to suck up the last of the flies that had sought refuge on the far corners of the ceiling when the phone rang.

It was my roommate and fellow cartoonist Dan O'Neill, calling from San Francisco. He was excitedly babbling about Winnebagos and Colorado, and when I finally managed to get him to speak coherently, I learned that the Mitchell brothers were planning to mount a full-scale assault on Aspen, to protest the persecution of Gonzo journalist Hunter S. Thompson. It would be a lavish expedition including two motorhomes, a replica of the Great Red Shark featured in Thompson's book "Fear and Loathing in Las Vegas," as many strippers and journalists as we could stuff into the vehicles, and a film crew to document the entire episode. We would sweep across the desert and descend on the Pitkin County courthouse creating chaos, confusion, and hopefully much media attention.

At the time I was beset by deadlines and completely broke. I had to decline. A week later, I received another frantic call from O'Neill; he had me this time. The rogue had arranged a publishing deal involving a cash advance, something he knew I couldn't resist. What the hell? I needed a vacation anyway, so I took the bait and suddenly found myself involved in this messy little war.

I had some time to familiarize myself with the impending case against Dr. Thompson. News reports claimed that he had been contacted by a former thespian of titillation who wanted to "set him straight" on the much-maligned pornography business. She also allegedly wished to obtain the film rights to "Fear and Loathing in Las Vegas." Thompson agreed to meet with her, and invited her to his home in Woody Creek.

At some point during their meeting, she was invited to join Hunter in his hot tub. When she declined, the author allegedly became agitated and assaulted her by twisting her left nipple. Hunter, on the other hand (and presumably not the one used in this heinous crime), accused the former actress of bad manners and claimed he was merely ejecting her from his home.

Whatever the circumstances, she then retreated to the local authorities to report the supposed indignities heaped upon her. During the course of her statement, she said that Thompson poured

a quantity of white powder onto a countertop and stuck his face into it proclaiming, "That's what I love about this house! There's cocaine everywhere!"

This proved to be too tempting for local law enforcement officials, who had long endured reports of guns, drugs, and wild behavior at Thompson's compound, the Owl Farm. They managed to get the distraught woman to file a formal complaint, and five days later stormed the premises with a search warreant. After an exhausting eleven-hour search, they retrieved 4.5 ounces of maijuana, four valiums, thirty-nine hits of LSD, a tenth of a gram of cocaine, four sticks of dynamite, and three blasting caps. Thompson said the drugs were probably years old, left there by visiting dignitaries of the drug culture, but the damage was done and he was arrested. "I've been living in this house for twenty-four years, and every freak in the world has come through... well, not every freak," he stated. "And I'm sure it's possible they might have been able to scrape up something in an eleven-hour search."

Thompson's antics had long ago made him an Enemy of the State in Aspen. We had to get there to raise a fuss in his defense.

The Expedition became a reality on a particularly wet Sunday morning in Colfax, California. We partied in town the night before, so as to prepare ourselves for the rigorous journey ahead. Dan's

girlfriend Lorraine drove us to the Colfax bus depot, and after an hour of standing in the rain, the entourage arrived. There were two new Ford Tioga motorhomes, equipped with all the comforts of home and the Red Shark--a 1972 Chevy Caprice convertible exactly like the car depicted in "Fear and Loathing in Las Vegas." The only difference was the buffalo head.

The Mitchells, in a moment of inspiration, had acquired a huge, musty, one-hundred-year-old stuffed buffalo head somewhere in the wilds of Marin County. The mere sight of this bizarre combination of Detroit steel and moldering fur would drive the good folk of Aspen to a frenzy. The dead thing was concealed under a strained convertible top to protect it from the elements.

O'Neill climbed into the lead motorhome, while Rick and I stashed our gear and ourselves into the back-up vehicle. We swung onto Interstate 80 and headed east toward Colorado. It was snowing as we reached Kingvale, but the snow was slushy and we were waved through chain control. There was an incident in Truckee when the Red Shark, piloted by a crazed reporter named Alex, suddenly broke formation and sped off ahead of the pack only to be apprehended by the California Highway Patrol. The motorhomes pulled over a safe distance beyond the altercation and waited to see if the Shark would be allowed to rejoin the caravan. After a short time, the big red Chevrolet reappeared. Although the patrolman had originally

☆ EXCLUSIVE INTERVIEW WITH THE ☆

BUFFALOHEAD

SO IS IT TRUE THAT YOU WERE SHOT BY BUFFALO BILL?

YEP... WUZ BACK'N TH' SPRING OF '84

"NOT THET I MINDED... THE PRARIE WEREN'T A FUN PLACE T'BE IN THEM DAYS! ...HELL, TH' INJUNS WUZ BAD 'NUFF... STICKIN' YA WITH POINTY ARROWS AN' SUCH!"

...DO YA KNOW HOW IT FEELS TA HAVE HOT LEAD SHOT UP YER ASS?

HUH?

NO..? WELL, IT HURTS LIKE HELL, BUT IT'S QUICK, AN' THETS 'BOUT ALL A SOUL KIN HOPE FER.. A QUICK DEATH!

IT'S SURVIVAL OF THE SMARTEST OUT THAR.. ..A CHIPMUNK KIN WHIP A GRIZZLY B'AR IF'N HE KIN LEARN HOW T'PULL A TRIGGER!

UH...RIGHT! ..DO YOU HAVE ANY THOUGHTS ON THE UPCOMING TRIAL OF DOCTOR THOMPSON?

..JES' THET TH' SAME RULE APPLIES: IF'N HE'S A'GONNA DODGE THIS BULLET, HE'S GOTTA BEAT 'EM AT THUR OWN GAME!!

WE HAD A SAYIN' OUT THAR ON THE PLAINS...

"TODAY'S HUNTER IS TOMORROW'S TROPHY!"

stopped Alex for speeding, he became more concerned about the registration, a temporary permit that had been filled out wrong. The permit stated that we were allowed to transport the Shark to Woody Creek, California, rather than Woody Creek, Colorado. After being reassured by Alex that it was only a misprint, the officer then turned his attention to the buffalo head in the backseat and asked to see a permit for it. Alex explained that the buffalo had been shot by Buffalo Bill himself, long before permits were required to snuff out an endangered species. The cop, who was somewhat confused and irritated by this time, advised him to slow down and wished him luck in getting to Colorado without being cited for something.

It was decided that from that point on, the Shark would remain sandwiched between the motorhomes to avoid further incidents with the law. We crossed the border into Nevada.

[THE LONELIEST ROAD IN AMERICA]

We stopped at the local Radio Shack and outfitted the vehicles with C.B.'s and radar detection equipment to avoid misunderstandings with the Law and each other. While the contraptions were being installed, we made the acquaintance of two hookers who were driving aimlessly around the parking lot in search of some quick cash. They claimed to be from California and needed money to get home. Alex and Arthur tried to convince them to join our happy group, but

they seemed wary of our motives and expressed little enthusiams for our lofty cause. When they saw the buffalo head protruding from the backseat of the Shark, their minds were made up. One of them, a tall black woman who claimed to be a model, shreiked, "Ah ain't radin' in no cah wif no buff'lo haid," as they slowly backed away from us toward their beat-up Chevy Nova.

Finally, the caravan was ready to roll again. The first order of business was to assign a "handle" or code name to each of the three vehicles. The back-up motorhome started out as "London Fog" and the lead motorhome became known as "Rebel Leader." Eventually, I changed our handle to "Hind Tit," a title that seemed to better fit our station in the rear.

We were headed due east on Highway 50, which billboards proudly proclaim as "The Loneliest Road in America." This was no idle boast, as Highway 50 runs through some of the most desolate landscape this side of the moon. It is almost straight, except for the occasional montain range or outcropping of jagged rock. Every time we scaled one of these stone summits, there was anticipation

that the other side might reveal something new to look at, but it was always more of the same. At times I wondered whether we had made a wrong turn and were merely traveling in a large circle while mischeivous road crews ran out behind us and changed the mileage signs so we would actually think we were going somewhere. After we ran out of gas and starved to death, they could steal our vehicles and possessions and sell them. It seemed plausible. After all, how else could anyone make a living out there?

Every three or four hours, we would acually pass through a town, which squelched my continuous circle theory, since there weren't enough people around to tear down and rebuild an entire town in the time allowed. Every time we passed a schoolyard, Roxi would stare dreamily out the window and fantasize teenage seductions, but for the rest of us, a town meant gasoline, junk food, and a few minutes to stretch our legs. Late in the day, we passed through Eureka, which a large billboard proclaimed as "the loneliest town on the loneliest road in America." There wasn't a soul on the street.

It was night as we crossed the border into Utah. That was a blessing because Utah is not the kind of place that would welcome people like us with open arms. Utah is the home of the Osmonds and is almost as conservative as Iran when it comes to religion and politics. The entire state is run by Mormons, a strange religious clan founded by a man who claimed he talked to a white salamander. I was traveling with the Mitchell brothers, the most outrageous purveyors of porn west of the Mississippi. If they were to stop us--find out who we were and what our mission was--the only way out would be to trade the women for safe passage, but that would have ruined my plan. You see, one crime that Mormons approve of (at least privately) is polygamy.

That's right. Mormons despise gambling, communism, liquor, and sex, unless its done with many of their many wives. It's a great deal for the Mormen, and the Morwomen, the merrier.

I had been nipping at the Jack Daniels when the idea hit me: I was in a motorhome with two single women, so why not marry them both? The novelty of the potential situation was appealing to me in my drunken state. And if things didn't work out in this state, we would run for Mexico and a double divorce before the law and the estranged wife in California could catch up to us. I asked the girls what they thought of the idea, and they just laughed nervously. Maybe they thought I was looking for a serious relationship. Hell, I was just trying to get involved in the story.

So much for spontaneity.

During breakfast, I became acquainted with the other members of the group. There was O'Neill and Rocky, a cousin of the Mitchells, riding in the command vehicle. Alex piloted the Shark with a friend

named Arthur riding shotgun. In the backup motorhome there was myself, Rick, Vaughn, Richard, and the two girls, Gigi and Roxi. Vaughn was in charge of security, a position he also held at the O'Farrell. Richard, a gray-haired Englishman, was an experienced cameraman who also handles the lights and sound at the live shows at the O'Farrell. Rick was an agent who handled original comic art through his company, Comic Detective. Gigi was a short attractive woman of Cuban descent who worked as a lap dancer at the O'Farrell while trying to build a career as a legitimate actress. She also did a great Charo impersonation. Roxi was small, thin, and had an incredibly beautiful head of long black hair. She claimed to be twenty and had a fetish for teenagers of either sex.

The leaders and backers of this strange endeavor were Jim and Artie, the notorious Mitchell brothers. "The Brothers" as they were known to friends and family, made their break-through in the pornographic film industry with "Behind the Green Door" in the later '60's. They had taken an unknown model named Marilyn Chambers, whose face as a baby adorned boxes of Ivory Soap, and made her into the queen of X-rated films. Ironically, it was Chambers who was arrested during a live performance at the O'Farrell in 1985 for what the vice squad described as "allowing herself to be digitally penetrated by patrons of the theatre."

Of course, this was not an isolated incident. The Brothers had been under siege from politicians, police, and fundamentalist fringe groups for twenty years. After countless attempts to shut down their skin factory, they enjoyed a certain degree of respect from the community. They liked the outlaw image, and thought of themselves as a twentieth-century version of the James Gang; popular rogues who were constantly at odds with the establishment.

It was inevitable that they would join forces with Thompson, America's number one outlaw journalist. The boys remembered Hunter's efforts on their behalf during the trial in 1985 and were prepared to return the favor.

We were to arrive in Woody Creek the day before Hunter's preliminary hearing. There would be a formal presentation at the Woody Creek Tavern, where Jim and Artie would hand over the keys to the Great Red Shark to Hunter in front of hordes of reporters and TV cameras in a show of solidarity. This would serve to remind the authorities that they were not dealing with some frightened drug fiend who got too sloppy, but a famous and respected author with

many vocal supporters. The next day we would stage a protest at the courthouse to further agitate the proceedings. After all, this wasn't a simple drug bust--it was a question of whether the police had the right to break into your house on the hearsay of a drunken bimbo.

[THE JACKALOPE]

2 a.m. I slid into the front passenger's seat next to Vaughn, who had been driving for four hours. "Do you want me to drive for awhile?" I asked. "Maybe later," he replied, "I'm fine for now. Just find some decent music on the radio, okay?" I fumbled in the darkness for the proper buttons, but all I could find was Mantovani or late night bible thumpers. We were flying down the highway with full radar, but there were no police or cars of any kind. Suddenly Vaughn slumped down in his seat. The motorhome started to drift off the road but I was transfixed. My lips were like innertubes filled with lead and the rest of me was numb from cheap whiskey. I knew that unless something was done in a matter of seconds, we would be smashed into pulp and shipped home in ziplock baggies.

Finally, after an eternity of seconds, I screamed. Vaughn jolted into consciousness and jerked the steering wheel, pulling us back to the center of the road. After a few moments of awkward silence he looked my way and said, "Yeah, Maybe you should drive for awhile."

We broke radio silence and alerted the others, then pulled into a rest area somewhere along Interstate 70 where I took the reins of the lumbering Tioga. I did all right for an hour or so, but silently cursed myself for not taking the time to find a good rock 'n' roll station, if there was such a thing out there in the wilderness. It was cold out on the high desert that night, so I had the heater up full blast, but the warmth and hum of the mighty engine was lulling me to sleep. Every ten minutes or so I rolled down the window and stuck my head out into the freeze-dried air to keep my wits about me. Ahead in the distance, the rest of the caravan was barely visible and everyone else in the motorhome was asleep. That was when I first saw the jackalope.

It came as a complete shock to me. After years of searching the western states for a living specimen of Pedigres Leapusalopus without success, the biggest jackalope in the world was dancing down the road in front of me. It jumped from the left and darted into the headlights. It all happened so fast I was unable to see it clearly, but I guessed it was about the size of a German Shepherd with rough-point antlers and ears about two feet in length. I didn't even have time to swerve as it disappeared into the sagebrush on the far side of the road. I thought about

The Caravan arrives and strips for action.

stopping to look for tracks or some other evidence that I wasn't just losing my mind, but I was already a mile past the encounter and would be hard pressed to explain my actions to the rest of the party. No, better to forget the entire incident. I took another shot of whiskey and rolled down the window for fresh air when I realized the jackalope was still there, running alongside the motorhome. I glanced down at the speedometer and saw the red arrow hovering at 65.

Mother of pistons! This creature was as fast as a cheetah, and didn't seem to be tiring at all. In fact it was looking over at me, as if it were trying to communicate. I leaned out the window and yelled, "What is it?!!!" The mouth of the animal was moving, but I still couldn't make out the words with the cold air blasting my frozen face.

"What is it?!!!" I yelled again, ignoring my slumbering cargo. I stood up in the seat in an attempt to reach out the window far enough to hear its garbled message. It started to speed up, so I stretched my aching leg to the gas pedal and caught up with the speeding creature. The cold air had frozen my lungs, but I managed to scream out again...

"WHAT IS IT?!!!"

"WATCH WHERE YOU GO!" the jackalope growled as it sped off down the highway at about 150 miles an hour. Suddenly, I realized I was off the shoulder of the road. I swerved to the left, narrowly avoiding a watch for livestock sign, and straightened out in the center of the blacktop. I looked back into the motorhome, but all the other passengers were still asleep and my window was rolled up tight.

Was it all a dream? It seemed so real, but the evidence pointed to a different vicinity. And what did the jackalope mean, "WATCH WHERE YOU GO!"? Was it talking about my sloppy driving, or something up ahead in the cold dark distance at the end of the of the road?

[BRINGING ALTAMONT TO THE ROCKIES]

The Caravan pulled into the Woody Creek Tavern around 10 a.m. Monday morning. We staggered out of the motorhomes into the sunshine and crisp mountain air, trying to get our bearings. It was like we had been out to sea, and no one was quite able to adjust to having solid ground beneath our feet.

The Tavern was a typical backwoods roadhouse, just a bar and restaurant adjoining the local post office, with a patio in front and a trailer court behind. Above the entrance, a weather-worn stuffed boar stared blankly into the wilderness. Inside, the walls were covered with pictures and posters of Thompson and other celebrities mixed in with polaroids of locals posing with women and other big game trophies. There was a pool table in the far corner. The only

thing that distinguished this bar from a million others like it was that it was often the setting for Hunter's depraved adventures in his weekly syndicated column. However, at this hour of the morning there were no colorful cowboys and conmen lurking in the shadows, just the bartender and kitchen crew preparing for the daily lunch crowd. The Brothers wasted no time in arranging a running bar tab for the spaced-out crew.

As it turned out, they were expecting us. The bartender produced a copy of the *Aspen Times Daily*, where a headline boldly announced: UNLIKELY CONVOY HEADED TO ASPEN. Jim and Artie had sent out a press release prior to our departure and national journalists were converging on Aspen like sharks in a feeding frenzy. There was blood in the water. Sex! Drugs! Explosives! LAST GREAT OUTLAW GANG PREPARES FOR SHOOT-OUT AT HIGH NOON! Film at eleven!

The hearing was on Tuesday, and this was Monday morning. We ordered Bloody Marys and moved out to the patio to make plans. The first chore was to clean up the Great Red Shark. There was a faucet and hose in front of the post office, so Alex, Jim, and Artie washed and polished the big Chevy to sparkling shine. Then the Brothers, with Gigi, Roxi, and the buffalo head, motored off to parlay with Thompson at Owl Farm. The rest of us tried to clean up our act in the Tavern rest room while continuing to consume vast numbers of Bloody Marys. About an hour later, the scouting party returned.

"Hunter... does not wanna be disturbed," giggled Gigi as she rolled off the trunk of the massive convertible.

The crowd, which was starting to grow as lunch hour approached, mumbled about government plots and toxic chemicals in the water. Reporters from the local tabloids drove up and the show began in earnest. Roxi turned up a tape of rap music and leaped onto the hood of the Shark while baring her chest for the cameras.

Gigi joined in, exposing her hooters and humping one of the horns of the dead bison.

Shutters crackled like wildfire as the crowd gaped in awe and passing cars ran off the road.

"Of course, we won't be able to run these," said David Matthews-Price of the *Times Daily*, "but I want a few prints for myself."

A small white-haired woman ran out of the post office and shrieked, "What are you doing? You can't park here! This is government property!"

Being the model law-abiding citizens that we were, the girls covered their breasts while Arthur moved the Shark across the road. "God only knows," he muttered, shrugging his shoulders. A film crew from CNN pulled up, and Jim and Artie held an impromptu press conference in the dirt parking lot.

Reporter: Why have you come to Aspen?

Artie: We're here to give this replica of the Great Red Shark to Hunter Thompson in a show of solidarity against the government's effort to silence his voice.

Reporter: How many are there in your group?

Artie: Well, there are about twelve of us in the advance group.

Reporter: You mean others are coming as well?

Jim: Yes... Ken Kesey, the Grateful Dead, and the Oakland Hells Angels should be here tonight. They're coming overland, straight across the desert.

Artie: The dust can be seen for a hundred miles.

(The reporter's eyes widened. Several others began to drool on their recording equipment. There was a fist fight at the pay phone across the street.)

Reporter: Do you plan to disrupt Dr. Thompson's preliminary hearing tomorrow morning?

Jim: No, not at all. We are here to exercise our First Amendment rights of free speech. We will picket the courthouse, but we're not looking for trouble.

Of course, we knew that the Angels were still in Alameda County, and the Dead were probably playing a gig somewhere in Alaska, but what the hell, Jim and Artie were masters of media mayhem. Let them think that we were bringing Altamont to the Rockies. Common sense might suggest that you lie still when surrounded by sharks in the water, but the Mitchell Brothers always made waves.

Just then, the main player in this little docudrama drove up. Hunter warded off the press, telling them that he had no comment until his day in court. He looked tired and eyed the crowd like a wounded tiger, but he still managed to smile when the Brothers handed him the keys to the car while the strippers gyrated in front of the cameras. He inched the convertible out onto the empty road and attempted to lay some rubber for the cheering throng, but the automatic transmission refused to cooperate. Finally, he put it in neutral, revved the engine, and slammed the shifting lever into low gear. There was a brief squeal as the Shark shot off down the highway. The show was over for now, and the news sharks scattered to write their stories and edit their videotape for the evening news. We returned to the Tavern and continued to run up the bar tab until late in the night. Sheriff's deputies arrived around eleven, searching the trailer court for a suspect in some domestic dispute. At the same time, a drunken cowboy was attempting to pull his mount through the narrow doorway into the bar, but the animal refused. The cowboy was persistent, even when confronted by a guardian of Law and Order.

"Are you really going to try and take that horse in the bar right here in front of me?" asked the dumbfounded cop.

"Yep," replied the determined cowboy as he tugged and grunted and swore at his unwilling accomplice. Eventually, he gave up in disgust, and everyone went home and passed out.

We parked the motorhomes about a half-mile from the Pitkin County Courthouse and assembled the troops. The signs were ready, the cameras were loaded, and everyone was advised to memorize the route in case we were separated and forced to retreat. Artie unfurled a large American flag and we fell into a line behind him as we marched off to demonstrate. Innocent bystanders cheered as we passed, and pick-up trucks honked their horns. The press had done their job well, and we were recognized wherever we went. They were all supportive now, but what if things got ugly at the courthouse? Would they hide us in the basement if we were forced to run from waves of tear gas and nightsticks? Would young women willingly give their bodies to

the liberators, like they did in France? We could only hope. The press was our ally for the moment, but tomorrow they could portray us as drug-crazed child molesters if it meant higher ratings.

A Woman's View

We reached the courthouse without incident, and set up our picket line near the front steps. O'Neill held official press credentials, so he would cover the trial upstairs while I handled the story from the street. The prosecution's star witness, Gail Slater-Palmer, was scheduled to take the stand early, so Dan hurried into the tightly-packed courtroom, leaving me with my sketchpad and trusty polaroid to sample public opinion outside.

> **RL**: Excuse me, ma'am...I'm sampling public opinion on the Thompson trial. Are you familiar with the case?
> **Woman**: Only what I've read in the newspaper.
> **RL**: Do you think Dr. Thompson is being treated fairly?
> **Woman**: He should be locked up for assaulting that poor woman.
> **RL**: I see...Then you think the authorities were justified in searching his home.
> **Woman**: Absolutely. They found drugs, didn't they? That proves he's guilty.
> **RL**: But what about his rights? You know, the Fourth Amendment... The search was authorized on hearsay.
> **Woman**: She's a woman...a sister. Why would she lie about something like that?
> **RL**: Publicity?...She is an actress after all...or maybe she was set up by the Feds.
> **Woman**: Either way she's a victim, isn't she? Just a pawn in some sick macho jack-off fantasy.
> **RL**: Then you see it more as a battle between men and women.
> **Woman**: Honey, that's what it's always been...

[THE SUBCULTURE STAND]

RL: Are you here to protest the Thompson bust?
Hippie: Are you a narc?
RL: No, no... I'm a cartoonist. I'm doing a book on the trial.
Hippie: Really? Are you famous? Weren't you in *Zap*?
RL: No, that was some other guy? Have you read any of Hunter Thompson's books?
Hippie: Yeah. I read "Fear and Loathing in Las Vegas" back in the seventies. The guy is out there man.
RL: Yeah. He took a lot of drugs in that story, didn't he?
Hippie: Is this a set-up?
RL: It's cool. I swear. See... It even says who I am here in the paper... And there's my picture.
Hippie: A guy can't be too careful these days. Not that I have anything to hide. I don't do drugs. Is this being recorded?
RL: Not by me except for these sketches and notes.
Hippie: I don't want my picture taken. Do you want my name?
RL: Only if want to give it to me.
Hippie: Smith. My name is Joe Smith. That's the ticket.
RL: In that case, "Joe," what do you think about drugs?
"Joe": I think they should bust the Colombian cartels and leave the pot smokers alone.
RL: Do you smoke marijuana?
"Joe": No. I'm straight, man... Well, I did try it once in college, but I never inhaled... Honest.

[ENLIGHTENED GUY]

RL: Hi there. Are you here for the Thompson protest?
Guy: Actually, I just come here for lunch on nice days. I work at the bookstore down the street.
RL: Does the store carry any books by Hunter Thompson?
Guy: Not anymore. He's too violent for our clientele. Didn't they find some kind of arsenal in his house?
RL: I think it was a Gatling gun... An antique.
Guy: They should be banned and destroyed.
RL: What? Hunter's books?

Guy: No. Just guns. I'm not into drugs either, or killing animals.
RL: Dr. Thompson kills animals with guns and drugs?
Guy: The local SPCA is after him for torturing a fox. He even wrote about it in one of his columns. Disgusting.
RL: But later he said that he made it all up... A fable of sorts.
Guy: He's too pessimistic. People need to have a positive outlook on life: it's the only way we can save the planet.
RL: Don't you think Thompson is helping by exposing the hypocrisy in our government?
Guy: The only way to heal the planet is heal yourself first. He should meditate instead of taking drugs and drinking. He could join our Men's Encounter Group. We meet on Tuesdays at the bookstore.

[MZ. MYSTERY WITH A CAMERA]

I was wandering up and down the sidewalk looking for interviews when I noticed her. She was taking pictures from across the street, all alone. The other photojournalists were crowded around the entrance to the old brick courthouse, but she chose to stay at a distance, clicking away with her gigantic lens. There was a shyness about her... Maybe it was the dark glasses... Maybe it was the way

she constantly glanced from side to side, as if she was afraid of any chance encounter with a stranger. I had to meet her.

RL: Wait! Don't run away! I just want to ask you a few questions.

Mz: No… I have nothing to say. I was just leaving anyway.

RL: But I saw you taking pictures. What newspaper do you work for?

Mz: I'm freelance, just an amateur, really (She climbs into a white van with Utah plates. A man wearing dark glasses and a suit flips his cigarette out the window and starts the engine.)

RL: Wait. Dr. Thompson hasn't come out yet. You'll miss the story.

Man: Thompson? We've already got his picture. (Van drives away at high speed.)

The hearing was adjourned in the late afternoon. Hunter's lawyers managed to have the explosives charge dropped, but he would have to go to trial for the remaining drug and assault charges. The judge had decided there was enough evidence to continue the case, but there were so many holes in the story that the whole thing looked like the script for a Marx Brothers movie. The defense was confident that they would pound the prosecution like a dead fish, and everyone seemed upbeat. The press would have an ongoing trial to cover, and the Brothers vowed to return with another army of protesters.

[BACK AT THE TAVERN]

We returned to the Tavern where a victory celebration was about to begin. The journalists were gone, but a large group of locals crowded the patio in anticipation of a Hunter appearance. We were all tired and filthy, so one of the locals offered his shower. By the time I got there, the hot water was long gone, and I settled for a quick splash of water just to revive.

Back at the bar, Roxi was fending off bikers and cowboys and giving a radio interview over the phone. Artie was chasing Gigi around the pool table, and everyone in the place was looking for drugs, including me. The endless party had taken its toll on my ravaged body, and it would take more than cold water in the face or strong coffee to bring me out of it. After badgering the locals for an hour or so, a fat line of cocaine was produced and I rejoined the party with renewed interest.

Just then I heard a cheer go up from the patio. Hunter cruised up to the motorhomes on a big black BMW.

Puffing a cigar and wearing a baseball hat that resembled a shark. He stopped in front of Artie and me and started to say something, but the crowd swarmed over him like mosquitoes. He tried to ignore them at first, but when they persisted he growled at them menacingly. The startled well-wishers jumped back long enough for him to park the bike and duck in to the motorhome. He was still in a sour mood from the courtroom ordeal, but stayed long enough to thank everyone for their support before zipping back to the safety of Owl Farm.

Eventually, the party moved down the road to a giant log house that once belonged to rock singer Jimmy Buffet. Our hosts even provided a gaggle of teenage boys for Roxi, although her aggressive behavior frightened all but one of the leather-clad group. Meanwhile, Gigi was sliding down the stairway banister in the raw while Artie waited at the bottom to catch her with his tongue.

These spectacles were lost on me, though. I finally got my shower and staggered down the covered walkway to the motorhome, where I fell asleep the moment my head touched the pillow.

[HOMEWARD BOUND]

After performing our duties in Colorado, we packed up and headed back to California. We were total burnt out basket cases, and there was a thousand miles of desert between us and the safety of home. I remember getting a chuckle out of Artie when I announced that "the part of my brain that controlled fashion was dead." It was true. I looked like a clown that had been shot out of a cannon. Our tab at the Tavern went well into the four figures, which should give you some indication of our condition. All we needed to do was put the motorhomes on auto-pilot and aim them toward Salt Lake City, since Jim and Artie had wisely decided to take a different route home. It should have been easy.

We were cruising north on the freeway when we passed the suburbs of American Fork, Utah. It was the first time I had been in that area since my teen years in the mid-sixties, and I was thinking back to the summer when I tried to seduce a young Mormon girl in that neighborhood. I never got past second base, which was just as well, She turned out to be one of those women who get pregnant at a drop of a zipper, and today she is raising an army of rugrats somewhere in Arizona. That would have been a disaster for a young California

boy who could barely wait to escape his parents' home and wander the lonely highways of America. She kept her virginity, and I kept my wheels on the blacktop. Twenty-five years later, another woman would give me reason to remember American Fork, Utah.

Gigi and Roxi were constantly flashing their tits at passing motorists just to see their reaction. We encouraged them at first, but when we crossed the border into Utah, the game was put on hold. We were back in the land of Mormons and we had to be cool.

Ahead of us in the lead motorhome, Gigi decided to catch a few rays of the afternoon sun, so she removed her tanktop and spread out on a makeshift bed below a large side window. She couldn't be seen from a normal car, but the big rigs had a perfect view of her succulent melons. From our vantage point in the other motorhome, we witnessed a unique and frightening mating ritual.

At first, there was only one truck, The poor bastard must have been hornier than a half-fucked fox in a forest fire, because he stuck to the side of the motorhome like flypaper. When they reduced their speed to let him pass, he slowed down as well backing up traffic in two lanes. Then the idiot got on his C.B. and started quacking about the "nekkid woman" to his good buddies in the area. Within minutes, the motorhome was surrounded by giant trucks. The only thing I can compare it to was the wild elephant stampede that always saved the day in those old Tarzan movies. The boys in the motorhome freaked out and did their best to avoid being trampled, while we could only watch in horror. They finally managed to dart off into a rest area before the jumbo rigs could slow down enough to follow them. We were following a safe distance behind them, and were able to follow their lead.

We spent a short fifteen minutes at the rest area. Those who didn't wet their pants during the ordeal emptied their bladders and crawled nervously back into the vehicles. The women were told to stay away from the windows, at least until we cleared Salt Lake City. Alex took the wheel of the lead motorhome and Vaughn relieved Richard in our rig. We were no sooner out on the freeway when the lead car shot off down the road like a bullet.

"Jesus Christ," cried Vaughn. "What the hell is he doing?" "These things aren't made to do eighty miles an hour in this kind of traffic!" We tried to keep pace, but Alex was weaving thought traffic like he was in the Indy 500. We completely lost sight of them by the time we reached the city.

"Oh well, fuck it," said Vaughn. "I'm not going to get killed trying to keep up with those drug fiends. The only thing to do is stick with the plan and keep driving west."

We headed out across the salt flats, occasionally calling out on the radio, but the only response was the hiss of static. They finally caught up to us in Winnemucca, Nevada around sundown, where we stopped for our final pitstop before California. Alex had missed the Interstate 80 cut-off in Salt Lake and it took them an hour to get back on the right track.

There were no other major obstacles in our path, and we arrived in Nevada City shortly after 3 a.m. O'Neill called Lorraine to come rescue us from the empty, sleeping town, and we said our goodbyes. The twin motorhomes rolled back onto the freeway and faded into the night.

One week later, on May 30, 1990, Hunter Thompson was in the news again. The Pitkin County District Attorney's office filed a motion to dismiss all charges against the Doctor. District court Judge Charles Buss accepted the motion and dismissed the charges "without prejudice" meaning they could not be refiled at a later date.

In a press release the following day, Thompson denounced the dismissal as "pure cowardice" and vowed to appeal it to the Colorado Supreme Court. He went on to describe the D.A.'s staff as "liars, crooks, and human scum... These stupid brutes tried to destroy my life, and now they tell me to just forget it!"

The Pitkin County Courthouse

THE WOODY CREEK EXPEDITION

FROM LEFT- VAUGHN-ROXI-DAN-ME-GIGI-RICHARD-ARTIE
ALEX-ROCKY-ARTHUR DOWN IN FRONT-RICK AND JIM

WOODY CREEK
TAVE

Photo: Alex Benton

TOP: *Artie Mitchell & friend in Woody Creek..*
BOTTOM: *The Author with Gigi and Roxi.*

BOOK FIVE

Midnight Faxes

FROM: HUNTER S. THOMPSON
TO: JEFF ARMSTRONG, *Road Manager*

[INCLUDING THE WHITE BUCK PAPERS,
OTHER FAXES FROM HST TO EDITORS AND AGENTS
& HUNTER'S EDITING CORRECTIONS]

Hunter making a 55-foot putt in San Francisco. He dedicated this photo to Jeff Armstrong, his Bay Area "Road Manager."

Tuesday

Congress of the United States
House of Representatives
Washington, D.C. 20515

Hi! I'm Alfie

message follows

Jeff

Thursday 11/13

Congress of the United States
House of Representatives
Washington, D.C. 20515

Help

I need a VHS copy of That New Sex Film that you told me about....,

Plus any others that look like our kind of movie...

Plus a small case of RUSH (10-12 little bottles

Thanx
Doc

* — I located the shotgun — Soon come

Jeff

Congress of the United States
House of Representatives
Washington, D.C. 20515

Arriving 2:30
Continental # [1-303-923-5424]
(call Morris here for
details. . . (5424)
We could go
straight to the
waterfront. . .
from the airport.
If you don't
meet me, I'll slit
my wrists & crawl
onto the baggage
carosel with a
huge air-horn.
OK Doc

Woody Creek
ROD & GUN CLUB
HUNTER STOCKTON THOMPSON, EXECUTIVE DIRECTOR

4:03 p.m.

Jeff

Good news

Rest easy. I won't be there. Clearer heads prevailed. Do not go to the airport.

Xray right. It is a far far better thing that I do now than I have ever done before.

POST OFFICE BOX 220, WOODY CREEK, COLORADO 8165

SORRY
Doc

THE POLO REPORT

DISPATCHES FROM THE WORLD OF POLO

Jeff

Call me tonite at The Red Lion Inn Durango, Colo
1-800-547-8010
ask for "Mr. Stanky"
or Deborah, who will be handling the phone

Lecture

OK I'm half-alive – but I'm still not a "COP" you swine.
+ I'm not writing a book on This nightmare — unless I decide to finish The Night Manager
Ho, ho Call me
(H)

Insert

The 1976 Fleetwood Eldorado Caddilac convertible is a monument to some of the ugliest moments in American history -- the cruel & terrible journeys by mule trains & wagons & drag-sleds & wooden-wheeled "stage coaches" that hauled the great Westward Movement for 2000 miles from the Mississippi River to the Rockies & on to California where money grew on trees & the streets of San Francisco were paved with gold bricks.

Some people made it the easy way -- taking six or eight month journeys on wooden steam-sailboats around the bottom of Argentina between icebergs & sea-monsters & shipwrecks in the frozen Straits of Magellan -- where they had to stay well clear of any ice-floe or island where they might be lured ashore by false land-lights & then boarded at night by gangs of desperate, malaria-crazed survivors of some previous disaster who had been stranded there for nine months with no matches or water & only dead seal-blubber to feed on while they waited with sharp sticks & bludgeons for the next ship to come through & maybe pick them up -- & then up the other side, another 8000 miles

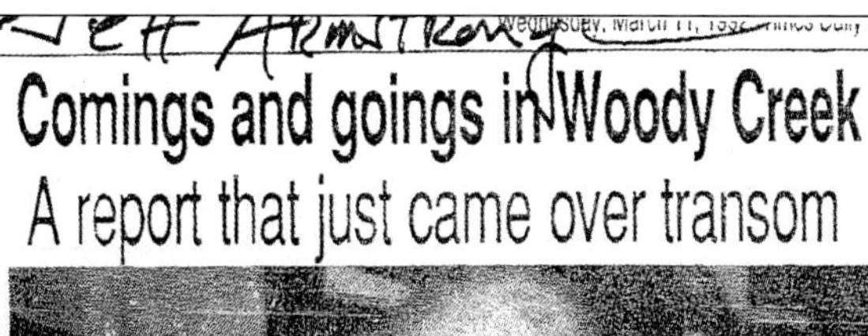

Jeff Armstrong

Wednesday, March 11, 199…

Comings and goings in Woody Creek

A report that just came over transom

Strange birth to Woody Creek couple

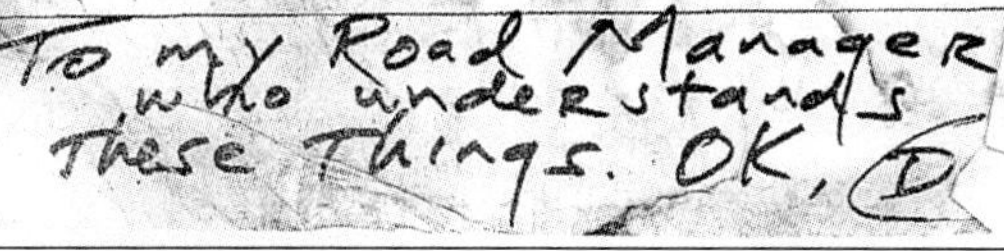

Woody Creek, Colo (March 10, 1992) — Famed Gonzo Journalist Dr. Hunter S. Thompson and celebrated Australian Lap Dancer Mme. Tara Ellison emerged from seclusion yesterday with their new-born 26-pound daughter, Mona, and announced to a frenzied press conference that the long-awaited "Love Child" will be sold to the King of Spain in July. Spokesman for the couple said they would "have no further comment."

To my Road Manager who understands these things. OK,

Thompson Gets Special Liquor Permit

DURANGO, Colo. (AP) — A special city permit has been granted to controversial journalist Hunter S. Thompson so he can imbibe in his usual scotch whisky while he lectures a college audience next month, officials said.

Thompson, whose most recent book "Songs of the Doomed" describes his run-in with the law over drugs last summer, is given to sipping Chivas Rigal scotch from the podium when he gives speeches.

His April 4 booking at Fort Lewis College posted a problem for some college officials, who questioned whether it would be appropriate for Thompson to drink at a college function.

THE AUTHOR INCLUDES the scotch provision in his contract, according to student union lectures chairman Jeff Lipshultz.

So last week, the Durango Liquor Authority granted Thompson a special-events liquor license, Lipshultz said.

It will be restricted to allow booze on the stage only, and police security will be present.

The drug charges against Thompson were dropped after prosecutors said they couldn't prove their case.

The White Buck Papers

[A TREATISE ON MANNERS, STYLE AND TIPPER GORE'S CENSORIOUS VALUES OCCASIONED BY JEFF ARMSTRONG SENDING HUNTER S. THOMPSON A SPANKING NEW PAIR OF WHITE BUCKS TO WEAR TO BILL CLINTON'S NOMINATION PARTY.]

(1)

Jeff Armstrong
Road Mgr.

July 13 '92
Owl Farm

AMENDMENT IV
to the U.S. Constitution

The right of the people to be secure in their persons, houses, papers, and effects, against unreasonable searches and seizures, shall not be violated, and no warrants shall issue, but upon probable cause, supported by oath or affirmation, and particularly describing the place to be searched, and the persons or things to be seized.

Remember this:
Ugliness Begins
at Home!

And where
do you Think you
were born?

Do your People
wear White Bucks?
I do. Because
I am smart—

over—

AMENDMENT IV
to the U.S. Constitution

The right of the people to be secure in their persons, houses, papers, and effects, against unreasonable searches and seizures, shall not be violated, and no warrants shall issue, but upon probable cause, supported by oath or affirmation, and particularly describing the place to be searched, and the persons or things to be seized.

— and you're not."

Ho, ho. Calm down — that's the name of a song I wrote for Bill Clinton. He plans to sing it on Wed. nite when he's nominated.

And I will be there with him — but only mouthing the words.

→

AMENDMENT IV
to the U.S. Constitution

The right of the people to be secure in their persons, houses, papers, and effects, against unreasonable searches and seizures, shall not be violated, and no warrants shall issue, but upon probable cause, supported by oath or affirmation, and particularly describing the place to be searched, and the persons or things to be seized.

And—actually—Bill won't be singing the words, either. Because they're obscene, + Mr. Tipper says No. At first he wanted to sing along with us—but his wife said No. She won't even let him mouth the words.

→

(4)

FORGET THE SHRIMP HONEY

I'M COMING HOME WITH THE CRABS

→ God only knows why, Jeff. On some days she acts like a monster. Why is she so weird?

The bitch has made a joke of my song. Me + Bill will be a laughing-stock, worse than ~~Vanilla Ice~~ Milli Vanilli??

Shit! Their names mean nothing now, anyway. At least not to us, right?

(5)

ROLLING STONE
Dr. Hunter S. Thompson: National Correspondent

→ Yes. Because we're obscene. That's what Mr. Tipper says, + sometime soon you might want to live in Mr. Tipper's neighborhood.

You bet. And you'll want to have yr. own pair of white Bucks, too. Because he will. And so will his wife. And also Bill. And Hillary — who has, oddly enough, frequently expressed a wistful desire to meet Jim.

Owl Farm, Woody Creek, Colorado 81656

over →

(3/6)

ROLLING STONE

Dr. Hunter S. Thompson: National Correspondent

Anyway, *yes* — I recalled yr elegant gift & immediately dyed them *black*, for my Wed. appearance in the Garden. New York is too ~~Filthy~~ Filthy for any other color. (or *lack* of..)

Indeed. ~~Black is Filthy; Filthy is Blacken~~ Obscene is Black; Black is Filthy.... therefore, I am—?

Well... shit. It won't *parse*, will it? *I* am *not* Black. But history might *portray* me that way.

Owl Farm, Woody Creek, Colorado 81656

I have no control over it. And, who knows? You don't have to be black to be a Nigger, These days. Take my word for it. The White Negro has evolved into—

Us.

Right.

So take care of yr. white Bucks. You're going to need them.

Okay. Thanx,

Hunter

Doc

Jeff Armstrong

COLLEGE SPECIAL

Ro Stone

LOLLAPALOOZA
On the Road With
The Chili Peppers,
Pearl Jam and
Soundgarden

CLINT EASTWOOD
He Shoots, He Scores

THE FIRST

ROLLING STONE
INTERVIEW
BILL
CLINTON
By William Greider,
P.J. O'Rourke and
Hunter S. Thompson

DEEE-LITE
MICHAEL JACKSON
BOBBY BROWN

Jeff thanx again for
the White Bucks
I wore them in
Little Rock. Okay
H

Other Faxes from HST to Editors and Agents & Hunter's Editing Corrections

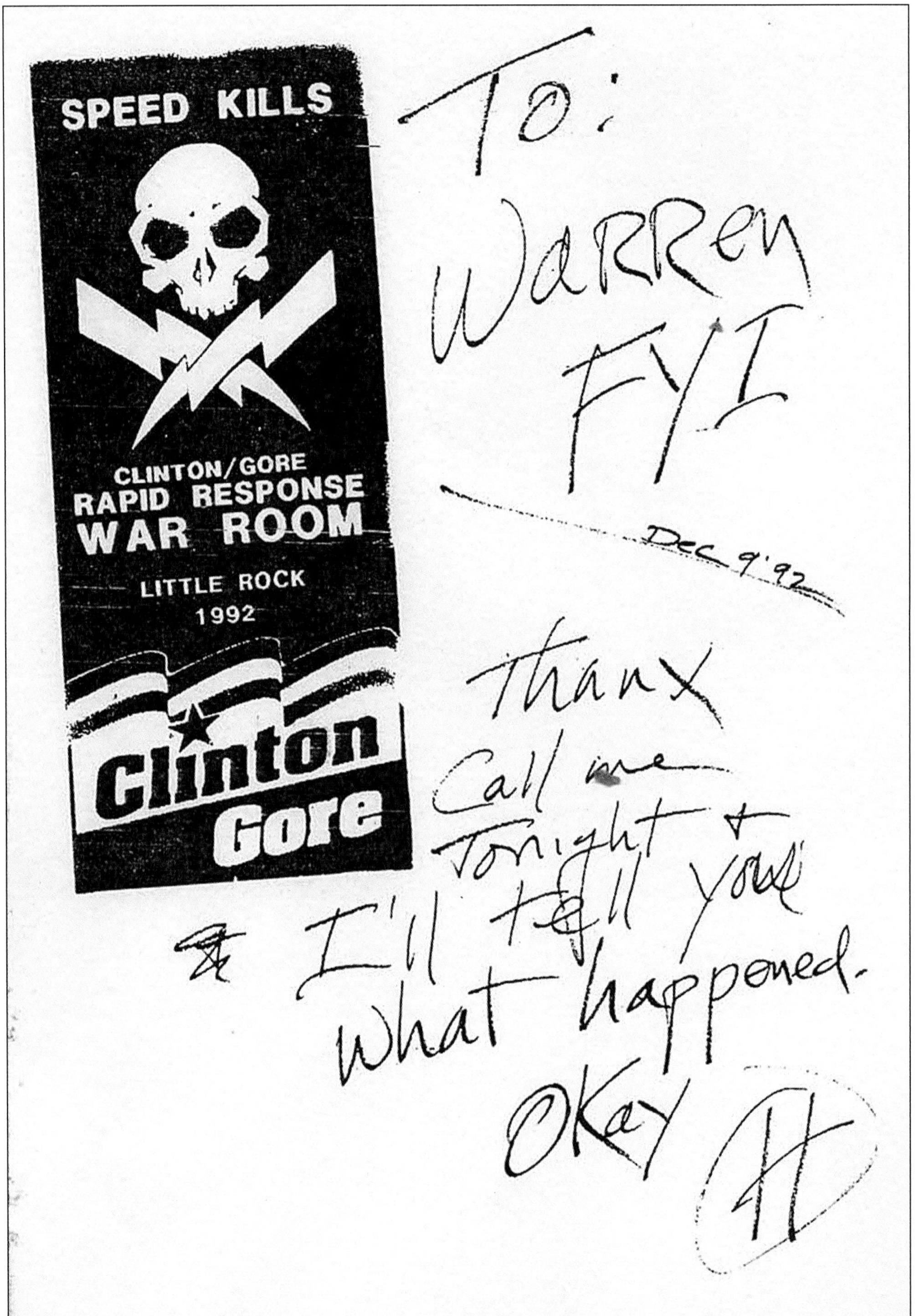

SPEED KILLS

CLINTON/GORE
RAPID RESPONSE
WAR ROOM

LITTLE ROCK
1992

Clinton
Gore

To:
Warren
FYI

Dec 9 '92

Thanx
Call me
Tonight +
I'll tell you
what happened.
Okay
H

A Hunter Midnight Fax to Warren Hinckle at the Argonaut.

Feb 13 '91
Owl Farm

38

Boys....

Inre: yr. giddy request for a "4x4 copy block before noon", pls. find enclosed the same of verses of the Book of Revelation,-which, as you know, speaks directly to my own view of the current war in Iraq & the end of the world as we know it..... We have spoken of this many times in the past (see NYTimes:Jan 1'74, op-ed/HST), and the only difference now is that time is getting shorter -- at least for you people.

I have warned you before & now I warn you again. The Time Has Come, O ye of little faith, yr. fat is now in the fire & yr. bones will be gnawed by the sons of Mesopotamia, who dwell in the dark of the desert....

Being against the ~~war now is like being~~ against the bombing of Guernica in 1937 (?) try 1939 (?) and trying to hold onto a good job ~~in Berlin~~ at the same time. Before this bomb frenzy is over, we will have dwarfed Guernica, as well as Dresden & Hiroshima.... and it was you, Charley, who paid for it. Bombs don't come from the stork; they come from the IRS, from Personal Income Taxes.... So think about it, Charley, when you fill out yr. forms next month.

ck?

And in the meantime, read the Book of Revelation, especially Chap. 6 and 9 and -- hell, read all of it; but here's a running start:

insert → REV 6: 1-17

REV 9: 1-21

OK. There's yr. copy block.
Good luck. HST

Hunter's deadline copy for the first edition of War News.

CLINTON/GORE
RAPID RESPONSE
WAR ROOM
LITTLE ROCK
1992

Clinton
Gore

Jann

12.9.92
Owl Farm

Dear Jann,

Your odious, bitchy little suggestion that I should chop 4000 words out of the middle of my Little Rock essay and let you publish a few lame fragments/leftovers in R.S. in some bogus fraudulent & utterly incomplete Scim of a silly "article" with my name on it just so you can sell a few more magazines is Unacceptable & wrong....

And I have to assume you know this, but it is hard to understand why why why you would even think about doing it, except to save a few dollars & cause me serious professional embarrassment.... It makes no sense to me & I'm sure it will make none to Lynn. I have worked very hard on this piece for a long time without any help from your end (on the ms.) except occasional nagging & prodding.

The article is clearly unfinished, but that is no reason or license for you to suddenly send the worst ten-percent of it to press & toss the rest away as offal. It has been many years, Jann, many years, since any editor was dumb enough to tell me that 90% of my work was so useless that the only way I could justify it was by publishing the worst 10% of it & feel lucky to sell that for a dime on the dollar & nevermind what it reads like—"just as long as you spell my name right in the Lede & nevermind yr.

Hunter to Jann Wenner on cuts to his copy.

Jann Wenner / cc

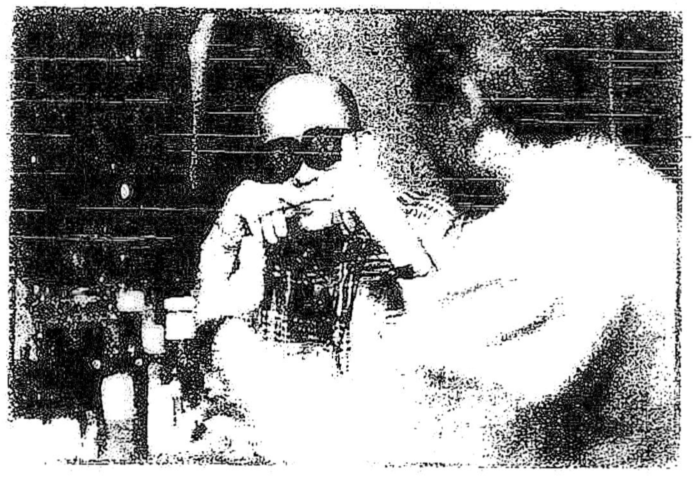

stupid little stories. And by the way, Bubba, why don't you wise up & toss that 'GONZO' bullshit back on the Junk-heap where it belongs??"

Right. Me & Bill Clinton -- two screwheads who never got smart.

Anyway, let's not have any confusion about this piece. It is not finished & I don't want to see a few dim chunks of it Rushed into print by anybody, for any reason, & certainly not with my name on it..... You could Do that, but it would be Wrong.

This is a good story and I have too much time, effort & keenly original thinking invested in it to let it go as a cheap imitation, just to get my name on the cover of Rolling Stone.

Why not move it up to the next issue & do it right? Why degrade ourselves in public so soon after yr. elegant celebration -- which consumed so much of our precious Time & our Health & our Brains & our Love & our Precious Bodily Fluids?

So much Time, Jann -- so much of our Precious Time. Why? I guess I'll ask Lynn. Okay. Later.

H

SPEED KILLS

CLINTON/GORE
RAPID RESPONSE
WAR ROOM
LITTLE ROCK
1992

Clinton
Gore

To: Lynn

URGENT

Dear Lynn,
I need your help with Jann, inre: my Little Rock article
see-over
pgs 2+3

I just sent it to him + I said you would CRUSH him if he TRIED to get away with it.
Fuck him. Why don't we sell it (when it's finished) - To Tina BROWN FOR $50,000!
Please help me!
Love, Hunter

Hunter to his agent, Lynn Nesbit. He attached his "Fuck You Fax" to Wenner (previous page.)

20:19 FROM ROLLING STONE EDITORIAL TO 9130392.0091 P.12

PART III... "WISDOM" SECTION

WELCOME TO THE GARDEN OF AGONY, BUBBA ... And Watch Yourself. We are a Smart, Well-Disciplined Organization ... And The Fat is in the Fire – ... Stand Back.... There is No Such Thing as Safe Sex, but it is Safer for Some People than Others... Will the New World Order be Ruled by Jesuits? ... Is Bill Clinton a Trojan Horse...Did the Real Jesus Freaks Run a Naked Reverse on Us?

"O they often call me Speedo
but my real name is Mister Earl ..."
– the Cadillacs, 1953?

THINK ABOUT IT, BUBBA. WHAT IF PRESIDENT CLINTON IS A MOLE FOR THE ORDER OF JESUS? WERE THE Preachers only a *decoy*? Will your children be turned into Slaves of a New Papist Dynasty? And who *is* the King of the Jesuits, these days?

These are serious questions, and the time has come to confront them. They are burning the midnight oil in the Jesuit war-room at Georgetown tonight, and not many of those boys are from Arkansas. . . Not hardly. Hell no. They are a gang of Bubbas from Rome – the Elite Troops of the Vatican, the Meanest of the Mean.

I don't know why it took me so long to figure this out, Jann – and you might be asking *yourself* the same question. Do you think it's some kind of goddamn hillbilly *coincidence* that Bill Clinton claims to have been born on a moonlit night to a single mother in some rural Ozark hamlet called Hope and then raised in a weird mountain town where the water is 4000 years old?

Some people have problems with that, Bubba. Some people know the *score*.

But not You, eh? No. It went *right past* Your goddam giddy eyes, but you were too crazy for Power to see it. All you cared about was whooping it up in the White House . . . after 25 years that was one long Rock and

Roll party, all you want now is One More Bash, an orgy of Greed and Ambition in the rooms where Abe Lincoln slept. Along with Judith Exner and Marilyn Monroe, on some nights. And God only knows who else. . ."

It gives me the Creeps, Bubba. I haven't had a wink of real sleep since the night before the election, when I suddenly saw it all very clearly. . .

INSERT P.

But not in *Little Rock*. Things are different there. People don't act the same way. They don't have the same kind of hopes & dreams & fears that people have in Boston & Reno & Texas. . . Hell, it's a whole *different world*, down in Little Rock. People are smart & they go down gracefully. . .

Or they get the fuck out of town, like Bill Clinton did. *Whacko!* Off to Washington, the White House, the Oval Office, black Limo's & Secret Service bodyguards, total power & a totally public life. Mr. President Boss. Leader of the Free World. . .

Hot damn! Fuck Little Rock. I was born for better Things. . . What? Don't ask. I must be about my father's Work. . . The business of America is Business; Don't ask me why. Fuck you. I was born in a bottomless Aquafilter, 4000 years deep – shot out from a crack in the mountain at tremendous pressure like a human cannonball who was aimed like a heat-seeking missile to be the President of the United States, or at least get out of Little Rock.

It's a grim town, Bubba. It's like a step down from Memphis, an easy place to wither up & die like a stupid flower. Little Rock is a serious Hick Town. Take my word for it.

Hunter always faxed his page proof corrections.

Jim

Congress of the United States
House of Representatives
Washington, D.C. 20515

Friday
1.18.91

What's this about Kramer fucking with Warren?

pls. advise soonest + tell me who should be flogged + when. Nevermind why.

OK
Doc

BEWARE

Today: the Doctor
Tomorrow: <u>You</u>

NO PASARAN

The Hunter S. Thompson Legal Defense Fund
Box 274, Woody Creek, Colorado 81656

Paid for George Stranahan and Michael Solheim

BOOK SIX

Requiem

SUZIE BRIGHT
JUAN THOMPSON
WAYNE EWING

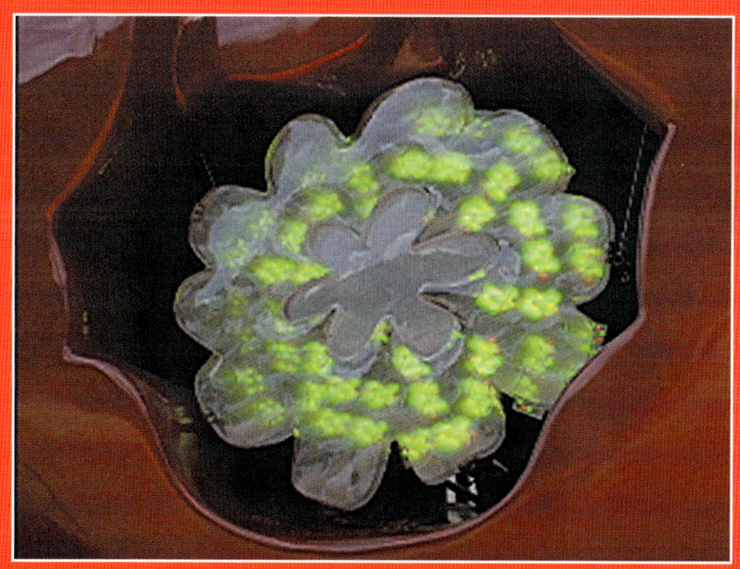

-30-

SUSIE BRIGHT

Hunter Thompson died last night, and I would say he planned it to a "T." He died of a self-inflicted gunshot wound to the head, but as friends and family will tell you, he was not depressed; he had not lost his passion for life, he didn't fit any description of a broken shell. This wasn't a guy who needed to call a hotline.

Hunter and I were both Irish Catholics, and on the occasion of his death, I opened the Roman Catholic Missal to this very day on the calendar to see what must be chanted at Mass. We are in Lent. I read the passage like an "I Ching" reading, substituting Hunter's name for "God":

> Let every heart that longs for Hunter rejoice, to Hunter have recourse and there find strength; beg continually for his presence. Praise Hunter and call upon his name, tell the story of his doings for all the nations to hear.

I believe, like many who knew him--and others who didn't know Hunter but are perfectly aware of the state of dying in this country--that the man checked out. By that, I mean self-deliverance, planned death, not an impulsive action.

Everyone close to Hunter knew he had health problems, and I don't mean the just the usual stuff that happens to you when you drink a lot! 'Course, alcohol in immoderate amounts doesn't help aging, but the man was stubborn, defined by his stubborness.

He had a constitution that left his peers in awe in his younger days. He has been plagued with excrutiating joint and bone problems for years. I don't know what else he was suffering from as he reached his sixties, and I doubt he told many people about it.

I called on Dr. Johnson one morning, when Mrs. Williams, the blind lady, was conversing with him. She was telling him where she had dined the day before. "There were several gentlemen there," said she, "and when some of them came to the tea-table, I found that there had been a good deal of hard drinking." She closed this observation with a common and trite moral reflection--which, indeed, is very ill-founded, and does great injustice to animals--"I wonder what pleasure men can take in making beasts of themselves."

"I wonder, Madam," replied the Doctor, "that you have not penetration to see the strong inducement to this excess; for he who makes a beast of himself gets rid of the pain of being a man."

--Samuel L. Johnson

If Thompson planned his death like other friends of mine have, he likely set a deadline; he might have confided to one or two. Because it's illegal to plan your death in Colorado, (and most people do want to die at home), the hardest task his family would face would be knowing that they couldn't be with him when he died, not without facing criminal charges.

Loved ones who collaborate with their dying friends' wishes either hide their presence, or they clear out. Can you imagine if you had to be born alone?--If it was against the law to have your family and friends close around you?

It was, by his lights, considerate for Hunter to shoot himself, although I wouldn't recommend it to just anyone. He made the sheriff's work cut and dried, and no one will charge that someone else held the weapon to his head. It spares his family scrutiny, it spares his body inquiry.

Hunter liked guns, used guns, didn't hesitate to aim and fire. The man was a Southern gentleman and a scholar. The reckless part about shooting yourself is that some people blow it, their technique is flawed, and they end up making themselves a vegetable instead of relieved death. Even done with discretion, the mess is left for someone else to deal with, which is a charge Hunter faced often his life.

I'm sure there may have been some dark jokes in his posse about whether HT would manage to take out the beast properly. A few years ago he took aim at a bear on his Colorado property and accidentally hit his secretary instead. When I heard that news, it already sounded apocryphal.

Hunter missed the grizzly that time, but the bear would be back.

I know Hunter because of Jim and Art Mitchell, who "hired" him to be their night manager at the O'Farrell Theatre in San Francisco in the 1980s, a job description that didn't exist before or since his tenure. He had similar position at Esalen. The gonzo muscle machine? I never saw him lift anything besides a glass and a card. I know I'm lucky, but he was extraordinarly gentle with me.

> *Wild men who caught and sang the sun in flight,*
> *And learn, too late, they grieved it on its way,*
> *Do not go gentle into that good night...*
> *Rage, rage against the dying of the light.*
>
> -- *Dylan Thomas*

This was during the years I was editing *On Our Backs*, and my business partner, Debi, stripped at the O'Farrell. It was a time when every woman who worked there seemed to be either a dyke on our magazine staff, or a member of the Rajneesh commune. Jim and Art had a running poker game upstairs, and also a running operation that published an antiwar rag with the contribution of every outlaw artist in town. The party and the propaganda went back and forth between the O'Farrell in the Tenderloin and the Tosca in North Beach.

Thompson wasn't that aware of me at the time. I wasn't dancing or playing poker--talking, watching, and muckraking were my chief occupations.

Our real connection wasn't until years later, after Artie died; after Thompson was back in Woody Creek. We shared some of the same publishing travails, and I have to say, Hunter always made me feel better, because he was endlessly militant towards publishers. I would think, "Hey, he's willing to fight these authoring justices tooth and nail--why am 'I' flinching?"

He enjoyed my writing, and would give me his review of the talent in my "The Best American Erotica" books. He would point out authors in the latest edition that were his favorites, and he invariably picked out the remarkable novitiates. His choices didn't tell me his erotic turn-ons; they showed me his writer antennae.

I am so proud of Hunter for dying the way he wanted to; for not succumbing to our sadistic "healthcare" traditions that keep you alive whether you like it or not; losing your dignity, your senses, and your independence.

"Checking out" is something that, if it was accepted, and decriminalized, would largely be a private affair, and the agents of the state would be there to support the survivors, not indict them.

I wish more people could be open about their plans, but it's difficult, isn't it? It's not like the legions of women who wrote their names down in the 60s saying, "I had an abortion, and I'm here to testify." They were still alive to fight against the laws of hypocrites.

When a man plans an intentional death, not out of despair but out of self-determination, the only ones left to talk about it are friends and family, who are suffering the loss. It's a hard time to be a right-to-die activist when you can hardly see through your grief.

Nevertheless, a change is gonna come, and the generation that threw a party at Woodstock and brought the war home isn't going to lay down gently. People don't want to die the way they've watching their elders go, they aren't going to put up with it anymore.

But I am so blue that Hunter is gone. No one else is going to call me at 3am and quote John Steinbeck, the Old Testament, and Nixon's Enemy List--reminding me why psychedelic subversiveness is a triumph of spirit.

[*A Story about Hunter, Praying...*]

One day Hunter held out a jar. "Here's where I keep my prayers and dreams," he said. He took the lid off the jar.

"I have to keep the top on," he said, "or my dreams and my prayers will escape."

There was a long pause while he stood there, holding the lid in one hand and the jar in the other.

"I'm waiting," Hunter said, "for the jar to fill back up."

Then he got impatient, and slammed the lid back on.

"Well," he said, "for now, prayers and dreams don't respect the simple laws of physics. They go right through."

He was... easy to love. Ha! Yes, more than the hardship of his mercurial disposition. When friends gather to mourn him, I have a feeling the greatest emotion will be tenderness. He had such a great big bear of a heart under all that bite. He was Someone Who Gave A Shit, who would not let his own fear and loathing defeat him, EVER. Brother Thompson wrote to live, and lived to write. I admire him, as usual, for clawing his way out of here, entirely by his own design.

--February 21, 2005

After-Word

JUAN THOMPSON

It has been two years since my father, Hunter S. Thompson, ended his life. I still miss him very much. I have thought a lot about him over the past two years as I've written about him, talked about him, read old letters, and gone through a significant portion of his papers. I've been trying to understand him more clearly, as my father, a writer, and a man. Though there are many things about him I miss, there are three qualities especially: his idealism, his sense of fun, and the warmth of his love.

It may seem strange to many people to think of Hunter as an idealist, but that was one of his defining characteristics. He had strong and clear ideas about the promise of our political system, about the need to act rather than be a passive victim of the greedy and power-hungry, and about the need to vigorously defend individual freedom. The disparity between the ideal and reality made him angry, and he was a man of action, a warrior and a leader. In an earlier age perhaps he would have taken up arms, but in this age he chose the written word as both his weapon and his art.

It was part of Hunter's gift to distort the actual facts of a situation to reveal its essential truth.

He had the talent, skill and convictions to draw you into his moral vision, and that vision was stark and uncompromising. There was good and there was evil, and there were no bystanders. To those

that agreed with him, he gave the chance to be part of something important, to do something meaningful with their time, money and talents. That kind of clear moral vision has tremendous power and appeal in our time of great moral confusion. When he called on his friends and acquaintances to help him with the Lisl Auman case, he was calling them to battle a great wrong. Lisl was not just an unfortunate legal mishap; what happened to her was Wrong, and we had the chance to make it Right. Nixon was not just one more crooked politician; he was the apotheosis of the arrogant, ruthless tyrant and the flagrant betrayer of the hope of the American political experiment. Our society in the age of so-called global terrorism is now a society somewhat more concerned with security than with civil rights; he called it "The Kingdom of Fear."

And he was right. I miss his vision, and the boldness, humor and conviction with which he described it to us. There are never enough such people, and now there is one less.

I miss his sense of fun.

Hunter liked to have fun. Having fun was serious business, because for him life without fun was no life at all.

I remember the folder of fake fax forms which included insect extermination notices, international stock transactions, court summonses, lingerie order confirmations, and fake fax error sheets. Late at night he would fill out one of the forms and fax it to the home or office of a friend or acquaintance, and laugh as he imagined how they would explain it to their wives, bosses, or lawyers.

I remember the story of a practical joke gone horribly wrong, that of Jack Nicholson and the bleeding Elk Heart, in which Jack cowered in the darkened house with his children, his phone cut off by awful coincidence, listening to the gunshots and the screams of a wounded pig played over and over through a megaphone outside the house.

I remember the story of a time his Japanese publishers came to visit and were given a demonstration one night of what Hunter said were nuclear-tipped bullets. A friend secretly ignited a stick of dynamite under the target, a large aluminum beer keg, at the same moment Hunter fired with the stainless-steel, scope-mounted, .454 Casull pistol. There was a tremendous explosion and the beer keg flew several hundred feet in the air, over the heads of the awestruck visitors who had never seen a gun before, much less nuclear-tipped

bullets. He was a fine storyteller, and enjoyed recounting the tale as much as he enjoyed the prank itself.

There are stories of fireworks, of bullets fired through the ceiling of the kitchen, of shotguns fired across the room. He loved masks, fireworks, fire, smoke bombs, hammers that screamed or made the sound of breaking glass when struck. Just about everyone who ever met Hunter has a story about his sense of fun, though not all of them laughed at the time.

I think for Hunter fun was also political, and therefore about more than just fun. His sense of humor often exceeded the boundaries of law, convention, and good taste, and his enjoyment came as much from breaking boundaries as from the reaction of his victims. It was fun for the hell of it, but it was also to shake people up, rock the boat, wake people from their routines, and make them uncomfortable or scared for a moment. That kind of fun requires a larger vision. He was a kind of "mad trickster" whose madness conveyed wisdom. I think, at bottom, Fun was a kind of practice for him that kept him in touch with the real and vibrant pulse of life, and to be in proximity to him was to be in proximity to that pulse. I miss that.

Finally and foremost I miss the warmth of his love. I miss sitting in the kitchen at Owl Farm watching a football game or an old Bogart movie, or talking to him on the phone about the latest political insanity, or driving up the Lenado road for a late-night swim. We didn't talk about our relationship, we simply enjoyed being together.

It took a long time to get to that point, a lot of hard and unspoken work on both our parts over many years, but we got there, so that by the time he died we knew where we stood with each other and we were satisfied.

He was a complex man with many, many facets. One of those aspects was his great tenderness.

He had the capacity for tremendous generosity, compassion, and personal loyalty when it cost something to be loyal.

When he gave his love it was intense and pure, and I felt blessed. God knows he was no saint, but his love was the real thing, not the cheap watered-down imitation most of us are familiar with. I miss the warmth of his love.

But these are just my recollections and opinions. Fortunately, Hunter S. Thompson was first a writer, and that is how he wanted to be remembered--as a Great American Writer.

He left a substantial body of work. Whatever you might think of the preceding paragraphs, I ask you to read what he wrote--start with "Hell's Angels"--and decide for yourselves who he was, what was significant about his work, and what is worth emulating and carrying on.

In my opinion his achievement and talent were considerable, but you will have to make up your own mind. He certainly did.

-- Denver, Colorado, April, 2007

Burial In The Sky

WAYNE EWING

Photo: Kathleen Ewing

Neighbor/filmmaker Ewing and Hunter in Woody Creek.

Documentary filmmaker Wayne Ewing, Hunter's friend, neighbor in Woody Creek and film biographer, met Hunter in 1985 at the Mitchell Brothers' O'Farrell Street Theatre in San Francisco when Hunter was in his Night Manager mode. At Hunter's invitation, Ewing in 1986 began a cinema verité account of Hunter's adventures, originally to be titled The Gonzo Tour.

It would take Ewing 18 years to complete filming "Breakfast With Hunter"-the 91-minute feature film produced and directed by Ewing that evolved from their collaboration and is the best of the films on Hunter. Released in 2003, it documents Hunter at work and play with Johnny Depp, Benicio del Toro, John Cusack and Warren Zevon, among other luminaries. It recounts Hunter"s struggles to bring "Fear and Loathing in Las Vegas" to the big screen and features his battles with the Aspen law enforcement and political establishment who attempted to jail Hunter to keep his "freak power" values from political ascendancy in Aspen politics. Ewing released a second film from his extensive footage of Hunter shot over two decades, "Animals, Whores & Dialogue: Breakfast With Hunter, Vol. II.," in the Fall of 2010. (See www.HunterThompsonFilms.com).

Ewing also worked closely with Thompson editing "Kingdom of Fear," Hunter's 2003 memoir, and went on to make two more documentary films about Hunter, "Free Lisl," about Hunter's last crusade--to free the wrongfully imprisoned Lisl Aumun, and "When I Die," a documentary about the planning and complex construction of the 153-foot gonzo memorial (taller by a few feet than the Statue of Liberty), topped by a peyote fist, that was built in Woody Creek to shoot Hunter's ashes into the sky on August 20, 2005.

This extraordinary project was paid for by Hunter's friend Johnny Depp, who played Thompson in the movie of "Fear and Loathing in Las Vegas," because Depp wanted his friend to have his often-expressed wish to have cannons and fireworks and his ashes blasted into the sky after his death. The following photographs show the construction of the memorial, including a close-up of the psychedelic peyote bud in the gonzo fist, and the final fireworks explosion. The photos were taken from frames of "When I Die" and were prepared for this book by Mr. Ewing.

PYROTECHNICIAN-IN-CHIEF: Funeral fireworks coordinator Matt Wood seeks approval from Pitkin County Fire officials.

WOODY CREEK CAUCUS: "Burial in the Sky" organizer Jon Equis explains the logistics of shooting Hunter's ashes into the sky--the FAA restricted traffic over Owl Farm the night of the memorial--to some of Hunter's Woody Creek neighbors.

[CONSTRUCTION BEGINS ON HUNTER'S BURIAL MONUMENT, WOODY CREEK, COLORADO 2005]

Hunter's Last Words: "No more games. No more bombs ...

[BUILDING THE TWO-THUMBED GONZO FIST]

... no more walking ...

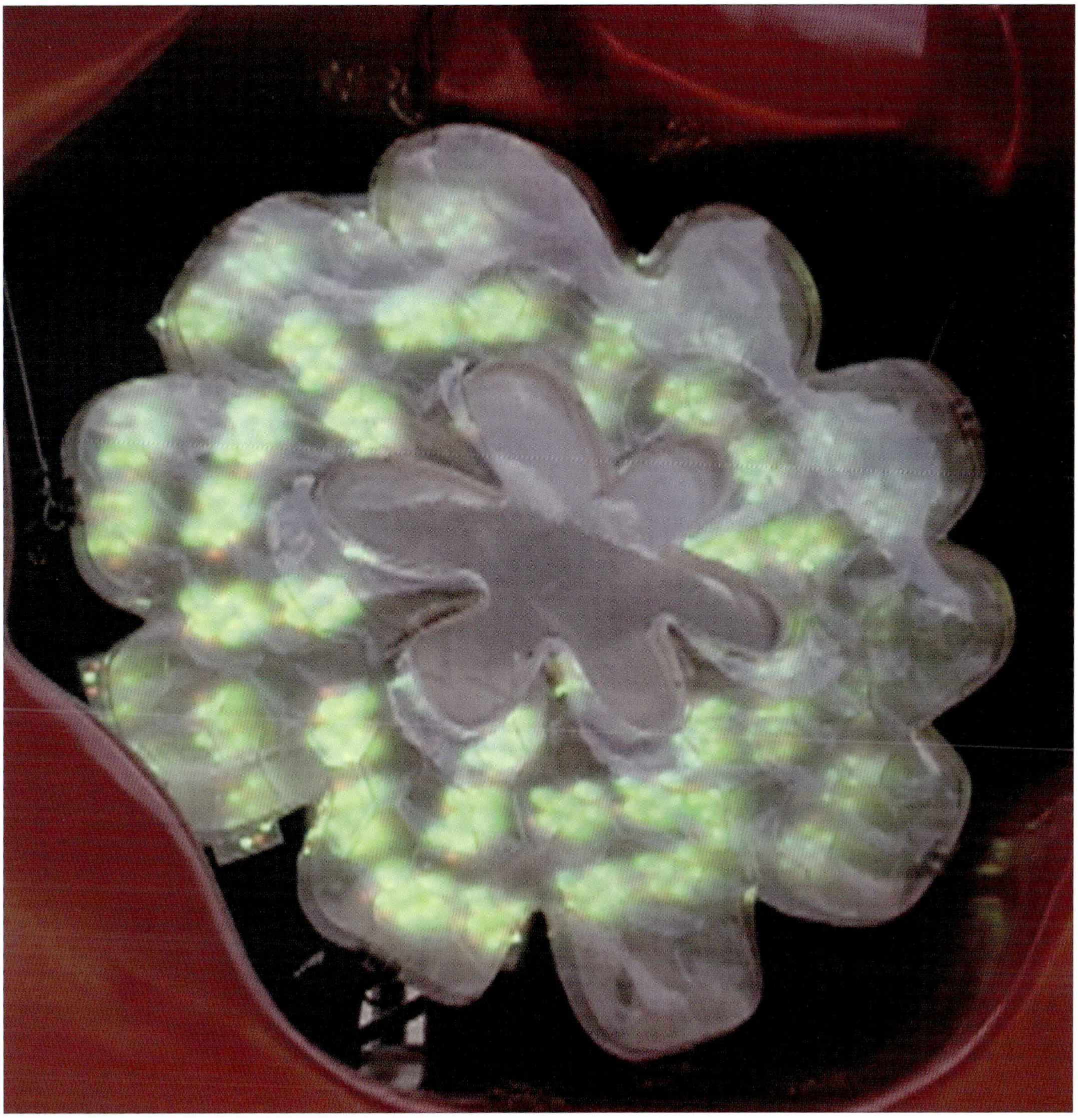

[INSIDE NEON PEYOTE BUD FIST]

... no more fun ...

[GONZO FIST MOUNTED]

... no more swimming ...

[ROADWAY TO MONUMENT]

... sixty-seven. That is seventeen years past fifty ...

[BLAST-OFF DAY: AFTERNOON]

... seventeen more than I needed or wanted ...

[THE MONUMENT AT DUSK]

... I am always bitchy ... no fun for anybody. Sixty-seven ...

[EVENINGTIDE]

... you are greedy ...

[BURIAL FIREWORKS LIFTOFF]

... act your old age. Relax--this won't hurt."

The Edge ... There is no honest way to explain it because the only people who really know where it is are the ones who have gone over.

The others--the living--are those who pushed their control as far as they felt they could handle it, and then pulled back, or slowed down, or did whatever they had to when it came time to choose between Now and Later.

--Hell's Angels

Roger Black is the highly esteemed, internationally known art director who designed *Rolling Stone*, *Newsweek*, and countless magazines and newspapers on several continents. He received the Lifetime Achievement award from the Society for News Design in 2013. Black designed the cover for this book, "Who Killed Hunter S. Thompson," and penned "Waiting for Copy." www.RogerBlack.com

Susie Bright is the author/editor of 30+ books specializing in erotic forensics and sexual politics, and was a friend of Hunter and the Mitchell Brothers. She wrote the essay "-30-" for this book the day after Hunter died. She misses Hunter dearly and sometimes blogs about him and other friends at www.SusieBright.com.

Phil Bronstein is executive chair of the board for the Center of Investigative Reporting in Berkeley. He was formerly with the Hearst Corporation for over 30 years, executive editor of the *San Francisco Chronicle* and the *San Francisco Examiner*. He is known for his work as a war correspondent and investigative journalist. In 1986, he was a finalist for the Pulitzer Prize for his reporting on the fall of Philippine dictator Ferdinand Marcos.

He recalls that at the *Examiner*, he was Hunter Thompson's least successful editor, ever. Despite six hours of debauched negotiations at the Waterfront restaurant over the best idea of Bronstein's life--to have Hunter cover the O.J. Simpson trial for the *Examiner*--nothing ever appeared in print. Years later, Bronstein convinced Hunter to agree to a series of political columns on the 2004 election season. Hunter never wrote them. Bronstein was able to get Hunter to fax a brief, nearly indecipherable appreciation when Richard Nixon died, which appeared in the paper. Over the years, Hunter left long messages on Bronstein's voicemail, offering commentary on world events or teasingly threatening to come to San Francisco and work as a police reporter.

Bronstein wrote "A Night at Hunter's."

Jerry Brown is the longest-serving governor in California history. He was first elected in 1974 and 1978, then again in 2010 and onto a fourth term in 2014. He is also a former U.S. presidential candidate, Mayor of Oakland, and Attorney General of California, in a long list of political career accomplishments. These thoughts on Hunter S. Thompson were originally written in 2005 and appeared in his blog, www.JerryBrown.typepad.com.

Bill Cardoso is the author of the "Maltese Sangweech & Other Heroes," an anthology. An elegant stylist, Mr. Cardoso's richly evocative articles appeared in such publications as the *Boston Globe, Rolling Stone, Harper's Weekly, Playboy, Ramparts* and *Esquire*. He assured himself a page in journalism history when he used the word "gonzo" in a note congratulating Hunter on his Kentucky Derby piece for *Scanlan's*. The term is now credited to him in the Oxford English Dictionary. The two became fast friends and developed their own language while covering the Foreman/Ali fight in Zaire, and were known there as the "Frick" and "Frack" of Counter Culture Journalism. The real event was not inside the ring but in the streets of Africa as told by Mr. Cardoso in his classic gonzo fight piece, "Zaire."

He was formerly the political editor of the *Boston Globe* and later became editor of the *Boston Globe Sunday Magazine*, which prompted Hunter to comment that the "freaks" were being moved "into power against their will. Cardoso is the reality of the New Journalism."

He left the *Globe* in 1972 to live and work in Europe. He could be seen, according to Hunter, amidst reporters interviewing Mandy Rice Davies in Israel, and later in the Canary Islands where he then ran a Jazz club. He later moved to Los Angeles and wrote for regional publications, but after the break-up of his marriage, resided for a time with Hunter and family in Aspen, Colorado. When he moved to San Francisco, he met Mary Miles Ryan, with whom he lived for the rest of his life, primarily at their home in Sausalito. In 1996, after collaborating with Hells Angel leader Sonny Barger on his autobiography, Mr. Cardoso was diagnosed with vocal cord cancer. He was treated successfully and maintained his voice, prompting a move to the wine country lakeside town of Kelseyville, where he continued to write, and completed a novel, "Blue Sausalito," shortly before he died of cardiac arrest in February, 2006--one year after the death of Hunter Thompson. He wrote the essay "The Origin Of Gonzo" for this book. He once pitched a no-hitter.

Dr. John G. Clancy was a lawyer, law professor, and writer, best known for his tireless work in social justice and gonzo mayhem. Born in the Bronx of Irish parents, he was the oldest of three and graduated from Fordham University and Columbia University Law School ('59). At 23, he met his lifelong friend and colleague, Hunter S. Thompson. The two shared a basement apartment on Perry Street, in NYC in the late 50s. They reunited in San Francisco in the early 60s after both had fled Gotham. Dr. Clancy was instrumental in conceiving the Esalen Institute with Dick Price and Michael Murphy. He worked as a tax and entertainment lawyer; some of his clients included Boz Scaggs, Ida Rolf, and various players from the Oakland Raiders. He helped David Meggyesy negotiate for The Players Union in 1982. He successfully represented famous photographer Tim Page against *Time Life*, which set a precedent for fair compensation for freelance artists. Quentin L. Kopp and Marc Libarle were his law partners.

He wrote a weekly sports column called "Diogenes" in Francis Ford Coppola's *City Magazine* during the mid-70's and published articles in *Harper's Magazine, Playboy, The Atlantic*, and other periodicals. In the early 80's, he took a sabbatical from his law practice to focus on writing. He moved to Durango, Colorado in 1984 where he and his wife Judy Campbell raised two daughters, Katie and Claire, on a peacock farm. Clancy taught political science at Fort Lewis College for 14 years and spent much time researching and writing about prison reform, his passion. He died in a freak auto accident on October 1st, 2005, near Ghost Ranch, New Mexico (Georgia O'Keeffe's sanctuary) exactly forty days after Hunter's blast-off memorial. He wrote the essay "A Master of Tools" for this book.

R. L. Crabb is a writer and cartoonist. His first newspaper cartoon appeared the day after Ronald Reagan was elected president. Since that time his crude and vulgar works have appeared in countless publications including *Weirdo, Rip Off Comix, Grateful Dead Comix, Snarf, Loompanics Live in Las Vegas, The Comics Journal,* and the *San Francisco Chronicle*. He considers himself a "Groucho Marxist," rejecting membership in any party that would have him as a member. Crabb is responsible for Book Four of this book-- he created the cartoons in "They Came For Blood ... We Gave Them Ink" and wrote and illustrated "The Caravan." His work can be found at www.RLCrabb.com.

Robert Crumb is the prolific cartoonist from the 60's underground comix movement, and founder of *Zap Comix*. He created counter culture icons Fritz the Cat and Mr. Natural, and the *Keep on Truckin'* strip. Crumb was inducted

into the comic book Hall of Fame in 1991, the same year he moved to France. Art critic Robert Hughes declares Crumb "the Bruegel of the second half of the 20th century."

Johnny Depp is the internationally acclaimed actor, producer, and musician, born in Kentucky. Hunter chose Depp to play himself in the 1998 Terry Gilliam film, "Fear and Loathing in Las Vegas." Depp lived in the basement at the Owl Farm for a few months before filming to research and observe Hunter. They became good friends. Depp's production company released "The Rum Diary," a 2011 film based on Hunter's novel of the same name. He blew Hunter's ashes out of a cannon. And contributed to Jonathan Shaw's essay in this book, "The Gift of the Severed Fingers."

Emory Douglas was the Minister of Culture for the Black Panther Party from 1967 until the Party disbanded in the 1980s. His graphic art was featured in most issues of the *The Black Panther* newspaper. As the art director, designer, and main illustrator for *The Black Panther*, Douglas created images that became icons, representing black American struggles during the 1960s and 1970s.

Dennis P. Eichhorn is a writer best known for his autobiographical comic book series, *Real Stuff*, illustrated by cartoonists he chose. He died of complications of pneumonia on October 8, 2015. Last Gasp published his most recent anthology, "Extra Good Stuff." Eichhorn submitted his cartoon tribute "Bill Cardoso: The Godfather Of Gonzo," for this book.

Wayne Ewing is an Emmy Award winning film maker who made several documentaries on Hunter Thompson; "Breakfast with Hunter" (2002), "When I Die" (2005), "Free Lisl: Fear & Loathing in Denver" (2006), and "Animals, Whores & Dialogue; Breakfast With Hunter Vol. 2" (2010). He lives in Aspen, Colorado. In this book he wrote "Never Call 911" and closes it in "Requiem" with "Burial In The Sky." www.EwingFilms.com

Christopher Felver is a photographer and filmmaker who Amiri Baraka called a "skilled photo-terrorist." His work as a documentarian and photographer of the Beat Generation has been exhibited at the Centre Georges Pompidou (Paris), Torino Fotografia Biennale Internazionale (Italy), the Fahey/Klein Gallery in Los Angeles, the New York Public Library and The National Gallery of Art in Washington, D.C. His many films include "John Cage Talks About Cows" (1991), "Donald Judd's Marfa, Texas" (1998),

and "California Clay in the Rockies" (1983), and "Ferlinghetti" (2009). His latest books are "Beat" (2007) and "American Jukebox: A Photographic Journey" (2014). Felver wrote "Shooting Hunter In f8" for this book. www.ChrisFelver.com.

Timothy Ferris is America's best science writer. His book "Coming of Age in the Milky Way" was nominated for a Pulitzer Prize. He has also written and narrated several documentaries on the universe, including "Seeing in the Dark" (2008). He was an editor at *Rolling Stone* and helped produce the Voyager Golden Record, an artifact containing music and sounds and images of earth, that was launched aboard the Voyager 1 spacecraft in 1977.He wrote the foreword to Hunter Thompson's book "Kingdom of Fear" (2003). He wrote "Fear And Loathing" for this book. www.TimothyFerris.com.

Ben Fong-Torres is an almost famous rock journalist, broadcaster, and author. He was a writer and senior editor at *Rolling Stone* when Hunter began writing for the magazine. He wrote the "Radio Waves" column for the *San Francisco Chronicle* for many years. His books include "The Rice Room: Growing up Chinese American from Number Two Son to Rock N' Roll" (1994), "Not Fade Away: A Backstage Pass to 20 Years of Rock & Roll" (1999), and "Becoming Almost Famous" (2006). His essay "Janis Joplin Knew What She Was Doing, Too" originally appeared in The *San Francisco Examiner's Focus* magazine in 1980.

Deborah Fuller was Hunter Thompson's assistant from 1982-2003. She did it all. In 2000, Hunter wounded her accidentally while shooting at a bear near her cabin at Owl Farm. She recovered. She contributed the "Owl Farm Album" for this book.

Jeff Goodby is a founder of the famed advertising firm Goodby, Silverstein & Partners in San Francisco. He wrote for the *Harvard Lampoon* in college, and his work as a director and illustrator has appeared in *TIME* and *Mother Jones*. He wrote "Hunter Makes a Commercial, Sort of" for this book.

William Randolph Hearst III is chairman of the board of the Hearst Corp. and President of the Hearst Foundation. He also has affiliations with numerous other boards and institutions. The grandson of William Randolph Hearst, he left the family business in 1976 to become managing editor of *Outside* magazine, started by *Rolling Stone*. Will returned in 1980

and was the editor and publisher of the *San Francisco Examiner* when he wooed Warren Hinckle and Hunter S. Thompson to his team. Hunter wrote a column for the paper. They inter-reacted. Hearst wrote "How The Doctor Rated The Game" for this book.

Warren Hinckle is a recipient of the H.L. Mencken Award--best newspaper columnist in the nation (1988)--and the Thomas Paine Award. He is the former editor of *Ramparts, Scanlan's Monthly*, and Francis Coppola's *City of San Francisco* magazine. His pairing of Hunter Thompson and Ralph Steadman to cover the Kentucky Derby for *Scanlan's* launched gonzo journalism. Hinckle is the author of seven books and was a longtime editor and columnist for the *San Francisco Chronicle*, the *San Francisco Examiner*, and the *San Francisco Independent*. He is editor and publisher of the *Argonaut*, an occasional periodical founded in San Francisco in 1877 and resurrected by Hinckle in 1991. His books include the memoir, "If You Have a Lemon, Make Lemonade" (1974), "The Fish is Red: the Secret War Against Castro" (1981), "GaySlayer! The Story of How Dan White Killed Harvey Milk and George Moscone and Got Away With Murder" (1985).

California historian Kevin Starr described Hinckle as "the flamboyant, pirated-patched writer-editor (he lost an eye in a boyhood accident), pub-crawler and larger-than-life legend. Literate, opinionated, genuinely eccentric (patent leather dancing pumps with grosgrain bows, a French basset hound in constant attendance), Hinckle is San Francisco's only living link with its colorful nineteenth-century past: a curious San Francisco blend of elegance and raffishness, left-wing radicalism and Tory bohemian style."

Hinckle wrote the massive introduction, "The Crazy Never Die including "The Night Manager," and most importantly, hit up all the other writers and artists for their contributions. His only belly flop was his failure to get longtime Hunter friend Jeannette Etheredge to contribute a written piece to this book. It's all his fault.

PUBLISHERS NOTE: *Hinckle died August 25, 2016 of complications from pneumonia, just hours after the final proofs for this book were delivered.*

William Kennedy quit journalism several times to write fiction. He published his first novel, "The Ink Truck," in 1968. He followed this with eight novels in his Albany Cycle on the fictional Irish-American Phelan family in Albany, NY, including "Billy Phelan's Greatest Game" (1978), the Pulitzer Prize winning "Ironweed" (1983), and eighth, "Changó's Beads

and Two-Tone Shoes" (2011). Kennedy wrote screenplays for Francis Ford Coppola's "The Cotton Club" (1986), and for the film of his own novel, "Ironweed" (1987). For Hunter, Kennedy wrote "A Box Of Books."

Paul Krassner edited The *Realist* from 1958-2001, but when *People* magazine called him "father of the underground press," he immediately demanded a paternity test. An award-winning stand-up comedian and writer, Krassner has six albums as well as a dozen + books under his belt. His latest is "One Hand Jerking: Reports From an Investigative Satirist," with an introduction by Lewis Black and a foreword by Harry Shearer. His most recent, 2016, is "The Realist Cartoons," a collection of the best. PEN's Oakland branch awarded him the Lifetime Achievement Award in 2010. He wrote "Blowing Deadlines With Hunter" for this book. He publishes the *Disneyland Memorial Orgy* poster, available from PaulKrassner.com..

John R. MacArthur is president and publisher of *Harper's Magazine* since 1983 and an award-winning journalist and author. In 1993 he received the H.L. Mencken Award for best editorial/op-ed column for his *New York Times* exposé of "Nayirah", the Kuwaiti diplomat's daughter who helped fake the Iraqi baby-incubator atrocity. He writes a monthly column for the *Providence Journal* and, in French, for *Le Devoir* (Montreal) on a wide range of topics, from politics to culture. He published his third book, "You Can't Be President: The Outrageous Barriers to Democracy in America," in 2008. MacArthur lives in New York City. He recorded his recollections of Hunter in "A Night On The Town."

Terry McDonell is a writer, editor, publisher, and former longtime editor of Time Inc. Sports Group, which includes *Sports Illustrated.* In the early 80s he was managing editor at *Rolling Stone*, which he followed with posts at *Esquire, Newsweek, US Weekly* and many more magazines. His 2016 memoir, "The Accidental Life: An Editor's Notes on Writing and Writers" captures many legends, including Hunter and Hinckle. McDonnell wrote "No More Smoking" for this book.

Matthew Naythons is a photojournalist, physician, and publisher. He documented the Fall of Saigon, the Yom Kippur War, the revolution in Nicaragua, and the Jonestown Massacare. He is the founder and CEO of Epicenter Communications, a multimedia company, in Sausalito, California. He wrote "16 Alexander Avenue" for this book.

Martin F. Nolan is a longtime ink-stained wretch for The *Boston Globe* where he covered nine presidential campaigns as Washington bureau chief, editorial page editor, and reporter. Nolan was a 1991 Pulitzer Prize Finalist for his editorial series, "Why Politics Stinks." He now lives in San Francisco.

Dan O'Neill is a cartoonist, creator of the "Odd Bodkins" syndicated comic strip and founder of the Air Pirates, an underground comic artists collective that went to court with the Walt Disney Company in a famous copyright/free speech case in the 70s. He lives in Nevada City, California, where he is on the board of the Original Sixteen to One Mine. www. DanOneillComics. blogspot.com

Stephen R. Proctor is the former managing editor of the *Houston Chronicle*. He joined the paper in 2012, after nine years at the *San Francisco Chronicle*, where he was also managing editor. Before moving to San Francisco, he spent 23 years as a reporter and editor at the *Baltimore Sun*. In both Baltimore and San Francisco, he has overseen coverage that won the Pulitzer Prize, one for feature writing and one for photography.

Jonah Raskin is a writer, journalist, and teacher. He joined Abbie Hoffman, Jerry Rubin and Paul Krassner in 1967 to form the Yippie party and was named Minister of Education. His books include, "American Scream: Allen Ginsberg's Howl and the Making of the Beat Generation" (2006), "The Radical Jack London: Writings on War and Revolution" (2008), and "Marijuanaland: Dispatches from an American War" (2011). He taught at Sonoma State University from 1981 to 2011.

Eugene Schoenfeld, M.D. gave medical advice as the popular '60s syndicated sex and drugs columnist and radio personality known as Dr. Hip. He was Hunter's friend, and occasionally when demand dictated, his doctor. He is a forensic psychiatrist, author, syndicated columnist, radio personality and yachtsman (he skippers High Hopes out of Sausalito, California), and a recent father. His 1967 medical column as "Dr. Hip" in the underground newspaper, *Berkeley Barb*, pioneered the first published advice column on patients' medical and sexual problems and he was the first psychiatrist to answer such questions live on the radio—a prototype for the popular "Frasier" TV series. Schoenfeld's books include "Dear Dr. Hip Pocrates" (1969) and "Jealousy: Taming the Green-Eyed Monster" (1980). His essay in this book was adapted from his forthcoming memoir, "Expert Witness."

Jonathan Shaw is a tattoo artist and writer who has inked Johnny Depp, Iggy Pop, and Jim Jarmusch. His books include, "Narcisa: Lady of Ashes," "Scab Vendor," and "Vintage Tattoo Flash." His motto is "Born to lose. Live to win."

Winston Smith is a Punk Art Surrealist and master of "hand-carved" collage. He began taking "safe" images from magazines and combining them to create politically charged works of art that challenge the viewer to confront incongruities and political paradoxes of modern society. www.WinstonSmithArt.com

Barbara Stauffacher Solomon is a San Francisco-based architect, landscape designer, artist, and writer. A ballet dancer before studying painting and sculpture at the San Francisco Art Institute, she moved to Switzerland as a young widow in 1955 to study graphic design at the Basel Art Institute with Armin Hofmann then later architecture at U.C. Berkeley. As Art Director of *Scanlan's Monthly*, she gave it a bold and modern design. Her iconic style of mixing Swiss Modernism and West Coast Pop pioneered a new look of California Cool, a departure from the psychedelic look of the day. She invented California Supergraphics at the Sea Ranch development in the 1960s and created the "Ribbon of Light" permanent installation along San Francisco's Embarcadero Promenade in 1991. She was a 1983 fellow at the American Academy in Rome. Her works have been exhibited everywhere from Paris to New York, and currently on permanent exhibition at SFMOMA. She is the author of "Green Architecture and the Agrarian Garden" (1989), "Good Mourning California" (1992), and her autobiography, "Why? Why Not?: 80 Years of Art & Design in Pix & Prose, Juxtaposed" (2013). www.BarbaraStauffacherSolomon.com

Ralph Steadman is a British artist and illustrator who defined Gonzo through his many years collaborating with Hunter, starting with "The Kentucky Derby is Decadent and Depraved" for *Scanlan's Monthly* in 1970 and continuing through "Fear & Loathing in Las Vegas," "The Curse of Lono," and numerous articles and adventures. While most known for his gonzo work with Hunter, Steadman has worked with other writers, including Ted Hughes, Adrian Mitchell and Brian Patten, and illustrated some classic editions-- "Alice in Wonderland," "Treasure Island," and "Animal Farm." He's designed postage stamps, album covers, won multiple awards, and is the star in the 2012 documentary, "For No Good Reason" (2012) www.RalphSteadman.com

Michael Stepanian is a renowned criminal defense trial lawyer in San Francisco, whose client list has included Hells Angels, Grateful Dead, and other harassed outlaws and hippies. A longtime friend of Hunter's, Stepanian was one of the inspirations for the character of Hunter's lawyer in the movie, "Where the Buffalo Roam."

Dugald Stermer, Art Director at *Ramparts* from 1964-1970, was responsible for giving the magazine its classic, bookish Times-Roman design – a design style picked up by *Rolling Stone* and many New York magazines. As art director he oversaw covers critical of the C.I.A. and opposing the Vietnam War. One provocative antiwar cover, in 1967, showed the hands of four men burning their draft cards. The hands belonged to Stermer and three fellow editors who were called before a federal grand jury in New York, accused of instigating action harmful to the best interests of the United States by encouraging civil disobedience. Stermer also persuaded Norman Rockwell to contribute a portrait of the peace activist and philosopher Bertrand Russell for a 1967 cover.

Stermer left *Ramparts* to pursue his passion for illustration, rendering exquisitely detailed color drawings of endangered animals, plants and insects, even Jerry Garcia. His illustrations appeared in numerous publications, including the *San Francisco Chronicle*, *TIME*, the *New York Times*, the *Los Angeles Times*, the *New Yorker*, *GQ*, *Rolling Stone* and *Mother Jones*. He chaired the illustration department at the California College of the Arts in San Francisco and served on the city's Art Commission. For 30 years he was on the board of directors for Delancey Street Foundation, a San Francisco organization that helps former substance abusers, ex-convicts and homeless. He authored four books, and was asked to update the design of the Olympic medals for the 1984 Games in Los Angeles. Dugald died in December 2011. www.DugaldStermer.com

Jack Thibeau is a writer and actor. When not acting or writing, Thibeau can be found in a box at the Santa Anita finish line. This essay is excerpted from his memoir-in-progress, "Happy Hour in the Garden of Agony."

Juan Thompson is Hunter's son. His memoir was published in 2016, "Stories I Tell Myself: Growing up with Hunter S. Thompson."

Garry Trudeau is the first cartoonist to win a Pulitzer, for his Doonesbury comic strip launched in 1970 while attending Yale. It became syndicated nearly immediately and runs daily in over 1400 newspapers. Trudeau first

introduced the fictional Doonesbury character Uncle Duke modeled on gonzo journalist Hunter S. Thompson, in 1974. Trudeau's newest project making waves is his 2016 book of cartoons, "Yuge!: 30 Years of Doonesbury on Trump."

John Walsh, the Godfather of ESPN for nearly 30 years before his 2015 retirement, was Hunter's editor there. Walsh also has held top editorial and sports editorial roles at *Newsday*, *Rolling Stone*, and the *Washington Post*, among many others. He is the editor of three sports books, including "The Heisman: A Symbol of Excellence" (1984). And not to forget, the creator and conductor of the famed San Francisco "A to Z Bar Tour" (26 bars in one day) in the 1970s.

Wavy Gravy is a well-known performance artist. He held the stage at Woodstock, hung with the Merry Pranksters, and is the unofficial king of 1960s counterculture (*Newsweek*). Wavy wrote a haiku to Hunter for this book. His haiku to Ken Kesey reads:

They say Kesey's dead
But Never trust a Prankster
Even if he's Underground.

S. Clay Wilson is an American underground cartoonist and central figure in the underground comix movement. Wilson attracted attention from readers with aggressively violent and sexually explicit panoramas of lowlife denizens, often depicting the wild escapades of pirates and bikers. He was an early contributor to *Zap Comix*.

Barbara Wohl-Luttringer was an early member of the San Francisco Mime Troupe. She lives in the Bay Area.

Tom Wolfe is a journalist and author who pioneered "New Journalism" in the 60s. His book "The Electric Kool-Aid Acid Test" in 1968 was a gospel on the 60s hippie movement, focusing on Ken Kesey and his Merry Pranksters. Other contemporary classics by Wolfe include "The Right Stuff" (1979), and "The Bonfire of the Vanities" (1987).

INDEX

ABOUT THE TYPE ON THE COVER

This is an updated version of Times Roman, called Starling. It was designed under the direction of the great Mike Parker, who was conviced that this was not an English typeface (created for Monotype's Stanley Morrison) but an *American* font designed by Starling Burgess. The *Financial Times* did a story about this theory, which I subscribe to, like the newspaper, without reservation.

I used it because Dugald Stermer made Times the typeface of *Ramparts*, where he was Warren's art director, and then for *Sunday Ramparts*, the strike newspaper which begat *Rolling Stone*.

Of course Warren paired Hunter and Ralph at *Scanlan's*, which used, horribly, Helvetica. --RB